STATS™ 1991 BASEBALL SCOREBOARD

John Dewan, Don Zminda, and STATS, Inc.

Foreword by Peter Gammons

Illustrations by John Grimwade

Statistical Compilations by Robert Mecca
with Dr. Richard Cramer and David Pinto

D1213986

STATS, Inc. (Sports Team Analysis & Tracking Systems, Inc.) – Chicago

STATS is a registered trademark of Sports Team Analysis and Tracking Systems, Inc.

First Edition: February 1991

Cover Design by John Grimwade

ISBN 0-9625581-2-5

Dedication

To Sharon Zminda, a .400 hitter every year,
and Jason Dewan, Rookie of the Year, 1991.

ACKNOWLEDGEMENTS

Stop! Don't skip this page. I know you are probably in a hurry to get to the guts of the book, but before you get there let me give you a little background on what goes into making this book. There are many more people involved than the names on the title page, but let me start there.

Bob Mecca is the person responsible for most of the statistical compilations which form the basis of this book. With STATS' raw data and the computer in hand, Bob went to work pulling out the answers to our many questions.

Dr. Richard Cramer is the founder and Chairman of the Board of STATS. He built the foundation for STATS' current baseball system which is so flexible and contains so much information that it allows us to answer virtually any question in baseball. He is constantly working to keep the system at the forefront of technology. In another role, he uses his analytical skill to develop and answer many of the questions you find in this book.

During the baseball season, David Pinto supplies STATS' statistical support for ESPN. In the off-season, he put his baseball and computer talents to work uncovering more of the answers to our questions. His assistance was invaluable. We thank him for spending time away from his family on the East Coast to help us here in the Chicago home office.

The one thing that probably jumps out at you as you page thru the book is the graphics by John Grimwade. If a simple picture is worth a thousand words, then his graphics are worth ten thousand. We are thrilled to have John join us again on this second edition of this book.

Arthur Ashley, Assistant Vice President at STATS, is invaluable at getting the collection and processing of the baseball data organized. Without that process, this book would not be possible.

Thanks to the rest of the STATS staff who not only assisted on the book, but also kept the STATS organization running at peak performance. They include: Susan Dewan, Robert Meyerhoff, Ross Schaufelberger, Marge Morra, Matt Greenberger, Carmen Corica, Suzette Neily, Marge Wucki, Nadine Sanchez, Andrew Berman, Michael Canter and Jon Passman.

Special thanks to all the STATS reporters around the country, who diligently and accurately supplied each game's play-by-play to our computer system.

Finally, thanks to Bill James for laying the groundwork for this type of baseball analysis, and also for his personal consultation and support of STATS, Inc.

Table of Contents

II. QUESTIONS ON OFFENSE   71

III. QUESTIONS ON PITCHING   156

IV. QUESTIONS ON DEFENSE   217

APPENDIX   241

FOREWORD

By **Peter Gammons**

Almost every day I was in the ESPN studio last season, poor David Pinto had to run some oblique statistical study. "Could you give me the starters' ERA, team by team, with innings per start?" Or, "who are the most and least productive at scoring runners from second base?" Or, "do you have some way — other than Earl Weaver's winning percentage — to prove that the sacrifice bunt is one of the most overrated plays?"

David Pinto is the STATS, Inc. man at ESPN in Bristol, Ct. It is he that provides the network with so much of its superb statistical data working with the database put together just outside of Chicago by John Dewan, Don Zminda and rest of the gang at STATS. For instance, one time, in putting together a visual display of the change in Roger Clemens' delivery in bi-annual bits from 1984 through 1990, Pinto walked over and, unrequested, dropped off a list of pitchers' 130-pitch starts over the last four years; it was an interesting addendum to the Clemens piece to note that not only had he made the most 130-pitch starts in the majors, but that in those four years he had more of those starts than Dave Stewart, Bob Welch, Frank Viola and Bret Saberhagen . . . combined. Ever since I first came in contact with STATS, Inc. at *Sports Illustrated*, that sort of statistical proof behind a subjective, intuitive or educated supposition has been invaluable. For instance, in doing a story on Carlton Fisk in January, 1990, it seemed that the White Sox pitchers were far more effective with Fisk catching them. I had been fascinated with the concept of the catchers' earned run average — relative to catchers on the same team — since a night in 1978 in the old Bards' Room at the late Comiskey Park when Paul Richards explained why he kept it when he managed, and in the 1978-79-80 seasons the difference between the Red Sox pitchers when Fisk caught and when he didn't was nearly two runs. Well, minutes after I mentioned my catchers' ERA idea to *Sports Illustrated* baseball editor David Bauer, the three year data was in my *S.I.* queue. And, yes, Fisk had more impact on the White Sox staff in those years than any other catcher in baseball.

It is this combination of the practical with the statistical that makes this *STATS Baseball Scoreboard* such an invaluable and fascinating book. We who covered the game from the inside out had always kept statistics. The late *Boston Globe* columnist Harold Kaese was a man years ahead of his time, and, in fact, when I first worked at the *Globe* in the early Seventies, most other writers made fun of his constant use of statistical data kept in small black notebooks in writing that only Kaese himself could read. Newspapermen's stats included books kept on all major league starters, plus some data on the teams we covered: getting runners in from third base with less than two out, relievers' run prevention and save/hold ratios, catchers' ERA, counts on which the manager ran, hit-and-ran and squeezed, etc.

But by the late Seventies, Bill James changed all that with his marvelous *Abstracts*, and by the mid-Eighties the computer world was so large that statistics became an integral part of the baseball world. The problem that some of us had from our view on the inside out was that a lot of the data was simply that — data, with no real practical purpose. There was a feeling that players were being judged only from the eyes of computers, and, no matter what any rotisserian says, you do have to watch Barry Larkin or Alan Trammell to appreciate just how wonderful each is.

When the *STATS Baseball Scoreboard* arrived last spring, it was the perfect, practical marriage between the statistical, intuitive and educated views of baseball, from the inside and from that lofty level to which James ascends. At the time, I was working on a *Sports Illustrated* piece on Rickey Henderson and the art of baserunning, and several experts on stealing had talked about the advantages and disadvantages of Henderson playing all his career on natural grass home fields. Open last year's *Scoreboard* to the first study . . .

"Do base stealers have an advantage on artificial turf?" Now, personal reference aside, how many times do we hear from a television announcer or a player that it is easier to get a jump on the turf? The *Scoreboard* addressed it, with individual breakdowns for the 40 base stealers.

The *Scoreboard's* essence is that it addresses questions that arise every day in baseball, be they from a fan, journalist or even front office executive. At the start of every game, we hear players talk about the home plate umpire's strike zone, and whether or not he is a pitchers' or hitters' ump; the *Scoreboard* gave us the umpiring leaders for batting average, slugging and strikeouts per nine innings. They addressed the flyball pitcher vs. ground ball hitter debates, told us which parks have the most foul outs and which teams bunt most in the early innings. How often in April do we hear that the hitters can't hit until it gets warm (or Wade Boggs theorize that the ball can't start jumping off his bat until it's warm enough so the molecules in his bat expand)? The *Scoreboard* showed how temperature affects offensive production.

We constantly hear managers, pitching coaches and pitchers say, "you have to throw first pitch strikes." They showed how important it is. Among the most interesting defensive studies was which parks produce the most errors, which can silence every other home team's infielders' complaints that they are playing on rock piles. It's just plain fun to know which pitchers throw over to first base the most often.

What I find is that I keep the *Scoreboard* with me while watching games, either in front of the television, in press boxes or in my seat behind home plate at Fenway Park. The problem is that since I began covering major league baseball on a travelling basis in 1971, my briefcase has become more and more of a travelling library. The *Bill James/STATS, Inc. Major League Handbook* published in November has left one with a choice between that and the *Baseball Register,* but one of them must travel. So must the large paperback *Sports Encyclopedia-Baseball.* The *Baseball America Almanac* has become a trade staple. Somewhere stuck in with my own current season stat notebooks, regular notebooks, address books and Tandy 1500 now is the *Scoreboard.*

Really, now, what happens if I'm watching Bobby Witt's pitch count roll up to 115 in the seventh inning and I'm thinking, "what chances do pitchers have when they get to high pitch counts?" Where else can I answer that question on the spot but the *Scoreboard?* Nowhere.

We are sometimes stat-ed to death these days, be it meaningless political polls, absurd *USA Today* charts showing us things like the number of cans of tunafish opened by American housewives in 1931/61/91. But *The STATS Baseball Scoreboard* is the most practical application of baseball numbers ever assembled, answering a number of questions before we can ask them.

INTRODUCTION

Hi, and welcome to the second edition of *The STATS Baseball Scoreboard*.

Many of you purchased the first edition of this book a year ago; if so, you're already familiar with our format. For you first-timers, what we do here is pretty simple. We try to think up 101 questions from the world of baseball, questions the astute fan — like you — is always asking. Which relievers get the cheap saves, and which ones the toughies? Which shortstops are best at going into the hole? Why did the hitters take control at Toronto's SkyDome last year? Which umpires are pitchers' friends, and which ones favor the hitters? That's just a sample.

Of course, anyone can ask questions like that; not many can provide accurate answers. That's why only STATS, Inc. can produce a book like this. Our database — which includes the result of every pitch from every major league game — is unmatched for both accuracy and sheer scope. We don't claim to know all the answers . . . but we have the store of information to begin to find them.

We separate our book into four sections: one on baseball in general, one on offense, one on pitching and one on fielding. We're proud of the whole book, of course, but we especially think you'll enjoy the new stats we provide on defense — the most overlooked aspect of the game. Since many of the questions from the first edition proved very popular with the readership, about 60 of them are repeated — with entirely new data and analysis, of course. But being the inquiring types that we are, we've tried to break a lot of new ground as well. We appreciated the letters and comments we received on the first edition, and many of these new questions (and the new index, as well) are in response to readers' requests.

But though we provide as much information as we can, we've done our best to make a fun book as well. This isn't a scientific treatise, and our touch is light, and at times irreverent. We think you'll agree that John Grimwade's splendid illustrations add to the fun — as well as give you a visual feel for the points we're trying to make.

Enjoy!

John Dewan and Don Zminda

I. GENERAL BASEBALL QUESTIONS

WHAT GOOD IS AN INTENTIONAL WALK?

Some managers like the intentional walk, some shy away from it. But every skipper uses it at least occasionally. There are usually two rationales for the purpose pass: to avoid facing a dangerous hitter and instead pitch to one who's likely to do less damage, or to set up a double play situation. The idea, in either case, is to get out of the inning with as little damage as possible.

Those are reasonable rationales, but let's see what actually happened in game situations last year, starting with the American League. The columns list how often each team ordered an intentional walk, how many runs scored subsequent to the walks, the average number of runs scoring for each intentional walk, and the number of times the walked batter himself wound up scoring:

Team	IW	Runs	Runs per IW	Walked Batter Scores
Baltimore	43	26	.60	3
Boston	47	33	.70	6
California	25	28	1.12	4
Chicago WSox	27	15	.56	3
Cleveland	38	39	1.03	7
Detroit	86	61	.71	9
Kansas City	45	28	.62	2
Milwaukee	39	38	.97	7
Minnesota	40	30	.75	6
New York Yanks	40	38	.95	7
Oakland	19	25	1.32	3
Seattle	55	73	1.33	14
Texas	39	44	1.13	11
Toronto	44	43	.98	6
American League	587	521	.89	88

As you can see, nearly one run, on average, scored subsequent to each intentional walk. There's a lot of variance — some managers seemed better able to minimize the damage than others. (Torborg, you're a genius.) While we can't really say how many runs would have scored without the IW, the idea that this is the way to "escape" undamaged from an inning is pretty well refuted. We also discover that 15 percent of the time, the walked batter himself eventually came around to score!

Here's the National League data:

Team	IW	Runs	Runs per IW	Walked Batter Scores
Atlanta	64	66	1.03	11
Chicago Cubs	85	75	.88	15
Cincinnati	60	37	.62	6
Houston	74	87	1.18	18
Los Angeles	49	36	.73	9
Montreal	76	33	.43	6
New York Mets	35	27	.77	5
Philadelphia	81	51	.63	9
Pittsburgh	48	21	.44	4
St. Louis	72	54	.75	9
San Diego	69	55	.80	13
San Francisco	84	65	.77	14
National League	797	607	.76	119

Fewer runs, on average, scored following a National League intentional walk. The reason is simple: NL managers often walk the eighth hitter to get to the pitcher. Even so, the damage following a National League IW is not that much less than after one in the American; and in NL games, as well, 15 percent of the time the walked runner comes around to score.

We also looked into situations where the walk sets up a double play situation. How often does a DP actually result? Only 13 percent of the time . . . meaning that the odds of getting a double play are lower than the odds of the walked batter eventually scoring!

This is good strategy?

IS THE STREAK RUINING RIPKEN?

Cal Ripken began his remarkable consecutive game streak on May 30, 1982, back when Earl Weaver was still managing the Orioles and Jim Palmer was still the ace of the Baltimore staff. Other American League shortstops at the time included Tim Foli, U.L. Washington, Todd Cruz and Fred (Chicken) Stanley. All are long gone, but Ripken survives, enduring day after day at a very transient position.

Ripken now has the second-longest consecutive game streak in major league history, and he's still more than four seasons away from Lou Gehrig's record 2,130. Lately people have begun to wonder whether the streak is worth continuing. Increasing the pressure is the fact that Ripken's offense has declined as the streak has gone on:

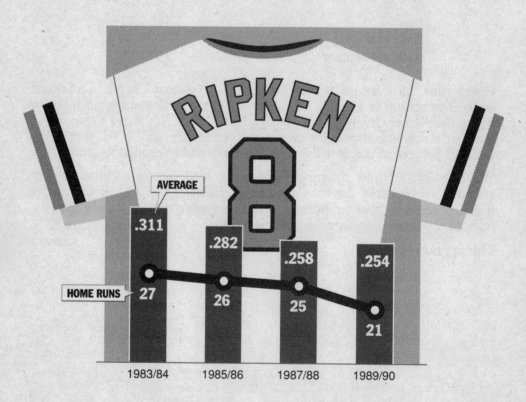

	1983/84	1985/86	1987/88	1989/90
AVERAGE	.311	.282	.258	.254
HOME RUNS	27	26	25	21

Ripken remains a fine offensive player, especially for a middle infielder. He attributes his hitting decline to mechanical problems that he can correct. But given the constant downward trend in his numbers, it's hard to buy that.

From a strictly mathematical perspective, one would find it impossible to defend the streak. Bill James and others who have studied the subject feel that a superstar can contribute somewhere between six and ten extra wins to his team — that is, if the '27 Yankees had been forced to go without Babe Ruth for the whole season, they probably would have won around 100 games instead of 110. (Poor babies.) But that's if he missed the whole season; on average, he'd have to miss about 15 games before it would cost the Yankees a single win. Cal Ripken is no Ruth. Doesn't it seem silly to put him out there day after day, when the evidence strongly suggests that an occasional rest — even five or ten games a year, with a few as a designated hitter — would increase his overall performance?

Decreased overall effectiveness is only one argument against the streak. Another is that it may well be shortening Ripken's career. Five other players have played in at least 1,000 consecutive games; all had premature fadeouts. Of course one was Gehrig, who was felled by a terrible disease. But look at the other four:

Everett Scott (1,307 games), a slick-fielding shortstop, played his last season as a regular at age 31, hitting .250 in 153 games. Never a great hitter, Scott remained at his same weak level after the streak ended. But he was no longer able to hold a regular position and was used strictly as a utility man, probably due to loss of range. Scott played only 55 and 44 games the next two years, then retired at age 33.

Scott 1920-24 (age 27-31): 153 gms/yr, .259 avg.
Scott 1925-26 (age 32-33):   50 gms/yr, .260 avg.

Steve Garvey (1,207 games) was probably the most serious challenger to Gehrig; he had the desire to break the streak, and it took a serious injury (a badly dislocated thumb in 1983) to get him out of the lineup. But Garvey had his last outstanding season at age 31 in 1980: .304 with 200 hits, 26 homers and 106 RBI. The '80 season was Garvey's third straight year with 200 or more hits, the seventh time in eight seasons he'd batted .300 (the other year he just missed, at .297), the third time in four years he'd hit at least 25 homers, and the third straight year he had over 100 RBI. Garvey continued to be a good player in the seven seasons he played after his 32nd birthday, but he was never again a great one: he never hit .300 again, never had more than 184 hits in a season, never drove in more than 86 runs, and hit over 17 homers only once (in 1986, when he had 21). A comparison of two four year periods (the streak ended with a 1983 injury):

Garvey 1977-80 (age 28-31): .308 avg., 27 HR per year
Garvey 1981-84 (age 32-35): .284 avg., 15 HR per year*

* 1981-84 homer totals are per 650 at bats (Garvey's average per year from '77 to '80) for purposes of comparison.

Billy Williams (1,117 games) lasted longer than Garvey, with an outstanding season at age 34: .333, 37 HR, 122 RBI. But in four more seasons Williams never hit more than 23 homers, never drove in more than 86 runs, and his last four batting averages were .288, .280, .244 and .211. Williams retired at age 38.

Williams 1969-72 (age 31-34): .311 avg., 32 HR per year
Williams 1973-76 (age 35-38): .259 avg., 23 HR per year*

* 1973-76 homer totals are per 612 at bats (Williams' average per year from '69 to '72) for purpose of comparison.

Joe Sewell (1,103 games), a singles-hitting shortstop and third baseman, had his last outstanding season at age 30 in 1929, batting .315. At that point Sewell had hit .315 or better for seven straight seasons. He lasted four more years, hitting over .300 only once (.302 in 1931), and retired before his 35th birthday.

Sewell 1926-29 (age 27-30): .319 avg.
Sewell 1930-33 (age 31-34): .283 avg.

Most players show declines in performance as they get into their thirties, and perhaps the fadeout of these players is simply attributable to age. However, it's hardly unusual for superstars to continue to perform at a top level up to age 35 and even beyond. It's also unusual not to have at least one great year after reaching age 31 or 32 . . . but Garvey, Scott and Sewell couldn't manage it.

Billy Williams had the best longevity, but that may have been due to his own good sense. Williams began to feel that the streak was hurting him, and finally, at age 32, told Leo Durocher to scratch him from the lineup. Ripken, with Gehrig's record now in sight, seems unwilling to do that. He'll probably need an even sharper decline in offensive performance — say a full season at the .230 level — before the Orioles would consider benching him.

The evidence suggests that Ripken could well drop that low.

WHICH PLATOONS WERE IN COMPANY "A"?

Platooning two players at one position has been around baseball for a long, long time. Bill James suggests that Hughie Jennings of the Tigers fashioned the first left/right platoon in the early days of this century; less than a decade later, George Stallings was winning a world championship with the 1914 "Miracle Braves" by juggling his lineup at several positions. Casey Stengel was famous for his platoons with the champion Yankees of the fifties, and Earl Weaver made the "Lowicke" combination of John Lowenstein and Gary Roenicke a feared power combo for years in the seventies and eighties. As recently as 1983, the World Series between the Orioles and Phillies was a chess game between two managers, Baltimore's Joe Altobelli and Philadelphia's Paul Owens, each constantly looking for a platoon advantage.

But in 1990, platooning seemed out of fashion. Both Tony LaRussa of the A's and Lou Piniella of the Reds, last year's rivals in the World Series, preferred to stick with a set lineup; each looked for a platoon advantage at times, but it was hardly a major part of their offense. Of the four division winners, the only one who liked to platoon was Jim Leyland of the Pirates. Leyland usually rotated players at catcher (Mike LaValliere/Don Slaught), first base (Sid Bream/Gary Redus) and third (Wally Backman/Jeff King). But the Pirates have let both Bream and Backman escape via free agency, so even they don't seem committed to continuing their platooning ways. In baseball, teams tend to imitate the successful clubs — which probably means even less platooning in 1991.

So when we pick the best platoons of 1990, we may be talking about a species that is, for the moment, in decline (stats are players' totals when playing that position only):

Pittsburgh Pirates — C	AB	H	HR	RBI	Avg
Mike Lavalliere	277	71	3	31	.256
Don Slaught	214	64	3	24	.299

When clubs platoon these days, it's often behind the plate, since it's tough for a catcher to play every day. This was a good one last year. But weirdly, Lavalliere, once hopeless against lefties, hit .375 in 56 at-bats against them last year. Since he's the better defensive catcher, he'll probably see more work against lefties this year.

Los Angeles Dodgers — 3B	AB	H	HR	RBI	Avg
Lenny Harris	281	93	1	24	.331
Mike Sharperson	279	84	2	25	.301

This was a surprisingly effective platoon. Tom Lasorda went to it in desperation when Jeff Hamilton got hurt, and — surprise — both guys hit. It didn't quite last the season, as Harris was often needed at second base. But it was a good one.

Pittsburgh Pirates — 1B	AB	H	HR	RBI	Avg
Sid Bream	375	103	15	67	.275
Gary Redus	187	46	6	22	.246

A very effective platoon, especially late last year, when Redus found his hitting stroke. Earl Weaver would have probably kept it intact for several years. It says something about how platooning is now perceived that the Pirates let Bream escape to Atlanta.

Pittsburgh Pirates — 3B	AB	H	HR	RBI	Avg
Wally Backman	245	71	2	26	.290
Jeff King	351	86	13	50	.245

The third of the Pirates' platoons, this worked well for much of the year. But Backman had defensive problems at third, and when King began to hit better, he became the regular. He looks to have the job for 1991.

San Francisco Giants — C	AB	H	HR	RBI	Avg
Terry Kennedy	290	80	2	26	.276
Gary Carter	214	56	7	22	.262

Roger Craig has a veteran pitching staff, and last year he had two veteran catchers to handle it. Offensively, it only worked for awhile; Carter hit for a half season, but then his bat died. The Giants didn't re-sign him, and now their righty-swinging catcher appears to be rookie Steve Decker. But word is that they're hoping Decker will become the regular — another sign that platooning is on the wane.

Texas Rangers — C	AB	H	HR	RBI	Avg
Geno Petralli	293	77	0	18	.263
Mike Stanley	123	34	1	10	.276

This platoon would probably work better if Petralli could stay healthy and

Stanley could improve his catching. Petralli's always been a good hitter against righties, so this one has some potential.

Toronto Blue Jays — C	AB	H	HR	RBI	Avg
Greg Myers	243	57	5	22	.235
Pat Borders	322	94	15	46	.292

Yet another catching platoon — and another which didn't last the season. What happened was that Borders finally showed he could hit righties, eliminating the need for the platoon.

All in all, these are sad days for platooning; hardly anyone seems to go into a season figuring that they'll rotate two players at a position. Whatever happened to Benny Ayala?

WHO BLOWS THE MOST LEADS?

By now, people are beginning to understand that any club which takes a lead into the eighth inning is very likely to win the game. Which is not to say the differences between teams can't be significant. Last year, for instance, the Atlanta Braves were 50-10 (.833) in games in which they led after seven innings; those numbers look pretty good, but the Braves had the **worst** percentage in baseball in the category. The best club — no surprise, considering everything, but especially their superior bullpen — was the Oakland A's (87-2, .978). If the Braves had performed like the A's when leading after seven, they'd have won nine more games, which is nothing to sneeze at. That was only one of many differences between the two clubs, but it was an important one.

Here's how the American League clubs performed last year when leading, trailing or tied after seven:

AL Team	Ahead			Behind			Tied		
	W	L	Pct	W	L	Pct	W	L	Pct
Orioles	55	7	.887	6	71	.078	15	7	.682
Red Sox	66	8	.892	8	55	.127	14	11	.560
Angels	66	3	.957	5	70	.067	9	9	.500
White Sox	81	7	.920	5	52	.088	7	9	.438
Indians	63	4	.940	6	75	.074	7	6	.538
Tigers	69	6	.920	3	69	.042	7	7	.500
Royals	66	8	.892	5	70	.067	4	8	.333
Brewers	64	9	.877	4	71	.053	6	8	.429
Twins	62	3	.954	2	77	.025	10	8	.556
Yankees	53	6	.898	5	79	.060	9	9	.500
Athletics	87	2	.978	7	53	.117	9	4	.692
Mariners	62	6	.912	6	64	.086	9	15	.375
Rangers	65	4	.942	7	65	.097	11	10	.524
Blue Jays	75	2	.974	6	63	.087	5	11	.313
AL Total	934	75	.926	75	934	.074	122	122	.500

In examining these figures, one finds some fascinating material. Let's look at the race in the American League East. The Red Sox lost eight games in which they were leading after seven — a clear sign of a shaky bullpen. But the Sox made up for that with their late-inning punch. Boston won eight games when trailing after seven — most in the league — and won 14 of the 25 games in which they were tied after seven, recording the second-most victories and the third-best percentage in the league in that category. In other words, the Sox were odds-on to win any game that was up for grabs.

Contrast that with Boston's chief divisional rival, the Blue Jays. Toronto, with a good bullpen, was almost invincible when leading after seven (75-2); they won the games they were supposed to win. The Jays were also respectable coming from behind (6-63). But when the game was tied after seven and there for the Jays to win or lose, Toronto fell apart, going only 5-11. Does this look like a club which "choked"? One would be tempted to say so. Looking at the record, one would also be tempted to say that Oakland — invulnerable when leading after seven, dangerous when trailing, overwhelming when tied — was about as perfect as a club could get.

Now let's look at the National League:

NL	Ahead			Behind			Tied		
Team	W	L	Pct	W	L	Pct	W	L	Pct
Braves	50	10	.833	8	77	.094	7	8	.467
Cubs	56	10	.848	6	68	.081	14	5	.737
Reds	74	5	.937	4	56	.067	13	9	.591
Astros	50	6	.893	8	63	.113	17	18	.486
Dodgers	67	6	.918	9	62	.127	10	8	.556
Expos	66	7	.904	9	58	.134	10	12	.455
Mets	74	4	.949	8	57	.123	9	10	.474
Phillies	57	5	.919	9	68	.117	11	12	.478
Pirates	73	4	.948	6	54	.100	13	9	.591
Cardinals	62	9	.873	4	70	.054	4	13	.235
Padres	57	9	.864	6	64	.086	11	14	.440
Giants	67	9	.882	7	56	.111	11	12	.478
NL Total	753	84	.900	84	753	.100	130	130	.500

The figures here are a lot less neat. The second- and third-best clubs in the league when both tied and ahead after seven were the division-winning Pirates and Reds. But before we call this a "clutch" category, note that the best team when tied after seven were those mighty Chicago Cubs, who went 77-85. You'll also note that the Reds were the second-worst club in the league when trailing after seven, behind only the punchless Cardinals. Cincinnati won only four games all year in which they were trailing after seven innings. And remember that Oakland lost only two games all year when leading after seven. So what happened in the World Series? The Reds were trailing the supposedly-invincible A's after seven innings in both Games 2 and 4, but won both, and with it the Series. It's a lesson that you shouldn't go overboard in using stats like these — or any stats, really — to evaluate a club's "character."

WHO'S REALLY OUT IN LEFT FIELD?

Girls once had a description for an inadequate, unaware loser of a guy —
"he's really out in left field." On the amateur level this never seemed quite
correct; as some people know from their own embarrassing experiences
(well, maybe **you** know it, but not the incredible jocks here at STATS,
Inc.), most hitters are right-handed, and the weakest player usually goes to
right, not left field.

But judging by 1990, that old "out in left field" slur applies very nicely to
major league teams. For all but three of the 26 clubs, left field was the
fielding position where either the most or the second-most different
players were tried. Here is a list of the number of players at catcher and left
field on all teams in 1990. The first of the two figures shown at each
team-position is the number of different players who started, and the
second the number who played at any time during the season.

American League

Team	Catcher Starting	Catcher Playing	Left Field Starting	Left Field Playing
Baltimore	3	3	8	8
Boston	3	3	2	5
California	4	4	5	5
Chicago	2	3	4	8
Cleveland	2	2	5	6
Detroit	4	4	9	10
Kansas City	4	4	9	10
Milwaukee	3	3	4	4
Minnesota	3	3	8	9
New York	5	5	9	10
Oakland	4	4	7	10
Seattle	3	4	6	7
Texas	4	5	5	9
Toronto	2	4	7	8

| | National League | | | |
| Team | Catcher | | Left Field | |
	Starting	Playing	Starting	Playing
Atlanta	5	6	4	7
Chicago	4	5	7	10
Cincinnati	4	5	8	9
Houston	5	5	11	13
Los Angeles	3	5	6	7
Montreal	4	4	6	8
New York	6	7	7	10
Philadelphia	4	4	8	9
Pittsburgh	4	5	7	9
St. Louis	3	3	8	9
San Diego	4	5	6	7
San Francisco	5	6	6	7

It seems almost predictable that the most volatile position of all was left field for the weakest hitting major league team, the Astros. Franklin Stubbs, their most often used left fielder, played barely a third of Houston's defensive innings and is now a Brewer. We will spare you the names of the other twelve also found wanting.

In contrast the Red Sox, whose last half century of left fielders is mostly Williams, Yastrzemski, Rice, and Greenwell, may not have used 13 left fielders in a decade! The Fenway tradition of stability under the Green Monster continued in 1990 with only two different starters in left.

Usually one thinks of catcher as the position where change is most likely, but last year every single team had more left fielders than catchers. In fact, three American League clubs started only two catchers all year; the White Sox with Fisk/Karkovice, the Indians with Alomar/Skinner, and the Blue Jays with Borders/Myers. Toronto and Chicago also had the most stable starting lineups overall, each needing only two starters at two other positions.

Only one team had a player who started every game at the same position — but Cal Ripken did let three other shortstops divide 31 defensive innings at shortstop. Must be slowing down.

A complete listing for this category can be found on page 243.

Is the SkyDome Home Run Heaven?

We pride ourselves on getting things right, but, like even the best ballplayers, we can pull an occasional rock. Last year we discussed the Toronto Blue Jays' midseason move from Exhibition Stadium to the new SkyDome. We concluded, based on 55 games worth of data, that "the SkyDome looks like it's going to be the one of best pitchers' parks in the majors."

Ouch. When 1990 came, the home run balls began flying out of the SkyDome, and people began talking about the Dome as one of the best **hitters'** parks in the majors. Now the dust has cleared, and we finally have a full season's worth of data on the new park. Let's look at it in terms of Bill James "ballpark factors," which compared how the home club AND their opponents do in games at the home yard versus how the clubs do in the road parks. Doing it this way eliminates a bias that would be created by having exceptionally good (or bad) pitchers or exceptionally good (or bad) hitters on the home team. What you do is divide the figures in the home games by the figures in the road games and multiply by 100 to create an index. An index of 100 would indicate a neutral park; one over 100 would indicate a hitters' park, one below 100 a pitchers' yard. Anyhow, here's how the SkyDome rated for 1990 in scoring, batting average and home runs:

	Sky-Dome	Road	Index
Runs/Game	9.0	8.7	103
Batting Average	.265	.260	102
HR/Game	2.16	1.67	129

The Dome, as you can see, has proven itself as a great home run park . . . but it's not that much above average when it comes to batting average and overall scoring. Now let's add another factor. The SkyDome, of course, has a retractable roof, and the Jays sometimes play with it closed (45 games last year), sometimes with it open (36 games). Whether the roof is open or closed has a huge effect on what kind of park the SkyDome is (averages are per game):

	Dome Open	Road	Index	Dome Closed	Road	Index
Runs/Game	8.2	8.7	94	9.6	8.7	110
Batting Average	.259	.260	100	.269	.260	103
HR/Game	1.64	1.67	98	2.58	1.67	154

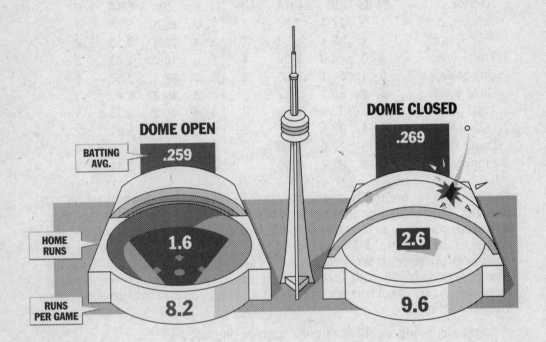

DOME OPEN

BATTING AVG. — .259

HOME RUNS — 1.6

RUNS PER GAME — 8.2

DOME CLOSED

.269

2.6

9.6

Closing the Dome turns the park into Home Run Heaven. That helped some players more than others; for instance, it turned Kelly Gruber from a 97-pound weakling into Babe Ruth:

Player	Dome Closed					Dome Open				
	AB	HR	RBI	Avg	Slg	AB	HR	RBI	Avg	Slg
George Bell	168	8	31	.262	.452	106	3	10	.245	.368
Pat Borders	110	7	16	.273	.573	54	3	12	.278	.500
Junior Felix	149	7	23	.248	.477	87	0	6	.241	.379
Tony Fernandez	178	1	18	.326	.444	143	1	20	.287	.469
Kelly Gruber	169	17	44	.361	.763	136	6	18	.206	.368
Manny Lee	95	2	9	.305	.432	95	0	10	.221	.242
Fred McGriff	138	6	17	.268	.428	126	8	21	.286	.524
John Olerud	98	5	17	.265	.490	89	6	9	.281	.506
Mookie Wilson	152	0	13	.230	.296	119	0	7	.269	.353

Pitcher	Dome Closed					Dome Open				
	W	L	IP	ERA	HR	W	L	IP	ERA	HR
Jim Acker	1	0	27.1	2.30	2	1	3	25.1	5.33	1
John Cerutti	3	4	38.1	6.34	10	2	1	32.2	4.13	4
Tom Henke	1	0	24.0	2.25	4	1	0	13.2	2.63	2
Jimmy Key	5	1	51.1	5.08	8	2	2	37.1	3.62	5
Dave Stieb	5	2	53.1	2.87	3	4	3	49.2	3.44	3
Todd Stottlemyre	4	4	57.1	5.02	8	3	4	45.2	3.35	1
Duane Ward	0	1	37.1	2.41	2	0	3	28.1	3.81	2
David Wells	0	0	37.0	2.68	5	3	2	45.2	2.56	4
Frank Wills	3	3	35.2	5.30	7	0	1	26.1	3.42	3

Our mistake — not really a mistake, but an assumption that turned out to be false — was that we thought that the Jays would keep the Dome open whenever possible, as they did in 1989. But the Jays' brass noticed that the club was 10-0 with the Dome closed, and in 1990 they kept the lid shut whenever possible. It worked, too: the Jays were 28-17 at home with the Dome closed, 16-20 with it open. So if you're watching a Toronto home game this year, expect to see the dome closed . . . or expect to see Kelly Gruber closing it.

A complete listing for this category appears on page 244.

WHO DOES WHAT THE MOST?

A zillion things happen in major league baseball over the course of a season, and we ought to know — we caught every one of them. We thought you might enjoy seeing how often each event we count happened, and who the major league leader was. Here they are: 3 Leagues

Play	No.	Leader	
Run Scored	17,919	Rickey Henderson, Oak	119
Single	26,099	Brett Butler, SF	160
Double	6,526	George Brett, KC	45
		Jody Reed, Bos	45
Triple	865	Tony Fernandez, Tor	17
Home Run	3,317	Cecil Fielder, Det	51
Game-Winning RBI	1,958	Bo Jackson, KC	19
Sacrifice Hit	1,437	Jay Bell, Pit	34
Sacrifice Fly	1,252	Bobby Bonilla, Pit	15
Hit by Pitch	861	Phil Bradley, Bal-WSox	11
Walk	12,468	Mickey Tettleton, Bal	103
Intentional BB	1,384	Andre Dawson, Cubs	21
		Eddie Murray, LA	21
Strikeout	23,753	Cecil Fielder, Det	181
Stolen Base	2,947	Vince Coleman, StL	73
Caught Stealing	1,490	Eric Yelding, Hou	25
Ground DP	3,064	Ivan Calderon, WSox	26
1B/Interference	15	R.J. Reynolds, Pit	3
1B/K+Wild Pitch	72	George Bell, Tor	4
1B/K+Passed Ball	25	Craig Worthington, Bal	2
		Barry Larkin, Cin	2
1B/K+Error	3	3 tied with	1
1B/Failed FC	90	Charlie O'Brien, Mil-Mets	3
1B/Error	1,546	Ryne Sandberg, Cubs	14
2B/Error	261	Charlie Hayes, Phi	5
3B/Error	28	28 tied with	1
1B/SacBunt+FC	37	Jay Bell, Pit	3
1B/SacBunt+Err	85	Bill Ripken, Bal	6
1B/Ball Hits Runner	10	George Brett, KC	2
Flied Out	23,000	Robin Yount, Mil	133
Foul Fly Out	469	Ozzie Guillen, WSox	8
Ground Out	31,711	Steve Sax, Yanks	224
Line Out	6,263	Tony Gwynn, SD	54
Bunt Out	454	Brett Butler, SF	17
Pop Out	6,785	Howard Johnson, Mets	60
Foul Pop Out	3,423	Chris Sabo, Cin	31
Force Out	4,255	Dickie Thon, Phi	35
Bunt/Force Out	101	Jay Bell, Pit	5
GDP on Bunt	21	3 tied with	2
Bunt Fly DP	11	11 tied with	1

Play	No.	Leader	
Line DP	322	Tony Fernandez, Tor	6
Grd Triple Play	3	3 tied with	1
Line Triple Play	1	Willie Randolph, LA-Oak	1
Bunt Fly Out	176	Brett Butler, SF	5
CS + Error	20	Mike Devereaux, Bal	2
		Tom Brunansky, StL-Bos	2
Fly DP	83	5 tied with	2
Double Steal	254	Tim Raines, Mon	6
SB + Error	89	3 tied with	4
SF+Error	9	9 tied with	1
Batter Obstruction	31	Eric Yelding, Hou	3
Pickoff	209	Rickey Henderson, Oak	6
Out Advancing	844	Tony Fernandez, Tor	10
Out Obstruction	8	8 tied with	1
Advance-No Play	57	Gary Sheffield, Mil	3
		Willie McGee, StL-Oak	3
Error on Pick Off	75	5 tied with	2
Advance on Throw	460	Andres Galarraga, Mon	7
		Ryne Sandberg, Cubs	7
Advance on Error	969	Barry Larkin, Cin	11
		Jerry Browne, Cle	11
Error on Foul Fly	60	Eddie Murray, LA	3
Adv. on Obstruction	2	Dan Pasqua, WSox	1
		George Brett, KC	1

The list is pretty self-explanatory, and we're braced for all those critics who want to know why we count the leaders in getting to second base on an error. We will now confess the truth. We work for Charlie Hayes' agent, and it's worth an extra $200,000 to him. Not to mention the endorsement possibilities. Next question.

A few quick observations:

1. Jay Bell had over twice as many sacrifice bunts (34) as any other major league player last year. Does this make him the Babe Ruth of the bunt?

2. Will R.J. Reynolds be teaching the Japanese his specialty — reaching first base on interference?

3. You'll notice that George Brett reached first base twice when his batted ball hit the runner. A little cheap, but that's two more hits. Do you think he did it deliberately just to win the batting title?

4. Steve Sax retained his crown as the major league player who grounded out the most times.

5. Did the Blue Jays give up on Tony Fernandez because he lines into too many double plays?

6. Hmm, Chris Sabo hit more foul popouts than any major league player. And Oakland has more foul territory than any major league stadium. Didn't those Oakland scouts know his weakness?

7. Isn't causing the fielder to make an error on a foul fly just the kind of heady play you'd expect a veteran like Eddie Murray to be the master of? Must be that scary scowl of his.

8. Gary Sheffield looks like the emerging master of the "Advance-No Play." As soon as Willie McGee hangs up his spikes, of course.

9. Did you notice there were exactly 23,000 flyouts hit in the major leagues last year? Not 22,999 and not 23,001. Now doesn't that make all our counting seem worthwhile?

IS IT IMPORTANT TO SCORE FIRST?

A good motto for every major league team would be: "Get on the scoreboard first." To remake an old point, we are constantly reminded of the importance of late inning performance; the Elias boys are the strongest voices in **that** particular choir. It's almost as though they're saying you could sleep through the first six innings, because nothing vital happens in them. Yet last year the club which scored first — one measly little run — went on to win the game over two-thirds of the time. Can we pretend that means nothing?

We thought you'd like to see how each club performed last year when they scored first, when their opponents scored first, and what the difference was between the two. Here are the figures for each of the 26 teams for 1990:

AL Team	Club Scores First				Opponents Score First				
	G	W	L	Pct	G	W	L	Pct	Diff
Baltimore	77	48	29	.623	84	28	56	.333	.290
Boston	77	56	21	.727	85	32	53	.376	.351
California	86	57	29	.663	76	23	53	.303	.360
Chicago	87	59	28	.678	75	35	40	.467	.211
Cleveland	79	53	26	.671	83	24	59	.289	.382
Detroit	78	51	27	.654	84	28	56	.333	.321
Kansas City	80	56	24	.700	81	19	62	.235	.465
Milwaukee	84	53	31	.631	78	21	57	.269	.362
Minnesota	90	57	33	.633	72	17	55	.236	.397
New York	68	43	25	.632	94	24	70	.255	.377
Oakland	91	75	16	.824	71	28	43	.394	.430
Seattle	84	55	29	.655	78	22	56	.282	.373
Texas	73	50	23	.685	89	33	56	.371	.314
Toronto	79	57	22	.722	83	29	54	.349	.373
American League	1133	770	363	.680	1133	363	770	.320	.360

NL Team	Club Scores First				Opponents Score First				
	G	W	L	Pct	G	W	L	Pct	Diff
Atlanta	75	41	34	.547	87	24	63	.276	.271
Chicago	78	49	29	.628	84	28	56	.333	.295
Cincinnati	88	66	22	.750	74	25	49	.338	.412
Houston	64	43	21	.672	98	32	66	.327	.345
Los Angeles	92	65	27	.707	70	21	49	.300	.407
Montreal	85	49	36	.576	77	36	41	.468	.112
New York	89	63	26	.708	73	28	45	.384	.324
Philadelphia	74	45	29	.608	88	32	56	.364	.244
Pittsburgh	86	61	25	.709	76	34	42	.447	.262

St. Louis	81	51	30	.630	81	19	62	.235	.395
San Diego	83	51	32	.614	79	24	55	.304	.310
San Francisco	77	54	23	.701	85	31	54	.365	.336
National League	972	638	334	.656	972	334	638	.344	.312
Major Leagues	2105	1408	697	.669	2105	397	1408	.331	.338

Obviously any team which posts the first run has a great chance of winning the game. The interesting cases are the clubs which perform exceptionally well — or exceptionally poorly — when they post the first run. Or when the opponents strike first. The best teams when scoring first last year were ones you'd expect: Oakland, Boston and Toronto in the American League, and Cincinnati, Pittsburgh, New York and Los Angeles in the National. But how about when the opponents make the first score? That's where the Expos (.468) and White Sox (.467) — two below-average teams when they get on the board first — really shine. What's the reputation of those two teams? They're thought of as overachievers . . . they win, but people aren't always sure how. The Expos and White Sox, and especially Montreal (only 112 points) have the smallest difference between winning percentage when they score first and when their opponents do.

So can we look on clubs that have a big difference as underachievers? It's an appealing notion, that some teams are fine when things are going well and they get out ahead, but they fold their tents when faced with coming from behind. When we add that the club with the biggest score first/opponents score first difference was the Kansas City Royals — Underachievement City! — you might be ready to jump on this notion. The only problem is that the number two and three clubs in biggest difference were the World Series opponents, the Athletics and Reds.

However, there's an important distinction. The A's and Reds had big differences primarily because they were exceptionally good when scoring first; when the opponents recorded the first tally, both Oakland and Cincinnati were still above the major league average. The Royals, though, were comfortably above average when scoring first (.700), but close to 100 percentage points below the norm (.235) when their opponents did. If you want to say that everything was not up-to-date in Kansas City last year, we'll find it hard to dispute you.

AL WEST: CAN THE A'S COME BACK?

Nothing in the 1990 baseball season was quite as shocking as what took place during the World Series: the Reds beat the favored A's in four straight games. To lose four straight contests is a rare — and perhaps ego-shattering — experience. We decided to examine the 13 teams which have been swept, and look for signs of scars. (Two additional teams, the 1907 Tigers and the 1922 Yankees, didn't win a game, but did play a tie. Since those two weren't completely whitewashed, we left them out of the study.) Here are the other 12 besides the 1990 A's, with a brief synopsis of what happened to them afterward:

Team	What happened
1914 A's	Last place every year 1915-21; next pennant 1929
1927 Pirates	Fourth in 1928; next pennant 1960
1928 Cardinals	Fourth in 1929; pennant 1930
1932 Cubs	Third in 1933; next pennant 1935
1938 Cubs	Fourth in 1939; next pennant 1945
1939 Reds	World champs in 1940
1950 Phillies	Fifth in 1951; next pennant 1980
1954 Indians	Second in 1955; still waiting for next pennant
1963 Yankees	Won pennant in 1964 (lost Series in seven games)
1966 Dodgers	Eighth in 1967; next pennant 1974
1976 Yankees	World champs in 1977
1989 Giants	Third place in 1990

The report is not very comforting for the A's; the average club faded to fourth place the next year. Four of the clubs went into a sort of long exile. Connie Mack's 1914 A's, a team which had won its fourth pennant in five years, went from first to last in 1915, and stayed there for six more seasons. However, this was largely because Mack, who felt he could no longer meet his stars' salary demands, sold most of them to other teams. But the '27 Pirates, after losing four straight to the mighty Yankees of Ruth and Gehrig, wouldn't appear in the Series again for 33 years; the Phillies didn't reach the Series for 30 years after their 1950 blowout at the hands of the Yanks; and the Indians haven't even won a division title since being shockingly humiliated by the 1954 Giants.

However, the damage wasn't that great for everyone. Three of the twelve made the Series the very next year, and two — the 1939 Reds and the 1976 Yankees — would turn things around completely, winning the world championship the very next year. Should that comfort the A's? Probably not. Both the '39 Reds and '76 Yankees were surprise pennant winners who'd made the Series for the first time in 20 and 12 years, respectively. They were clubs on the way up, very different from the A's situation.

Were there any clubs with strong parallels to the '90 A's? There were; you could find similarities to the '28 Cardinals, the '63 Yanks and the '66 Dodgers. Branch Rickey's Cardinals won their first world championship in 1926, and weren't thrown off stride much by being blown out in '28. St. Louis would take a year to recover, but then won the National League pennant again in 1930, and the world championship in both 1931 and '34. The Yankees of 1963, a longtime dynasty, weren't thrown by being the first Yankee club to lose the Series in four straight games; they returned to the Series the very next year despite an aging roster, though they would lose in seven games to the Bob Gibson-Cardinals.

On the other hand, the '66 Dodgers, a team which had won the world title in both 1963 and 1965, lost the Series to the Orioles in a four-game shocker that was every bit the surprise that Oakland's 1990 loss was. That Dodger club fell all the way to eighth place in the ten-club National League in '67, and wouldn't return to postseason play until 1974. The Dodgers had an excellent excuse: their best player, Sandy Koufax, retired after the '66 blowout. But even the loss of such a great player would not figure to make that enormous a difference. The combination of losing first the Series, then Koufax, threw LA off-stride for a long time. Fortunately, the A's have only one trauma to deal with.

Though not the victim of a blowout, one more World Series loser seems eerily similar to the 1990 A's: the 1971 Orioles. Like the Athletics, the O's had dominated the American League for three straight years. In year one, 1969, the Oriole were heavily favored over a supposedly-weak National League opponent, the Mets . . . but they lost to the underdogs in five contests, just as the 1988 A's would bow to the Dodgers. In year two, both the 1970 Orioles and the 1989 A's played with a vengeance all year, and didn't stop until they'd won the championship: the '70 O's overwhelmed a good Reds club in five contests, and the '89 A's destroyed their opponents, the Giants, in four straight games. In year three, both the '71 Orioles and the '90 A's once more marched through the regular season and the playoffs with seeming invincibility. But each club was shocked once again in the Series: the Orioles lost in seven games to the Pirates (after winning the first two), and of course the Reds shocked the '90 A's.

What happened to those Orioles? They fell to fourth in 1972, and wouldn't return to the Series until '79: they'd be heavily favored in that Series, also, but would lose once again to the Pirates. Though the Orioles would remain a strong club, with division titles in 1973 and '74, the air of invincibility was gone forever.

That may or not happen to the A's, who still possess an imposing roster. But history suggests that if Oakland wants to reclaim their mantle of greatness, they'll have their work cut out for them.

IS A WALK AS GOOD AS A HIT?

It was the old pitcher-turned-broadcaster Waite Hoyt, we believe, who introduced a familiar lament to radio listeners: "Oh, those bases on balls!" Or maybe it was Frankie Frisch. (Help us on this one, Alert Readers.) Whoever the wise old sage was, the point he was making has been oft-repeated — when the leadoff man in an inning reaches base via a walk, he's almost certain to score.

True or false? Certainly we know that every leadoff walk doesn't result in a run scoring . . . although it certainly seems that way when it's your team that surrenders the free pass. But we wondered about those leadoff walks. If a pitcher yields a base on balls to start an inning, is it more of a sign of weakness than if he starts it out by giving up a hit? Which is more likely to score, the runner who reaches base on the walk or the one who hits his way on? And how about if one of his trusty fielders starts off the inning by booting one? Will that unnerve the pitcher more than if the batter had hit or walked his way on? (Yes, we're thinking of you, Dave Stieb.)

Well, that's why we have our database. Here's how often at least one run scored after a batter reached base under varying circumstances in 1990:

	Scored	Occurences	Scored pct.
SINGLE	2,822	6,357	44.4%
DOUBLE	1,073	1,633	65.7%
TRIPLE	165	198	83.3%
WALK	1,353	2,967	45.6%
1ST ON ERROR	163	346	47.1%

As you can see, a runner who reaches via a walk is indeed more likely to score than one who reaches on a hit. However, the difference is very small — only a little more than one percent, and that could easily be the result of chance. Indeed, the league data was split: in the National League a leadoff walk resulted in a run more often than a single did (46.9% to 43.2%), but in the American League the results were reversed (walk resulted in a run 44.6% of the time, single resulted in a run 45.4%). It's possible that the pitchers in the American League are manlier men than the ones in the National, and thus less likely to let a little old walk bother them — but's it much more likely the results were simply due to chance. So the Waite Hoyt lament is hardly proven: it doesn't seem more damaging, to any significant degree, whether the pitcher starts out the inning by yielding either a walk **or** a single. The best advice, still, is get the man out!

However, the data did reveal a couple of other interesting tidbits:

1. There could be something to the old Dave Stieb Syndrome. When an inning started with an error, it was more likely to result in a run than when the inning started with either a walk or a hit. Again, the differences were fairly small, but the data is fascinating. After all, starting off the inning by giving up either a walk or a hit is a sign of pitching weakness, whereas starting with a fielder's error indicates no such thing. Still, the runner was more likely to score after the error. Hurlers, control thy tempers!

2. We were surprised, as we're sure you were, that when an inning starts off with a triple, the defensive team escapes without allowing a run about one sixth of the time. Either major league hitters are a lot worse at fundamentals than even we thought, or else this situation — man on third, none out — is a lot less certain than people think. Maybe Waite Hoyt should have said, "Oh, those triples with nobody scoring!"

WHICH TEAMS HAVE NIGHT VISION?

When night baseball was new, a lot of people felt that the pitchers had a clear advantage under the lights. That may well have been true — unfortunately, we have only sketchy data on the subject. But how about nowadays, when most games are played at night and the lights are generally considered excellent? Here's American League data on the subject for 1990:

American League — 1990

	Avg	OBP	Slg
Day	.259	.327	.383
Night	.259	.327	.387

There's virtually no difference between the day and night figures. However, there is a good deal of team-to-team variance. Here's how each AL club batted during the day and at night last year:

American League — 1990 Batting

Team	Day Avg	OBP	Slg	Night Avg	OBP	Slg
Baltimore	.263	.343	.391	.239	.324	.362
Boston	.287	.360	.431	.266	.337	.379
California	.247	.318	.368	.264	.333	.399
Chicago WSox	.256	.319	.374	.259	.320	.381
Cleveland	.274	.324	.401	.264	.323	.386
Detroit	.262	.338	.400	.258	.337	.412
Kansas City	.269	.327	.425	.266	.328	.386
Milwaukee	.235	.296	.344	.266	.331	.402
Minnesota	.272	.340	.393	.262	.317	.382
New York Yanks	.260	.319	.362	.233	.293	.368
Oakland	.245	.330	.374	.260	.340	.402
Seattle	.247	.319	.362	.264	.338	.377
Texas	.252	.338	.361	.260	.329	.379
Toronto	.261	.319	.417	.266	.332	.420

The Orioles, Red Sox and Yankees all hit more than 20 points better in day games; the Brewers hit more than 30 points better at night. Do these clubs simply have hitters who have night-adjustment problems, or is there some kind of home park factor at work, maybe poor lighting? If the latter were the case, you'd expect the O's, BoSox and Yank pitchers to also have an advantage under the lights. Here's how each club's pitchers fared in the day/night comparison last year:

American League — 1990 Pitching

Team	Day Avg	OBP	Slg	Night Avg	OBP	Slg
Baltimore	.263	.327	.416	.264	.329	.407
Boston	.252	.323	.343	.265	.329	.382
California	.274	.336	.394	.265	.333	.374
Chicago WSox	.250	.318	.380	.241	.315	.351
Cleveland	.260	.317	.416	.273	.341	.418
Detroit	.263	.343	.406	.257	.341	.402
Kansas City	.259	.342	.371	.265	.332	.390
Milwaukee	.273	.331	.405	.276	.332	.396
Minnesota	.270	.331	.383	.274	.333	.418
New York Yanks	.261	.342	.392	.261	.334	.410
Oakland	.225	.296	.341	.247	.306	.377
Seattle	.250	.326	.390	.241	.320	.348
Texas	.267	.350	.371	.244	.322	.370
Toronto	.274	.328	.411	.253	.312	.392

If poor home park lighting is a factor in Baltimore, Boston and New York, you sure can't see it from their pitchers' data. The Oriole and Yankee pitchers have only a tiny day/night difference, and the Red Sox hurlers were actually better during the daytime.

When we look at the National League data (excluding pitchers' hitting), we find something a little surprising — NL teams overall perform much better in the daytime:

National League — 1990

	Avg	OBP	Slg
Day	.270	.334	.409
Night	.261	.329	.390

One guess you might make is that the Cubs, with their great hitting park and numerous day games, might be the primary reason for the daytime advantage. Here are the breakdowns for each NL club's offense:

National League — 1990 Batting

Team	Day Avg	OBP	Slg	Night Avg	OBP	Slg
Atlanta	.260	.318	.401	.255	.317	.411
Chicago Cubs	.283	.334	.425	.255	.305	.384
Cincinnati	.278	.341	.429	.275	.335	.413
Houston	.266	.337	.383	.243	.316	.348
Los Angeles	.272	.343	.409	.268	.336	.390
Montreal	.262	.336	.411	.258	.333	.374

National League — 1990 Batting

Team	Day			Night		
	Avg	OBP	Slg	Avg	OBP	Slg
New York Mets	.270	.336	.427	.259	.329	.422
Philadelphia	.253	.333	.380	.266	.338	.375
Pittsburgh	.273	.341	.452	.267	.341	.411
St. Louis	.269	.324	.381	.258	.328	.360
San Diego	.265	.332	.389	.264	.328	.394
San Francisco	.279	.336	.418	.269	.334	.412

The Cubs, not surprisingly, hit 28 points better in day games. But every other club except the Phillies also fares better during the day, though sometimes the differences are quite small. Wrigley is probably a factor, and so is Candlestick Park: the Giants play a lot of day games, and it might be tougher to hit there at night, when the hitters' hands are even more frozen. In addition, the Houston Astrodome and New York's Shea Stadium have a reputation for poor lighting; Met hitters did somewhat worse at night, and Houston hitters a **lot** worse. All those could be possible explanations as to why NL hitters fare better in the daytime.

If any of those explanations are valid, you'd expect the clubs' pitching staffs to show the same biases. Here's the data for NL pitching staffs:

National League — 1990 Pitching

Team	Day			Night		
	Avg	OBP	Slg	Avg	OBP	Slg
Atlanta	.283	.347	.424	.272	.342	.396
Chicago Cubs	.283	.346	.430	.258	.332	.370
Cincinnati	.236	.313	.357	.249	.317	.374
Houston	.262	.321	.405	.252	.317	.374
Los Angeles	.267	.329	.401	.242	.303	.369
Montreal	.253	.313	.389	.242	.310	.356
New York Mets	.255	.308	.374	.241	.302	.359
Philadelphia	.253	.337	.368	.253	.333	.390
Pittsburgh	.247	.303	.380	.252	.306	.381
St. Louis	.258	.314	.383	.262	.323	.380
San Diego	.259	.323	.400	.258	.319	.386
San Francisco	.270	.329	.405	.264	.335	.386

The Cub, Astro, Met and Giant pitching staffs are indeed more effective at night; however, only the Cubs have a really big difference. Wrigley Field appears to be the biggest reason why National League clubs hit better during the daytime. In addition, the theory about lighting problems in the Astrodome and Shea still seems to hold water.

A complete listing for this category appears on page 245.

HOW WOULD PYTHAGORAS PREDICT THE PENNANT RACES?

The Pythagorean Theorem, one of the Bill James' first contributions to the world of baseball statistics, is pretty simple. It projects a club's winning percentage by how many runs they score, and how many they allow. The formula is:

$$\frac{\text{(Runs squared)}}{\text{(Runs squared)} + \text{(Opposition Runs squared)}} = \text{Won-Lost Percentage}$$

The formula is usually very accurate in measuring how many games a team wins during a season. It ordinarily comes within three wins of the actual victory total . . . but as we'll explain in a minute, the interesting cases are the ones where the formula is off. Let's look at how the formula predicted the won-lost totals for teams in 1989:

1989

	Runs Scored	Opponent Runs	Actual W	Actual L	Projected W	Projected L	Diff.
AL East							
Blue Jays	731	651	89	73	90	72	–1
Orioles	708	686	87	75	84	78	3
Red Sox	774	735	83	79	85	77	–2
Brewers	707	679	81	81	84	78	–3
Yankees	698	792	74	87	71	91	3
Indians	604	654	73	89	75	87	–2
Tigers	617	816	59	103	59	103	0
AL West							
Athletics	712	576	99	63	98	64	1
Royals	690	635	92	70	88	74	4
Angels	669	578	91	71	93	69	–2
Rangers	695	714	83	79	79	83	4
Twins	740	738	80	82	81	81	–1
Mariners	694	728	73	89	77	85	–4
White Sox	693	750	69	92	75	87	–6
NL East							
Cubs	702	623	93	69	91	71	2
Mets	683	595	87	75	92	70	–5
Cardinals	632	608	86	76	84	78	2
Expos	632	630	81	81	81	81	0
Pirates	637	680	74	88	76	86	–2
Phillies	629	735	67	95	68	94	–1

		1989					
	Runs Scored	Opponent Runs	Actual W	L	Projected W	L	Diff.
NL West							
Giants	699	600	92	70	93	69	−1
Padres	642	626	89	73	83	79	6
Astros	647	669	86	76	78	84	8
Dodgers	554	536	77	83	84	78	−7
Reds	632	691	75	87	74	88	1
Braves	584	680	63	97	69	93	−6

As you can see, the actual totals were generally very close to the projected totals, particularly in the American League. Only six clubs were off by more than four wins, four of them in the volatile NL West: the White Sox, Mets, Padres, Astros, Dodgers and Braves. What happened with those clubs? More than likely, they were simply unlucky; they lost a lot of close games they would normally be expected to win. Baseball people, of course, don't like to talk about things like luck. When a club wins a title, they say it was because the team had "character." Then, presumably, the players spend the off-season with gamblers and women of ill repute (which sounds okay to us). Anyway, when the next season begins, all that character is suddenly lost, along with the chance to repeat. Well, if you substitute the word "luck" for character, you don't have to surmise about off-season activities.

The point of all this is that the Pythagorean theorem is sort of like the Leading Economic Indicators. Luck swings back and forth, and lucky clubs (or teams that had "character," if you prefer) in one season tend to be unlucky in the next. Which brings us to 1990. Here are the Pythagorean projections, and the actual victory totals, for the 1990 clubs:

		1990					
	Runs Scored	Opponent Runs	Actual W	L	Projected W	L	Diff.
AL East							
Red Sox	699	664	88	74	85	77	3
Blue Jays	767	661	86	76	93	69	−7
Tigers	750	754	79	83	81	81	−2
Indians	732	737	77	85	80	82	−3
Orioles	669	698	76	85	78	84	−2
Brewers	732	760	74	88	78	84	−4
Yankees	603	749	67	95	64	98	3

	Runs Scored	1990 Opponent Runs	Actual W	L	Projected W	L	Diff.
AL West							
Athletics	733	570	103	59	101	61	2
White Sox	682	633	94	68	87	75	7
Rangers	676	696	83	79	79	83	4
Angels	690	706	80	82	79	83	1
Mariners	640	680	77	85	76	86	1
Royals	707	709	75	86	81	81	−6
Twins	666	729	74	88	74	88	0
NL East							
Pirates	733	619	95	67	95	67	0
Mets	775	613	91	71	100	62	−9
Expos	662	598	85	77	89	73	−4
Cubs	690	774	77	85	72	90	5
Phillies	646	729	77	85	71	91	6
Cardinals	599	698	70	92	69	93	1
NL West							
Reds	693	597	91	71	93	69	−2
Dodgers	728	685	86	76	86	76	0
Giants	719	710	85	77	82	80	3
Astros	573	656	75	87	70	92	5
Padres	673	673	75	87	81	81	−6
Braves	682	821	65	97	66	96	−1

The White Sox, the AL unluckiest team in 1989, more than made up for it in 1990 — after winning six games fewer than expected, they won seven more. The Royals, plus-four in 1989, were minus-six in 1990, and the Padres went from plus-six in year one to minus-six in year two. On the other hand, the system wasn't perfect. The Astros exceeded expectations in both seasons, and the Mets — big surprise — did less than expected both years.

Can you use the Pythagorean theorem to project how clubs will do in 1991? You can, though we have to caution that luck doesn't always even out over a two year span. We'd venture that in '91, the White Sox figure to win fewer games, the Royals and Padres more. The Astros, after two years of overachieving and a 1990 off-season in which they seemingly lost every valuable player they had, seem a mortal cinch to crash to earth in '91. And the Mets and Blue Jays finally figure to get lucky. But don't bet on it.

WHICH TEAMS ARE BEST IN THE CLUTCH?

In 1990, about 29 percent of all major league games were decided by one run. How important is that? Well, in 1989, the Red Sox went 13-25 in one run contests and missed the American League East title by six games. In 1990 the Sox were 31-22 in one run games — a ten and a half game improvement — and won the East by two. The main difference from '89 to '90 was that the Red Sox improved their hitting in the late innings of close games by 14 points. Boston ended up leading the league in late-and close situations with a .283 mark. The AL figures for 1990:

American League
Late Innings of Close Games

Team	Avg	Opp. Avg	1-Run Games W	L
Texas	.261	.257	37	22
Boston	.283	.249	31	22
Chicago	.245	.215	30	22
Oakland	.269	.190	23	18
Minnesota	.252	.271	21	19
California	.248	.260	23	21
Detroit	.228	.263	22	22
Toronto	.254	.262	24	27
Kansas City	.258	.280	21	26
Milwaukee	.237	.267	18	23
New York	.237	.251	23	29
Baltimore	.245	.250	22	28
Seattle	.248	.258	20	28
Cleveland	.249	.247	16	24

In the National League, the best hitting club in late-and-close situations was the lackluster Philadelphia Phillies. The champion Reds were well down the list — tied for next-to-worst, in fact — but Cincinnati made that up in the pitching department:

National League
Late Innings of Close Games

Team	Avg	Opp. Avg	1-Run Games W	L
Los Angeles	.257	.262	26	16
Pittsburgh	.252	.237	28	20
San Francisco	.267	.239	25	23
Philadelphia	.285	.252	28	26
Cincinnati	.246	.233	20	19
Houston	.247	.250	24	23
Montreal	.258	.263	30	30
St. Louis	.250	.289	21	24
Atlanta	.216	.276	18	21
Chicago	.278	.270	24	29
New York	.255	.233	23	28
San Diego	.246	.259	19	27

We argued last year that stopping the opposition in the late innings was a key factor in the makeup of a good ballclub. There's nothing in the 1990 stats to dispute that notion. In the American League, the champion A's held the opposition to an unreal .190 average in late-and-close situations. The next best team was the White Sox, winners of 94 games.

In the National League, the most effective pitching club in the late innings of close games was the world champion Reds. The worst teams were the last-place finishers, the Cardinals and Braves. One club badly hurt in the late innings was the Montreal Expos. The 'Spos allowed 35 late-and-close home runs, the most in the majors by far. As a result, Montreal was only 30-30 in one-run games and 9-12 in extra innings, despite a good late-inning offense.

There is a well-studied theory which states that performance in one-run games (and late-and-close situations) is governed to a good extent by luck. Bill James originated the idea, but the Elias boys have quoted it so much that people like Tim McCarver think they invented it. (Hey Tim, get it straight!) Anyway, the theory would indicate that the following teams should do better in 1991, all other things being equal, which of course they're not: Mets, Cubs, Padres, Indians and Mariners. These should regress: Dodgers, Pirates, Rangers, Red Sox, White Sox. Free agent signings, trades and injuries would affect those predictions, but we think it's safe to say that the Cubs and Padres are very likely to be much better in 1991, and the Pirates, Rangers and White Sox should be worse. When you see it on CBS, remember where you heard it first.

A complete listing for this category can be found on page 246.

WHY THROW TO FIRST?

You might recall that, a year ago, we looked into the question of whether pitchers' throws to first are a waste of time. The answer was a disappointment to anyone who hates a three hour game: there seemed to be a real correlation between throwing to first and cutting down the chances of a successful steal.

That was one year's worth of data, and it's natural to wonder whether the numbers would hold up when given another look. We did the same comparison for 1990, and the answer was the same — those maddening tosses to first really do work. An '89-'90 comparison (data for both leagues):

	1989			1990			Both Years		
	SB	CS	%	SB	CS	%	SB	CS	%
No Throws Made	1401	526	73	1422	560	72	2823	1086	72
Throws Made	1175	681	63	1321	721	65	2496	1402	64

The data held up very well in 1990. This time there was a seven percent difference in the success rate instead of ten, but that's still pretty sizable. For the two years together, the steal success rate is eight percent lower when a toss to first is made. And that's a big difference. Every stolen base

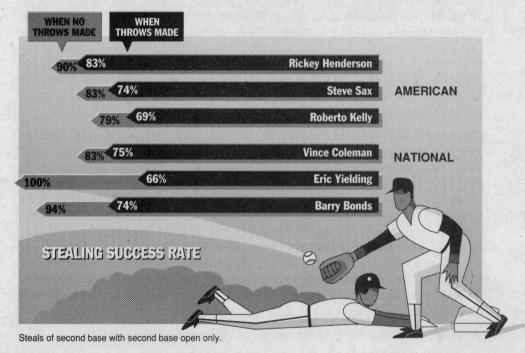

WHEN NO THROWS MADE **WHEN THROWS MADE**

90%	83%	Rickey Henderson	AMERICAN
83%	74%	Steve Sax	
79%	69%	Roberto Kelly	
83%	75%	Vince Coleman	NATIONAL
100%	66%	Eric Yielding	
94%	74%	Barry Bonds	

STEALING SUCCESS RATE

Steals of second base with second base open only.

study we've seen indicates that at a 64 percent success rate — the rate when pitchers tossed to first in the two years combined — stealing is a losing proposition.

One other thing you might notice from the data is that pitchers were throwing to first a little more often in 1990. In 1989, there was at least one toss to first in 49 percent of the steal attempts; in 1990, the figure rose to 51 percent. We'd like to think this indicates that major league pitchers were reading our book; in fact there's rumor — started by us — that Orel Hershiser suffered his arm injury pulling his copy of the *Scoreboard* out of his back pocket. That rise in tosses to first was a small one, however, and may have been just a random occurrence. But we'll keep an eye on it for the future.

The other thing the 1989 data showed was that throwing to first worked even better against the top base stealers than it did against average runners. The graphic shows that this was still the case in 1990. Here's a more detailed look at the 12 runners who stole 40 or more bases in 1990:

	No Throw Made			Throw Made		
American League	**SB**	**CS**	**%**	**SB**	**CS**	**%**
Henderson, Oak	19	2	90	29	6	83
Sax, Yanks	15	3	83	17	6	74
Kelly, Yanks	11	3	79	24	11	69
Cole, Cle	6	0	100	25	9	74
National League	**SB**	**CS**	**%**	**SB**	**CS**	**%**
Coleman, StL	25	5	83	33	11	75
Yelding, Hou	15	0	100	39	20	66
Bonds, Pit	15	1	94	25	9	74
Butler, SF	21	8	72	28	10	74
Nixon, Mon	16	2	89	21	9	70
Raines, Mon	24	7	77	14	6	70
Roberts, SD	12	2	86	27	6	82
DeShields, Mon	13	5	72	22	15	59
TOTALS (Top 12)	192	38	84	304	118	72

In 11 of the 12 cases, the success rate was lower when the pitcher tossed to first (all except Brett Butler). Overall, the top stealers stole at a rate 12 percent lower when the pitcher threw to first at least once. That wasn't as big a difference as in '89, when the 40-plus stealers had a success rate 24 points lower when the hurler threw to first, but it's still a pretty large difference. The moral, much as we hate to say it, is still: keep tossing to first!

A complete listing for this category can be found on page 247.

NL WEST: WHAT'S THE FUTURE FOR THE REDS?

After several years of being labeled underachievers, the Cincinnati Reds are on top of the baseball world. But baseball is a game of "What have you done for me lately?" Now the question is whether the Reds can repeat, and develop into the sort of dominant team that people expected Oakland to be.

We'll say this right off: history is on Cincinnati's side. In our article on the A's, we tell what happened to the twelve teams which lost the World Series in four straight games. How about the teams which **won** four straight? Generally these clubs proved that their victories were no flukes. Four of them made the Series again the next year, and three of those repeated as world champions. Four more finished second the following year, and two were third. The only two clubs that flopped the year after a winning four straight were the 1963 Dodgers and the 1966 Orioles, who both dropped to sixth place (in ten-team leagues). But that was mostly due to injuries, and both teams quickly recovered — the Dodgers would win pennants in 1965 and 1966, and the Orioles would win flags in 1969, 1970 and 1971. In addition, the two other teams which went undefeated in the World Series (each played a tie game) also remained dominant: both the 1907 Cubs and the 1922 Giants would win pennants the next year.

So that part of the prognosis is good. But it might be more revealing to compare the Reds with the dominant teams of the more recent past. Since the leagues split into divisions in 1969, these clubs might be considered "dynasties;" all won at least four division titles and one world championship, with no more than a three-year gap between one crown and the next:

- The Baltimore Orioles won pennants in 1969-70-71, with the world championship in 1970, and division titles in 1973-74.

- The Oakland Athletics won division titles in 1971-72-73-74-75, with world championships in 1972-73-74.

- The Cincinnati Reds won division titles in 1970-72-73-75-76-79, with pennants in 1970 and '72 and the world championship in 1975-76.

- The New York Yankees won pennants in 1976-77-78-81, with world championships in 1977-78.

- The Los Angeles Dodgers won division titles in 1974-77-78-81-83-85-88, with league pennants in '74, '77, and '78, and world championships in 1981 and 1988

Were there any common traits that all these teams had? We thought you'd never ask:

1. All had strong, though sometimes volatile, ownership and management — marked by an excellent eye for talent.

2. All had excellent pitching. Sparky Anderson's Reds might be considered an exception to this rule, but the Big Red Machine had outstanding bullpens, and usually ranked in the National League's top three in team ERA.

3. All had excellent home run power.

4. All had two or three "superstars" — players who would win, or be strong contenders for two or more MVP or Cy Young Awards, and wind up as viable Hall of Fame candidates. About the only exception might be the Dodgers, who, in the Hollywood tradition, had short-term superstars: Garvey/Mike Marshall the Pitcher (not to be confused with Mike Marshall the Disabled) in 1974, the 30-Homer Bunch (Garvey-Cey-Baker-Smith) in 1977, Valenzuela in 1981, Gibson/Hershiser in 1988.

5. All had, supporting the superstars, several players who would be considered longterm stars — among the best in the league at their position for a decade or more. An example would be the Sparky Reds: Bench-Morgan-Rose-Perez (superstars), Concepcion-Griffey-Foster-Gullett-Nolan (stars). Or the Earl Weaver Orioles: B.Robinson-F.Robinson-Palmer (superstars), Johnson-Belanger-Blair-McNally-Cuellar (stars).

How do the Reds stack up? Well, Cincy has the sort of owner who brings back memories of Finley and Steinbrenner — it's almost as though they win just to spite her (him). Nothing wrong with a little creative tension. The Reds' pitching is outstanding, but not their home run power; they were only seventh in team homers last year. Stars and superstars? Too early to tell, because this is still a pretty young club. But you could see Davis (if he stays healthy)-Larkin (the next great shortstop)-Dibble (the first superstar setup man?) as superstars, Rijo-Myers (these two could move up)-Browning-Sabo-O'Neill as the dependable longterm stars. The potential is there.

However, the Reds have to contend with the now-revived Dodgers. Remarkably, Los Angeles hasn't gone more than three years without a division title since the early seventies, when Walter Alston was still their manager. Now **that's** a dynasty. This year the Dodgers will present Murray-Strawberry-Martinez (unless his arm falls off) as superstars, Daniels-Butler-Scioscia and possibly Valenzuela-Samuel-Hershiser as stars. Should be an interesting race.

WHICH TEAMS HAVE LEAD FEET?

The Boston Red Sox have long had the reputation for having a "country club" offense — blast the ball as far as you can, saunter down the fairway and don't get that nice outfit mussed up. Our baserunning stats indicate that this reputation is well-deserved. We keep track of the number of extra bases each team takes on hits and outs, and compare that with the number of chances they had. For the second year in a row, Boston was the most conservative baserunning club in the majors. Here are the 1990 figures for the American League, along with the total runs scored by each team, and their rank in each category:

Team	Extra-Base Pct	Rank	Runs	Rank
Chicago	45.8	1	682	9
Milwaukee	45.2	2	732	4T
Oakland	44.2	3T	733	3
Toronto	44.2	3T	767	1
Texas	44.0	5	676	10
Kansas City	43.1	6	707	6
Cleveland	43.0	7	732	4T
Baltimore	42.6	8	669	11
California	42.4	9	690	8
Minnesota	41.8	10	666	12
Detroit	40.6	11	750	2
Seattle	39.4	12	640	13
New York	38.8	13	603	14
Boston	38.0	14	699	7

Do teams which run aggressively score more runs? You can't prove it by the White Sox, the most aggressive baserunning club in the league but only ninth in runs scored. Or by the Tigers — 11th in extra base percentage, second in scoring. There seems to be a strong relationship, however, between the size of the ballpark and how aggressive teams are. The most daring teams — the White Sox, Brewers, A's and Blue Jays — all play in pretty big parks. The least aggressive clubs — the Twins, Tigers, Mariners, Yankees, and Red Sox — all play in parks with shorter dimensions. The Red Sox may be a conservative baserunning club, but the big reason for that is Fenway Park, where the Green Monster dominates the game. No club playing in Fenway, with balls caroming off The Wall into the left fielder's hands, would be taking a lot of extra bases.

Now let's look at the National League:

Team	Extra-Base Pct	Rank	Runs	Rank
Los Angeles	47.2	1	728	3
New York	46.2	2	775	1
Cincinnati	45.0	3	693	5
Montreal	44.9	4	662	8
San Diego	43.6	5	673	7
Pittsburgh	43.1	6	733	2
San Francisco	42.7	7	719	4
Houston	42.2	8	573	12
Chicago	42.0	9	690	4
St. Louis	41.1	10	599	11
Philadelphia	40.3	11	646	10
Atlanta	38.7	12	682	9

In the National League most of the parks are mostly good-sized, so there's not the same kind of relationship between park and aggressiveness that we saw in the AL. But there is a stronger relationship between extra-base percentage and runs scored. This was also true with 1989 data. This consistent with the notion that the National League is the "speed" league while the American is "power."

The surprise in the NL in 1990 was the Dodgers, who moved from eighth to first in baserunning aggressiveness, and — not completely coincidentally — from twelfth to third in runs scored. That could be a portent of better things to come for the Bums in 1991.

A complete listing for this category can be found on page 248.

WHICH UMPIRES ARE OFFENSIVE?

One of the crucial factors in every game is one most people never even consider: the home plate umpire. When Terry Cooney worked the plate last year, American League hitters batted .272, and each team averaged 4.9 runs per game — hitters' paradise. When Mark Johnson was behind the plate, on the other hand, the hitters batted only .246, and the teams averaged 4.0 runs per game — pitchers' battles. Since each ump works behind the plate only 35 to 40 times per year, those figures will fluctuate from year to year. But our stats over the past two seasons leave little doubt that there really are "pitchers' umpires" and "hitters' umpires."

We thought you might be interested in how different umpires perform at various points in the ball-and-strike count. Okay, the first pitch has been made and the batter took it — which umpires are more likely to call it a strike?

Batter Takes First Pitch

American League		National League	
Pitchers' friends	Called Strike %	Pitchers' friends	Called Strike %
Larry McCoy	41.9	Harry Wendelstadt	40.2
Greg Kosc	41.4	Bob Davidson	39.7
Larry Barnett	40.1	Eric Gregg	38.8
Hitters' friends	Called Strike %	Hitters' friends	Called Strike %
Rocky Roe	31.6	Bruce Froemming	33.5
Tim McClelland	32.9	Dana DeMuth	34.0
Dan Morrison	33.3	John McSherry	34.0
		Jerry Crawford	34.0

If you're a pitcher who likes to nibble, you'd sure want Larry McCoy behind the plate. When the batter was taking last year, McCoy called the first pitch a strike 41.9% of the time; not surprisingly, pitchers in McCoy games had "great control," averaging only 2.7 walks per nine innings. But hurlers with borderline control must have dreaded the sight of Rocky Roe, who called first-pitch strikes only 31.6% of the time the batter was taking. Pitchers in games umpired by Roe allowed 48 percent more walks (4.0 per nine innings) than pitchers in McCoy games.

Okay, let's move ahead in the count. The pitcher's having trouble, and he misses with his first three offerings. The batter's taking this one all the way. Will our pitcher get that "automatic strike" on 3-0? It depends on who's umpiring:

The Automatic Strike — Batter Takes 3-0 Pitch

American League		National League	
Pitchers' friends	Called Strike %	Pitchers' friends	Called Strike %
Mark Johnson	69.5	Eric Gregg	76.6
John Hirschbeck	64.8	Dutch Rennert	68.0
Mike Reilly	64.1	Bob Davidson	66.7
Hitters' friends	Called Strike %	Hitters' friends	Called Strike %
Don Denkinger	49.6	Joe West	50.4
Derryl Cousins	52.0	Bill Hohn	51.7
Jim McKean	52.4	Jerry Layne	53.0

There's no automatic strike when the veteran Don Denkinger's working — over half the time last year, he called it a ball . . . fairly astonishing when you consider that most pitchers are just laying it in there on 3-and-0. But when big Eric Gregg is behind the plate, the pitcher gets a strike called more than three-fourths of the time.

Now the count is 3-2. The batter doesn't want to strike out looking, so he's apt to swing at anything close. But when the pitch is borderline, he might make a point of remembering who the plate umpire is:

Swing if it's Close — Batter Takes 3-2 Pitch

American League		National League	
Pitchers' friends	Called Strike %	Pitchers' friends	Called Strike %
Tim Welke	23.8	Bob Davidson	26.8
Don Denkinger	23.0	Mark Hirschbeck	24.7
Tim Tschida	21.7	Gerry Davis	22.6
Hitters' friends	Called Strike %	Hitters' friends	Called Strike %
Al Clark	8.8	Eric Gregg	9.6
Rocky Roe	9.2	Randy Marsh	11.2
Steve Palermo	10.2	Steve Rippley	11.5

What a huge difference! The National League's Bob Davidson punched out the hitter nearly 27 percent of the time on 3-2. Davidson was more than three times as likely to call a third strike on 3-2 than the American's Al Clark, the only major league umpire who has his name on his cap.

So this season, when it's a crucial game and the contest comes down to two out in the ninth, 3-and-2 count, don't be surprised if the hitter eyes the ump, steps out and says, "Time out . . . I gotta check my *Scoreboard!*"

A complete listing for this category can be found on page 249.

WHEN CAN A MONTH SEEM LIKE A YEAR?

Baseball is a daily struggle, and not surprisingly, a game of streaks. A hitter or pitcher can get hot for a month or more, and carry his club along with him. (Of course, he can get cold, too, and drag his club down along with him. But we'll get to that later.) The following players, and pitchers, were the heroes who turned in the best monthly performances of 1990:

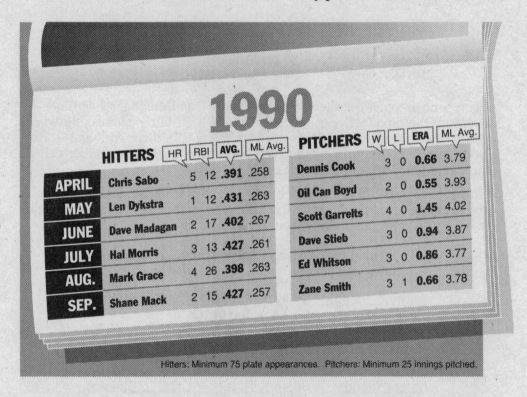

1990

HITTERS		HR	RBI	AVG.	ML Avg.
APRIL	Chris Sabo	5	12	.391	.258
MAY	Len Dykstra	1	12	.431	.263
JUNE	Dave Madagan	2	17	.402	.267
JULY	Hal Morris	3	13	.427	.261
AUG.	Mark Grace	4	26	.398	.263
SEP.	Shane Mack	2	15	.427	.257

PITCHERS	W	L	ERA	ML Avg.
Dennis Cook	3	0	0.66	3.79
Oil Can Boyd	2	0	0.55	3.93
Scott Garrelts	4	0	1.45	4.02
Dave Stieb	3	0	0.94	3.87
Ed Whitson	3	0	0.86	3.77
Zane Smith	3	1	0.66	3.78

Hitters: Minimum 75 plate appearances. Pitchers: Minimum 25 innings pitched.

Though none of the players could sustain this type of performance for very long, one can immediately see how important their hot streaks were both to themselves and their teams. Chris Sabo's break from the starting gate was crucial to the Reds' setting the pace in the National League West. Just as important was the way Zane Smith pitched down the stretch for the Pirates, when they outlasted the Mets to win the NL East. Dave Magadan's June sparked the Mets back into contention, as did Dave Stieb's July for the Blue Jays. Mark Grace's August turned around what 'til then had been a disappointing season, and Shane Mack's September spurt put him squarely in the Minnesota Twins' plans for 1991.

The following players didn't quite make the leaders list, but they were month-long heroes for their clubs last year:

June	Sandberg, Cubs	.377, 14 homers, 25 RBI
June	Strawberry, Mets	.376, 10 homers, 27 RBI
May	Fielder, Det	.369, 11 homers, 23 RBI
May	Canseco, Oak	.353, 13 homers, 35 RBI
August	Clemens, Bos	6-0, 1.09 ERA
September	Stewart, Oak	5-0, 1.32 ERA

As far as taking control of a race was concerned, no effort was as crucial as Roger Clemens' August. Clemens was undefeated during that crucial part of the race, striking out 48 men in 49.1 innings without allowing a home run. Though Clemens would develop a sore shoulder soon afterward, his August performance gave the Red Sox just enough momentum to hold on and win the American League East.

Well, those were the great months. How about the guys who suffered through the tough months of 1990? It's a list which includes some pretty famous names:

	Player, Team	HR	RBI	Avg	Pitcher, Team	W	L	ERA
April	O'Brien, Sea	1	7	.151	Robinson, Det	1	2	5.83
May	Martinez, WSox	1	8	.145	Garrelts, SF	1	4	8.54
June	Rivera, Bos	1	6	.167	Ballard, Bal	0	4	7.34
July	Pendleton, StL	1	6	.127	Blyleven, Cal	1	3	8.58
August	Gaetti, Min	2	8	.158	Robinson, Det	2	1	9.12
September	Dunston, Cubs	1	2	.148	Harris, Bos	1	4	8.68

The stickout is Scott Garrelts — the worst National League pitcher in May, the best in June. No wonder the Giants went after the relatively consistent Bud Black. Pete O'Brien's debut after signing a big free-agent contract with the Mariners was just the start of a rocky campaign. April has always been feast or famine for O'Brien; in the last six Aprils he's been over .390 three times ('86, '88, '89) and under .200 the other three times. Terry Pendleton's July and Gary Gaetti's August were big factors in their clubs' decisions to let them go free agent. And what a forgettable campaign Jeff Robinson of the Tigers had!

A complete listing for this category appears on page 250.

NL EAST: WHAT GIVES WITH THE METS?

What a maddening club this must be to root for. Since 1984, whenDwight Gooden broke in and Davey Johnson became the manager, the New York Metshave averaged 95 wins per year (the best in baseball), have had a winning percentage of .588 (also the best) and have never finished more than six and a half games out of first place. The Mets have been in contention in September during each of the last seven years. Yet they have only one world championship to show for it, along with a division title in 1988. During both of their first-place years, the Mets took command of the race by August, and coasted in to win by 22 games (in 1986) and 15 (in 1988). But every time they've been in a close pennant race, the Mets have fallen short.

Is there a statistical reason why they've continually fallen short? We can find several. With a pitching staff based on power, and catchers with weak arms, the Mets have been vulnerable to other contenders, like the '85 and '87 Cardinals, who run well. (Last year was no different, as New York surrendered a whopping 201 stolen bases.) The Met defense has never been very good; last year they were tied for ninth in team fielding, and showed their usual weakness around second base. Hitting with men in scoring position has been a Met problem in the past, though it wasn't in 1990 (.272). But another problem often exaggerated in the past — weakness against left-handed pitching — proved all too real. The Mets were 27-33 against left-handed starters last year, the worst record in the National League. They were also 23-28 in one-run games, the second worst mark in the league. Clubs with poor one-run records in one season tend to reverse the trend in the next. That should give the Mets some hope.

One thing we've looked for in these "division essays" is historical precedents. Has there ever been with a similar record of frustration? Sure:

- In 1948, the Cleveland Indians won a surprise pennant in a three-team race with the Red Sox and Yankees, won a pennant playoff from the Red Sox, and then took the World Series from the Boston Braves in six games.

- The Indians were expected to battle the Red Sox again in 1949. Instead they finished third, eight games out, to Casey Stengel's first Yankee team.

- In 1950, the Indians were involved in a torrid four team pennant race with the Yankees, Tigers and Red Sox. Though they finished fourth, the Indians were only six games out and won 92 games. Nevertheless, the Tribe fired their manager, Lou Boudreau.

- In 1951, now under Al Lopez, the Indians again battled the Yankees, but finished five games out.

- In 1952, it was the same story: another close race with the Yankees, another frustrating season as the Yanks won by two.

- In 1953, the Indians chased the Yankees again, losing by eight and a half games.

- In 1954, the Tribe finally broke through, winning a league record 111 games and vanquishing the Yanks by eight. The Indians were heavily favored in the World Series, but were humiliated in four straight games by the NewYork Giants.

- In 1955, the Indians battled the Yanks again all season. But NewYork passed them in September, winning by three games.

- In 1956, it was the old routine: second to the Yanks by nine games.

What happened to the Indians after that? They decided that they needed to try something new. They let Lopez resign and go to the White Sox. Their solid general manager, Hank Greenberg, also moved on to the White Sox. They pushed Bob Feller and Al Rosen, two of their longtime stars, into retirement; both, but especially Feller, had been in decline, but Indian fans (and players, too) were left feeling that the club didn't fully appreciate either player's efforts. The Tribe traded their best power hitter, Larry Doby, before the '56 season, and their durable right-handed ace, Early Wynn, after the '57 campaign. Their farm system was still producing players like Rocky Colavito, Roger Maris, Mudcat Grant and Gary Bell, but not the great pitchers to replace the aging starting rotation of Wynn, Bob Lemon, Mike Garcia and Feller. They didn't show much patience with their young stars, and traded both Maris and Colavito after a couple of years. The Indians faded to sixth in 1957, and except for a strong run in 1959, they haven't been contenders since.

The Mets, similarly frustrated, have fired Davey Johnson, let Joe McIlvaine move on the Padres, let Darryl Strawberry sign with the Dodgers. With a new cast still woefully weak in defense (Hubie Brooks in right, Howard Johnsonat short, Mackey Sasser behind the plate, Greg Jefferies anywhere) and the Straw Man gone, there's little reason to think 1991 will be their year. A dangerous club, yes; a championship club, probably not. At least they don't have to worry about the Yankees.

WHO ARE THE SLOWEST-STARTING BATTERIES?

If Jack McDowell's and Carlton Fisk's agents haven't gotten their clients a share of the concessions at the new Comiskey Park, they're missing a good bet. McDowell averaged a tedious three hours and nine minutes for his 33 starts last year, the most for any major league pitcher who made 20 or more starts. And Fisk, who continues to explore new depths in "deliberateness," averaged a leisurely 3:03 for his 112 starts behind the plate. With McDowell pitching and Fisk catching, a fan could continually stock up on goodies — some No-Doz tablets might be a good idea — without missing very much of the "action." They averaged 3:14 when working together.

We pointed out last year that, despite the pleas of managers, broadcasters and fans, major league games keep getting longer. In the American League, where Fisk seems to set the tone, the average time of a nine-inning game has risen from 2:26 in 1974 to 2:51 in 1990 — a full 25 minutes in only 16 years. Baseball people always say that, when pitchers work slowly, the fielders start to sit back on their heels and miss getting that good jump on the ball. Or that they commit more errors. Yet when you look at the slowest working pitchers and catchers in the majors last year (all from the American League, not surprisingly), you can find some well-respected workmen:

Slowest Working Pitchers	Starts	Average
Jack McDowell, WSox	33	3:09:27
Pete Harnisch, Bal	31	3:08:38
Bob Milacki, Bal	24	3:07:20
Jeff Robinson, Det	27	3:06:37
Frank Tanana, Det	29	3:06:02
(Note — minimum 20 starts)		

Slowest Working Catchers	Starts	Average
Mickey Tettleton, Bal	85	3:04:27
Carlton Fisk, WSox	112	3:03:18
Bob Melvin, Bal	70	3:02:30
Lance Parrish, Cal	125	2:59:24
Mike Heath, Det	99	2:58:47
(Note — minimum 50 starts)		

All those White Sox, Oriole and Tiger players — it seems obvious that either the manager or the number-one catcher **likes** a deliberate pace. Can we really say that Fisk and Frank Robinson don't know what they're doing? Not really; those are some pretty smart baseball men. All we can really say is, "That's just their style."

The point becomes clearer when you look at the **fastest**-working pitchers and catchers:

Fastest Working Pitchers	Starts	Average
Bob Tewksbury, StL	20	2:28:36
Greg Maddux, Cubs	35	2:33:30
Ed Whitson, SD	32	2:33:50
Kevin Tapani, Min	28	2:36:30
Tom Browning, Cin	35	2:38:36

Fastest Working Catchers	Starts	Average
Brian Harper, Min	116	2:41:43
Joe Oliver, Cin	107	2:42:35
Don Slaught, Pit	61	2:42:57
Tom Pagnozzi, StL	59	2:43:15
Joe Girardi, Cubs	120	2:44:07

If working quickly was such a key to success, Bob Tewksbury would have been a Cy Young candidate, and Brian Harper would be regarded as the smartest catcher in baseball. Which they're not. It really is just a matter of style. It's no coincidence that Tewksbury pitches for the Cardinals, where the go-go style of Whitey Herzog still dominates. Or that Greg Maddux, the second-fastest working pitcher, toils for Don Zimmer, who is similarly inclined. (Sometimes we think Zimmer doesn't want his hitters to draw walks because they take too long). These are fast-paced people, and so their teams tend to move more quickly. As fans who like to get out of the ballpark before midnight on occasion, we'd like to say, "This Bud's for you, Tewks." But there's no real evidence that working quickly has anything at all to do with winning games.

A complete listing for this category can be found on page 251.

DO FREE AGENTS BUST OUT WITH THEIR NEW CLUBS?

With the collusion era finally over and a number of players granted "new look" free agency, the 1990 off-season was a bountiful one for free agents. Players the caliber of Darryl Strawberry, George Bell, Mike Boddicker, Vince Coleman, Jack Clark, Brett Butler and Willie McGee — among others — all signed big-bucks contracts with new teams. All things considered, it was the biggest shift of talent since the first crop back in 1977, when Sal Bando, Don Baylor, Lyman Bostock, Bobby Grich, Reggie Jackson and Rollie Fingers were some of the big names shifting clubs.

That sort of talent movement excites fans, and has probably had a lot to do with baseball's increased popularity in recent years. But does it win ballgames? There's a school of thought — call it the "take the money and run" school — which says that free agents are usually flops with their new teams, and don't perform up to their previous level. Is that a bum rap? We decided to examine 14 years worth of free agent movement to examine the question. The question we ask is fairly narrow: do free agents do better or worse in their first year with their new clubs than they did in the last year with their old one?

Let's begin with the hitters. Here's how all free agents, both big names and small, performed in their last year with their old clubs, and then in the first year with their new ones:

Free Agent Signing History: Major League Hitters

	Avg	AB	R	H	HR	RBI	SB	Per 100 AB HR	RBI	SB
Before	.261	55,756	7,101	14,568	1,425	6,960	1,241	2.6	12.5	2.2
After	.264	50,249	6,505	13,286	1,329	6,341	954	2.6	12.6	1.9

The free agents actually hit for a better average with their new clubs; on a per at-bat basis, their power figures are almost identical; stolen bases are down, however. But the big difference is that the hitters logged 10 percent fewer at-bats in their first season with their new clubs. Signs of goldbricking and "convenient" trips to the disabled list, as some have charged?

We don't want to be the apologists for modern ballplayers, but in this case we can point out a couple of things in their defense. First, most free agents are veterans, and older players are more apt to get hurt. Second, it sometimes happens that the injuries are a result of simply playing hard, of trying to earn that big new salary: Joe Rudi of the first free agent crop was a good example. It's also true that a large number of free agents are getting close to the end of their careers (the Rick Dempsey/Bob Boone type) and become part-time players for their new teams. Still, you don't produce when you don't play, and in terms of overall effectiveness, the free agents did somewhat less for their new clubs than they did for their old ones.

How about the pitchers? Here's their before/after comparison:

Free Agent Signing History: Major League Pitchers

	ERA	W	L	Pct.	Sv	IP
Before	3.72	913	866	.513	430	15,403.1
After	3.71	847	780	.521	368	14,178.2

The same story: the pitchers had about the same ERAs, and their winning percentages were actually higher for their new clubs. But they worked about eight percent fewer innings. Clubs were sometimes more cautious about protecting their big new investments, but injuries and aging were also factors. As with the hitters, the pitchers performed at about the same level as before when they were in the game — but they were in it less often.

Was there one free agent group that stood out? In terms of offense, the first one of 1976-77, already described, not only had big names, but big performance: their overall average jumped from .265 in 1976 to .278 in '77, and their home run total rose from 160 to 221 — this despite the fact that both Bobby Grich and Joe Rudi missed much of the '77 season with injuries. The 1990-91 group has the talent to rival this group . . . but they'll have to stay healthy!

A complete listing for this category can be found on page 252.

DO THEY STEAL BETTER ON TURF?

In the first edition of this book a year ago, we studied the question of whether base stealers have an advantage on artificial turf. Based on the data we were examining then, the answer clearly seemed to be yes. For three straight seasons (1987-89), stealers on turf had recorded a success rates at least 4.4 percent better each year than stealers on natural grass fields — with an average of 5.6 percent a year. The leading base stealers of 1989 had also shown a clear advantage on turf (6.4 percent).

However, after gathering data for another season, we find the evidence a little less compelling. In 1990, once again, stealers on turf had a definite overall advantage. The four-year success rates:

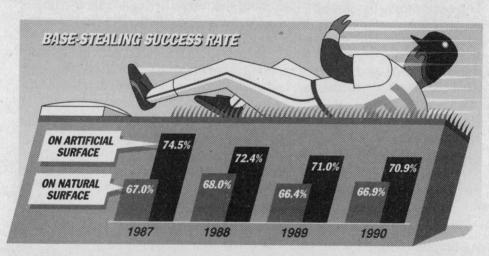

Base-Stealing Success Rate 1987-1990	
Turf	72.3%
Natural	67.1%

Looking at it this way, the advantage to stealers on turf seems quite clear. However, let's do something we didn't consider a year ago — separating the data by leagues:

	1987	1988	1989	1990	4 yrs
American League					
Turf	74.4	70.5	67.9	65.5	69.8
Natural	67.0	67.9	68.9	65.8	57.4

	1987	1988	1989	1990	4 yrs
National League					
Turf	74.6	73.2	72.7	73.4	73.5
Natural	67.1	68.2	62.3	68.3	66.6

National League stealers continue to have a clear advantage on turf. However, American League stealers were actually better on natural grass fields in both 1989 and 1990; the difference was very small, but it conflicts with the idea that base stealers automatically do better on turf.

What's the difference between the American and National Leagues? The obvious one is that half of the NL fields are turf, while 10 of the 14 AL fields are grass. An alert reader, Willie Runquist of Union Bay, British Columbia, has suggested the possibility that stealers might tend to do better on the surface they normally play on — that is, stealers who play their home games on grass fields might steal better on dirt, and turf stealers might steal better on turf. The American League data for the last two years would tend to support that idea. So would a look at the leading base stealers of 1990 (40 or more steals):

Player, Team	Home Surface	Natural			Turf		
		SB	CS	%	SB	CS	%
Vince Coleman, StL	Turf	14	7	66.7	63	10	86.3
Rickey Henderson, Oak	Natural	53	9	85.5	12	1	92.3
Eric Yelding, Hou	Turf	19	7	73.1	45	18	71.4
Barry Bonds, Pit	Turf	12	4	75.0	40	9	81.6
Brett Butler, SF	Natural	39	15	72.2	12	4	75.0
Otis Nixon, Mon	Turf	11	2	84.6	39	11	78.0
Tim Raines, Mon	Turf	12	4	75.0	37	12	75.5
Bip Roberts, SD	Natural	34	8	81.0	12	4	75.0
Steve Sax, Yanks	Natural	38	7	84.4	5	2	71.4
Delino DeShields, Mon	Turf	8	6	57.1	34	16	68.0
Roberto Kelly, Yanks	Natural	40	16	71.4	2	1	66.7
Alex Cole, Cle	Natural	37	6	86.0	3	3	50.0
Total		317	91	77.7	304	91	77.0

The top 1990 stealers actually stole better, overall, on natural grass fields than they did on turf. More interestingly, eight of the 12 — and all four of the American League leaders — stole better on the surfaces they played their home games on, whether they were turf or dirt. This supports the idea that stealers might do better on the surface they were more familiar with.

However, the differences were often slight, and the number of attempts frequently very small.

Let's take a more complete look at the subject. We separated every player since 1987 into two groups — those who played the majority of their games over the last four years on grass fields, and those who played most of their games on turf. Here's the four-year data for each group:

	Natural			Turf		
	SB	CS	%	SB	CS	%
Played Primarily on Natural Grass	5847	2813	67.5	2249	934	70.7
Played Primarily on Turf	2142	1116	65.7	3874	1404	73.4

Each group stole better on turf, which supports the idea turf is the better stealing surface — you can simply run faster on it. We've never really doubted that contention. However, the point that reader Runquist raises seems to be validated. Players whose primary playing surface is grass have a much smaller turf edge (3.2% to 7.7%) than players whose primary surface is turf. What the player is most familiar with indeed seems to make a difference.

A complete listing for this category can be found on page 253.

WHO GOT THE BEST OF THE BLUE JAY-PADRE DEAL?

They called it the "fantasy-league trade" because it involved so many big names: Fred McGriff and Tony Fernandez of the Blue Jays for Joe Carter and Roberto Alomar of the Padres. An international swap of All-Stars! It was the talk of the winter meetings, and the talk still continues. But now that the dust has settled, who got the best of it?

Only time will give the definite answer, of course. But let's do our best to give it a balanced look. Here's the argument in favor of the Padres getting the best of it:

1. Both McGriff and Carter are fine power hitters, but McGriff is a better overall offensive performer. He hits for a much higher average (.300 to .232 last year), gets on base many more times via the walk (94 to 48), and has shown a steadier home run bat (35 last year, to 24 for Carter). It's true that Carter has driven in more runs, but that's mainly because he's had more opportunities. And anyway, McGriff's overall skills, plus five years in age, more than make up for the RBI difference.

2. Both Fernandez and Alomar are outstanding middle infielders, but Fernandez is the steadier one. He makes far fewer errors, draws more walks, and showed late last year that he's finally recovered from his fearful beaning of 1989. Fernandez batted .322 after August 1 last year, and .341 after September 1.

Others argue in favor of the Blue Jays:

1. Sure McGriff hits, but Carter hits when it counts. RBIs are what you want from a power man, and Carter has averaged 109 over the last five seasons; McGriff has never driven in more than 92.

2. Fernandez may be steadier than Alomar, but that's mainly because he's older. Alomar is only 23, and studies have shown that players who produce at an early age — as Alomar has — usually will have outstanding careers.

Let's examine the trade in two parts, Carter vs. McGriff and Fernandez vs. Alomar.

Carter vs. McGriff

The knock against McGriff is a valid one. Despite his imposing numbers, he has not produced in the clutch; over the last four years with men in scoring position, he's 30 points below Carter:

Batting Average with Runners in Scoring Position

Year	McGriff	Carter
1987	.191	.249
1988	.227	.291
1989	.252	.274
1990	.264	.266
1987-90	.239	.269

McGriff is closing the gap, but he's still not in Carter's league in this category. Last year Carter drove in 26 percent of his runners from scoring position; McGriff drove in only 21 percent.

But is this enough to overcome McGriff's overwhelming edge in most other offensive categories? We think not. One problem with Carter is that he **only** seems to produce with men on base:

	With Bases Empty	With Men On
Joe Carter, 1989-90	.223	.252

There are people who will point to a breakdown like this as proof that Carter "hits when it counts;" the Elias boys, in particular, are fond of making this assertion. But since about half a player's plate appearances come with the bases empty, how can you pretend they don't matter? We were talking to Hall of Famer Joe Morgan about Carter last year, and what Joe said got right to the point: Carter's only doing half his job. The other half involves getting on base so that his teammates will also have someone to drive in.

Carter not only doesn't hit for average with the bases empty; he seldom draws a walk, either. Getting on base is something McGriff does very well — and we think it more than makes up for whatever shortcomings he's had in clutch situations. Despite that gaudy RBI total, the Bill James estimate is that Carter created only 72 runs for his team last year. McGriff, with his much wider breadth of skills, created 124. That's a huge difference, and you can't tell us that a .232 hitter who "produces in the clutch" is somehow better.

Alomar vs. Fernandez

We've pointed out the studies which indicate that players who perform well at a young age are very likely to have outstanding careers. Roberto Alomar hit .295 and stole 42 bases at age 21 in 1989. His offensive potential is outstanding. However, Alomar's numbers either stayed the same, or dropped a little, in 1990. He drew only 48 walks, not what you want from a "top of the order" player. Alomar also led the National League in errors at second base with 17. He's a very good player now, but the word for Alomar is still "potential."

Fernandez, six years older, is much more polished. He's won four Gold Gloves at shortstop; though he lost out to Ozzie Guillen last year, he led the AL in chances, putouts and assists while committing only nine errors. Fernandez has hit as high as .322, that was back in '87. His hot finish last year notwithstanding, he only batted .276. But he had 17 triples, most in the American League, and drew a career-high 70 walks. The Bill James estimate is that Fernandez created 88 runs last year, Alomar 77 (which was five more than Joe Carter).

There's little question that, as 1991 begins, Fernandez is better, both offensively and defensively. However, that doesn't matter much. A year ago, Bill James wrote, "This is my number one tip for this guide (*The Baseball Book* Draft Advisor): GET ROBERTO ALOMAR. (The caps are Bill's.) No matter who you are — rotisserie, card collector, whatever; get Alomar." Bill then goes on to mention the great second basemen in history (Morgan, Eddie Collins, Rogers Hornsby et al) and says, "I think by the time he is through, Roberto Alomar is going to be talked about with those guys."

Well, that's good enough for us; the Blue Jays win this side of the trade. But do they win it by enough to make up for McGriff's advantage over Carter? Probably not for 1991. But if Alomar is going to be as good as Bill James thinks, this may eventually look like a very even deal, or even a net gain for Toronto.

AL EAST: WHAT HAPPENED TO THOSE SLUGGING SOX?

Playing in cozy Fenway Park, the Boston Red Sox have traditionally had a reputation as a slugging club with a high-powered offense. But though Boston continues to be a winning club, the Sox have not done it by slugging in quite awhile. Let's look at how the six pennant- or division-winning Boston clubs since World War II have ranked in runs scored, batting average and home runs:

Boston Red Sox
American League Rank

Year	Runs	Avg	HR
1946	1	1	2
1967	1	1	1
1975	1	1	4
1986	5	2	11
1988	1	1	10
1990	7	1	11

All six first-place clubs ranked either first or second in batting average. But while the 1946, 1967 and 1975 clubs all ranked near the top of the American League in home runs, the three division winners since 1986 have ranked near the bottom, and the 1986 and 1990 teams had only middling offenses in terms of scoring runs. Since you expect a club playing in Fenway to do a lot of scoring, one could argue that the '86 and '90 clubs won **in spite of**, not because of, their offenses.

Why have recent Red Sox clubs been so underpowered? A lot of the blame has gone to a man who's not even in Boston any more — former hitting coach Walt Hriniak. Hriniak is a Charlie Lau disciple, and his critics charge that he preaches hitting for average at the expense of home runs. Hriniak has moved on to the White Sox, and the same charge continues to dog him, sometimes to a ridiculous degree. For instance, the White Sox' Frank Thomas has been a major leaguer for less than half of one season (.330 in 191 at-bats last year), and people have already complained that Hriniak has taken away Thomas' home run stroke!

That's one theory. But another is Fenway Park. One thing we're discovering as we analyze park data is that it doesn't always take moving in fences or shifting the location of home plate to change the way a park plays. Since the early eighties the Red Sox have built private suites atop Fenway's left and right field stands and then constructed a stadium club above the grandstand behind home plate. Those changes appear to have had a big effect, because players are no longer hitting homers at Fenway the way they used to. Using the Bill James "park factor" system, here's how many homers the Red Sox and their opponents have hit in Fenway Park games over the last six years, and how many they've hit in Boston road games:

Year	Homers at Fenway (both teams)	Homers in Boston Road Games (both teams)
1985	137	155
1986	140	171
1987	161	203
1988	141	126
1989	122	117
1990	105	93

Over the last six years, more homers have been hit in Boston **road** games than at Fenway. The 1985-87 data would actually mark Fenway as a very poor home run park. For the last three years — which was the period when the "600 Club" was put in — more four-baggers have been hit at Fenway than on the road, but not a lot more; ratios like those of 1988-90 would mark Fenway as a good home-run park, but definitely not a Homer Heaven like Wrigley Field or Fulton County Stadium.

So Hriniak has gotten something of a bum rap for Boston's lack of power in recent years. However, Fenway remains a good park for hitters in terms of overall offensive potential, and a team playing there should rank higher than seventh in runs scored. The Red Sox used to be famous for importing right-handed sluggers like Jimmie Foxx, Rudy York, Vern Stephens, Dick Stuart and George Scott to take advantage of The Wall. For 1991, they've gone back to their old tradition and signed Jack Clark as a free agent. It looks to us like a good move; the only problem is that Clark won't be hitting in the same old Fenway.

WHAT'S THE OPPOSITE OF A GRAND-SLAM HOME RUN?

You know those intelligence tests where they show you a word and ask you to select one of five that's most nearly opposite? Well, you could call the opposite of a grand slam homer a "grand-slam double play." Instead of bringing home four runs, it would produce a big, fat zero. A grand slam DP would be a double (or triple) play with a runner on every base and no runs scoring.

A double play, of course, can occur only if there are none or one out. When a team has the bases loaded with less than two out, on average it will score 1.5 runs. Thus the grand slam double play saves 1.5 runs for the defensive team. That's enough to make the difference in a lot of games, so we think the grand slam double play deserves attention, just as the grand slam homer does.

What can we learn about the grand slam double play? First, it's a much more common play than the grand slam home run. In 1990 there were 162 such double plays, but only 72 grand slam homers. On defense, the Brewers pulled off 12 grand slam DP's and the Giants 10, while the Cardinals and Mets wiggled out of bases-loaded jams only three times with a DP. With their power-pitching, flyball-throwing mound staff, the Mets were obviously at a disadvantage in this category.

On the other side of the ledger, just as the lead-footed Red Sox recorded historic performances in grounding into triple and double plays last year, they also grounded into 14 grand slam double plays. We don't know if that was historic, but it was the worst total in the majors. Kansas City, the next-worst club, grounded into 10 grand slam DPs. At the other end of the spectrum, the Yankees, Expos, Pirates, and Giants were each victimized only three times. If we assume each grand slam DP do be worth 1.5 runs on defense and each 10 runs to be worth a game in the standings, the Giants' plus-seven in grand slam DP's — the result of leadership in both offense and defense — won the Giants one extra game. Here's how the teams fared in the department:

Making the Grand Slam DP on defense — 1990

American		National	
Baltimore	5	Atlanta	8
Boston	6	Chicago Cubs	8
California	5	Cincinnati	5
Chicago White Sox	8	Houston	5
Cleveland	8	Los Angeles	4
Detroit	7	Montreal	8
Kansas City	6	New York Mets	3

Milwaukee	12	Philadelphia	6
Minnesota	4	Pittsburgh	4
New York Yankees	4	St. Louis	3
Oakland	5	San Diego	7
Seattle	9	San Francisco	10
Texas	7		
Toronto	5		

Making the Grand Slam DP on offense — 1990

American		National	
Baltimore	8	Atlanta	6
Boston	14	Chicago Cubs	8
California	9	Cincinnati	8
Chicago White Sox	3	Houston	9
Cleveland	6	Los Angeles	7
Detroit	4	Montreal	3
Kansas City	10	New York Mets	4
Milwaukee	6	Philadelphia	6
Minnesota	6	Pittsburgh	3
New York Yankees	3	St. Louis	8
Oakland	6	San Diego	6
Seattle	6	San Francisco	3
Texas	5		
Toronto	5		
AL Total	**91**	**NL Total**	**71**

Among individuals, three was the magic number. Matt Young and Bill Swift accounted for six of the nine Seattle escapes themselves; that tied them for the major league lead with Teddy Higuera, Joe Klink, Mike Lacoss, and Les Lancaster. Four batters, all American Leaguers, were goats three times: Brian Downing, Mike Gallego, Mike Greenwell, and Dave Valle. These are very low league-leading totals; in 1989 Carmelo Martinez stifled five Padres teammates' rallies in only 267 AB's. No wonder San Diego dumped him.

A complete listing for this category appears on page 254.

WHO TAKES 'EM, WHO SWINGS AT 'EM, WHO FOULS 'EM OFF?

A plate appearance is a continual battle between the pitcher and batter. The hitter wants the best possible pitch to hit; the pitcher wants him to settle for less. Some hitters will take a lot of pitches in hopes they'll get the right one. Other hitters tend to think **every** pitch is the right one. Let's break down the 1990 major league plate appearances by the result of each pitch:

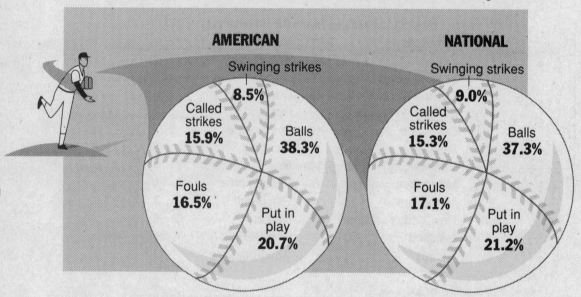

AMERICAN

Swinging strikes **8.5%**
Called strikes **15.9%**
Balls **38.3%**
Fouls **16.5%**
Put in play **20.7%**

NATIONAL

Swinging strikes **9.0%**
Called strikes **15.3%**
Balls **37.3%**
Fouls **17.1%**
Put in play **21.2%**

You'll notice that there's a slight, but definite difference between the leagues: American League hitters take more pitches. This is right in line with the old theory which says pitchers "challenge the hitters" more in the NL, while they nibble the corners more in the AL. This has less to do with macho posturing than with the ballparks. In the bigger NL parks, a pitcher can throw one down the middle and let the batter hit it with less fear that it'll end up in the seats. You can overstate this difference — National League hitters don't swing at **that** many more pitches — but it's there.

Here are the hitters who saw the highest percentage of called balls, and the pitchers who threw the most:

Ball % (Batters)	
Mickey Tettleton, Bal	46.3
Barry Bonds, Pit	45.4
Rickey Henderson, Oak	45.4
Alvin Davis, Sea	44.5
Mark McGwire, Oak	44.4

Ball % (Pitchers)	
Charlie Hough, Tex	42.5
Mike Moore, Oak	41.4
Scott Garrelts, SF	41.0
Melido Perez, WSox	41.0
Matt Young, Sea	40.8

Not much of a surprise here — guys who walk a lot, pitchers with bad control in '90. One wonders, however, how Tettleton, with the discipline to lay off bad pitches, could hit only .223.

A more interesting set of leaders are the batters and pitchers who had the highest percentages of called strikes:

Called Strike % (Batters)	
Jody Reed, Bos	23.5
Eric Yelding, Hou	23.5
Edgar Martinez, Sea	23.2
Dave Magadan, Mets	22.9
Wade Boggs, Bos	21.4

Called Strike % (Pitchers)	
Mike Boddicker, Bos	20.1
Frank Tanana, Det	19.9
Ron Robinson, Cin-Mil	18.8
Zane Smith, Mon-Pit	18.5
Bob Welch, Oak	18.3

The hitters here are all very disciplined: they hit for good averages (all except Yelding) but not much home run power. The pitchers are tricky, finesse types with great location. It takes great stuff to make the hitter take a lot of strikes, and not surprisingly, four of the five pitchers had terrific seasons. But what's Frank Tanana — with his 5.31 ERA — doing in this distinguished company?

Swinging Strike % (Batters)	
Pete Incaviglia, Tex	19.1
Sammy Sosa, WSox	18.4
Jim Presley, Atl	17.9
Matt Williams, SF	17.6
Cecil Fielder, Det	17.2

Swinging Strike % (Pitchers)	
Nolan Ryan, Tex	14.7
David Cone, Mets	13.3
Ramon Martinez, LA	12.0
Jose DeLeon, StL	11.3
Sid Fernandez, Mets	11.3

Is there such a thing as "smash-mouth baseball?" If there is, this no-nonsense group is it. It was Johnny Logan, we believe, who offered the classic advice, "Swing hard in case you hit it." Pete Incaviglia remains his greatest protege.

Fouls % (Batters)	
Ozzie Guillen, WSox	23.7
Joe Carter, SD	22.6
Garry Templeton, SD	22.5
Mookie Wilson, Tor	22.0
Willie McGee, StL-Oak	21.9

Fouls % (Pitchers)	
Danny Darwin, Hou	24.6
Pete Harnisch, Bal	22.7
Sid Fernandez, Mets	21.9
Terry Mulholland, Phi	20.6
David Wells, Tor	20.2

A great White Sox tradition: slick shortstops who hit a lot of foul balls. Ozzie Guillen is a worthy successor to the late, great Luke Appling. The San Diego Padres, with America's greatest "foul ball deficit" problem, have taken drastic action: they traded Carter, and phased out Templeton. Southern California souvenir hunters are in mourning.

The pitchers in this group are generally tough to make good contact against. Darwin, Fernandez and Wells were all among the leaders in lowest oppenents' batting average — a lot of hitters probably felt fortunate to hit a foul against them.

In Play % (Batters)	
Ozzie Guillen, WSox	30.2
Lance Johnson, WSox	27.5
Brian Harper, Min	27.2
Jeff Treadway, Atl	26.8
Garry Templeton, SD	26.5

In Play % (Pitchers)	
Tom Browning, Cin	26.3
Terry Mulholland, Phi	25.4
Ed Whitson, SD	25.3
Bill Gullickson, Hou	25.3
Dave Johnson, Bal	24.9

Guillen, we wrote several years ago, belongs to the Will Rogers School of Hitting: he never met a pitch he didn't like. (Jim Murray later used this line, but as usual, we were first. You could look it up.) Ozzie's ideas are catching on — Lance Johnson comes out of the dugout swinging as well. But if this is the new fad at Comiskey, why do White Sox games still take forever?

The pitchers whom batters most often put the ball in play against are what you'd expect — finesse hurlers who don't strike out a lot of batters. That doesn't mean they can't be effective. Browning is no slouch, and Whitson was one of the best starters in the majors last year.

A complete listing of balls put in play on each count can be found on page 255.

WHO'S BEST WITH DUCKS ON THE POND?

Batting

We always hear how important it is for an offense to produce with runners in scoring position. So it's a little bewildering to note that the best American League team with ducks on the pond — in terms of runs scored, and also in batting average (tied for the lead with the White Sox) — was that juggernaut, the Cleveland Indians:

American League
Batting with Runners in Scoring Position

Team	Avg	OBP	Slg	R	HR
Cleveland	.278	.341	.389	595	23
Chicago	.278	.352	.413	556	26
Boston	.271	.358	.392	579	27
Toronto	.270	.339	.429	582	40
Kansas City	.262	.342	.385	588	25
Minnesota	.262	.336	.380	535	26
Seattle	.261	.345	.372	512	28
Texas	.259	.347	.371	528	22
Milwaukee	.258	.340	.389	586	30
Oakland	.251	.347	.347	531	25
Detroit	.248	.345	.402	568	45
California	.248	.332	.382	536	36
Baltimore	.243	.350	.354	530	28
New York	.234	.309	.343	435	26

The Indians, despite their 77-85 record, did have an effective overall offense: tied for second in team batting, tied for third in runs scored. The surprise in these stats was how poorly the league champion Oakland A's did in runner-in-scoring-position situations.

The National League offensive stats are a little more predictable:

National League
Batting with Runners in Scoring Position

Team	Avg	OBP	Slg	R	HR
Pittsburgh	.275	.360	.422	569	35
New York	.273	.351	.434	588	44
Los Angeles	.267	.359	.385	594	32
Philadelphia	.262	.351	.366	510	24
San Francisco	.261	.338	.380	545	31
Chicago	.258	.331	.381	533	28
San Diego	.255	.345	.383	532	32
Atlanta	.255	.336	.391	500	35
Cincinnati	.252	.331	.370	550	25
Houston	.243	.334	.349	459	27
St. Louis	.242	.322	.339	502	14
Montreal	.238	.337	.363	532	30

The best National League clubs with runners in scoring position were the Pirates (in terms of batting average) and the Mets (in terms of runs scored and home runs). These were also the best NL teams in overall runs scored, so these results aren't very surprising. It's a mild surprise that the world champion Reds were pretty far down the list — especially since Cincinnati led the league in team batting. But the Reds, only fifth in overall runs scored, and seventh in home runs — really didn't have that great an attack.

Pitching

The A's offense might have been a disappointment with men in scoring position, but not their pitching staff. The A's had the best AL staff in those situations, but watch the young Seattle staff, which turned in an impressive performance last year:

American League
Opposition Batting with Runners in Scoring Position

Team	Avg	OBP	Slg	R	HR
Oakland	.239	.314	.370	329	28
Seattle	.241	.332	.354	407	25
Detroit	.243	.349	.388	431	46
Chicago	.250	.337	.374	375	21
Kansas City	.251	.342	.375	412	34
New York	.253	.348	.401	391	38
Baltimore	.255	.332	.397	361	39

American League
Opposition Batting with Runners in Scoring Position

Team	Avg	OBP	Slg	R	HR
Texas	.255	.353	.365	434	26
Toronto	.267	.336	.407	340	29
California	.268	.351	.380	423	22
Milwaukee	.272	.340	.376	440	25
Cleveland	.273	.350	.385	429	26
Boston	.276	.352	.372	449	19
Minnesota	.279	.346	.408	394	29

Even better than the A's — see, this really is a good category — were the Cincinnati Reds. Cincy allowed opponents only a .230 average with men in scoring position, the best figure in baseball. The Mets, Expos and Pirates, all with strong staffs, were the next three:

National League
Opposition Batting with Runners in Scoring Position

Team	Avg	OBP	Slg	R	HR
Cincinnati	.230	.325	.328	354	19
New York	.231	.297	.338	361	25
Montreal	.239	.331	.348	342	29
Pittsburgh	.248	.322	.370	369	31
Los Angeles	.251	.338	.386	379	31
Houston	.252	.334	.383	358	32
Philadelphia	.253	.349	.389	436	35
San Diego	.255	.341	.382	390	30
San Francisco	.274	.358	.397	433	37
St. Louis	.276	.350	.383	424	18
Chicago	.277	.370	.418	483	29
Atlanta	.286	.370	.425	493	41

No 1990 club was as pathetic as the '89 Yankees, who allowed opponents a .307 batting average with men in scoring position. But the Atlanta Braves made a good effort. We wouldn't be surprised to see Jane Fonda take the hill for the Braves sometime in '91. How could they do worse?

A complete listing for this category can be found on page 256.

II. QUESTIONS ON OFFENSE

WHO'S BEST IN THE PINCH?

Back in 1961, when the Cincinnati Reds were winning their first National League pennant in 21 years, the club's motto was "Hutch in the Clutch and Lynch in the Pinch." Hutch was Reds manager Fred Hutchinson; Lynch was ace pinch-hitter Jerry Lynch, who came through with 19 pinch knocks in 47 at-bats — most of them in crucial situations — for a hefty .404 average.

In 1990, when the Reds broke through to win their first National League pennant — and their first world championship as well — in 13 years, they didn't have a nifty motto, but they might not have made it without the contributions of the unsung Luis Quinones. Quinones is no Jerry Lynch, but he did belt 13 pinch hits over the course of the regular season, the third-best total in baseball, and batted .361 in pinch roles. Better yet, Quinones came through with the crucial pinch hit in Game 6 of the National League playoffs, the one that put the Reds in the World Series.

Though the DH rule has cut down severely on the use of pinch-hitters in the American League, a player who can come through in the pinch is still an awful valuable guy. The following players were the leading pinch hitters in the major leagues in 1990 (minimum 20 at-bats):

Player, Team	AB	H	HR	RBI	Avg
Dave Magadan, Mets	22	9	0	4	.409
Terry Puhl, Hou	20	8	0	8	.400
Craig Wilson, StL	23	9	0	4	.391
Rance Mullinicks, Tor	22	8	0	7	.364
Luis Quinones, Cin	36	13	1	9	.361
Carlos Baerga, Cle	31	11	1	9	.355
Tommy Gregg, Atl	51	18	4	17	.353
Rick Leach, SF	20	7	0	3	.350
Fred Lynn, SD	32	11	1	6	.344
Hal Morris, Cin	21	7	0	2	.333
Casey Candaele, Hou	30	10	1	6	.333

Not surprisingly, nine of the top 11 pinch swingers played for National League clubs. American League pinch hitters don't get as much chance to hit because of the DH rule, and most pinch-swingers tell us they have to hit often to stay sharp. That's why the performance of Toronto's Rance Mullinicks (8 for 22 last year, including several crucial knocks in the heat of the pennant race) was all the more impressive. Mullinicks, whose career was considered in jeopardy at the start of the year, wound up re-signing with the Jays as a free agent at year's end. To us, it seemed like a very smart move. Among all players in major league history with more than 150 pinch hit at-bats, Mullinicks is one of only five with a lifetime average over .300. The alltime leaders:

Player	Avg
Tommy Davis	.320
Frenchy Bordogaray	.312
Frankie Baumholtz	.307
Rance Mullinicks	.304
Red Schoendienst	.303

Another veteran pinch swinger, Denny Walling of the Cardinals, came through with 11 pinch hits last year. In the process Walling became one of the rare players to record 100 lifetime pinch hits, and by year's end he was tenth on the alltime list. Walling was still unsigned as this book went to press, but he has a chance to move up on the alltime list. The career leaders in pinch hits:

Player	Lifetime Pinch Hits
Manny Mota	150
Smoky Burgess	145
Greg Gross	143
Jose Morales	123
Jerry Lynch	116
Red Lucas	114
Steve Braun	113
Terry Crowley	108
Gates Brown	107
Denny Walling	104

A complete listing for this category can be found on page 257.

WHO CREATED THE MOST RUNS?

Runs Created is a tool invented by Bill James to evaluate the number of runs contributed by each player on a team. By now it's been accepted as an accurate measure of a player's offensive contributions, and it's routinely quoted in numerous baseball books. There are several versions of the runs created formula; we use the technical version, the definition of which appears at the end of this article. As with runs scored and RBIs, a player with 100 runs created is having a heck of a year. The 1990 leaders by league and overall:

THE RUN MAKERS

RUNS CREATED

AMERICAN		NATIONAL	
Rickey Henderson	137	Barry Bonds	128
Cecil Fielder	129	Ryne Sandberg	124
Fred McGriff	124	Lenny Dykstra	121

Henderson and Bonds each were voted their league's most valuable player.

Player, Team	Runs Created
Rickey Henderson, Oak	137.1
Cecil Fielder, Det	128.5
Barry Bonds, Pit	128.0
Fred McGriff, Tor	123.8
Ryne Sandberg, Cubs	123.7
Lenny Dykstra, Phi	121.1
Eddie Murray, LA	117.7
Ron Gant, Atl	109.3
Brett Butler, SF	108.1
George Brett, KC	106.0

You could hardly find a better list of the offensive stars of 1990. It starts off with the American League's Most Valuable Player, and continues with the AL runner-up for MVP and then the National League Most Valuable Player. Fred McGriff, Ryne Sandberg, Lenny Dykstra, Eddie Murray et al? These were the biggies of 1990.

Lest Henderson and company let their laurels go to their heads, however, we'd like to offer a list of the best totals of runs created by a player in one season since 1920. Because of different stat-keeping in the old days, we used the simplest — but still accurate — version of the formula:

Player, Team	Year	Runs Created
Babe Ruth, Yanks	1921	233
Babe Ruth, Yanks	1923	216
Lou Gehrig, Yanks	1927	211
Rogers Hornsby, StL	1922	206
Jimmie Foxx, Phi (AL)	1932	206

Well, Rickey got within 100 runs of the best season, anyway.

****

James has a refinement of runs created called "offensive winning percentage," the definition of which is also included below. We can't describe it any better than we did last year, except to revise the example. Offensive winning percentage attempts to answer this question: if all the players on a team performed like Rickey Henderson did in 1990, what would the club's winning percentage be? The answer is .869, meaning that a team of Rickey Hendersons would have a record of about 141-21. Just like Little League, which is how Rickey makes the game look at times. The 1990 leaders in offensive winning percentage (minimum 250 plate appearances):

Player, Team	Off. Win %
Rickey Henderson, Oak	.869
Barry Bonds, Pit	.819
Jack Clark, SD	.812
Fred McGriff, Tor	.778
Lenny Dykstra, Phi	.777
Eddie Murray, LA	.767
Jose Canseco, Oak	.758
Kal Daniels, LA	.758
Dave Magadan, Mets	.754
Cecil Fielder, Det	.747

Fielder moves down in these ratings, but you can't quarrel with the leaders, Henderson and Bonds. Here are the 1990 trailers in offensive winning percentage:

Player, Team	Off. Win %
Andres Thomas, Atl	.181
Frank White, KC	.237
Carlos Martinez, WSox	.243
Scott Bradley, Sea	.243
Randy Velarde, Yanks	.288

Thomas was also the worst player in offensive winning percentage in 1989 — not exactly the best example of "offensive consistency." A frightening thought: a team of Rickey Hendersons playing a team of Andres Thomases. Now **there's** a competition the A's might win.

Technical Version Of Runs Created Formula

Runs created is A times B divided by C where

A = Hits plus walks plus Hit Batsmen minus Caught Stealing minus Grounded into Double Plays

B = Total Bases plus (.26 times the Sum of Hit Batsmen and Unintentional Walks) plus (.52 times the sum of Sacrifice Hits, Sacrifice Flies and Stolen Bases)

C = At Bats plus Walks plus Hit Batsmen plus Sacrifice Hits plus Sacrifice Flies

Simple Version of Runs Created

A = Hits plus walks

B = Total Bases

C = At Bats plus Walks

Offensive Winning Percentage

To figure a player's offensive winning percentage, start by figuring the number of runs the player created per 27 outs. Then find the offensive context of his team by adding the number of runs scored by his team to the number they allowed (say 700 plus 650) and divide that total by 324 (162 games X 2). Divide the number of runs created per 27 outs by the offensive context figure.

Square this new figure. Then divide the squared figure by the sum of itself with one to obtain the offensive winning percentage.

A complete listing for this category can be found on page 258.

WILL JACK CLARK LIKE FENWAY?

Thanks to the research of people like Pete Palmer and Bill James, most fans know that some parks (like Wrigley Field) favor batters and some (like the Astrodome) favor pitchers. But not all ballparks are symmetrical — the Fenway Green Monster comes to mind. And different fence distances may not affect batting averages in the same way that they influence power hitting.

For each of the 26 home parks, we asked our computer to figure out what happened to all right-handed batters and to all left-handed batters — both home and visitors — when they came to town. We also separated power hitting from batting average, as "power percentage," or slugging percentage minus batting average. These results are presented in two tables, the first studying batting average effects by ballpark, the second power percentage. Each table is sorted so that the parks which most favored left-handed batters are at the top of each table; the parks at the bottom are the ones which most favored righties. As an example, Yankee Stadium increased lefties batting averages by 23 points. It decreased righties' averages by 12 points, so the net advantage to lefties was 35 points. A positive difference in the last column means the park favors lefties; a negative difference means it's better for righties.

Here's park data on batting average for the last four years, with two exceptions. We limit the Toronto data to 1990 only, since that was their first full year in the new SkyDome, and do the same for Seattle, since the Mariners changed their park configuration last year:

Home Park By Effect on Batting Average (1987-90)
(Sorted by Net Advantage to LH Batters)

	On LHB	On RHB	LHB - RHB
New York Yankees	+.023	−.012	+.035
Boston	+.031	+.013	+.018
Seattle (1990 only)	+.005	−.011	+.016
New York Mets	−.004	−.019	+.015
Detroit	−.013	−.024	+.011
Oakland	−.009	−.018	+.009
Chicago Cubs	+.023	+.016	+.007
Montreal	+.005	+.000	+.005
Houston	−.009	−.013	+.004
Cincinnati	+.011	+.007	+.004
San Francisco	−.001	−.004	+.003
Toronto (1990 only)	+.006	+.003	+.003
San Diego	−.008	−.009	+.001
St.Louis	+.003	+.003	+.000

Kansas City	+.006	+.006	+.000
Cleveland	+.002	+.002	+.000
Atlanta	+.017	+.017	−.000
Milwaukee	−.002	−.001	−.001
Chicago White Sox	−.001	+.003	−.004
Minnesota	+.006	+.011	−.005
Philadelphia	−.006	−.000	−.006
Pittsburgh	−.011	−.001	−.010
Baltimore	−.021	−.009	−.012
California	−.010	+.006	−.016
Los Angeles	−.018	+.001	−.019
Texas	−.010	+.018	−.028

And here's four-year data on power percentage, again with the exception of Toronto and Seattle:

Home Park By Effect on Power Percentage (1987-90)
(Sorted by Net Advantage to LH Batters)

	On LHB	On RHB	LHB - RHB
New York Yankees	+.015	−.012	+.027
Pittsburgh	+.011	−.011	+.022
Detroit	+.018	+.004	+.014
Philadelphia	+.017	+.007	+.010
Montreal	+.004	−.004	+.008
Cincinnati	+.022	+.014	+.008
St.Louis	+.001	−.005	+.006
Milwaukee	−.001	−.007	+.006
New York Mets	−.010	−.012	+.002
Chicago Cubs	+.012	+.011	+.001
Kansas City	−.009	−.010	+.001
Minnesota	+.010	+.010	+.000
Baltimore	−.001	+.000	−.001
California	+.008	+.010	−.002
Houston	−.032	−.030	−.002
Atlanta	+.006	+.010	−.004
Oakland	−.029	−.023	−.006
Seattle (1990 only)	−.002	+.006	−.008
San Francisco	−.005	+.015	−.010
San Diego	+.004	+.015	−.011
Chicago	−.023	−.010	−.013
Texas	−.007	+.007	−.014
Boston	+.005	+.019	−.014
Cleveland	−.028	−.009	−.019
Toronto (1990 only)	+.006	+.028	−.022

Well, there are a lot of numbers here, let's pick out some interesting ones. The most interesting, as always, is Fenway Park. Where power is concerned, Boston of course favors right-handed batters — only Cleveland and the new SkyDome penalize lefties more. But in terms of batting average, Fenway favors left-handed batters, more so than any park other than Yankee Stadium.

People have been commenting that Fenway helps lefties' averages for a few years, but even we didn't realize the degree. In truth, we probably should have noticed this long ago. In the fifty years since 1941, six different left-handed Boston hitters have won 18 batting titles; they also got a championship from a righty, Carney Lansford, in 1981. Except for the 11 titles won by Carew, Oliva and Puckett in Minnesota, no other American League team in that time has recorded more than four batting championships. Sure, Yaz, Ted, and Wade didn't need much help, but how about Pete Runnels or Billy Goodman?

The "real" Fenway — in terms of favoring righties in both categories — is Texas' Arlington Stadium, and its opposite is Yankee Stadium, long known as a haven for lefty hitters. You may know that Detroit also favors left-handers, but why do the perfectly symmetric Pittsburgh and Philadelphia parks pump up left-handers' power numbers?

The study does not uphold St.Louis' reputation as a pitcher's park. Busch is a tough home run park, to be sure, but it's neutral as far as batting average is concerned, and it actually has minimal affect on power percentage because players hit a lot of doubles and triples there. In contrast, despite the numbers put up by Canseco, McGwire, and the Hendersons, Oakland is the worst park in the American League for power.

How come some parks have advantages to lefties or righties that are not immediately apparent? Often it's a wind current blocked or helped by something like the location of the scoreboard. (This is the case in Texas, where there's a huge scoreboard in right.) Other factors are more subtle — for example the hitting background, or the lighting.

So will Jack Clark like Fenway? Well, sure. But not quite in the same way that Wade Boggs (and Pete Runnels and Billy Goodman) have liked it. Don't expect a batting championship this year, Jack — unless you decide to hit lefty.

WHO'S NO. 1 AT NO. 1?

Funny how times change. A few years ago, when Rickey Henderson was having problems with the Yankees, some New York writers were referring to him as "baseball's biggest underachiever." Now Henderson's had two glorious seasons in Oakland, topped by the American League's Most Valuable Player Award for 1990. He's also on the brink of eclipsing Lou Brock's career stolen base record. Suddenly Henderson's getting a new label: the best leadoff hitter in major league history.

We couldn't agree more. Not that he needed to prove himself, but Henderson was once again at the top of the leadoff list in 1990. We rank No. 1 hitters by on-base percentage, since the leadoff man's primary job is to get on base. Here are the major league leaders for 1990 (minimum 150 plate appearances while batting first):

Player, Team	OBP	AB	R	H	BB	SB
Rickey Henderson, Oak	.439	485	119	158	95	63
Lenny Dykstra, Phi	.419	588	106	192	89	33
Lonnie Smith, Atl	.419	315	53	107	41	5
Wade Boggs, Bos	.402	353	52	106	61	0
Brett Butler, SF	.398	621	108	192	90	51
Brian Downing, Cal	.382	128	24	35	20	0
Delino DeShields, Mon	.380	401	57	118	54	34
Alex Cole, Cle	.379	227	42	68	28	40
Luis Polonia, Yanks-Cal	.377	346	48	116	24	18
Bip Roberts, SD	.377	503	92	158	47	43

Does this sound like a good leadoff man to you? Apart from ranking first in on-base percentage, Henderson

- Scored 119 runs while hitting in the top spot, leading both leagues

- Drew 95 walks, again the best total

- Stole 65 bases (63 while in the #1 slot), ranking second only to Vince Coleman (77)

- Had 28 home runs, twice as many as any other leadoff man. The Reds' Chris Sabo ranked second with 14

- Had 64 extra base hits, by far the best total; Dykstra was second with 47

- Had a .579 slugging average, easily the best mark

- Drove in 61 runs, the top total among leadoff men

- Had a .326 leadoff batting average, fourth best behind Lonnie Smith (.340), Luis Polonia (.335) and Lenny Dykstra (.327)

Henderson will probably remain baseball's best leadoff man for as long as he wants to be. But there are some youngsters who show a lot of promise. Delino DeShields, 22 this season, and Alex Cole, 25, displayed both speed and on-base ability in their rookie seasons. Bip Roberts, who's still only 27, proved that his strong showing in 1989 was no fluke. And Luis Polonia, 26, hit his way into the top ten. Polonia would rank higher if he could draw more than an occasional walk.

The booby prize goes to the leadoff men with the **worst** on-base percentages:

Player, Team	OBP	AB	R	H	BB	SB
Juan Samuel, LA	.249	158	15	29	14	18
Jeff Huson, Tex	.271	226	33	45	21	4
Lance Johnson, WSox	.274	261	35	61	15	12
Junior Felix, Tor	.288	198	30	47	15	7
Sammy Sosa, WSox	.296	258	33	65	17	15

One of the baseball publications had a "best leadoff man ever" poll last year, and a Chicago writer came up with Luis Aparicio, the old White Sox hero. Didn't the guy notice that Aparicio played 18 years without ever having a 100-run season — even when he was batting in front of Frank Robinson, Brooks Robinson and Boog Powell for the Orioles? Aparicio had the smaller part of the leadoff package, speed, but not the big part, ability to reach base. Lance Johnson and Sammy Sosa (and, at times, Ozzie Guillen) seem to be carrying on this dubious Chicago tradition. The Chisox acquisition of Tim Raines could easily reverse the trend.

Hey, Tommy Lasorda: just think of Juan Samuel as "Ultra Out-Fast."

A complete listing for this category can be found on page 259.

WHO ARE THE AARONS OF TOMORROW?

We hate to be the sort of guys who romanticize the past, but what happened to all the great sluggers? Between 1960 and 1987 a total of 11 players reached the sacred 500-homer mark: Ted Williams, Willie Mays, Henry Aaron, Mickey Mantle, Frank Robinson, Harmon Killebrew, Willie McCovey, Eddie Mathews, Ernie Banks, Reggie Jackson and Mike Schmidt. But looking at the current list of lifetime home run leaders, all we see are a bunch of graybeards who are a long, long way from that lofty level:

Player	Opening Day Age	HR
Dwight Evans	39	379
Eddie Murray	35	379
Dave Winfield	39	378
Dale Murphy	35	378
Carlton Fisk	43	354
Andre Dawson	36	346
Dave Parker	39	328
Gary Carter	36	313
Jack Clark	35	307
Fred Lynn	39	306

There is, at least, a fascinating race for the top spot, with only a single homer separates the top four sluggers. Evans has definitely slipped, but Murray, Winfield and Murphy all finished strongly last year, and have decent chances of reaching 400 during the coming season. Murphy, 17 days younger than Murray, is the most youthful member of the list, and the odds are pretty slim of any of the top ten reaching the 500 mark.

There are, fortunately for the younger generation, a few players who may ultimately reach that goal. Bill James has a formula called "The Favorite Toy" which measures the chances of a player reaching milestones like 500 homers or 3000 hits. The formula is a little complicated, but it goes like this. First you measure a player's established level of performance by using the last three seasons as a basis; the most recent season is weighed most heavily. Then you estimate how many homers (or hits, or whatever) the player figures to hit over the rest of his career. That will give him a projected lifetime total, and from that you can estimate his chances to reach different lifetime goals. The formula for The Favorite Toy, with an example, is at the end of this article.

Using The Favorite Toy, the following players have the best chances to reach 500 homers (and 600 or 700):

Chance of reaching 600 or 700 home runs		
	600	700
Strawberry	16%	1%
McGwire	13%	1%
Canseco	10%	--

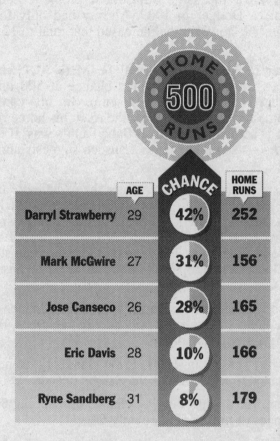

	AGE	CHANCE	HOME RUNS
Darryl Strawberry	29	42%	252
Mark McGwire	27	31%	156
Jose Canseco	26	28%	165
Eric Davis	28	10%	166
Ryne Sandberg	31	8%	179

A few comments on the projections:

1. Aaron's lifetime mark of 755 looks about as safe as anything can be.

2. Though no player is an odds-on choice to reach 500 homers, the odds are extremely strong (over 75%) that at least **one** of them will make it.

3. The projections point up what a great career the much-maligned Strawberry is having. Darryl has 252 homers — more than halfway to 500, an almost-automatic qualifier for the Hall of Fame — at age 29.

Compare his lifetime totals, not only with the other players on the above list, but with other sluggers who are the same age:

Player	Opening Day Age	HR
Darryl Strawberry	29	252
Don Mattingly	29	169
Kevin Mitchell	29	135
Kelly Gruber	29	83

The Strawman dwarfs them all, with as many homers as Mattingly and Gruber combined.

However, Strawberry's future pace may be slowed by Dodger Stadium, which is a much tougher home run park than his old yard, Shea. In eight years and 40- plus games as a visiting player in L.A., Strawberry has hit only five homers. He may have the same adjustment problem Eddie Murray did when he became a Dodger in 1989. Murray had only four homers in Dodger Stadium in '89; however, he increased that total to 12 in 1990.

4. The best home run hitter in baseball may well be Mark McGwire. McGwire ranks behind Strawberry in his estimated chance at 500 only because he's sorely penalized by Oakland Coliseum. In his career McGwire has hit only 60 home runs at home, 96 on the road; his home run percentage away from home is actually better than Babe Ruth's was. If the A's ever move in their fences — something Jose Canseco suggests about every other day — look out!

5. You might find it odd that Canseco, a year younger than McGwire but with nine more homers, is projected to hit fewer over the course of his career. There's only one reason: McGwire stays healthy, Canseco doesn't. Jose played in only 65 games in 1989 and 131 in 1990; that lowered his projected totals for the future by a considerable degree. If Canseco can stay healthy for a few years, he'll soar to the top of the list. But so far he hasn't done so.

6. Injury problems have also hampered Eric Davis, whose slim chance of reaching 500 would increase greatly if he could only stay in one piece. But the chances of that happening are equally slim.

7. After his big 40-home run season in 1990, Ryne Sandberg is now projected to have a slight chance to reach 500. A very slight chance.

8. Among the current top ten, Murray has the best chance of reaching 500 at 10%. Dale Murphy's chances of hitting 500 are only 6%.

FORMULA FOR THE FAVORITE TOY

1. Begin by figuring an established level of performance in the category you're studying. For current players, we use 1988, 1989 and 1990 as a basis, with 1990 weighed most heavily. The formula is:

Established level = [1988 total plus (2 X 1989 total) plus (3 X 1990 total)] divided by six.

To get Will Clark's established home run level for the last three years, you add his 1988 total (29) plus twice his 1989 level (23 X 2 = 46) plus three times his 1990 total (19 X 3 = 57). Then you divide that total by six: 132

divided by six is 22, so Clark has an established home run level of 22 per year.

2. Next you factor in the player's age to estimate the years remaining in his career. The formula is

Years remaining = 24 minus (.6 x Age)

Clark will be 27 on opening day, so the formula estimates he has 7.8 seasons remaining. A 30-year old has 6.0 estimated seasons left, and so on. This is sort of like an actuarial table; Clark may play more years then 7.8, but he might also play less.

3. Next we multiply the established level by the years remaining to project how many homers the player will hit over the rest of his career. We estimate Clark will hit 172 more homers (22 X 7.8 = 171.6) over the rest of his career. Clark currently has 117 career homers, so we project him to end up with 289.

4. The final step is to compare the player's projected total with a goal (like 400 homers), and estimate his chances of reaching it. The formula for this is

[Projected Remaining Homers minus .5 x (Homers Needed)] divided by Homers needed.

This is set up so that if the player is estimated to hit more homers than he needs, his chances of reaching the goal will be greater than 50 percent; the farther under the goal he is, the slimmer his chances. Let's say we want to estimate Clark's chances of reaching 400 homers. He's projected to hit 172 more, and needs 283. The formula would be

[172 - (.5 x 283)] divided by 283

Clark has an estimated 10.6 percent chance of reaching 400 homers (30 divided by 283).

WHO SOARED TO THE SKIES — AND WHO CRASHED AND BURNED — IN 1990?

Welcome to STATS, Inc., brokers. You say your fantasy league team didn't do very well last year? You say you're looking for some hot tips for 1991? You say your Uncle Harry just died, and you have a lot of money to invest? We can help you do that. Heh heh heh.

First, for those of you who like to ride the bull market, we present the following commodities, undervalued in 1989, very hot in 1990:

Batting Average Improved Most

Player, Team	1989	1990	Change
Ron Gant, Atl	.177	.303	+126
Lenny Dykstra, Phi	.237	.325	+88
Eddie Murray, LA	.247	.330	+83
Bill Doran, Hou-Cin	.219	.300	+81
Matt Williams, SF	.202	.277	+75
Lenny Harris, LA	.236	.304	+68
Darren Daulton, Phi	.201	.268	+67
John Shelby, LA-Det	.183	.248	+65
Wally Backman, Pit	.231	.292	+61
Alan Trammell, Det	.243	.304	+61

Ron Gant is for those of you who like the "junk bond" market. Ron was solid when he joined the exchange in 1988 (.259, 19 homers), had a little bad luck in 1989 — hey, everybody has a .177 season now and then — but now he's sound, a very solid investment. Oh excuse me, there are Federal investigators outside? Maybe we should revise this opinion. Let's just say that we like Ron Gant, we like his ballpark even better, but if you want to bet heavily that Ron Gant will hit .303 with 32 homers again this year, we really do hope your uncle died, and that you'll come and see us. With no questions asked.

We'll be honest about the others on this list of commodities. The odds that Lenny Dykstra will hit .325 or Eddie Murray .330 again are about as good as our chances of winning the Nobel Prize for Literature — we still have a place cleared on the mantelpiece, but we're not counting on it. Matt Williams has finally lived up to his press clippings, and we think he's the real thing, though he may not hit as high as .277. Wally Backman — he whined his way out of the American League after one year, and now he thinks he's too good for the Pittsburgh Pirates. Was there ever a man more born to wear a New York Met uniform? Stay away from him. Bill James has this piece of advice for 1991: <u>Don't Draft Darren Daulton.</u> The underlining is Bill's.

We know some of you prefer a bear market, and like to look for undervalued stocks. For you we present the players who had hard times in 1990, and figure to be bargains this spring:

Batting Average Declined Most

Player, Team	1989	1990	Change
Carlos Martinez, WSox	.300	.224	−76
Milt Thompson, StL	.290	.218	−72
Robin Yount, Mil	.318	.247	−71
Carney Lansford, Oak	.336	.268	−68
Dwight Smith, Cubs	.324	.262	−62
Alvaro Espinoza, Yanks	.282	.224	−58
Steve Sax, Yanks	.315	.260	−55
Scott Bradley, Sea	.274	.223	−51
Harold Reynolds, Sea	.300	.252	−48
Don Mattingly, Yanks	.303	.256	−47

Some good professional hitters here. Most of them figure to bounce back to at least some degree in '91. The big gambles are Yount (a Hall of Famer, but on the decline?), Mattingly (ditto, but only if healthy) and Dwight Smith (very talented, but buried in Don Zimmer's dog house last year). One of them might be worth a chance. So might Steve Sax, who swore to John Benson, our Yankee *Scouting Report: 1991* writer, that he hit the ball hard, but in miserable luck, in 1990.

A word of warning for you speculators out there. Carney Lansford was on the "improved most" list last year, the "declined most" in this edition, and is now out for most, if not all, of the 1991 season. Gant, Backman, and Trammell were on the "declined" list after the '89 season, the "improved" list after 1990. Caveat emptor, as they say.

A complete listing for this category can be found on page 260.

WHO HAS THE BEST "KNOCKOUT PUNCH"?

In the boxing ring, a Mike Tyson punch can end a fight at any time. In baseball, the equivalent of a knockout punch is a big home run with men on base. Though the game goes on, a multiple-run homer often puts the game out of reach for the opposition — whatever inning it happens in. "Baseball is pitching, defense and three-run homers," said Earl Weaver. As usual, Earl knew what he was talking about.

We argued last year that RBI per home run is a decent measure of clutch hitting. The rationale is fairly simple. Producing with men on base is always crucial, and the players who can homer with men on are coming through at exactly the time when they can do the most damage. That said, here are the 1990 leaders in RBI per home run (minimum 15 homers):

Player, Team	HR	RBI on HRs	RBI per HR
Kal Daniels, LA	27	54	2.00
Gary Gaetti, Min	16	31	1.94
Lou Whitaker, Det	18	35	1.94
Bo Jackson, KC	28	52	1.86
Tim Wallach, Mon	21	39	1.86
Joe Carter, SD	24	44	1.83
Dale Murphy, Atl-Phi	24	44	1.83
Robin Yount, Mil	17	31	1.82
Tom Brunansky, StL-Bos	16	29	1.81
Andres Galarraga, Mon	20	36	1.80

This is not as impressive a group of hitters as was the case in 1989, when the top three were Eddie Murray, Dale Murphy and Jack Clark. But it's still a pretty good one, and there was good year-to-year consistency from 1989, always a sign of a good stat. Murphy, Gaetti and Galarraga all made the top ten in both 1989 and 1990, and Jackson, Wallach and Brunansky just missed making it both years. Matt Williams, seventh in 1989, was 11th in 1990. Paul O'Neil, fifth in '89, tied for 13th in 1990.

Though the figures for the leaders were outstanding, no one approached the 1989 totals of Murray, Murphy and Clark, all of whom averaged more than two RBI per homer. When you think about that — their **average** four-bagger was between a two and three-run shot — you realize how impressive it is.

Less impressive were the totals of the players who trailed in this category in 1990:

Player, Team	HR	RBI on HRs	RBI per HR
Steve Balboni, Yanks	17	20	1.18
Harold Baines, Tex-Oak	16	19	1.19
Roberto Kelly, Yanks	15	18	1.20
Jim Presley, Atl	19	23	1.21
Randy Milligan, Bal	20	25	1.25

There are some careers in a little bit of trouble here. Roberto Kelly, who's young and often bats at the top of the lineup, can be excused for appearing on this list. But Kelly's teammate Steve Balboni has had his problems during his second stint with the Yankees, and this is just another sign of them. Harold Baines has now been traded twice since the middle of '89, and though the A's seem happy with him, he'll have to prove he's still a top-quality player. One year was enough to convince the Braves that Jim Presley was not their third baseman of the future; they went out and signed Terry Pendleton as a free agent. A lot of that was due to Presley's poor defense, but his weak performance in this category couldn't have helped him. Randy Milligan had a 1.83 RBI-per-homer ratio in 1989, and his poor ratio last year can probably be discounted.

A complete listing for this category can be found on page 261.

WHO HITS FLYBALLS?

We have no way of proving it, but "Fly Me to the Moon," a Frank Sinatra favorite of the early sixties, may well have been the bedtime lullaby for a Southern California tyke named Mark McGwire (born in 1963). The San Francisco playpen of young Willie McGee (born 1958), on the other hand, was probably filled with the lyrics from a different Sinatra ballad, "The Second Time Around." Little Willie, they say, always joined in at the part where Frank crooned, "Love is lovelier with both feet on the ground." Francis Albert Sinatra — Hitting Coach of the Stars!

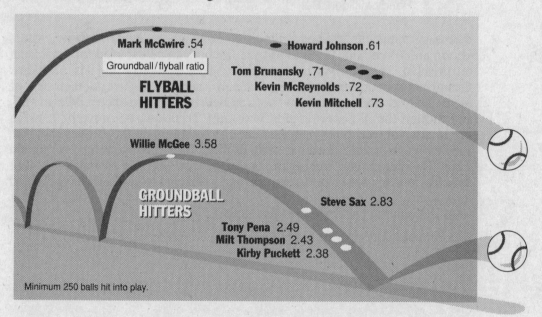

Mark McGwire .54   Howard Johnson .61

Groundball / flyball ratio   Tom Brunansky .71

FLYBALL   Kevin McReynolds .72
HITTERS   Kevin Mitchell .73

Willie McGee 3.58

GROUNDBALL   Steve Sax 2.83
HITTERS

Tony Pena 2.49
Milt Thompson 2.43
Kirby Puckett 2.38

Minimum 250 balls hit into play.

McGwire, as the chart shows, was the most pronounced flyball hitter in the majors in 1990, hitting the ball in the air almost twice as often as he hit it on the ground. McGee, meanwhile, did things the opposite way: more than three and a half grounders for every fly ball. Who was better? Each could put up a good argument for his own personal style. McGwire, the flyball basher, lifted 39 balls out the park last year, the second-best total in the American League. McGee, just as good at the opposite game, scorched enough grounders to lead the National League in hitting with a .335 mark. Late in the year, they had to chance to compare styles face-to-face when McGee was dealt to McGwire's A's. No doubt each faced the other and belted out a chorus of, "I did it my way!"

Enough already. All we're trying to say is that there is more than one way to be a successful hitter. In general, home run sluggers like to uppercut the ball at least a little; the result is more flyballs than grounders. The singles-hitting types, like McGee, are better off trying to beat the ball into the ground, especially if they have good speed. But there may be a danger in being too extreme one way or the other. Take McGwire, for instance. While he continues to be a prolific home run hitter, Mark has seen his batting average decline from .289 as a rookie in 1987 to the .230 level the last two years. Some people are arguing that he's trying to uppercut everything, and hitting way to many lazy flies. With his style, McGwire will always hit a lot of homers. But he's become a low-average slugger — Dave Kingman, except with more walks — and that seems a shame for a hitter of his talents.

It's also instructive to look at the other leaders among the "flyball" group: Howard Johnson, Tom Brunansky, Kevin McReynolds, Kevin Mitchell. Only one of them, Mitchell, hit over .270 last year. Of the top 20 flyball hitters, only one, Barry Bonds, batted over .300. Now compare that with Fred McGriff and Ryne Sandberg, who had fairly even groundball/flyball ratios (1.06 and 1.07). Both McGriff and Sandberg hit for power (35 and 40 homers, respectively), and both batted .300 as well. We're not saying that every home run hitter could bat .300. But he should be able to hit higher than McGwire's .235.

It's also possible to be too much of a groundball hitter. A year ago, one of the most pronounced groundball hitters in the majors was Baltimore's Bill Ripken. The only problem was that it didn't help him — Ripken batted an anemic .239 in 1989. In 1990 Ripken hit the ball in the air a lot more. He was still a groundball hitter, but not an extreme one, and his average soared to .291.

Then there's Kirby Puckett. A line-drive type, Kirby's never been a real flyball hitter, but in the past he lifted the ball out of the park enough to hit as many as 31 homers. The last two years, however, Puckett's been a very pronounced groundball hitter. His homer totals dropped to nine and 12, and even his average slipped to .298 — his lowest in five years — in '90. Puckett might have to go back to his old hitting stroke, because the one he's using now just isn't working as well. Maybe the Twins organist could break into "Fly Me to the Moon" when Puckett comes to bat — just to remind him.

A complete listing for this category can be found on page 262.

WHO PLAYS FOR THE BIG INNING?

When a runner reaches base to start an inning, major league managers don't all respond in the same way. Some skippers see the opportunity for a big rally, and let their hitters whale away. Others are more conservative; they'd rather score one run than none at all, and so they'll use up outs — even at the cost of a possible big inning — in order to get the man home.

There's a simple way to measure which are the big-inning clubs, and which ones play for one run at a time. It's called "outs invested in one-run strategies." The building blocks of one-run strategy are the stolen base and the sacrifice bunt. Both the steal and the sac hit can move a runner closer to home, but at the cost of an out (in the case of the bunt) or the potential cost of an out (if the runner is caught stealing). Those outs are "investments" — the price paid to try to get the runner home. One-run clubs will invest a lot of outs in those strategies; big-inning clubs won't. Here's how the 26 teams ranked last year in inverse order of outs invested in one-run strategies. That would put the big-inning clubs first. You'll notice a clear difference between the leagues:

Outs Invested in One-run Strategies

Team	League	CS	SH	Outs
Toronto	AL	52	18	70
New York	AL	45	37	82
New York	NL	33	54	87
Seattle	AL	51	41	92
Kansas City	AL	62	31	93
Detroit	AL	57	36	93
Minnesota	AL	53	40	93
Philadelphia	NL	35	59	94
Boston	AL	52	48	100
California	AL	43	58	101
Texas	AL	48	54	102
Atlanta	NL	55	49	104
Cleveland	AL	52	54	106
Chicago	NL	50	61	111
Oakland	AL	54	60	114
Baltimore	AL	52	72	124
Milwaukee	AL	72	59	131
San Francisco	NL	56	76	132
Los Angeles	NL	65	71	136
San Diego	NL	59	79	138
Pittsburgh	NL	52	96	148
St. Louis	NL	74	77	151
Cincinnati	NL	66	88	154
Houston	NL	83	79	162
Chicago	AL	90	75	165
Montreal	NL	99	87	186

Six of the top seven clubs, and nine of the top eleven, play in the American League. This makes perfect sense: with the designated hitter rule and generally-smaller ballparks, AL games are usually higher scoring. If you need a lot of runs to win, you're less apt to give up a chance for a big inning by stealing or bunting. On the other hand, clubs which play in big parks — the Expos and Astros, for example — are much more likely to play for one run.

The two clubs which stick out on the list are the Blue Jays and Mets — the leading big-inning teams in each league. Many people would simply say that these teams — usually labeled underachieving — have "weak fundamentals," and leave it at that. But it's easy to see why Cito Gaston and Bud Harrelson don't bunt or steal much — the Jays were second in the American League in homers, and the Mets tied the Tigers for the major league home run lead. And it's hard to quarrel with success: the Jays and Mets led their leagues in runs scored.

On the other hand, the Mets were 23-28 in one-run games, the Blue Jays 24-27, which suggests that maybe they should have been playing for one run more often. In the case of the Mets, you have to wonder why they didn't try to steal more. The Metsies had the best stolen base percentage in the National League (.769), but ranked ninth in total steals. Under Davey Johnson — usually considered a big-inning manager — the Mets took advantage of their baserunning skills; in 1989, Johnson's last full year, New York was second in the league in steals. If the chance of getting thrown out isn't all that great, why not take it?

Another club hard to understand is the other New York team, the Yankees. A woefully weak offense, some base stealing threats . . . why did the Yanks keep playing for big innings which never came?

IF LINEOUTS WERE HITS . . . ?

Who says there are no .400 hitters? Let's pretend all those hard, scorching, screaming, tear-the-glove-off-your-hand, why-did-he-have-to-hit-it-right-at-the-fielder lineouts belted by major league batters in 1990 had dropped in for hits. Suddenly we'd be back in the 1920s, when men were men and the great sluggers were hitting .400. If lineouts were hits, Dave Magadan and Tony Gwynn would be the Rogers Hornsbys of today. The "New-Avg" column shows who the batting average leaders would have been if only their lineouts had fallen for hits:

American League

Player, Team	AB	H	Avg	LO	New Avg
Alan Trammell, Det	559	170	.304	45	.385
Rafael Palmeiro, Tex	598	191	.319	36	.380
Wade Boggs, Bos	619	187	.302	48	.380
George Brett, KC	544	179	.329	18	.362
Rickey Henderson, Oak	489	159	.325	18	.362
Jody Reed, Bos	598	173	.289	43	.361
Julio Franco, Tex	582	172	.296	37	.359
Ken Griffey, Sea	597	179	.300	32	.353
Brook Jacoby, Cle	553	162	.293	30	.347
Brian Harper, Min	479	141	.294	25	.347

National League

Player, Team	AB	H	Avg	LO	New Avg
Dave Magadan, Mets	451	148	.328	40	.417
Tony Gwynn, SD	573	177	.309	59	.412
Lenny Dykstra, Phi	590	192	.325	34	.383
Eddie Murray, LA	558	184	.330	29	.382
Mark Grace, Cubs	589	182	.309	39	.375
Willie McGee, StL-Oak	501	168	.335	18	.371
Bip Roberts, SD	556	172	.309	31	.365
Ryne Sandberg, Cubs	615	188	.306	34	.361
Jeff Treadway, Atl	474	134	.283	35	.357
Barry Larkin, Cin	614	185	.301	34	.357

Wow, Alan Trammell really shoulda hit .385! Pretty neat, huh? (We're sorry, but we should point out that STATS, Inc. is located in the Chicago area, and that "let's pretend" is a pretty popular game around here. There's,

"Let's pretend Dave Stewart and Dennis Eckersley can't lift their arms above their waists next year," and "Let's pretend there's a big plane crash involving the Pirate, Met and Expo ballclubs," and "Let's pretend Elle MacPherson walks into the STATS office and says, 'Wow, guys who love baseball statistics really turn me on!' " This is a popular one around book-deadline time.)

But lest you think this is just an exercise in futility, let us set you straight. We ran this same study a year ago, and several alert readers subsequently pointed out that most of the players who hit into a lot of lineouts wound up increasing their batting averages in 1990. And most of the players who hit into very few lineouts wound up with lower averages. Here are the top six in each category last year:

Most Lineouts per At-Bat — 1989

Player, Team	LO/AB	1989 Avg	1990 Avg	Change
Gregg Jefferies, Mets	.108	.258	.283	+.025
Tommy Herr, Phi-Mets	.089	.287	.261	−.026
Darryl Strawberry, Mets	.084	.225	.277	+.052
Alan Trammell, Det	.076	.243	.304	+.061
Jeff Treadway, Atl	.074	.277	.283	+.006
Johnny Ray, Cal	.074	.289	.277	−.012
Average Change				+.018

Least Lineouts per At-Bat — 1989

Player, Team	LO/AB	1989 Avg	1990 Avg	Change
Shawon Dunston, Cubs	.021	.278	.262	−.016
Eric Davis, Cin	.026	.281	.260	−.021
Danny Tartabull, KC	.027	.268	.268	-----
Jeffrey Leonard, Sea	.028	.254	.251	−.003
Chili Davis, Cal	.030	.271	.265	−.006
Glenn Davis, Hou	.031	.269	.251	−.018
Average Change				−.011

The players who hit into the most lineouts wound up increasing their batting averages by an average of 18 points last year. And the players who hit into the fewest wound up dropping by an average of 11. Is this compelling evidence? Not if you talk to Tommy Herr. But we'll keep an eye on this subject for the future; certainly it makes logical sense that guys who hit into tough luck one year would find better luck the next. Here's the 1990 players with the most and least lineouts per at-bat:

Most Lineouts per At-Bat — 1990
(Expect an increase in batting average)

American League		National League	
Player, Team	LO/AB	Player, Team	LO/AB
Trammell, Det	.081	Gwynn, SD	.103
Boggs, Bos	.078	Magadan, Mets	.089
Reed, Bos	.072	Hayes, Phi	.077
Fletcher, WSox	.067	Lind, Pit	.076
Browne, Cle	.064	Treadway, Atl	.074

Least Lineouts per At-Bat — 1990
(Expect a decrease in batting average)

American League		National League	
Player, Team	LO/AB	Player, Team	LO/AB
D.White, Cal	.018	Presley, Atl	.020
Tettleton, Bal	.020	Brooks, LA	.025
Canseco, Oak	.021	Williams, SF	.026
Deer, Mil	.025	Thompson, SF	.032
McGriff, Tor	.025	Van Slyke, Pit	.033

For you fantasy players out there, we'd strongly recommend trying to obtain Tony Gwynn if you can get him for a good price. This is no .309 hitter, and you don't have to play "let's pretend" to figure **that** one out.

A complete listing for this category appears on page 263.

WHAT'S THE TRIPLE CROWN OF LEADOFF MEN?

If you had to pick the ideal qualities for a leadoff man, you'd look for dominance in on-base average, stolen bases and runs scored — what we call the "Leadoff Triple Crown." You're probably wondering, as we did, how many players have led in all three categories in the same season. What we found was more proof of Rickey Henderson's status as the best leadoff man ever, a subject we discuss in another essay. Last year Henderson became the first American League leadoff man to win the leadoff triple crown — but there's a catch.

The catch is that the great Ty Cobb, who had most of the traits of a good leadoff man, but — like Rickey — the power to hit lower in the order, was batting in the power slots when he led in all three categories in both 1909 and 1915. We should add that 1909 was a "double triple," since Cobb also took the traditional triple crown by leading in batting, homers and RBI. That's a feat unmatched in baseball history. (Cobb also led the AL in hits and total bases in his "double triple" season, but not, unfortunately, in either doubles or triples.) His figures in 1909 were a .431 on-base average, 76 stolen bases (then the AL record), and 116 runs. In 1915, Cobb had a .486 OBA (his career high, due to 118 walks, the only time he drew over 85 BB), 96 SB (the modern record until Maury Wills), and 144 runs.

If we include the nineteenth century, there are three leadoff triple crowns in the NL among two men, both players who batted first. The only post-1900 crown belongs to George Burns, an outfielder for the Giants, Reds and Phillies from 1911 to 1925, who's not to be confused with either George Burns, the comedian, or "Tioga George" Burns, the American League first baseman of the same period. (Burns the National Leaguer was born in 1889, Burns the American Leaguer in 1893, and Burns the comedian in 1896. The baseball-playing Burnses are dead, but it's no wonder people get confused.) While playing for the Giants in 1919, this George Burns led the NL with a .396 OBA, 86 runs (the lowest leading total in the NL since 1880 except for the strike year '81), and 40 SB.

Now basically forgotten, Burns was an excellent leadoff man who led the National League five times in runs scored — it helped that McGraw's Giants were always a good-hitting team. Only Rogers Hornsby and Stan Musial, who also led the NL in runs five times each, could match Burns in that category. Burns also led the league in steals in 1913, with 62, and had 334 with the Giants; both are all-time Giant franchise records. *Total Baseball* gives him three Bill James' runs created championships: 1913, 113; 1917, 102; 1919, 96. According to Shatzkin's *The Ballplayers,* Burns was also a good fielder, with "a special knack for playing the notorious sun field in left (at the Polo Grounds)." He was also highly regarded as a man; Frank Graham in *McGraw of the Giants* writes about Burns' trade to the Reds (for Heinie Groh), "George was one of the few players for whom he (McGraw) ever had indicated a warm personal regard." And McGraw, as we'll see, knew more than a little about the art of leading off.

Probably the best leadoff man before Rickey Henderson, and according to Shatzkin, "perhaps the best player of the 1890s," was "Sliding Billy" Hamilton of the Phillies and Boston Beaneaters. Hamilton won the leadoff triple crown in 1891 (.453 OBA, 111 SB, 141 runs), and in 1894 (.523 OBA, 96 SB, and 192 runs). Along with Ed Delahanty and Sam Thompson, he was one of three Hall-of-Fame Phillie outfielders who played together from 1891 to 1895. Hamilton's lifetime marks are extraordinary; his batting average of .344 is seventh alltime; his OBA of .455 is exceeded only by Babe Ruth, Ted Williams, and John McGraw; his runs/game total of 1.06 is #1; his 912 stolen bases are #3.

The 1894 season was the all-time hitting year in ML history (the league batted .309 as a whole, and the average team scored more than seven runs a game), and Hamilton's record 192 runs were scored in only 128 games. Other features of this season were seven steals in one game and a 36-game hitting streak, sixth longest in NL history. His 1894 batting average of .404 *(Total Baseball)* was fourth in the NL, and third among Phil outfielders (or perhaps even fourth; utility outfielder Tuck Turner hit .416 in 339 AB). The Phillies as a team batted .349, but finished only fourth in the standings (and second in runs scored with 1143 to Boston's 1222 — Boston hit "only" .331 but out-homered the Phils 103 to 40 in a bandbox park — the Phils' Baker Bowl was actually a "pitcher's park" by 19th century standards.)

OK, so much for yesteryear. Here are some AL leadoff hitters who won two-thirds of the Triple Crown (unless stated otherwise, the missing leg was on-base average; just as the HR/RBI crowns are often paired, but BA goes to someone else, players often lead in steals and runs scored, but not in OBA):

Wade Boggs in 1988 (yes, he missed in SB)

Rickey Henderson in 1981, 1985, and 1986 (in OBA, finished #4 in 1985 and #3 in 1981)

Ron LeFlore in 1978

Dom DiMaggio in 1950 (leading the AL with all of 15 SB)

Snuffy Stirnweiss in both 1944 and 1945

George Case in 1943

John "Bananas" Mostil in 1925 (You mean you don't remember this ChiSox center fielder? His nickname indicated his fate.)

In the National League:

Tim Raines in 1983 (finished #4 in OBA)

Lou Brock in 1967

Arky Vaughan in 1943 (Arky was usually very strong in OBA too, but not in 1943)

Augie Galan in 1935

Pepper Martin in 1933

George Burns in 1914

Max Carey in 1913

Bob Bescher in 1912

John McGraw in 1899 (missed in SB only, finishing second with 73, two behind Jimmy Sheckard; his leading .547 OBA is the highest ever for a leadoff man and his .391 BA was the highest ever for a third baseman. It was also his first year as a manager (with Baltimore), and he finished fourth, surprisingly well since all the best Baltimore players had been "traded" to the pennant winner Brooklyn (Brooklyn and Baltimore were owned by the same man).

Billy Hamilton in 1895 (#2 in OBA) (More on that Phil OF. Hamilton finished #5 in league BA in '95 and still #3 among Phillie outfielders, since Tuck Turner "slumped" to .386. In 1893, the Phillie outfielders finished #1, #2, #3 in league BA, but this time Hamilton finished #1 in BA and OBA. In all Hamilton, as mentioned, was #7 in lifetime BA, Delahanty was #5, and Thompson a mere #26, at .331.)

Rickey Henderson greatly exceeds Hamilton in power-hitting — and indeed exceeds all other leadoff men in baseball history, since his .577 slugging average in 1990 tops any mark of Bobby Bonds (peak of .530 in 1973) or Felipe Alou (.533 with a leadoff record 31 HR in 1966). All in all, Rickey's 1990 season was the finest leadoff season in history by the finest leadoff hitter in baseball history.

WHO SHOULD BE PLATOONED?

It's no secret that, as a rule, hitters perform better against pitchers from the opposite side. There are always, however, some guys who just **have** to be different. The list of hitters with the biggest left/right differentials (minimum 50 plate appearances against each side) in 1990 includes two players who did better against hurlers who throw from the same side. Here are the top ten in batting average differential against lefties and righties; a minus difference means they do better against hurlers from the same side:

Player, Team	Bats	Vs. Left			Vs. Right			
		AB	HR	Avg	AB	HR	Avg	Diff
Mariano Duncan, Cin	R	188	4	.410	247	6	.227	+183
Jack Clark, SD	R	114	9	.377	220	16	.209	+168
Hal Morris, Cin	L	76	0	.224	233	7	.378	+154
Mike LaValliere, Pit	L	56	2	.375	223	1	.229	−146
Cecil Fielder, Det	R	178	25	.371	395	26	.235	+136
Willie Randolph, LA-Oak	R	116	0	.353	272	2	.221	+132
Mackey Sasser, Mets	L	53	1	.208	217	5	.332	+124
Rob Deer, Mil	R	140	16	.293	300	11	.170	+123
Kevin Maas, Mets	L	67	3	.164	187	18	.283	+119
Dave Justice, Atl	L	131	10	.366	308	18	.247	−119

We'll get into the exceptions — Mike LaValliere and Dave Justice — in a moment. The other eight have the traditional bias in favor of opposite-side throwers . . . but that doesn't necessarily mean they need to be platooned. You wouldn't want to sit down Kevin Maas and Hal Morris against southpaws just yet, since both were rookies who showed great promise in 1990. Righty sluggers Jack Clark and Cecil Fielder simply destroyed lefties last year; they batted for a low average against righties, but with great power, and their clubs need them in the lineup every day.

However, good candidates for platooning would include Mariano Duncan, Willie Randolph and Rob Deer; Mackey Sasser is already a platoon catcher, for the most part. Duncan, a former switch-hitter, has never shown ability to hit righties whether he switches sides or not. Randolph, an aging player, has seen his batting skills erode, but he can still make an offensive contribution if spotted against lefties. As for Rob Deer, he probably should have been a platoon outfielder all along.

As for Dave Justice, the National League's Rookie of the Year, and Mike LaValliere, a guy who's been around for awhile, the odds are against their continuing to hit better against lefties in 1991. Look at what happened to the three hitters who had the biggest reverse-platoon differentials in 1989:

Player	Bats	1989			1990		
		LHP	RHP	Diff	LHP	RHP	Diff
Gerald Perry	L	.337	.198	-139	.209	.272	+63
Greg Brock	L	.333	.244	-89	.209	.260	+51
Randy Milligan	R	.225	.306	-81	.330	.240	+90

All three reversed the trend in 1990, hitting much better this time against pitchers from the opposite side. That's what you normally expect, so you'd have to think their '89 figures were a fluke. But before we say that Justice and LaValliere won't hit lefties better again in '91, it's worth noting that B.J. Surhoff, a lefty swinger, did just that in both 1989 and 1990:

Player	Bats	1989			1990		
		LHP	RHP	Diff	LHP	RHP	Diff
B.J. Surhoff	L	.310	.233	−77	.317	.265	−52

Surhoff is a strong exception to the rule, however.

A few players were jewels of consistency in 1990, hitting for almost the same average against lefties and righties:

Player, Team	Bats	Vs. Left			Vs. Right		
		AB	HR	Avg	AB	HR	Avg
Kent Hrbek, Min	L	129	2	.287	373	20	.287
Willie McGee, StL-Oak	S	225	2	.324	389	1	.324
Mike Felder, Mil	S	80	3	.275	157	0	.274
Rafael Ramirez, Hou	R	192	1	.260	253	1	.261
Julio Franco, Tex	R	179	3	.296	403	8	.295

Hrbek, a traditional lefty slugger, still hits for much more power against righties. But wouldn't every manager like to have a 1990-style Willie McGee, a switch-hitter who performed identically against lefties and righties?

A complete listing for this category can be found on page 264.

CAN HITTERS CAUSE ERRORS?

There are volumes and volumes of stats these days, but one you never see is "times reached base on error." Of course not, you say; errors are committed by the fielder and have nothing to do with who hits the ball. But is this completely true? Let's build a hypothetical model of a player who might reach base on errors a lot:

1. He'd be a right-handed hitter. Righties usually hit the ball to the left side of the diamond, and more errors are committed by third basemen and shortstops — who have to make a longer throw — than anyone else.

2. He'd have good speed, forcing the fielder to hurry his toss and sometimes throw the ball away.

3. He'd have good line drive power, with the ability to hit the ball hard enough to tie up a fielder.

4. He'd probably be a good bunter; fielders forced to make a quick play on a bunt would be more likely to make an error.

Now let's look at the players who reached base most often on errors last year, as a percentage of total at-bats (minimum 502 plate appearances):

Percentage of time reaching base by an error — 1990

Player, Team	Errors	AB	Pct.
Shawon Dunston, Cubs	16	545	.029
Charlie Hayes, Phi	15	561	.027
Devon White, Cal	12	443	.027
Bip Roberts, SD	14	556	.025
Ryne Sandberg, Cubs	15	615	.024
Joe Carter, SD	15	634	.024
Gary Gaetti, Min	14	577	.024
Billy Hatcher, Cin	12	504	.024
Andre Dawson, Cubs	12	529	.023
Jay Bell, Pit	12	583	.021
Jerry Browne, Cle	11	513	.021
B.J. Surhoff, Mil	10	474	.021

Amaze your friends at cocktail parties with this one: Shawon Dunston reached base more often on errors last year (16) than he did on walks (15)!

Our model, it seems, holds up rather well. Eight of the twelve players bat righty; three (Roberts, White and Browne) are switch-hitters. The only lefty swinger is B.J. Surhoff, who's not much of a pull hitter. Players who have both power and speed — usually both — are represented; the ones who aren't very fast, like Gaetti and Dawson, are known for hustling down the line. Jay Bell, one of baseball's best bunters, is on the list.

Why would Dunston excel in this category? He has most of the essentials: he's righty, he hits the ball hard, he has fine speed. There's another reason — he plays in Wrigley Field. Our stats a year ago showed that more ground ball errors are committed at Wrigley than at any other park. That might surprise you, since Ryne Sandberg has set numerous fielding records there. Nonetheless it's true. Thus it's no shock that three Cubs (Dunston, Sandberg and Dawson) were among the players who reached most often on errors. Another Cubbie, Mark Grace — a lefty swinger — also ranked close to the top.

Is reaching base on errors a skill? In a way it is: players who match our profile have a much better chance of reaching than others do — especially if they play in a park with a tricky infield. But Shawon Dunston's request — that reaching on errors be incorporated into his on-base average — is hereby denied. You'll just have to try cracking that 20-walk barrier this year, Shawon.

A complete listing for this category can be found on page 265.

WHO ARE THE "HUMAN AIR CONDITIONERS"?

If it's a hot day at the ball park, you might be grateful to see Cecil Fielder come to bat. Not only is there a good chance that Cecil might lauch one into the stratosphere; there's an even better one that he'll cool off the stadium with a mighty swish. Last year Fielder blasted 51 dingers — but he completely missed the ball 465 times, more than nine times as often. Given the kind of season Fielder had overall, the Tigers weren't complaining.

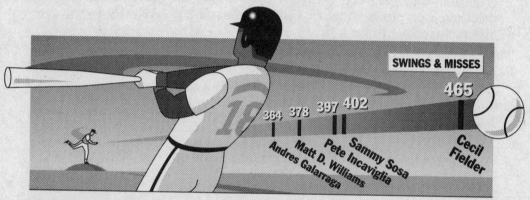

This chart lists the major league players who swung and missed most often in 1990. If you recall our article on this subject last year, you probably only have one question: where's Bo? Bo Jackson was the swing-and-miss champion in 1989 with 452, but last year he was well down the list, tied for seventh with a lowly total of 334. Not to worry. Bo still knows air conditioning; it's just that he was injured last year, and got into only 111 games.

Bo's injury problems prompted us to look at this subject in another way. As the legendary Dave Nicholson (1419 lifetime at-bats, 573 strikeouts) might have put it, "You can't miss the ball if you don't swing at it." We decided to rank players on the basis of percentage of swings missed. Here are the 1990 leaders in percentage of their swings that missed (minimum 700 swings):

Player, Team	Swung	Missed	Pct
Pete Incaviglia, Tex	1,058	397	37.5
Bo Jackson, KC	918	343	37.4
Cecil Fielder, Det	1,273	465	36.5
Sammy Sosa, WSox	1,172	402	34.3
Jose Canseco, Oak	1,021	343	34.0
Rob Deer, Mil	919	303	33.0
Jim Presley, Atl	1,098	354	32.2

Mickey Tettleton, Bal	848	268	31.6
Greg Vaughn, Mil	778	245	31.5
Ron Kittle, WSox-Bal	708	218	30.8

Bo looks a lot more like himself using this system, though he still yielded first place in a photo finish to Pete Incaviglia. It's a plenty interesting list. There's Jackson, Fielder and Jose Canseco, three of baseball's most legendary sluggers. There's Incaviglia, Jim Presley, Rob Deer and Ron Kittle, four players whose careers have been considered disapointments. There's Mickey Tettleton, a unique hitter who, like Jack Clark, both strikes out and walks a lot. And there's Sammy Sosa and Greg Vaughn, young hitters who still have holes in their swings. The one constant among all ten is great power. The moral is, you can get away with this style of hitting — but only if you put up some big numbers.

How about the other side of the coin, the hitters with the best bat control? The following players missed with the **lowest** percentage of their swings in 1990 (again, minimum 700 swings):

Player, Team	Swung	Missed	Pct
Lenny Dykstra, Phi	1,055	62	5.9
Tony Gwynn, SD	913	59	6.5
Jody Reed, Bos	944	66	7.0
Ozzie Smith, StL	837	59	7.0
Wade Boggs, Bos	1,147	84	7.3
Edgar Martinez, Sea	808	67	8.3
Brett Butler, SF	1,268	108	8.5
Dave Magadan, Mets	734	64	8.7
Tommy Herr, Phi-Mets	965	86	8.9
Steve Sax, Yanks	1,045	97	9.3

Another interesting list, one which includes some of 1990's best hitters. If you could use one word to describe the previous group of players, it would probably be "powerful." The word for this group would be "intelligent." Three of the top five National League leaders in on-base percentage are represented, and two of the top six in the AL. Boggs has won five batting titles, and Gwynn four. You can't find many better hitters than these guys. One thing to point out: Boggs went from 5.4% missed in '89 to 7.3% in '90. This partially explains his sinking batting average.

The absolute kings of futility last year were two relief pitchers, Drew Hall of the Expos and Marvin Freeman of the Phils. Each swung the bat 12 times, and missed the ball on 10 of them. Even Dave Nicholson wasn't quite **that** bad!

A complete listing for this category appears on page 266.

WHO LEADS THE LEAGUE IN LOOKING?

In life, everyone has his personal style, and the same is true in baseball. Some hitters are fuss-budgets, waiting for exactly the right pitch. Others are more impatient, and whack at the first offering that looks reasonable (which is often the first thing that leaves the pitcher's hand). Our preference is for the more patient type, and we think you'll agree with us after looking at the list of players who used the most pitches per plate appearance in 1990 (minimum 300 plate appearances):

Player, Team	Plate App.	No. of Pitches	Pitches per PA
Mickey Tettleton, Bal	559	2,482	4.44
Wade Boggs, Bos	713	3,067	4.30
Rickey Henderson, Oak	594	2,540	4.28
Jack Clark, SD	442	1,870	4.23
Randy Milligan, Bal	456	1927	4.23
Craig Worthington, Bal	501	2,096	4.18
Brian Downing, Cal	390	1,621	4.16
Jesse Barfield, Yanks	570	2,371	4.16
Jose Canseco, Oak	563	2,317	4.12
Rob Deer, Mil	511	2,107	4.12

Boggs-Henderson-Clark-Canseco? We'll take this as a reasonable list of some of the best hitters in baseball. They'll do a lot with a good pitch — but they're not afraid to take a walk when the pitcher won't give them anything good to hit. Their value is usually more than expressed in mere batting or even slugging percentages.

Whereas if you look at the hitters who average the **least** pitches per plate appearance, you'll mostly find players whose value is almost entirely expressed in their batting averages:

Player, Team	Plate App.	No. of Pitches	Pitches per PA
Mackey Sasser, Mets	288	743	2.58
Joe Girardi, Cubs	447	1,199	2.68
Ozzie Guillen, WSox	563	1,604	2.85
Scott Bradley, Sea	257	761	2.96
Jose Uribe, SF	448	1,348	3.01

Except for Sasser ("Mackey the Hacker"), who can occasionally unload a long one, these are punch-and-judy types who could generally do as much damage with a walk as they could with a single. You'd think they'd smarten up a little, but they never seem to.

Are some teams more patient than others? They certainly are. Here is a team-by-team ranking of the clubs which used the most pitches per plate appearance last year:

American League	Plate App.	No. of Pitches	Pitches per PA
Orioles	6,223	23,478	3.77
Tigers	6,224	23,463	3.77
Angels	6,267	23,420	3.74
Rangers	6,177	22,995	3.72
Athletics	6,240	23,020	3.69
Red Sox	6,234	23,031	3.69
Blue Jays	6,223	22,667	3.64
Mariners	6,207	22,620	3.64
Yankees	6,037	21,746	3.60
Royals	6,099	21,721	3.56
Brewers	6,185	21,901	3.54
White Sox	6,038	21,277	3.52
Indians	6,087	21,207	3.48
Twins	6,086	20,512	3.37

National League	Plate App.	No. of Pitches	Pitches per PA
Expos	6,189	22,562	3.65
Astros	6,076	22,077	3.63
Mets	6,182	22,390	3.62
Pirates	6,161	22,184	3.60
Padres	6,218	22,248	3.58
Cardinals	6,127	21,901	3.57
Phillies	6,245	22,189	3.55
Braves	6,084	21,575	3.55
Giants	6,216	22,005	3.54
Dodgers	6,179	21,902	3.54
Reds	6,163	21,653	3.51
Cubs	6,149	20,776	3.38

On a team-wide basis, patience is not everything. The Orioles drew 660 walks, the most in baseball, but their offensive effectiveness was blunted by a .245 team batting average. The Reds, on the other hand, drew only 466 walks — second fewest in the NL — but were able to mount an effective offense because they led the league in hitting. (Just ask the A's about their offense.) Being selective isn't everything ... but it's a lot.

A complete listing for this category can be found on page 267.

IS "GIVING YOURSELF UP" A GIVE-UP PLAY?

Runner on second base, nobody out. We all know what the batter's job is supposed to be — hit that ground ball to the right side so that the runner can advance to third base. If the ground ball finds its way through the infield for a hit, so much the better. But woe to the batter who instead pops up, especially if the next batter hits a long fly to the outfield. The announcers moan about "poor fundamentals," and sometimes hint of doubtful moral character!

Few events in baseball cause more negative discussions than this simple little play. We are often told that "it's the little things that win pennants," and this is always one of the prime examples. Old-time baseball men frequently argue that, with free agency, batters seek to pad their statistics and don't do those little uncounted things. Which is why the home team will not be in the World Series (again).

Well, STATS is in the business of counting things, even the little ones. We thought we'd take a look at the runner on second base, nobody out, situation. In 1990 there were 2,753 chances for the "give-up" play. For the average team that meant about two occurrences for every three games. Kansas City had the most chances, 140, and San Diego the least, 93.

In 936 of those 2,753 situations — only a little over a third of the time — the batter produced a ground ball. We can hear those announcers moaning already. Whittling it down even further, only 523 of the 936 grounders (56 percent) were hit to the right of second base (and past the pitcher). When that happened, the advance to third was almost automatic: the ground balls to the right side advanced the runner 512 of the 523 times. Knowledgeable fans applauded politely, nudged each other, and said, "He did his job." As a bonus, the batter reached base on 142 of those occasions (including errors and fielders choices as well as hits) — 27.2 percent of the time.

What can we learn from all that? Well major leaguers only produced the appropriate ground ball in 523 of 2,753 chances, or 19.0% of the time. Even if many batters are weak or careless on fundamentals, this result suggests that those little ground balls are not that easy to steer. That of course, makes sense: the defensive team wants to prevent the advance, and the pitcher will often throw a pitch that's tough to hit to the right side.

We can also tell you that the most effective club in giving itself up was the World Champion Cincinnati Reds (26.0% of the time) and that the weakest club was the disappointing Chicago Cubs (11.7% of the time). So far you might decide that, hey, even if this is harder to do than it looks, it's obvious that those give-up plays do mean championship play. However, we should raise some counter-arguments. The top two teams in the American League in this category, Kansas City and Toronto, are not noted either for over-achievement or clubhouse camaraderie. And even if you make the extreme assumption that the runners left on second base never score and the runner moved to third base always scores, the difference between the Reds and the Cubs would have been 21 runs over the season — two games in the standings. It would have taken much more improvement than that to make George Will happy and get the Cubs to the World Series!

We did one more study. What happened on the 2,230 occasions when the batter was NOT successful in hitting a ground ball to the right side?

The answer is this: on 1,184 of those occasions, either the runner reached third base or the batter reached first, a success rate of 53.1%. That's admittedly less than the 97.9% for the ground ball to the right side. However, there was a significant bonus: the batter reached safely 759 times, or 34.0% of the time, which is significantly better than the 27.2% rate for batters who try to "give themselves up."

Is the "give-up" play a good play? There's little statistical evidence that it is. In *The Hidden Game of Baseball,* Pete Palmer and John Thorn estimate the run potential of a man-on-second, no-out situation at 1.07 — meaning that a club in this situation will average a little over one run per inning. The run potential of a man-on-third, one-out situation is less, not more: 0.90 runs per inning. In that sense, the play is just like the sacrifice bunt — the chances of scoring one run are better, but the chances of scoring more than one are worse. Of course, it's different from a sacrifice because the batter has a decent chance of reaching base (27.2%, according to last year's data). But he has a much better chance of reaching (34.0) if he **doesn't** go to the right side.

Clearly, if one run is critical, moving the runner to third tends to be more important. But if as many runs as possible are wanted, the additional base runners are more valuable. Putting all this together. we think that "giving oneself up to advance the runner" may be selfless, but it's often an undesirable strategy; it's something of a "give-up" play for the batting team as well as the batter. Probably a legitimate question to ask when the situation comes up is whether you'd be bunting. In the late innings, needing a run, it's a good move. Otherwise, though, it doesn't make much sense.

In any case, it's obviously not an easy thing to do consistently, assuming most batters are trying. For these reasons, a popup with a runner at second and none out really shouldn't be singled out as being any weaker a batting effort than a popup at any time. Too much is made of this play.

Team data on this subject appears in the appendix on page 268.

WHAT'S AN AVERAGE LINEUP?

Based on 600 plate appearances.

Major league lineups are constructed along classic lines: a speedy player who can (hopefully) get on base at the top, then a good contact man, the power guys in the three-through-six slots, and finally the weaker hitters at the end. Looked at by leagues, we see little variation on the pattern. But an AL-vs-NL comparison nonetheless yields some very interesting results.

	Avg	OBP	Slg	AB	R	H	2B	3B	HR	RBI	BB	K	SB
American League — per 600 PA													
Batting #1	.265	.334	.374	534	78	141	23	6	8	47	54	76	25
Batting #2	.265	.332	.371	532	72	141	25	4	8	58	52	68	16
Batting #3	.271	.343	.420	531	71	144	27	3	15	74	58	80	10
Batting #4	.263	.338	.442	529	71	139	26	2	22	85	60	106	4
Batting #5	.265	.336	.427	533	71	141	27	3	18	69	56	98	7
Batting #6	.252	.326	.386	534	65	135	23	3	14	63	56	97	7
Batting #7	.261	.325	.385	537	59	140	24	3	12	67	49	90	6
Batting #8	.242	.307	.342	537	61	130	23	3	8	58	48	94	7
Batting #9	.243	.299	.331	538	59	131	23	3	6	51	42	88	10
National League — per 600 PA													
Batting #1	.286	.357	.401	533	85	153	27	5	8	44	57	71	36
Batting #2	.279	.342	.402	534	79	149	27	4	10	56	51	69	19
Batting #3	.283	.351	.426	532	74	150	25	4	15	76	56	80	19
Batting #4	.272	.340	.467	536	76	146	27	3	24	90	55	94	9
Batting #5	.258	.323	.413	539	68	139	24	3	18	80	52	89	13
Batting #6	.255	.317	.381	541	59	138	26	3	12	64	49	89	11
Batting #7	.251	.317	.371	538	57	135	25	2	12	58	51	86	9
Batting #8	.239	.303	.330	539	51	129	22	4	6	50	49	81	5
Batting #9	.223	.292	.320	533	59	119	17	4	9	57	51	135	8

Note: NL figures do not include pitchers' hitting

When we looked at this subject a year ago, we commented on how much

LEAD-OFF	2	3	CLEAN-UP	5	6	7	8	9
			NATIONAL					
.286	.279	.283	.272	.258	.255	.251	.239	.223

AVG.

1989 .246
1990 .256

LEAGUE BATTING AVERAGE

Based on 600 plate appearances.

more punch the American league lineups had. What a difference a year made! In 1990 the NL got better decidedly better production out of each of the top four spots in the lineup; the AL led after that, but except for the ninth spot, where the National League pitchers bat, the difference wasn't all that great. What happened? In 1990 American League offense stayed at about the same level as in '89; National League offense got a lot better.

Just look at the league averages in the charts.

How extreme was the National League's ten point rise in batting average? Well, in the last 60 years, the NL has had a bigger jump only once, in 1953. Your guess is as good as ours as to why it happened, or whether it will continue. The American did have the better offensive figures again last year, but that was only because of the DH rule. On the whole, the National was the better-hitting league last year. They sure looked like it in the World Series, didn't they?

Some other observations on the batting order:

1. Despite the NL's legitimate claim to being the better-hitting league last year, there was still greater depth to American League lineups. The average number seven hitter in an AL batting order was much more dangerous than his National League counterpart.

2. The National League's edge in speed is very obvious.

3. Managers still place a lot of importance on contact hitting from the number-two spot, which makes sense since they're trying to protect their base-stealing leadoff men. In each league, the number-two hitters struck out less than any other lineup position.

4. We always hear how tough it is to bat eighth in the NL — with the pitcher coming up next, he won't get much to hit, the story goes. But National League number-eight hitters were only slightly worse than their American League counterparts last year.

5. Over the course of a season, each succeeding spot in the order will come up fewer times than the spot before it. Notice that neat descent in batting average from the third to the ninth spot in the NL? Smart fellows, those National League managers.

A complete listing for this category appears on page 269.

DOES THE COLISEUM HURT MARK McGWIRE?

If you can muster any sympathy for a multi-millionaire, you might want to feel a little sorry for Mark McGwire. We point out elsewhere that McGwire is one of the great young sluggers in baseball, with 156 homers in just a little over four seasons. But McGwire slugs away while being severely penalized by his home park — 96 of his homers have come on the road, only 60 at the Oakland Coliseum. Here's a point that bears repeating — McGwire, at this point of his career, is hitting homers on the road at a faster pace than Babe Ruth did:

McGwire on the road — one homer every 11.7 at bats
Ruth on the road — one homer every 11.9 at bats

At home, however, it's a different story:

McGwire at home — one homer every 17.4 at bats
Ruth at home — one homer every 11.6 at bats

McGwire's plight caused us to wonder whether any player in modern history has been so badly penalized by his home park. We don't have the whole answer; complete home/road home run data only extends back to 1950. That's still the biggest part of the home run era — Willie Mays and Mickey Mantle both debuted in 1951 — so let's look at this fascinating data. We took all the players who have hit 150 home runs since 1950, and figured a home/road index as follows:

Index = (Home runs at home) divided by (home runs on the road) X 100

If a player hit 75 home runs at home and 75 on the road, his index would be 100 (75 divided by 75 X 100 = 100). If he hit 60 at home and 90 on the road, his index would be 67 (60 divided by 90 X 100 = 67). If he hit 95 homers at home and 55 on the road, his index would be 173 (95 divided by 55 X 100 = 173). Here are the players whose careers began after 1950 with the **lowest** indexes — meaning they were the ones most penalized by their home parks (150 lifetime homers minimum):

Batter	Home	Road	Index
Howard, Elston	54	113	48
Cruz, Jose	59	106	56
Clendenon, Donn	58	101	57
Watson, Bob	67	117	57
McGwire, Mark	60	96	63
Davis, Willie	70	112	63
Wallach, Tim	71	111	64

Adcock, Joe	137	199	69
Skowron, Bill	86	125	69
Porter, Darrell	77	111	69

McGwire, to our surprise, didn't top the list; in fact he was down in fifth place, tied with the old Dodger outfielder, Willie Davis. The leader, by far, was Elston Howard, who spent most of his career slugging long fly balls into "Death Valley" at Yankee Stadium. Bill Skowron, another righty slugger with the fifties and sixties Yankees, was tied for eighth place on this list. They have some good company. Joe Dimaggio, one of the pre-1950 players for whom there is complete data, also had an index of 69 (148 homers at home, 213 on the road).

Along with Howard, Skowron and McGwire, the list gives us renewed appreciation for hitters like Jose Cruz and Bob Watson, whose slugging was muted by the Astrodome, and for Joe Adcock, mostly of the Braves, who might have had a 400-homer career if he'd played in friendlier parks. Among today's stars, Montreal's Tim Wallach has been penalized by his home yard almost as much as McGwire has.

How about the players who won the lottery and got to play in chummy home parks? They end up looking better than they really were, thanks to their ability to take advantage of their home dimensions:

Batter	Home	Road	Index
Horner, Bob	142	76	187
Carty, Rico	132	72	183
Petrocelli, Rico	134	76	176
Santo, Ron	216	126	171
Bailey, Ed	95	60	158
Lemon, Jim	100	64	156
Mattingly, Don	102	67	152
Dropo, Walt	91	61	149
White, Bill	120	82	146
Furillo, Carl	94	65	145

Bob Horner and Rico Carty rode Atlanta's Launching Pad to fame — for awhile, anyway. So, in a smaller way, did Henry Aaron, who was penalized during his years in Milwaukee (home run index 87), but rewarded during his years in Atlanta (home run index 131). Aaron almost certainly wouldn't have topped Ruth if the Braves hadn't moved to Atlanta. Moving down the list, we see how the reputations of Rico Petrocelli and Ron Santo were aided by Fenway and Wrigley Field.

In all of baseball history, only 17 players have hit 475 or more homers. We thought you might like to see their home-road breakdowns (thanks to the *Bill James Historical Baseball Abstract* for data on pre-1950 players):

Batter	Home	Road	Index
Ott, Mel	324	187	173
Banks, Ernie	290	222	131
Foxx, Jimmie	299	235	127
Robinson, Frank	321	265	121
Musial, Stan	252	223	113
Aaron, Henry	385	370	104
Gehrig, Lou	251	242	104
McCovey, Willie	264	257	103
Mays, Willie	335	325	103
Killebrew, Harmon	291	282	103
Jackson, Reggie	280	283	99
Mantle, Mickey	266	270	99
Ruth, Babe	347	367	95
Schmidt, Mike	265	283	94
Williams, Ted	248	273	91
Mathews, Eddie	238	274	87
Stargell, Willie	221	254	87

No great slugger was helped by his home park more than the Giants' Mel Ott, whose home run total was almost obscenely padded by the Polo Grounds. On the other hand, Eddie Mathews and Willie Stargell reached the top echelon **despite** their home parks.

A complete listing for this category appears on page 270.

WHO BUNTS THE BEST?

Rating bunters can be a little complicated because a successful bunt can be either a hit (if the batter's trying to reach base) or an out (if he's attempting a sacrifice). So we've come up with two rankings — one for sacrifice attempts, one for obvious bunt-hit attempts. You might wonder how we can differentiate, but it's fairly simple: the circumstances tell us. For instance, although National League pitchers will sacrifice with one out, position players almost never will be sacrificing unless there's nobody out. We make the best educated guess if there's any ambiguity, but ordinarily the situations are self-evident. Here are the major league leaders last year in successfully performing the sacrifice (minimum 10 bunts in play):

Bunting For a Sacrifice

Batter, Team	Sac Bunts	Sac Atts	Pct.
Mike Gallego, Oak	17	17	1.000
Dick Schofield, Cal	13	13	1.000
Oil Can Boyd, Mon	12	12	1.000
Jerry Browne, Cle	12	12	1.000
Bryn Smith, StL	11	11	1.000
Marty Barrett, Bos	11	11	1.000
Gary Pettis, Tex	11	11	1.000
Phil Bradley, Bal-WSox	11	11	1.000
Alvaro Espinoza, Yanks	11	11	1.000
Jody Reed, Bos	11	11	1.000
Devon White, Cal	10	10	1.000

Of course these figures don't count the times a player bunted foul twice and then had to abandon the attempt, but National League pitchers Oil Can Boyd and Bryn Smith can be proud of themselves — they were two of only eleven players who got at least 10 sacrifice attempts down, and were successful every time. Boyd, an American League refugee who was batting regularly for the first time in his career, should be especially proud.

The AL players on this list aren't pitchers, of course, but most of them are fairly weak hitters who have an ability to move a runner along. Oakland's Mike Gallego — he's the one with the sinister "Born to Bunt" tattoo — heads the list. The one surprise was Boston's Jody Reed, a .289 hitter with 45 doubles. We're not the only people who can't figure out Reed's manager, Joe Morgan. . .

The following players had the best percentages when they were obviously bunting for a hit last year (again, minimum, 10 attempts):

Bunting For a Hit

Batter, Team	Bunt Hits	Atts	Pct.
Scott Fletcher, WSox	11	15	.733
Robby Thompson, SF	7	10	.700
Luis Polonia, Yanks-Cal	10	15	.667
Craig Biggio, Hou	13	20	.650
Billy Hatcher, Cin	10	16	.625
Rex Hudler, SL	8	13	.615
Tony Phillips, Det	8	13	.615
Eric Yelding, Hou	12	20	.600
Oddibe McDowell, Atl	15	26	.577

For the most adept and speedy batsmen, bunting for a hit is a high-percentage move — all ten of the leaders were successful over half the time. Not on the leaders list but just as impressive was San Francisco's Brett Butler, who had 24 bunt hits (nine more than anyone else) in a whopping 46 attempts for a .522 success rate. Though Butler's percentage wasn't as high as the leaders, he never had the element of surprise going for him; defensive teams **always** expect Butler to bunt, and position their third baseman accordingly.

The bunt-for-a-hit stats also clearly indicate that speed alone is no guarantee of success. Vince Coleman, still learning his trade, was 10-for-21, which was much better than Alex Cole (4-for-11), Harold Reynolds (5-for-15), Lance Johnson (4-for-14) and Steve Finley (5-for-19). Bunting may or may not be a lost art, but a lot of players sure have trouble mastering it.

A complete listing for this category can be found on page 271.

WHO SWINGS AT THE FIRST PITCH?

The first pitch is on its way, and you only have an instant to decide whether you're going to swing or not. If your name is Joe Girardi, you're probably going to say, "Gee, looks good," and start your swing . . . even if it's a throw to first. But if your name is Wade Boggs, the pitcher could walk up to the plate, put the ball on a batting tee in front of you (after first asking how high you like it set), get all his teammates to leave the field so you'll have more hitting room . . . and still you'd say, "Nah," and let the umpire call it a strike.

We're exaggerating a little, but only a little. Last year Girardi swung at 57 percent of the first pitches offered him, the highest ratio in baseball. Boggs, meanwhile, swung at the first offering only 3.9 percent of the time, less than one-fourteenth as often as Girardi. Which is the right philosophy? The swingers would point out that pitchers are anxious to get ahead on the count, and thus their first pitch is usually a good one to hit. Indeed, the major league average last year when putting the first pitch in play was .315. The takers would point out that, when you go after the first thing to leave the pitcher's hand, you're missing the chance to get an even better one later in the count . . . or if the pitcher won't give you anything to hit, you can always settle for a walk. Many studies have shown that the overall advantage is on the side of those who wait. But it's a matter of individual style, and there are lots of good hitters among the swingers.

Let's look at each group. The following players were the ones who swung at the first pitch most often in 1990 (minimum 400 first pitches). The first columns, labeled "How Often He Swung," lists the number of first pitches seen, the number of those pitches swung at, and the swung-at percentage. The second, "Results When He Swung," shows the number of first-pitch swings the batter put into play (as opposed to swinging and missing or hitting a foul ball), and then his batting average, slugging average, and number of home runs on those first pitches that were put in play:

| The Swingers | How Often He Swung | | | Results When He Swung | | | |
Name	First Pitches	Swung	%	In Play	Avg	Slg	HR
Joe Girardi, Cubs	433	247	57.0	126	.287	.402	1
Cory Snyder, Cle	464	238	51.3	81	.380	.646	5
Matt Williams, SF	655	329	50.2	125	.341	.512	5
Ozzie Guillen, WSox	576	289	50.2	144	.346	.446	1
Bo Jackson, KC	475	229	48.2	62	.377	.852	9
Lonnie Smith, Atl	550	265	48.2	103	.382	.618	3
Dave Parker, Mil	651	311	47.8	143	.324	.439	2
Gary Gaetti, Min	626	298	47.6	107	.286	.457	3

| Alvaro Espinoza, Yanks | 468 | 222 | 47.4 | 115 | .269 | .287 | 0 |
| Kirby Puckett, Min | 600 | 281 | 46.8 | 143 | .357 | .550 | 4 |

There are some quality hitters here: Matt Williams, Bo Jackson, Lonnie Smith, Dave Parker, Gary Gaetti, Kirby Puckett. All swung at the first pitch almost half the time, and several — notably Jackson, who hit .377, slugged .852, and belted nine homers when he put the first pitch in play — did some real damage. You could argue that these hitters know what their strengths are — most likely jumping on a first-pitch fastball — and that they're taking advantage of it. The downside is that they're jettisoning the rest of the plate appearance — and the chance that the count may allow them to do even more damage.

Here are hitters who took the first pitch most often:

The Takers	How Often He Swung			Results When He Swung			
	First			In			
Name	Pitches	Swung	%	Play	Avg	Slg	HR
Wade Boggs, Bos	692	27	3.9	12	.167	.333	0
Rickey Henderson, Oak	661	69	10.4	22	.227	.545	2
Alvin Davis, Sea	566	60	10.6	39	.342	.395	0
Edgar Martinez, Sea	555	72	13.0	33	.433	.600	1
Jody Reed, Bos	689	98	14.2	52	.327	.612	2
Julio Franco, Tex	687	98	14.3	47	.319	.489	2
George Bell, Tor	596	90	15.1	44	.273	.386	1
David Magadan, Mets	519	80	15.4	47	.432	.591	1
Todd Zeile, SL	550	86	15.6	43	.286	.595	4
Luis Salazar, Cubs	425	67	15.8	33	.455	.545	1

Some great hitters, here, also (Boggs, Henderson, Reed, Franco, Bell, Magadan) . . . and the presence of Martinez, Franco, Bell and Salazar ought to dispel the notion that all Latin players swing at everything. Because they're more selective, the hitters in his group often do more damage when they swing and put the ball in play, as you can see from the averages of Salazar (.455), Martinez (.433) and Magadan (.432).

Boggs continues his role as the player who swings at the first pitch less than any other hitter. When Wade was batting .368, no one could complain, but now that Boggs is down to the level of mere mortals (.302), people are wondering why he keeps letting the pitcher get an almost-automatic strike against him practically every time up. We'll make it easy on you, Wade: all you have to do is hit .368 again, and we'll shut up again.

A complete listing for this category can be found on page 272.

WHO'S HOT WHEN IT'S COLD?

You know how this one goes. It's spring training and your favorite player, Joe Shlabotnick, is tearing up the Grapefruit League. You think, wow, old Joe's going to have himself a great year. But then the big club comes north and the season starts, and old Joe's a big fat zero. And then you think, "Hey, this happens every year!"

There could be an easy explanation: some players can hit when it's cold out, others can't. We record the temperature at the start of every game, and we've discovered that there's a big difference in how players perform in frigid weather. The following players had the highest averages in games in which the temperature was 50 degrees or lower during the last four years (1987-90, minimum 75 total at bats):

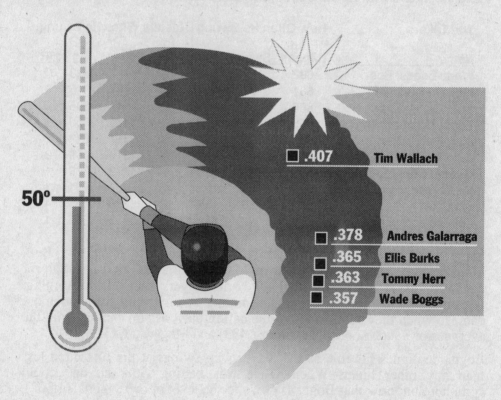

50°

.407	Tim Wallach
.378	Andres Galarraga
.365	Ellis Burks
.363	Tommy Herr
.357	Wade Boggs

6th thru 10th place	Avg
Kelly Gruber	.344
Tony Pena	.342
George Bell	.339
Paul Molitor	.330
Brook Jacoby	.329

Teams that figure to get off to a hot start if it's a cold spring: Montreal (with Wallach and Galarraga — if the domed Expos are playing on the road) and Boston (with Burks, Boggs and Pena). The notion that Latin players can't hit in cold weather is dispelled by the presence of Galarraga, Pena and Bell among the top cold-weather hitters. Players to add to this list would be Rob Deer (.286, seven home runs in 112 at-bats) and Bo Jackson (seven homers in only 98 at bats). Deer-hunting season comes when it's cold, and we'd be shocked if Bo didn't thrive in low temperatures!

These are the **worst** cold-weather hitters:

Player	AB	H	HR	Avg
Eddie Murray	90	10	0	.111
Cal Ripken	79	12	3	.152
Fred Lynn	82	13	1	.159
Shawon Dunston	101	18	2	.178
Mel Hall	92	17	0	.185
Frank White	80	15	1	.188
Jesse Barfield	101	22	2	.218
Chet Lemon	96	21	3	.219
Lloyd Moseby	120	27	2	.225
Willie Wilson	83	19	0	.229

Gee, no wonder the Orioles started out 0-21 in 1988; they had Eddie Murray **and** Cal Ripken **and** Freddie Lynn in their lineup. They couldn't miss, could they? You can also see why aging players like Lynn, White, Lemon, Moseby and Wilson might be checking the temperature gauge as soon they wake up this year.

Eddie Murray has long been know as a great clutch hitter, but, until now, his performance in the 1979 World Series (4-for-26, .154) has been a mystery. Now we can offer an explanation: it was too cold out. We wish you lots of warm weather on those road trips this year, Eddie.

A complete listing for this category appears on page 273.

WHO BRINGS 'EM HOME?

OK, stat fans, it's pop quiz time. Question: Who was the better RBI man in 1990, Joe Carter or Kirby Puckett? Some of you have smug looks on his faces, because you know that Carter drove home 115 runs last year, while Puckett only brought home 80 — Kirby's worst total in five years. The answer, you say, is Joe Carter, easily. Stop looking so self-assured; we're about to show you that if the fates of the two players had been reversed, Puckett would have driven in more than Carter.

That 35-RBI gap between Carter and Puckett in 1990 was, more than anything, due to opportunity. In the San Diego lineup, Carter was coming up behind Bip Roberts, Roberto Alomar and Tony Gwynn, all of them on-base aces. In the Minnesota lineup, Puckett usually batted behind guys like Dan Gladden and Nelson Liriano, neither of whom will remind you of Rickey Henderson. What difference did that make? Well, last year Carter came up with a total of 289 men in scoring position, the most in the majors; he drove home a respectable 26 percent of those runners, thereby accounting for 75 of his 115 ribbies. By contrast Puckett was starving for chances to bring runs home. Kirby came up with only 182 men in scoring position all year — more than 100 fewer than Carter. Puckett come through when he had the chance, bringing home 29.1 percent of the runners — a higher percentage than Joe did.

Overall, we'd still have to rank Carter, with 12 more homers, as the slightly better run producer; Joe was more of a threat when runners **weren't** in scoring position. But it was the extra chances that accounted for most of the 35-RBI difference. Given Carter's total of opportunities, Puckett would have driven home 25 more runs, or a more Kirby-like 105. Given Puckett's starvation diet of baserunners, Carter would have driven in 26 fewer, or only 89. Aren't you glad you didn't get traded to the Twins, Joe?

The point of this discussion is that RBIs depend on opportunities — and some players, because of the strength of the club's lineup, and where they hit in it — get many more chances than others. We thought you might like to see the players who made the most of their opportunities in 1990. Here are the hitters who brought home the best percentage of runners from scoring position last year (minimum 150 opportunities):

RBI with Men in Scoring Position

Batter, Team	RBI	Opp.	Pct.
Dave Magadan, Mets	59	159	37.1
Kelly Gruber, Tor	69	215	32.1
Matt Williams, SF	67	211	31.8
Barry Bonds, Pit	66	212	31.1
Alan Trammell, Det	64	210	30.5
Ruben Sierra, Tex	69	226	30.5
Lance Johnson, WSox	46	153	30.1
George Brett, KC	59	199	29.6
Gary Sheffield, Mil	50	170	29.4
Rafael Palmeiro, Tex	59	203	29.1
Kirby Puckett, Min	53	182	29.1

Dave Magadan, RBI man? With only six homers last year, it seems incongruous. But Magadan was a terror when the opportunity presented itself last year. Given his production rate and Carter's 289 baserunners, he'd have driven in 120 runs last year! That's not likely to happen in 1991, just as Lance Johnson shouldn't be expected to repeat his lusty clutch hitting this year. But both were much more than just slap hitters last year.

Which players produced **least** with men in scoring position last year? We thought you'd never ask:

RBI with Men in Scoring Position

Batter, Team	RBI	Opp.	Pct.
Kevin Seitzer, KC	24	164	14.6
Mickey Tettleton, Bal	28	190	14.7
Todd Zeile, StL	32	199	16.1
Devon White, Cal	28	163	17.2
Edgar Martinez, Sea	32	186	17.2

Some well-known names here, but not much production. Just a fluke? We'll see in 1991, but Seitzer, Tettleton and White were all weak in this category (under 21 percent) in both 1989 and 1990.

A complete listing for this category can be found on page 274.

WHAT HAPPENS IN THAT LAST AT-BAT?

One of the legends told about Pete Rose has to do with his fighting spirit and his incredible concentration. If Pete would come up to bat for the fourth time in a game with no hits on the day, the story goes, he was bound and determined to get his hit for that day — and he'd usually get it.

That got us wondering about what happens to hitters in that last — let's just make it their fourth — at-bat. If a player has been hitless thus far, is he more likely or less to come through? How about if he's had one, two or three hits? Of course, high average hitters are always more likely to hit safely than low average hitters. So let's look at two groups of hitters — those who hit higher than .290, and those who hit less than .240. Here's the overall data for those who batted higher than .290 since 1987 (minimum 250 plate appearances):

Batting by players after three AB
Average higher than .290

	AB	H	Avg
Had 0 hits:	5,355	1,555	.290
Had 1 hits:	7,643	2,365	.309
Had 2 hits:	3,554	1,131	.318
Had 3 hits:	538	165	.307
All other ABs	178,308	54,896	.308

As you can see, a good hitter with three hitless at-bats is **less** likely, not more, to come through with a hit the fourth time up. Since, as modern baseball goes, he's liable to be facing a different pitcher this time up, it's tempting to say the difference is psychological — if he's had no hits, he figures it's not his day; if he's had one or more, he feels in the groove, and he's more likely to come through again. Still, the differences are not that great; a good hitter is a good hitter **any** time up. It's also true that having one or more hits might indicate the hitter might simply have better mechanics that day — which has nothing to do with psychology. Let's examine how a few famous hitters did after three hitless at-bats last year:

AL Player, Team	AB	H	Avg	NL Player, Team	AB	H	Avg
Wade Boggs, Bos	40	15	.375	Barry Bonds, Pit	28	7	.250
George Brett, KC	25	5	.200	Will Clark, SF	38	15	.395
Julio Franco, Tex	27	3	.111	Kal Daniels, LA	28	9	.321
Mike Greenwell, Bos	41	9	.219	Lenny Dykstra, Phi	35	11	.314
Rickey Henderson, Oak	23	9	.391	Mark Grace, Cubs	35	12	.343
Fred McGriff, Tor	38	10	.263	Tony Gwynn, SD	42	10	.235
Rafael Palmeiro, Tex	36	11	.305	Dave Magadan, Mets	23	10	.435
Kirby Puckett, Min	35	8	.228	Eddie Murray, LA	25	5	.200
Alan Trammell, Det	32	11	.344	Ryne Sandberg, Cubs	49	16	.326

This is a very elite group of hitters . . . the best of the best, really. But as you can see, there's a lot of variance in how they perform after three hitless at-bats. Are Dave Magadan, Will Clark and Rickey Henderson of the Pete Rose school — that is, they concentrate extra-hard when they've come to the plate wearing the collar after three at-bats? It's nice to think so, but we must caution you that this data is based on a very small number of plate appearances.

Now let's look at the weak hitters — those whose average was lower than .240:

Batting by players after three AB
Average less than .240

	AB	H	Avg
Had 0 hits:	4,938	1,040	.211
Had 1 hits:	4,693	1,076	.229
Had 2 hits:	1,610	354	.220
Had 3 hits:	149	33	.221
All other ABs	144,072	32,429	.225

Interestingly, the weak hitters show the same type of pattern that the good hitters do. When they've had no hits for three at-bats, they're less likely to bang one out the fourth time. If they've had one or more hits, they're a little more likely (though not much for these guys). Psychological, or mechanical? Though it's very hard to say, we lean towards the mechanical explanation. The differences are fascinating.

WHO PULLS?

We pointed out last year that using the whole ballfield is one of the most common pieces of advice given by hitting coaches. We also pointed out that hitters don't always take it — they still pull the ball about 59% of the time — and that, in many cases, it's a good idea that they don't. The following players were the most pronounced pull hitters and opposite field hitters in baseball in 1990:

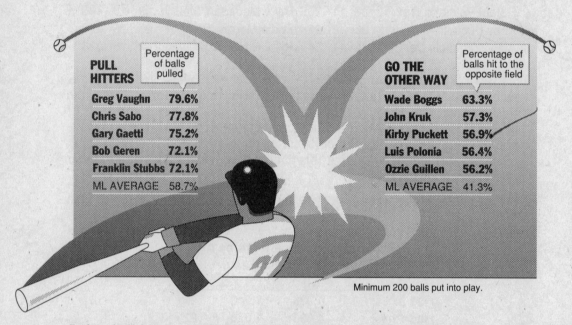

PULL HITTERS	Percentage of balls pulled		GO THE OTHER WAY	Percentage of balls hit to the opposite field
Greg Vaughn	79.6%		Wade Boggs	63.3%
Chris Sabo	77.8%		John Kruk	57.3%
Gary Gaetti	75.2%		Kirby Puckett	56.9%
Bob Geren	72.1%		Luis Polonia	56.4%
Franklin Stubbs	72.1%		Ozzie Guillen	56.2%
ML AVERAGE	58.7%		ML AVERAGE	41.3%

Minimum 200 balls put into play.

Is it a ball idea to pull? You can't prove that by Chris Sabo, who swung more aggressively in 1990 and had the best season of his career. Or by Franklin Stubbs, who parlayed pulling the ball into 23 home runs for the Astros (no mean feat) and a big free agent contract with the Brewers (no mean feat, either). Other pull hitters who soared in 1990 inclued Ron Gant (70%), Darren Daulton (70%), Cecil Fielder (70%) and Kevin Maas (69%). But what do they know?

On the other hand, if you asked any hitting coach what was wrong with Greg Vaughn or Gary Gaetti or Steve Balboni (72%) — or Charlie O'Brien (72%) or Tim Jones (71%) — he'd probably say, "He pulls the ball too much." Like anything else in baseball, what they think about you depends on the end results.

All right, then. The guys who go the other way drank their milk, left their cookies (bad for you, you know) and went to the opposite field the most times in 1990. We'd like to admit that we here at STATS, Inc. are as shallow as anyone in baseball today. Which means that we loved Wade Boggs when he was going the opposite way and hitting .368, but now that he's down to .302, we're thinking — hey, what's wrong with this guy? Whereas we think about Alex Cole (57% to the opposite field), who broke in with a bang by hitting .300 in a half season for the Indians, "What a clever young hitter this is."

We always like to look for consistency in year-to-year statistics, and it's interesting to note that Boggs, Kruk and Polonia were all in the top five players who went the opposite way in 1989.

Then there were the hitters who chose to spray their hits around:

Batter, Team	Percentage of Balls Pulled
Jay Bell, Pit	50.2
Robin Yount, Mil	50.1
Edgar Martinez, Sea	50.0
Mookie Wilson, Tor	49.9
Vince Coleman, StL	49.7
Mike Stanley, Tex	49.7

Some pretty good hitters in this group, also — don't you think?

A complete listing for this category appears on page 275.

WHICH HITTERS ARE AT HOME ON THE ROAD?

Some people love their homes; others can't wait to pack their suitcases. So it is in baseball, where a friendly home ballpark — or an unfriendly one — can make all the difference in a player's career. Exhibit A for 1990 was Tom Brunansky. Early last year Brunansky moved from Busch Stadium in St. Louis, a park which was destroying his power, to his all-time dream stadium, Fenway Park in Boston. As expected, Bruno became a force at Fenway; unfortunately, he dampened his impact by hitting like a minor leaguer when he went on the road. Brunansky, of course, wasn't the only player helped a lot by his home park in 1990. The ones who benefitted most:

BA Change	Player, Team	Home			Road		
		Avg	HR	RBI	Avg	HR	RBI
+153	Tom Brunansky, StL-Bos	.333	13	52	.180	3	21
+114	Wade Boggs, Bos	.359	3	32	.245	3	31
+110	Gary Carter, SF	.307	6	19	.197	3	8
+102	Ryne Sandberg, Cubs	.357	25	62	.255	15	38
+101	Dion James, Cle	.325	0	10	.224	1	12
+97	Ken Caminiti, Hou	.288	2	31	.191	2	20
+92	Kirby Puckett, Min	.344	6	47	.252	6	33
+91	Lee Stevens, Cal	.256	4	20	.165	3	12
+90	Willie Wilson, KC	.331	1	22	.241	1	20
+87	Chili Davis, Cal	.306	10	39	.219	2	19

One could say that all Brunansky needs to do to become a top hitter again is to hit decently on the road. But in his case, it's easier said than done. In his last full American League season, 1987, Bruno hit .300 in his home park, the Metrodome, but only .216 on the road. Then he went to St. Louis in the National League, where his home performance dropped but his road production got a lot better. Maybe what Brunansky needs is for the commissioner to let him play his home games at Fenway, his away games in National League parks. Hmmm, maybe if he's got a good agent . . .

Wade Boggs also deserves some comment. Boggs continues to decline, both at home and on the road. But it's been the road dropoff that's affected him most. Through 1989 Boggs had hit 61 points better at home than on the road (.383 to .322). The difference in 1990 was almost twice that. If Wade had batted .297 on the road in 1990 — 62 points lower than his home average — his overall mark would have been a more Boggs-like .328, not the .302 he ended up with.

Boggs will get no sympathy from the following players, who were the ones **hurt** most by their home parks in 1990:

		Home			Road		
BA Change	Player, Team	Avg	HR	RBI	Avg	HR	RBI
−133	Mackey Sasser, Mets	.245	3	21	.378	3	20
−121	Brady Anderson, Bal	.175	1	10	.296	2	14
−115	Bob Melvin, Bal	.174	3	13	.289	2	24
−94	Dave Magadan, Mets	.278	2	34	.372	4	38
−82	Gary Redus, Pit	.204	2	12	.286	4	11
−74	Cal Ripken, Bal	.213	8	42	.287	13	42
−72	Glenn Davis, Hou	.217	4	22	.289	18	42
−72	Travis Fryman, Det	.259	5	8	.331	4	19
−66	Danny Tartabull, KC	.232	5	25	.298	10	35
−63	Felix Jose, Tor	.233	5	27	.296	6	25

You'll notice that five of the top six players worked for either the Mets or the Orioles. One would be tempted to say that Sasser and Magadan are line-drive gap hitters, better suited for NL turf fields than for Shea Stadium, a spacious grass park. One would be tempted except that, in 1989, both players hit better in Shea than on the road (Magadan much better, in fact, as he had in 1988). As we stated last year, sometimes a player simply relaxes more when he doesn't feel the pressure to produce in front of the home folks. Look at the list. Tartabull is constantly part of trade rumors, Davis and Felix were in fact traded after the 1990 season, Ripken's always having to justify his playing streak, Anderson's a young player who's been considered a disappointment. Maybe these guys just felt more comfortable when they went on the road.

The following players had **no** difference in batting average between home and road last year — not that it was always such a good thing:

		Home			Road		
BA Change	Player, Team	Avg	HR	RBI	Avg	HR	RBI
0	Scott Fletcher, WSox	.242	1	29	.242	3	27
0	Carlos Martinez, WSox	.224	2	16	.224	2	8
0	Randy Velarde, Yanks	.210	1	9	.210	4	10
0	Randy Milligan, Bal	.265	11	31	.265	9	29
0	Ozzie Guillen, WSox	.279	1	25	.279	0	33

Now this one looks like a private White Sox club. Good preparation for switching to a new home ballpark in 1991, wouldn't you say?

A complete listing for this category appears on page 276.

EXCUSE ME, COULD YOU USE A .378 HITTER?

Whenever a runner is moving as a pitch is made, an infielder must move from his fielding position to take the catcher's throw. The batter then has a vacant territory to hit through. Often the result of "starting the runner" is baserunners on first and third bases.

Until now, no one has known just how much of an edge the moving fielder gives to the batter. Enter, of course, STATS. Our reporters are instructed to use a different pitch code whenever the runner is breaking as the batter hits the ball. The results for almost every major league hit-and-run in the last four years appears in the following table:

	AB	H	DP*	NoAdv*	Avg	Slg
1990 AL	1026	394	88	189	.384	.492
1990 NL	1102	407	62	228	.369	.491
1987-90 AL	3483	1312	293	614	.377	.479
1987-90 NL	3846	1457	223	744	.379	.493

* DP is any double or triple play; a NoAdv occurs when with less than two out the batter is out and the runner stays, or a force-out occurs.

Looks like an overlooked opportunity. Send your runner(s) and your average .260-hitting major league batter becomes a .378 hitter! Yet major league managers speak only of "sending the runner to stay out of the double play." What are we missing?

The catch is that this table does not include swinging strikes. If the batter strikes out with the runner breaking, he's out (and often the runner is, also). Since the reporters don't record the swings-and-misses as hit-and-runs, those particular hitless at bats aren't shown in our first table. How would major league hitters fare in all plate appearances with runners on base if strikeouts were left out?

	AB	K	AB-K	H	TB	"Avg"	"Slg"
1987-90 ML	139,192	38,706	100,486	36,307	54,448	.361	.542

The overall batting average is lower than the hit-and-run BA, .361 to .378, but slugging is much higher when the runner is not moving. Of course, this makes sense. With the runner breaking the batter must often swing at bad pitches, which he cannot hit as hard, but which may nevertheless become singles because of the moving infielder.

Two other points should be considered for a full picture. When the batter is forced to swing and does not put the pitch in play, there is a good chance that the pitch would have otherwise been taken for a ball. So the subsequent count will tend to favor the pitcher more than if the hit and run had not been tried. Furthermore our information about hit-and-run success compared to hitting away is biased. Managers presumably tend to use the hit-and-run with hitters who have little power, with batters who hit a lot of ground balls, and on favorable counts. STATS has the raw information and tools to explore all of these points and maybe in future years we will. But for now we thought it more interesting to see which managers and players use the hit-and-run most.

The hit-and-run is used much more often in the National League (an average of 93 tries per club in 1990) than in the American League (74 tries/club). In 1990 Roger Craig's Giants executed the hit-and-run most often (123 times) and also were the most successful (50 hits, for a .407 BA). At the bottom were Sparky Anderson's Tigers with 47 attempts (for 17 hits, also low, and a .362 BA). The highest BA on the H&R was the Indians' .462 (33/70) and the lowest the Cardinals' .280 (33/116).

How about defense against the hit-and-run? This is also a good time to address a question you are probably already asking, "Just how good are those STATS reporters in mentioning that the runner was breaking?" If apparent differences among teams result mostly from differences in reporter attentiveness, you would expect teams which seem to use the play a lot to also defend against it more. In looking at all the teams together, the most suspect data are for the White Sox, scored quite often by the home office (?!) The ChiSox have the second fewest attempts recorded on both offense and defense, and White Sox opponents have a BA of .516, by far the highest, suggesting that maybe some of those STATS boys neglected a few "runner breaking" pitch codes on outs. (The STATS boys deny this vehemently.) On the whole, the evidence suggests that our data is trustworthy.

On defense, then, the 1990 teams which yielded the most and fewest attempts were the Astros (116) and the Twins (53), the most and fewest hits allowed were by the Dodgers (49) and the Blue Jays and Twins (21), and the highest and lowest BA's were off the White Sox (.516) and the Angels (.262).

Over the last four years, no one will be greatly surprised to hear that the Cardinals executed the hit and run most, 506 times, whereas the Braves were last in the NL with 331 tries. Underscoring the difference in the leagues, Oakland led the AL with 333 attempts from 1987 to 1990, while the White Sox trailed with 188 recorded attempts.

Who are today's hit and run artists? It's interesting that no one in recent years has anything like the reputation of two National League shortstops of the '50's, Al Dark and Granny Hamner. There was even a joke about the typical Phillie rally, a leadoff walk to Ashburn, a hit-and-run single by Hamner sending Richie to third, and a GDP by Del Ennis scoring the run. Anyway, here are the leaders among current AL and NL players in attempts and hits, for both 1990 and 1987 to 1990:

1990 AL Hits per Hit & Run Attempts (13 or more)

4/18	Mike Gallego, Oak
7/15	Rafael Palmeiro, Tex
5/15	Dave Parker, Mil
6/14	Steve Sax, Yanks
5/14	Mookie Wilson, Tor
5/14	Alvaro Espinoza, Yanks
7/13	Jerry Browne, Cle

Other AL batters with seven hit-and-run base hits were Ivan Calderon (12 AB), Felix Fermin (11), Don Mattingly (12), and Kirby Puckett (8). Kirby hit .875 on the hit-and-run play!

1987-90 Hits per Hit & Run Attempts — both leagues — by 1990 AL batters (35 or more attempts)

17/51	Scott Fletcher
17/47	Kevin Seitzer
16/47	Carney Lansford
15/44	Rafael Palmeiro
24/43	Tony Pena
20/41	Willie Randolph
16/41	Steve Sax
13/39	Marty Barrett
19/38	Willie McGee
11/38	Tony Fernandez
15/38	Dave Parker
15/37	Robin Yount
19/36	Johnny Ray
10/35	Cal Ripken

There are six players on the 1987-1990 AL list also played a lot in the NL, and you might have supposed that their hit-and-run attempts reflect mainly NL experience. Actually, the opposite is true. Palmeiro, Sax, Parker, and Ray all try the hit and run far more often with their current teams. Perhaps they want to show their teammates this secret National League play, or maybe the AL managers assume this skill in former NL players.

1990 NL Hits per Hit & Run Attempts (14 or more)

7/22 Mark Grace, Cubs
7/20 Jose Lind, Pit
9/19 Willie McGee, StL
      (includes 2/2 in AL)
4/19 Tony Gwynn, SD
4/19 Barry Larkin, Cin
10/18 Tommy Herr, Phi
5/18 Tim Wallach, Mon
2/18 Ozzie Smith, StL
9/16 Rafael Ramirez, Hou
4/15 Jay Bell, Pit
8/14 Ryne Sandberg, Cubs
5/14 Mike Scioscia, LA
(Note: John Kruk was 9/11)

1987-90 Hits per Hit & Run Attempts — both leagues — by 1990 NL batters (40 or more attempts)

28/93 Ozzie Smith
24/69 Jose Lind
28/67 Tommy Herr
23/64 Robby Thompson
19/61 Tim Wallach
22/54 Mike Scioscia
19/54 Tony Gwynn
23/52 Jose Oquendo
24/51 Ryne Sandberg
14/51 Terry Pendleton
18/47 Mark Grace
15/46 Pedro Guerrero
18/40 Will Clark
12/40 Kevin Mitchell

Although Ozzie Smith had a poor 1990 with the hit and run play (also), the Wiz is the standout H&R threat over the last four years. His 93 attempts are almost 40% more than Jose Lind, his nearest competitor, and his 28 hits tie him for first with former DP partner Tommy Herr. Tommy also tied with Robby Thompson for the most H&R hits in 1990 with 10. The dominance of Cardinals and ex-Cardinals at the tops of these lists shows the uniqueness of Whitey-Ball, to an extent that even the St. Louis resident writing this essay (Dick Cramer) did not appreciate. But there's also Gerbil-Ball, with Cubs Grace and Sandberg showing up unexpectedly at the tops of lists. Sandberg also joins with Kevin Mitchell as 40+ home run hitters with offensive versatility. And would you have believed that Tim Wallach, once an NCAA home run leader, attempted the hit-and-run more than any active AL player?

WHO HAS OPPOSITE FIELD POWER?

We talk in other parts of this book about the prevailing theory of hitting, which says to use the whole field. But in truth most balls are pulled, and most home runs in particular — 88 percent of all homers were pulled in 1990. This stands to reason; the normal way to generate power involves getting out in front of the pitch and pulling it to left if you're a righty swinger or to right if you bat from the left side.

But, being the kind of guys we are, we find it fun to look at the players who are the exceptions to the rule. The following players hit the greatest percentage of their homers to the opposite field in 1990 (five opposite field home runs minimum):

Batter, Team	Bats	Total HRs	Opposite Field HRs	Opp%
Shane Mack, Min	R	8	5	62.5
Jack Howell, Cal	L	8	5	62.5
Robin Yount, Mil	R	17	10	58.8
Kal Daniels, LA	L	27	15	55.6
Roberto Kelly, Yanks	R	15	8	53.3
Harold Baines, Tex-Oak	L	16	8	50.0
Bo Jackson, KC	R	28	13	46.4
Pete Incaviglia, Tex	R	24	11	45.8
Eric Davis, Cin	R	24	8	33.3
Danny Tartabull, KC	R	15	5	33.3

You can quickly see that there are some quality hitters on this list, as well as some guys who have had their problems. Who would have guessed that Jack Howell and Pete Incaviglia, to name two, would hit a high percentage of their homers to the other side? In truth, Incaviglia made this same list a year ago, along with Harold Baines, Robin Yount and the man himself, Bo Jackson. The one hitter who may have changed his style is Jack Howell, a pronounced pull hitter in the past. Judging by Howell's 1990 results — a .228 average, only eight homers — we're not sure the change was worth it.

On the other hand, a number of players **never** hit a home run to the opposite field in 1990. These players hit the most:

Batter, Team	Bats	Total HRs	Opposite Field HRs	Opp%
Ron Gant, Atl	R	32	0	0.0
Chris Sabo, Cin	R	25	0	0.0
Kevin McReynolds, Mets	R	24	0	0.0
Howard Johnson, Mets	S	23	0	0.0
Dave Parker, Mil	L	21	0	0.0

Frankly, we think the hitters on this list are a little more impressive than the "opposite field" guys. Which tells us that pulling the ball is still a plenty good idea if you're trying to hit for power.

Here's how the two most extreme power hitters, Yount and Gant, compare graphically:

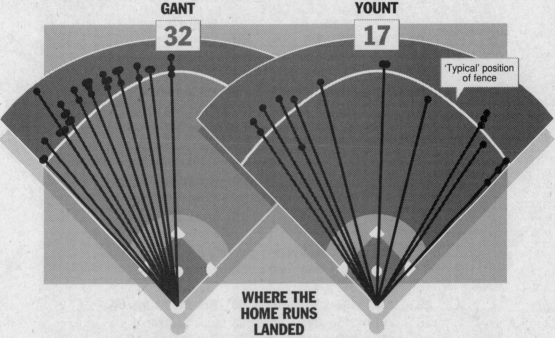

GANT 32

YOUNT 17

'Typical' position of fence

WHERE THE HOME RUNS LANDED

How about the guys who hit the most four-baggers? A look at the players who went deep most often in 1990 shows some variation in style, but a preference for pulling:

Batter, Team	Bats	Total HRs	Opposite Field HRs	Opp%
Cecil Fielder, Det	R	51	7	13.7
Ryne Sandberg, Cubs	R	40	1	2.5
Mark McGwire, Oak	R	39	9	23.1
Jose Canseco, Oak	R	37	6	16.2
Darryl Strawberry, Mets	L	37	7	18.9

Interestingly, however, four of the top five hit a higher percentage of opposite field home runs than the major league average (12.4%). Only McGwire, however, was significantly above the average.

A complete listing for this category appears on page 277.

WHAT'S AN AVERAGE FIRST BASEMAN?

One saying you often hear in baseball is, "He's a good hitter for a shortstop." Or catcher, or whatever. That's a fairly nebulous phrase, however, unless you have a context to put it in. So we present the average offensive output for each league at each position in 1990; as we did last year, we include the performer at each spot who was closest to the norm:

Pos	Avg	OBP	Slg	HR	RBI	Most Typical Performer
			American League (per 600 PA)			
C	.260	.321	.380	12	64	Tony Pena ✗
1B	.271	.353	.438	19	73	Kent Hrbek ✗
2B	.253	.320	.346	6	51	Harold Reynolds ✗
3B	.259	.333	.375	10	58	Tony Phillips OK
SS	.252	.314	.342	6	52	Kurt Stillwell ✗
LF	.268	.329	.406	14	65	Ivan Calderon ✗
CF	.270	.330	.408	12	63	Roberto Kelly OK
RF	.254	.321	.409	7	72	Junior Felix ✗
DH	.251	.326	.394	15	70	Dwight Evans ✗
			National League (per 600 PA)			
C	.246	.319	.358	10	58	Todd Zeile OK
1B	.276	.347	.438	17	79	Sid Bream ✗
2B	.274	.337	.393	10	56	Roberto Alomar OK
3B	.261	.315	.393	14	66	Luis Salazar ✗
SS	.250	.307	.347	7	51	Dickie Thon ✗
LF	.274	.351	.433	18	68	Kevin McReynolds ✗
CF	.277	.345	.403	10	55	Billy Hatcher ✗
RF	.269	.335	.435	19	78	Paul O'Neill ?
P	.138	.172	.170	2	27	

It's a bit of an eye-opener, isn't it, to discover that Roberto Kelly was just an average AL center fielder last year, or Roberto Alomar a typical NL performer at second. We ran this study last year, and can detect some trends:

1. Catcher and shortstop remain the weakest-hitting positions, which is expected because they're the spots where defense is most important. National League catchers hit less than AL receivers do, primarily because the need for a good throwing arm is more vital in the NL. But clubs seem less prone to simply stick a glove man out there than previously. National

League catchers hit only .236 in 1989; they batted ten points higher in 1990. American League catchers improved by 11 points over 1989.

2. The best power position, not surprisingly, is first base. Some clubs really weakened themselves with poor hitters at this vital spot (Milwaukee with Greg Brock, Seattle with Pete O'Brien, Cleveland with Keith Hernandez, to name three). But as in the previous comment, clubs no longer show much patience with a first sacker who doesn't hit. Brock gave way to Paul Molitor, O'Brien to Alvin Davis and Tino Martinez, Hernandez to Brook Jacoby. One of the smartest moves the Reds made last year was to replace Todd Benzinger at first with Hal Morris. They were astute enough to realize that Benzinger's stats, which appeared decent, weren't adequate for the position.

3. Many American League clubs, even after 18 years of the DH rule, still don't realize the importance of good production at this position. The Rangers, for instance, used 15 different designated hitters last year, none in more than 21 games. The most-used Tiger DH was Dave Bergman, an excellent fielder but no big threat at bat; the Royals used Gerald Perry at DH more than anyone else. Couldn't they do better than that?

4. A comparison of the two leagues at each position yields some interesting results:

 C Alomar, Fisk, Harper, Parrish, Pena, Surhoff — definite advantage AL
1B A tossup — maybe a slight advantage to the AL
2B Sandberg, Alomar, Jefferies, Doran — big advantage NL
3B Slight edge to NL, with a little more power
SS Another tossup — Ripken and Trammell give the AL a slight edge
LF Despite Rickey Henderson, NL has more overall strength
CF Very close — maybe a slight edge to the NL
RF Bonilla, Strawberry, Dawson, Justice, Gwynn — easy advantage NL

Overall, the National League has a clear edge at three positions: left field, right field and second base. The American League has a clear edge only behind the plate. The other four positions are a little closer, with no clear edge to either circuit. We argued a year ago that the National League is improving offensively, especially in the power department. What happened in 1990 — including what happened in the World Series — did nothing to change that opinion.

A complete listing for this category appears on page 278.

WHO'S PRIMARY IN SECONDARY AVERAGE?

We know that many of you are Bill James fans, so you may already be familiar with the concept of secondary average. For those of you who aren't, secondary average was created by Bill to highlight contributions not reflected in batting average. The idea is to reward players who hit for extra bases, draw walks and steal bases. The formula is:

Secondary Average= (2B + 3Bx2 + HRx3 + BB + SB - CS) / AB

Secondary averages are somewhat like batting averages — the major league average last year was .237, about 20 points lower than the major league average of .258. But the spread is greater; in secondary average, some players actually reach the .500 mark. The 1990 leaders:

Player, Team	Secondary Average
Jack Clark, SD	.581
Rickey Henderson, Oak	.562
Bobby Bonds, Pit	.518
Randy Milligan, Bal	.478
Cecil Fielder, Det	.469
Mark McGwire, Oak	.467
Jose Canseco, Oak	.437
Glenn Davis, Hou	.428
David Justice, Atl	.410
Fred McGriff, Tor	.402

Jack Clark has only reached a .300 batting average twice in his 16-year career, but he continues to swing a heavy bat nonetheless. Last year, while playing in only 115 games, Clark hit 25 homers and drew 104 walks — the most in the National League — before signing a big free agent contract with the Red Sox. Boston had to be as impressed as we were that Clark, who also led both leagues in secondary average in 1989, finished just in front of Rickey Henderson and Bobby Bonds, the league MVPs.

And look at the rest of that top ten. Cecil Fielder, Mark McGwire, Jose Canseco, Glenn Davis, Dave Justice, Fred McGriff . . . practically an All-Star team, although everyone would want to play first base or the outfield. Which leads us to a good point about secondary average — it measures a player's contributions in important categories, but the picture isn't quite complete. If you want a better feel for this, look at the 1990 trailers in secondary average:

Player, Team	Secondary Average
Alvaro Espinoza, Yanks	.084
Ozzie Guillen, WSox	.105
Felix Fermin, Cle	.111
Alfredo Griffin, LA	.113
Jose Uribe, SF	.116

All are shortstops. Their batting averages range from Guillen's .279 to Griffin's .210, but no matter what they hit, their offensive contribution is a light one. They don't draw walks, they don't hit for extra bases, their stolen base totals are usually balanced by caught stealings. This is familiar territory for Espinoza, Guillen and Fermin, who managed to rank in the bottom five in 1989 as well.

And that, in a way, is why it's called "secondary average." The primary contributions of Guillen, Griffin et al are defensive in nature. You couldn't have a successful team made up only of players like Jack Clark; you need guys who contribute in other areas as well. But a Clark's contributions are very vital, and that's what this category is meant to show.

A complete listing for this category appears on page 279.

WHO'S BEST WITH TWO STRIKES?

At its heart, baseball is nothing less than a chess game between the pitcher and the hitter. The best hitters are the ones who play that chess game well. They know that a plate appearance is more than one pitch long, and that they don't have to swing at the first offering. They have enough self-confidence to take a strike, realizing that a better pitch might come later. And they don't give in to the pitcher, even with two strikes. We expected that the best two-strike hitters of 1990 might be a distinguished group, and we were right. Here are the leaders (150 or more plate appearances):

Player, Team	Avg	HR	RBI
Rickey Henderson, Oak	.310	7	16
Dave Magadan, Mets	.309	0	20
Tony Gwynn, SD	.282	1	18
Brett Butler, SF	.275	2	19
Eddie Murray, LA	.273	4	30
Kevin McReynolds, Mets	.273	11	38
Edgar Martinez, Sea	.270	3	19
Gregg Jefferies, Mets	.269	5	21
Alan Trammell, Det	.260	4	25
Jody Reed, Bos	.256	0	10
Wade Boggs, Bos	.256	2	22

What do these hitters have in common? They're **smart**. For the most part, they're high-average hitters who also draw a lot of walks — not the sort to let a two-strike count bother them. A two strike count usually means shorten your stroke, but some of these guys even hit with power when their backs are against the wall. McReynolds was particularly thorough in that regard. He had 11 two-strike homers — tied with Ryne Sandberg and Jesse Barfield for the major league lead — and 38 two-strike RBI, the third best total (along with Kal Daniels) behind Joe Carter and Kelly Gruber, who each had 41.

You'll notice that, even for the best, it's tough to hit with two strikes. Only Henderson and Magadan were over .300 last year, and the major league average with two strikes was a paltry .184.

You're also probably wondering about Wade Boggs. For years Boggs had been one of the premier two-strike hitters in baseball, if not the very best. There was nothing wrong with the way he performed last year — except that it wasn't quite up to Wade Boggs standards. Boggs, as we know, hardly ever swings at the first pitch, and it may well be that he has to do a little more to keep the hurlers honest. It may also be that his personal problems of the last couple of years have simply distracted him. We'll be keeping an eye on Boggs in this and other categories in 1991.

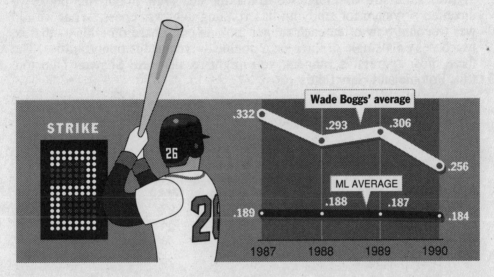

Well, if those are the smart hitters, what does that say about the other group — the players who had the lowest two-strike averages?

Player, Team	Avg	HR	RBI
Eric Anthony, Hou	.112	5	12
Pete Incaviglia, Tex	.126	8	31
Cory Snyder, Cle	.128	2	11
Mike Gallego, Oak	.129	1	12
Joe Oliver, Cin	.131	1	11

Eric Anthony and Joe Oliver are young players who might be expected to improve — you could forgive their inclusion in this group. And Mike Gallego is in the Oakland lineup for his glove, anyway, so neither we nor the A's are very upset that he struggled with two strikes. But Cory Snyder and Pete Incaviglia? Snyder was the fourth player selected in the 1984 draft; Inky was the eighth player chosen a year later. Yet neither has developed into the outstanding hitter he was projected to be. Incaviglia, at least, was a dangerous two-strike hitter last year, despite his low average. But Snyder was almost completely helpless. The White Sox acquired Snyder over the winter because they thought he was "coachable." We sure hope so.

A complete listing for this category appears on page 280.

WHO TAKES THE EXTRA BASE?

Last year we wrote: "Running the bases is one of baseball's hidden mysteries." It still is, though we're making headway. In our first book, we unveiled a system for studying baserunning aggressiveness. What we did was to count how often each runner took an extra base on a hit — that is, two bases on a single or three on a double — versus his opportunities. The three most aggressive runners, you might recall, were Shawon Dunston, Luis Polonia and Gary Pettis.

We ran the same study for 1990. Here were the ten most aggressive runners (30 or more opportunities):

Runner, Team	Opportunites to Take An Extra Base	Number of Times An Extra base Taken	Extra Bases Percent
Willie Wilson, KC	32	27	84.4
Lance Johnson, WSox	48	39	81.3
Walt Weiss, Oak	35	28	80.0
Daryl Boston, WSox-Mets	37	29	78.4
Julio Franco, Tex	69	53	76.8
Ron Gant, Atl	50	37	74.0
Lenny Harris, LA	42	31	73.8
Eric Yelding, Hou	38	28	73.7
Mike Sharperson, LA	34	25	73.5
Bo Jackson, KC	30	22	73.3
Major League Average			51.1%

You might wonder how the 1990 leaders list compares with 1989's. The answer is that it's completely different — not one of the 1989 top ten made the list again in 1990. The closest was Julio Franco, who ranked 11th in '89. As for Dunston, Polonia and Pettis — the big three of '89 — they were well down the list last year. Dunston dropped from 96.2 percent to 63.2, Polonia from 83.3 percent 63.9 and Pettis from 78.0 to 54.8. Jim Eisenreich, the eighth-most aggressive runner in '89 (72.2 percent) was Mr. Meek in 1990 (38.7).

What's going on here? It's hard to believe that Dunston, Pettis or the others just lost their aggressiveness from one year to the next. Indeed, all but Eisenreich were still above average in 1990. One complicating factor, however, is that this category is somewhat situation-dependent. A runner on second with no one out, for instance, is much more likely to hold up at third on a single than he would with two outs; with nobody out, the risk of being thrown out, and possibly spoiling a big inning, simply isn't worth it. The inning the opportunity comes in, the score of the game and the strength of the outfielder's arm are other factors which a baserunner has to take into account before he risks taking an extra base. So is the ballpark — runners at Fenway, to use a good example, will be less likely to take chances than runners at the Astrodome. And the type of team a runner plays for is a big factor. Rickey Henderson, for instance, doesn't rate as a very aggressive runner in our rankings. But that's probably because he sees little percentage in trying for one more base when he has hitters like Jose Canseco and Mark McGwire coming up behind him.

So the category doesn't tell us everything — but it does tell us something. We watched the White Sox all last year, and we can tell you for certain that Lance Johnson's high ranking was no fluke. More than anything, the category shows what a huge difference there is between the most- and least-aggressive runners. Wilson, the most aggressive in 1990, took the extra base 84 percent of the time; Jack Clark, the least aggressive, took it only 25 percent. Situation-dependency doesn't explain a difference like that.

Here were the least aggressive runners of 1990:

Runner, Team	Opportunites to Take An Extra Base	Number of Times An Extra base Taken	Extra Bases Percent
Jack Clark, SD	40	10	25.0
Sid Bream, Pit	32	8	25.0
Pedro Guerrero, StL	30	8	26.7
Lance Parrish, Cal	30	8	26.7
Jim Presley, Atl	33	9	27.3
Carlos Quintana, Bos	56	16	28.6
Dave Parker, Mil	39	12	30.8
Brian Downing, Cal	31	10	32.3
Kent Hrbek, Min	37	12	32.4
Paul O'Neill, Cin	37	12	32.4

This is pretty much what you'd expect — for the most part, aging players and guys with knee problems. These guys will seldom go unless they're sure they can make it.

A complete listing for this category appears on page 281.

WHO'S TOPS IN GO-AHEAD RBI?

The game-winning RBI, we noted a year ago, is no longer an official statistic. Too many people complained that guys were getting credit for "game-winning hits" in the early innings, and that therefore the stat wasn't really a measure of clutch hitting. We beg to differ with that part of the argument; we strongly disagree with the notion that the only "clutch" parts of the ballgame are the late innings. To give a perfect example: were there any bigger RBIs in 1990 than the two which came on Eric Davis' first-inning home run in Game One of the World Series?

Even so, we concede that there are problems with the game winning RBI. We'll re-state Bill James' objection from last year. As Bill points out, any good stat should measure a skill. But driving in the run which puts your club ahead to stay — the definition of a GW-RBI — depends not just on the hitter's skill in bringing home the run, but on the skill of his club's pitching staff, which may or may not be able to hold the lead. So we decided to just measure go-ahead RBIs — a ribbie which gives the player's club a lead, whether the team holds it or not. Here were the 1990 leaders in go-ahead RBI:

Batter, Team	Go Ahead RBI
Joe Carter, SD	36
Matt Williams, SF	33
Cecil Fielder, Det	30
Kelly Gruber, Tor	29
Cal Ripken, Bal	28
Gary Gaetti, Min	28
Kal Daniels, LA	28
Eddie Murray, LA	28
Andres Galarraga, Mon	27
Ellis Burks, Bos	27
Will Clark, SF	27
Jose Canseco, Oak	27

What this means is that, 36 times last year, Joe Carter drove in a run which gave the Padres the lead. We like to look from some year-to-year consistency in statistics, and several players made the leaders list both times. Carter ranked sixth in the majors in go-ahead RBI in 1989 with 29. (He was inadvertantly left off the leaders list in the text of last year's book, but he belonged there.) Cal Ripken, Eddie Murray and Will Clark also made the leaders list in both 1989 and 1990. Not a bad list of ballplayers, is it?

We like this as a "clutch" stat; it's obvious that any time a player drives in a run which gives his club the lead, he's doing something vital to put his team on the road to victory. Whether his pitching staff can hold the lead or not is fairly irrelevant; at that particular point of the game, the player was doing all he could to help win the game.

You might say, "Sure, Carter, Williams and Fielder had a lot of go-ahead RBIs. They had a lot of RBIs, period." Okay, so let's rank the players on a percentage basis. Since a player can get only one go-ahead RBI per plate appearance, we'll figure the percentage based on the number of plate appearances in which the player had at least one RBI. The leaders (players with 60 or more total RBI during 1990):

Batter, Team	Plate Appearances with 1+ RBI	Plate Appearances with a Go Ahead RBI	Pct.
Dwight Evans, Bos	48	24	50.0
Kal Daniels, LA	59	28	47.5
Bo Jackson, KC	54	24	44.4
Gary Gaetti, Min	65	28	43.1
Joe Carter, SD	84	36	42.9
Ellis Burks, Bos	65	27	41.5
Barry Larkin, Cin	56	23	41.1
Ivan Calderon, WSox	59	24	40.7
Carlton Fisk, WSox	54	22	40.7
Cal Ripken, Bal	69	28	40.6

Not all of these players drove in a lot of runs — Evans, for instance, had only 63 ribbies for the year — but they did have a lot of big ones. And Joe Carter still looks pretty good, doesn't he?

A complete listing for this category appears on page 282.

WHO HAS THE BEST "HEART OF THE ORDER"?

The "heart of the order" consists of the three, four and five spots in the lineup. These are the power slots, where the main home run and RBI men reside. If the big boppers in these spots are effective, the team is almost certain to have an offense to be feared. But if the club has "heart trouble," it won't have enough punch to mount an effective offense.

We keep track of production by lineup position, and we thought you'd like to see which clubs were best in the heart of the order. Here are the three best teams in each of the three main "3-4-5" categories: home runs, RBI and slugging percentage. Note that the stats include **all** players who batted in those spots over the course of the season. The "main 3-4-5 hitters" are shown in the appendix; they are the players who did most of the damage in the power spots for each club.

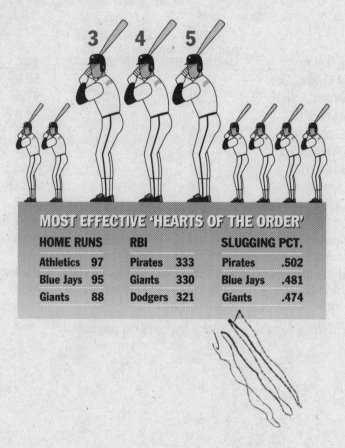

MOST EFFECTIVE 'HEARTS OF THE ORDER'

HOME RUNS		RBI		SLUGGING PCT.	
Athletics	97	Pirates	333	Pirates	.502
Blue Jays	95	Giants	330	Blue Jays	.481
Giants	88	Dodgers	321	Giants	.474

The best clubs averaged well over 100 RBI apiece from their power spots; the worst couldn't even average 80. We find it interesting that the top three RBI trios all came from the National League — it's yet another sign that the NL is regaining its oldtime power. The best of the best was the Pittsburgh Pirates. All Jim Leyland had to do was remember his outfield of Barry Bonds, Andy Van Slyke and Bobby Bonilla. Giving the Bucs a run for it was the great Giant trio of Will Clark, Kevin Mitchell and Matt Williams. It was quite a battle: in '89 Mitchell and Clark finished one-two in the league MVP voting, while in 1990 the top two were Bonds and Bonilla. The Dodger offensive revival was shown in their third place finish in RBI (they also had the best batting average). Credit GM Fred Claire for rebuilding his power spots: he added Eddie Murray and Kal Daniels in 1989, and signed Hubie Brooks in 1990. Now Brooks is gone, but he's being replaced by Darryl Strawberry. (Not a bad replacement.) Surprisingly, the champion Reds didn't fare all that well in this category, but of course, the heart of their order was a lot more potent when Eric Davis was healthy.

Sometimes you can see a club's plight just by examining how the heart of its order is doing. The Baltimore Orioles were surprise contenders in 1989, but with Randy Milligan injured, Mickey Tettleton slumping and Cal Ripken off his past form, the O's couldn't muster the power a top club needs in 1990. The mighty Yankees practically invented the concept of putting three straight home run hitters in a lineup, with Babe Ruth, Lou Gehrig and Bob Meusel in the twenties. But last year, with Don Mattingly hurt, Dave Winfield gone and such unlikely names as Oscar Azocar and Mel Hall often appearing in the power spots, the Yanks were really hurting. The Houston Astros got poor production from their power spots in 1990, and now their two best sluggers from a year ago, Glenn Davis and Franklin Stubbs, are gone. Sounds like it's going to be a long season in Houston.

A complete listing of this category appears on page 283.

WHO CAN POP IN THE CLUTCH?

There are all kinds of "clutch" situations in a ball game, but no one can deny the importance of hitting well in the late innings of close games. Our definition of a late-and-close situation is, to begin with, a plate appearance in the seventh inning or later. In addition, the batting team has to be either leading by a run, tied or within shouting distance of the lead; if the batter's club is trailing, the tying run has to be either on base, at bat or in the on-deck circle. Here are the batting leaders in the late innings of close games for 1990 (50 or more plate appearances in those situations). As we did last year, we add the leaders in home runs and RBI:

Player,Team	Avg	AB	H	HR	RBI
Benito Santiago, SD	.433	67	29	3	8
Rickey Henderson, Oak	.426	61	26	5	11
Randy Ready, Phi	.407	54	22	1	7
Walt Weiss, Oak	.405	74	30	0	10
Gary Sheffield, Mil	.397	63	25	2	9
Dave Magadan, Mets	.391	69	27	1	8
Greg Gagne, Min	.385	52	20	0	2
Terry Kennedy, SF	.378	45	17	0	3
Willie McGee, StL-Oak	.376	93	35	1	17
Harold Baines, Tex-Oak	.373	59	22	3	11

Home Run Leaders: Dwight Evans 8, Kevin Mitchell 8, Franklin Stubbs 7, Bo Jackson 6, Ryne Sandberg 6.

RBI Leaders: Harold Reynolds 26, Kelly Gruber 24, Joe Carter 22, Ruben Sierra 21, Howard Johnson 20.

Some observations on the list:

1. How many of the top ten hitters from 1989 also made it in 1990? None. That's right, zero. The only repeater on the homer and RBI lists was Kevin Mitchell, who had six late-and-close homers in '89. That does nothing to destroy the oft-stated contention that these clutch figures are based on too small a sampling of at-bats to be a reliable measure of consistent performance. We know from the figures that Benito Santiago produced in the clutch in 1990; but we can't argue with any certainty that he'll do so again in 1991.

2. Underscoring this notion, the Cincinnati Reds had no one on the clutch leaders list last year; the Oakland A's had Rickey Henderson, Walt Weiss, Willie McGee and Harold Baines, along with Mark McGwire, who

slugged .613 and had an unreal .549 on-base percentage in the late innings of close games. So which team choked in the World Series? Oakland, of course.

3. We add the homer and RBI leaders because batting average by itself never gives a complete picture of hitting ability. Joe Carter is a good example; he batted only .220 in the late innings of close games, but with 22 RBI, he obviously came up with a good number of important hits.

4. Both Dwight Evans and Harold Reynolds turned in remarkable late-inning performances last year. Evans hit only 13 homers, but eight of them came in crucial late-inning situations. Reynolds had only 55 RBI, but nearly half of them — 26 — came in the clutch. Reynolds was also a top late-and-close performer in 1989, batting .351 (but with only six RBI).

The list of worst clutch hitters in 1990 includes some very famous names:

Player, Team	Avg	AB	H	HR	RBI
Jeff King, Pit	.117	60	7	0	4
Kevin Elster, Mets	.125	48	6	1	7
Dale Murphy, Atl-Phi	.129	85	11	0	6
Jeffrey Leonard, Sea	.141	78	11	0	10
Carney Lansford, Oak	.152	66	10	0	9
Chet Lemon, Det	.156	45	7	0	8
Alfredo Griffin, LA	.159	63	10	0	2
Junior Felix, Tor	.160	75	12	1	7
Jose Canseco, Oak	.161	62	10	1	8
Al Newman, Min	.161	62	10	0	4

Fewest RBI: Billy Hatcher 1 (76 AB), Lou Whitaker 1 (67 AB), Mike Scioscia 1 (58 AB), Dave Valle 1 (49 AB), Dion James 1 (46 AB).

Dale Murphy? Jose Canseco? Carney Lansford? Canseco continued to struggle in postseason play last year. But Lansford was Oakland's best hitter in the playoff and Series (11-for-31, .357). Meanwhile Billy Hatcher, who hit only .224 with one measly late-and-close RBI during last year's regular season, was Mr. Everything (9-for-12, .750) in the World Series. It's another example of why one should not rely too heavily on late-inning clutch statistics.

A complete listing for this category can be found on page 284.

WHICH PLAYERS HAVE THE BIGGEST "IMPACT"?

Everyone knows the limitations of batting average. A .300 hitter can be a less effective offensive performer than a .240 hitter, if the .240 guy makes up for the low average by hitting with power, drawing walks or stealing bases. So we have stats — new and old — like slugging average, on-base percentage, runs created, total average and linear weights, all of which give one a clearer idea of a player's total offensive contributions.

Now a statistician named Paul Johnson has come with an appealing rating system, one which uses the familiar context of batting averages, called IMPACT. Johnson, we should tell you, is no neophyte. A few years ago, he came up with a formula called "Estimated Runs Produced" which was a variation on Bill James' runs created. James thought so highly of the system that he published it in the 1985 *Baseball Abstract,* calling it "an extraordinarily good method" and "more accurate than runs created for certain types of players." So Johnson clearly knows his stuff.

The appeal of Johnson's IMPACT rating, which uses his "estimated runs" as a base, is that the figure it computes reads like a batting average, and has the same mileposts: a .300 IMPACT is excellent, .260 is average, a .200 IMPACT very poor. The formula for the system is at the end of this article; it ends up adding or subtracting points to batting average according the run-producing potential of the player's power, walks and steals. To give you an idea of the system in action, here the 1990 IMPACT leaders (minimum 502 PA):

Player, Team	IMPACT
Rickey Henderson, Oak	.394
Barry Bonds, Pit	.364
Fred McGriff, Tor	.349
Cecil Fielder, Det	.347
Kal Daniels, LA	.342
Lenny Dykstra, Phi	.340
Dave Justice, Atl	.340
Dave Magadan, Mets	.339
Ryne Sandberg, Cubs	.337
Eddie Murray, LA	.335

You can see IMPACT's appeal — these could be the batting average leaders for a big-hitting season of the twenties. Henderson, who hit for average and power, stole bases and drew walks, is rightly at the top. Other players have a mixture of those skills, but none is so good across the spectrum. Johnson notes that's Henderson's IMPACT rating of .394 was the highest in the majors since George Brett had a .409 mark in 1980. (That, of course, was the year Brett had a .390 batting average.)

How does IMPACT match up with runs created? Pretty well. The 1990 top seven in runs created were Henderson, Fielder, Bonds, McGriff, Sandberg, Dykstra and Murray, all of whom are represented here; Daniels, Justice and Magadan had fewer runs created only because they had fewer plate appearances. So the system seems to work very well, though we really don't have the space to make a long critique of it. (One reason we include the formula is so readers can do just that).

The offensive duds of 1990 in IMPACT (minimum 350 PA) were:

Player, Team	IMPACT
Alfredo Griffin, LA	.170
Alvaro Espinoza, Yanks	.185
Mike Gallego, Oak	.185
Jose Uribe, SF	.192
Bill Spiers, Mil	.199

Four weak-hitting shortstops, one combination second-baseman shortstop. Johnson notes that last year, major league regulars at shortstop combined for a .235 IMPACT, catchers and second basemen .255, third basemen .265, outfielders .280, first basemen .295. Managers obviously expect more offensive production — more IMPACT — at first base than they do at shortstop, where defense is much more important.

Calculating IMPACT

1. Calculate estimated runs

   Estimated Runs = TB/3.15 + (BB+HP-IBB-CS-GIDP)/3 + H/4 + SB/5 - AB/11.75

2. Calculate outs charge to batter

   Outs = AB + CS + GIDP - H

3. Project estimated runs for a full season (474 outs: AB+CS+GIDP-H)

   Full Season of Runs = Estimated Runs / Outs x 474

4. Calculate theoretical at-bats for full season

   Theoretical At-Bats = Full Season of Runs x 1.5 + 495

5. Calculate theoretical hits for full season (based on 454 outs: AB-H)

   Theoretical Hits = Theoretical At-Bats - 454

6. Calculate IMPACT

   IMPACT = Theoretical Hits / Theoretical At-Bats

A complete listing for this category appears on page 285.

WHO WENT TO THE MOON IN 1990?

Few things in baseball match the thrill of a long home run. Watch a Cecil Fielder or Jose Canseco shot soar into the stratosphere, and you'll be talking about it for years. Since we keep track of virtually everything that happens on a baseball field, you won't be surprised that we've compiled a list of the longest home runs of 1990. Here they are:

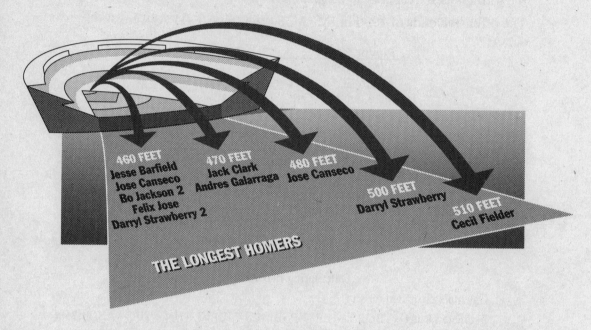

460 FEET
Jesse Barfield
Jose Canseco
Bo Jackson 2
Felix Jose
Darryl Strawberry 2

470 FEET
Jack Clark
Andres Galarraga

480 FEET
Jose Canseco

500 FEET
Darryl Strawberry

510 FEET
Cecil Fielder

THE LONGEST HOMERS

You might recall Fielder's mighty homer last August 25 off Oakland's Dave Stewart. It reached the left field roof at Tiger Stadium, only the third time in history that's been done; the other two were belted by a couple of pretty fair country hitters named Harmon Killebrew and Frank Howard. How do we know the ball travelled 510 feet? Well, we don't . . . at least not exactly. Measurements ranged from 470 to 550 feet on this ball. (Our 510 figure is right in the middle.) However, our home run distances are normally very accurate, and we can confidently assert that though they are estimates, they're very good ones.

That said, it's interesting to compare 1990 with 1989. We ran this same study a year ago, and the longest homer was only 470 feet, a blast by Canseco. We recorded three homers longer than that in 1990. We also logged a total of 19 homers that travelled at least 450 feet in '89; in 1990 the total was 32. Is this evidence that the ball was livelier last year? Not necessarily. But home run production was up by eight percent last year —

11 percent in the National League, five percent in the American — and that's a pretty sizeable jump. It's hard to buy the explanation that the pitching was simply lousier last year, though this could be evidence of a lockout affect.

So who was Mr. Longball of 1990? It was a pretty close competition. Darryl Strawberry led the way with five 450-foot-plus homers. But Canseco, Fielder and Kevin Mitchell each had four, and any of them could argue that he was the top guy. It probably wasn't Bill (Bubble) Bathe of the Giants, the most unlikely 1990 player to record a 450-foot shot.

The dubious honor of yielding the most long homers went to the Phillies' Pat Combs, who was taken deep by Felix Jose, Strawberry and Dale Murphy in a period of less than three months last year. No doubt Combs was grateful to see Murphy get traded to the Phillies later in the year.

A complete listing for this category can be found on page 286.

WHO CLEANS 'EM UP?

No matter how much baseball changes, one thing remains constant: the main slugger in the lineup usually bats cleanup. We rank number four hitters, sensibly enough, by slugging percentage. The following players had the best slugging percentages in baseball while batting in the cleanup position in 1990 (minimum 150 plate appearances):

Player, Team	Slg	Avg	OBP	AB	H	HR	RBI
Cecil Fielder, Det ✔	.585	.283	.391	424	120	36	96
Dave Justice, Atl	.565	.286	.387	147	42	10	31
Jack Clark, SD	.558	.279	.449	215	60	16	41
Kevin Mitchell, SF	.544	.289	.359	522	151	35	93
Mark McGwire, Oak	.544	.246	.368	349	86	31	84
Andre Dawson, Cubs	.541	.311	.362	501	156	27	95
Darryl Strawberry, Mets	.530	.277	.364	477	132	34	98
Eddie Murray, LA	.523	.332	.416	554	184	26	95
Glenn Davis, Hou	.521	.248	.354	326	81	22	63
Bobby Bonilla, Pit	.519	.280	.323	624	175	32	120

Some familiar names here — just about all of them are veteran sluggers who don't figure to be bothered by the pressure of a key RBI spot. The top two guys, however, were two of the major new stars of 1990. Cecil Fielder came back from Japan and made himself right at home, not only in Detroit but as the Tigers' number four hitter. And Dave Justice, a raw rookie, didn't seem to be awed by anything about major league baseball. Justice still has to prove that he can do it over the long haul, but you have to like the way he's started. Both Justice and Fielder filled glaring needs on their ballclubs last year; Atlanta (with Dale Murphy) and Detroit (with Keith Moreland and Alan Trammell) had terrible production from the cleanup spot in 1989.

You'll notice that most of the players on the leaders list are pretty complete hitters. Only two of the ten batted lower than .275 as a cleanup man, and all but #10 Bonilla had solid on-base percentages. That would, of course, figure — the number-four hitter is almost always one of the two best hitters on the team, along with the number-three.

The following hitters were anything but complete, however; they were baseball's poorest performers when hitting in the cleanup position last year:

Player, Team	Slg	Avg	OBP	AB	H	HR	RBI
Mickey Tettleton, Bal	.333	.198	.364	243	48	7	28
Gary Gaetti, Min	.338	.206	.257	228	47	6	28
Steve Balboni, Yanks	.367	.164	.270	177	29	11	22
Jeffrey Leonard, Sea	.368	.256	.300	386	99	10	66
Rickey Jordan, Phi	.375	.250	.292	192	48	4	28

Interestingly enough, both Tettleton (.537 slugging average) and Gaetti (.508) were two of the leading hitters at the cleanup spot in 1989. That was probably why their clubs gave them so many at-bats at the position last year before giving up on them. But by the end of year, all five of these guys needed to prove themselves as major league sluggers again.

Though Fielder was awesome in 1990, he didn't always bat cleanup and couldn't approach the kind of cleanup production that Kevin Mitchell of the Giants provided in 1989. That was almost a once-in-a-lifetime thing: Mitchell had 47 homers, 125 RBI and a mighty .636 slugging average while hitting fourth in '89. Mitchell had another fine year in 1990, proving that he was no fluke, but while he was among the leaders again, his figures couldn't approach his mighty '89 totals.

A complete listing for this category can be found on page 287.

III. QUESTIONS ON PITCHING

WHO GETS THOSE CHEAP SAVES?

Like many children of the sixties, the save rule has had a controversial life. The beginning was fairly simple: the rule was invented by a Chicago sportswriter, Jerome Holtzman, who wanted to show the world how good the Cub relievers, Don Elston and Bill Henry, were. (Not so good, as it turned out.) According to the original rules, the reliever had to face the tying run in order to get a save. Those rules were liberalized during the self-indulgent hippie era, so that even working the ninth to wrap up a 12-0 win was good enough for a save. Finally they were tightened again as times got more conservative, but they're still more liberal than the original ones. These days you can pitch a scoreless ninth with a three run lead — or work three innings with any lead — and log a save.

With a history like that, it's no wonder people are still arguing about the rule. They say Dennis Eckersley has it made, that he gets "cheap" saves. Or that Randy Myers has to work for his. To paraphrase Gertrude Stein, a save is not a save is not a save. We'd like to try to make some sense of this controversy. We begin by defining some terms:

- **Cheap Save:** first Batter Faced is not the tying run AND reliever pitches one inning or less. Example: Thigpen comes in with a 5-3 lead and no one on base to start the ninth. Under the current rules, this is a Save Opportunity. We call it a Cheap Save Opportunity.

- **Tough Save:** reliever comes in with the tying run anywhere on base. Example: Thigpen comes in with a 5-3 lead, two outs and the bases loaded in the ninth. This is a Tough Save Opportunity.

All other Saves fall into the "Regular Category."

Fair enough? You might disagree with the definitions, but you have to admit that a "tough" save is much harder to record than a cheap save, which by definition means the reliever has at least a two-run lead with no more than one inning to play. The "tough save" definition is also tougher than the original definition of a save — in this case, the tying run has be on base, not just at bat. If you need any further proof that our definitions are pretty strict, look at how often relievers converted each kind of opportunity in 1990:

League	Cheap			Regular			Tough		
	Sv	Opp	%	Sv	Opp	%	Sv	Opp	%
AL Average	208	224	93%	330	439	75%	99	215	46%
NL Average	92	104	88%	294	399	74%	90	172	52%
MLB Average	300	328	91%	624	838	74%	189	387	49%

The "cheap" save is fairly automatic, with relievers converting 90% of the opportunities. The "tough" save is exactly that, with the firemen failing half the time. Now let's see how the leading relievers of 1990 (minimum 20 saves) performed in each category:

Reliever	Cheap		Regular		Tough		Total	
	Sv	Opp	Sv	Opp	Sv	Opp	Sv	Opp
Rick Aguilera, Min	9	9	15	17	8	13	32	39
Tim Burke, Mon	4	5	15	18	1	2	20	25
Dennis Eckersley, Oak	21	21	21	23	6	6	48	50
John Franco, Mets	8	9	19	23	6	7	33	39
Bryan Harvey, Cal	10	10	8	13	7	8	25	31
Tom Henke, Tor	8	8	19	23	5	7	32	38
Tom Henneman, Det	4	5	16	20	2	3	22	28
Doug Jones, Cle	14	15	28	33	1	3	43	51
Craig Lefferts, SD	3	3	13	18	7	9	23	30
Roger McDowell, Phi	7	7	9	13	6	8	22	28
Jeff Montgomery, KC	8	8	14	19	2	7	24	34
Randy Myers, Cin	5	5	18	20	8	12	31	37
Gregg Olson, Bal	20	20	14	17	3	5	37	42
Dan Plesac, Mil	8	8	11	17	5	9	24	34
Jeff Reardon, Bos	9	9	9	13	3	6	21	28
Dave Righetti, Yanks	23	24	11	13	2	2	36	39
Mike Schooler, Sea	14	14	15	18	1	2	30	34
Dave Smith, Hou	9	10	12	15	2	3	23	28
Lee Smith, Bos-StL	7	8	22	24	2	5	31	37
Bobby Thigpen, WSox	29	32	20	23	8	10	57	65

Looking at this list, you get much a better idea of how relievers compile their save totals. The difference between Bobby Thigpen's 57 saves and Dennis Eckersley's 48 was almost entirely in the "cheap" category, where Thigpen was 29-for-32, Eckersley a perfect 21-for-21. Gregg Olson and Dave Righetti also had 20 or more "cheap" saves.

By contrast, no National League relief ace had more than nine cheapies, and NL pitchers overall had less than half the cheap saves that AL pitchers did. What's the difference between leagues? Simple: National League pitchers have to hit. An NL manager is less likely to bring in his ace with two- or three-run lead to start the ninth because if the other club rallies, the reliever might have to bat in the next inning or two. So the manager will hold off bringing in the ace just yet, except when he's had a chance to pinch-hit for the previous reliever in the eighth. Because of that, National League relievers have a tougher time compiling the big save totals that American League relievers do. That's something to remember when comparing save totals.

As for the "tough" saves, we were only mildly surprised that nobody had more than eight — we've commented several times that today's relief aces are usually brought in **before** the tying run gets on base. (When the game get this close, National League managers will still wait a little longer than American League managers before changing pitchers, but only a little. Last year the average AL team had 15 "tough save" opportunities, the average NL team 14). Look at Cleveland's Doug Jones — 43 saves, but only one in the "tough" category (in three opportunities). And Righetti had only two tough saves out of his total of 36.

Who was the best reliever of 1990? Despite Thigpen's record save total, it's hard not to pick Eckersley, who had six "tough saves' in six opportunities — the only perfect score in the category for any pitcher with more than two opportunities. But Thigpen (8-for-10 in tough save opportunities) and the Mets' John Franco (6-for-7) weren't far behind.

A complete listing for this category appears on page 288.

ARE GROUNDBALL PITCHERS MORE EFFECTIVE?

If we could leave you with one thought to hold in your mind after reading our book, this might be a good one: in baseball, there are all kinds of ways to be successful. That's an especially good thing to remember when studying major league pitchers. We always hear, "You can't throw the ball by major league hitters," and yet we see guys like Rob Dibble and Randy Myers who can do exactly that. We hear, "You've got to be able to hold baserunners," and yet some of the most successful pitchers in the majors (Dwight Gooden and Nolan Ryan, to name two) are among the easiest to steal on. You also hear, "You've got to keep the ball down in the strike zone," but the evidence that this is important is hardly overwhelming.

Groundball Pitchers

	Ground Balls	Fly Balls	HRs Allowed	Opp. Avg	G/F Ratio
Billy Swift, Sea	285	83	4	.272	3.43
Kevin Brown, Tex	361	105	13	.255	3.44
Mike Morgan, LA	419	158	19	.266	2.65
Greg Maddux, Cubs	425	164	11	.265	2.59
Matt Young, Sea	366	164	15	.237	2.23
Dana Kiecker, Bos	248	115	7	.253	2.16
Zane Smith, Mon-Pit	374	175	15	.245	2.14
Mike Witt, Cal-Yanks	205	96	9	.241	2.14
Duane Ward, Tor	186	95	9	.221	1.96
Jim Abbott, Cal	375	192	16	.295	1.95

Flyball Pitchers

	Ground Balls	Fly Balls	HRs Allowed	Opp. Avg	G/F Ratio
Chuck Cary, Yanks	135	217	21	.260	0.62
Sid Fernandez, Mets	135	232	18	.200	0.58
Jose DeLeon, StL	158	223	15	.246	0.71
Danny Darwin, Hou	158	215	11	.225	0.73
Roy Smith, Min	174	234	20	.313	0.74
Tom Browning, Cin	269	354	24	.266	0.76
Jim Deshaies, Hou	217	280	21	.245	0.77
Dave Johnson, Bal	220	278	30	.280	0.79
Steve Wilson, Cubs	149	184	17	.259	0.81
Teddy Higuera, Mil	174	214	16	.256	0.81

Keeping the ball down results in more double play balls and fewer home runs allowed, which is great. But does it also result in more victories? Two list are shown above. The first consists of the most pronounced groundball pitchers in the majors last year (minimum 250 balls in play); the second consists of the most pronounced flyball pitchers.

Some observations on the two groups:

1. There was a lot of year-to-year consistency in the leaders group. Fernandez was the top flyball pitcher in both 1989 and 1990; Brown and Swift were one-two among groundball pitchers in both '89 and '90, the spots reversed in 1989. Zane Smith, Morgan, Maddux, Browning, Roy Smith and Deshaies all made the top ten in their respective groups in both 1989 and 1990.

2. The won-lost records of the two groups were almost identical — the groundball pitchers were 87-107, the flyball pitchers 88-108. In 1989, the top ten groundball pitchers went 100-107, the top ten flyballers 107-82. If it's such a good idea to throw grounders, why can't the best pitchers with that style win more games than they lose?

3. However, the groundballers had a lower ERA, 3.53 to 3.91. In 1989, the groundball group also had the lower ERA, 3.21 to 3.58. Hmmm, maybe the lowball style isn't so bad after all.

4. The groundball group allowed far fewer homers, 118 to 193. That would figure — keep the ball low, keep it in the ballpark.

5. The flyball pitchers had a lower opponents' batting average, .254 to .257. That would also figure — pitchers who work up in the strike zone generally throw harder, getting more strikeouts and allowing fewer hits while giving up more home runs. The difference would have been greater if not for the presence of Roy Smith's .313 opponents' average in the flyball group. Smith, who doesn't throw very hard or get many strikeouts, is an unlikely (as well as unsuccessful) flyball pitcher.

6. Seven of the ten groundball leaders pitched for American League teams; six of the ten flyball pitchers worked in the National League. This suggests that the old saw that the American is the high-strike league, the National the low-strike, has it backwards. A more likely explanation is the ballparks: in the smaller AL parks, where it's easier to hit one out, it's more essential to keep the ball down. However, before we get too carried away with this kind of theorizing, we should point out that in 1989, both groups were dominated by NL pitchers.

On balance, the evidence suggests that the best groundball pitchers, with a lower ERA, are better than the best flyball pitchers. However, the difference is not all that great. The original point still holds: there are all kinds of ways to be successful.

A complete listing for this category can be found on page 289.

WHO ARE THE BEST-HITTING PITCHERS IN BASEBALL?

PITCHERS WHO CAN HIT

	HR	AVG.
Dan Schatzeder	5	.240
Don Robinson	13	.232
Tim Leary	1	.221

Minimum 150 plate appearances lifetime.

If more pitchers could hit, the American League wouldn't have the designated hitter rule. Unfortunately, the average National League moundsman is about a .130 hitter, and any hurler who can top the Mendoza Line (.200) is, by pitcher-hitting standards, another Wade Boggs. We argued a year ago that the good-hitting pitcher is becoming a thing of the past. Indeed, of the top ten among current major league pitchers (minimum 150 lifetime plate appearances), seven are 30 or older, including the top four. The leaders:

Pitcher	Avg	AB	H	2B	3B	HR	RBI
Dan Schatzeder	.240	242	58	8	2	5	29
Don Robinson	.232	573	133	19	0	13	64
Tim Leary	.221	163	36	6	0	1	19
Dennis Rasmussen	.205	215	44	7	0	0	14
Rick Aguilera	.203	138	28	3	0	3	11
Fernando Valenzuela	.202	807	163	22	1	8	72
Sid Fernandez	.199	377	75	10	2	1	29
Orel Hershiser	.189	456	86	15	2	0	29
Rick Sutcliffe	.189	507	96	20	1	4	52
Dwight Gooden	.183	513	94	7	2	3	39

We'll make another argument: it doesn't have to be this way. The leaders list is dominated by pitchers who have worked for two systems, the Mets and the Dodgers. (Two pretty good clubs, not coincidentally.) The Mets have produced Gooden, Aguilera, and Leary and can share credit with LA for Fernandez. New York also has David Cone (.178), who ranks 13th on the list. Even Frank Viola, who basically would wave at three pitches and then sit down when he first came over to the Mets from the American League, is no longer a joke. Viola batted a better-than-average .153 with seven sacrifice hits last year. The Dodgers also make sure their pitchers don't take their stick work lightly; five of the top ten (Leary, Valenzuela, Fernandez, Hershiser and Sutcliffe) either came up through the LA system, or saw extensive action with the Dodgers.

Unfortunately, the Mets and Dodgers are the exception. For that you at least can partially blame lack of practice. Any pitcher who comes up through an American League farm system is almost certain to reach the majors without getting a professional at-bat; pitchers who come up through National League systems only bat when they play other NL farm clubs. It takes a lot of hard work to overcome that handicap, and most teams simply don't bother. The Mets and Dodgers do, however, and they reap the benefits.

Most clubs, however, produce guys like these — the **worst**-hitting pitchers in baseball:

Pitcher	Avg	AB	H	2B	3B	HR	RBI
Don Carman	.059	204	12	0	0	0	4
Mike Bielecki	.076	197	15	0	0	0	5
Jim Deshaies	.077	297	23	0	0	0	12
Bruce Hurst	.080	137	11	0	0	0	1
Bruce Ruffin	.088	239	21	3	0	0	6

Dangerous Don Carman, who's earned a reputation as one of the worst-hitting pitchers ever, had his career year last year, hitting .273 (3-for-11). Don't expect it to happen again.

Carman has nothing on the Astros' Jim Deshaies, who has 297 lifetime at-bats, 23 singles, and 157 strikeouts. We state in another part of the book that Dwight Gooden and Deshaies pitched about the same last year, and that Gooden's superior record was largely a product of better offensive support. What we didn't say was that Gooden supplied some of that support himself. The 1990 hitting figures for the two:

Pitcher	Avg	AB	H	2B	3B	HR	RBI	SH	SO
Gooden	.187	75	14	1	1	1	9	14	15
Deshaies	.063	63	4	0	0	0	3	7	33

It's obvious that Gooden helped himself with the bat last year, and Deshaies didn't. Time for some work in the batting cage, Jimmy!

A complete listing for this category can be found on page 290.

WHICH PITCHERS SHOULD SUE THEIR FIELDERS?

We'll be the first to admit that the earned run average is a good stat. ERA bends over backward to be fair: it measures how many runs each pitcher has allowed per nine innings, but first it subtracts runs that were caused by fielding miscues ("unearned" runs). Of course, if the pitcher's fielders have no range, they'll let more balls drop in for hits, and **those** are considered earned, and that isn't fair either. But such limitations aside, ERA is a fine measure of pitching effectiveness.

Nonetheless, those fielding miscues happen, and the runs they cause count just as much as the earned ones do. Even if they don't show up in pitchers' ERA, they still might cause some extra losses. That caused us to wonder which pitchers were penalized most by their fielders in 1990. So along with the traditional earned run average, we computed an "unearned run average" — how many unearned runs per nine innings each pitcher allowed. The figures on the left of the leaders list below computes the UERA; the "Err" column is the number of errors which were committed while the pitcher was on the mound. The figures on the right are the traditional stats — won, lost, ERA — for comparative purposes. The pitchers most penalized last year (minimum 100 innings pitched):

Pitcher, Team	IP	R	UER	Err	UERA	W	L	ERA
Scott Erickson, Min	113.0	49	13	9	1.04	8	4	2.87
Greg Maddux, Cubs	237.0	116	25	27	0.95	15	15	3.46
Bill Krueger, Mil	129.0	70	13	19	0.91	6	8	3.98
Bryn Smith, SL	141.1	81	14	18	0.89	9	8	4.27
Billy Swift, Sea	128.0	46	12	15	0.84	6	4	2.39
Bill Gullickson, Hou	193.1	100	18	20	0.84	10	14	3.82
Charlie Leibrandt, Atl	162.1	72	15	18	0.83	9	11	3.16
Tom Gordon, KC	195.1	99	18	18	0.83	12	11	3.73
Mike Witt, Cal-Yanks	117.0	62	10	10	0.77	5	9	4.00
Dennis Rasmussen, SD	187.2	110	16	24	0.77	11	15	4.52

All the pitchers except two had ERAs of 4.00 or below. But their fielders' miscues added nearly another run of damage, and in Erickson's case, more than that. Even so, four of the ten managed winning records, and Maddux was a .500 pitcher — that indicates some pretty good pitchers here. As would figure with so much ineptitude behind them, all ten pitchers worked for clubs with losing records.

What's the common denominator, aside from pitching for lousy teams? It's that these are primarily ground-ball pitchers. Which makes perfect sense: most errors are committed by infielders, and ground-ball pitchers give the infielders more chances to screw up. We always hear about the benefits of keeping the ball down: fewer homers allowed, more DPs. Well, here's a hidden **dis**advantage, and a big one. (Advice to Maddux: make them hit the ball to Sandberg, not Salazar!)

How about the pitchers whose fielders were Gold Glovers with them on the mound? These pitchers had the lowest unearned averages last year:

Pitcher, Team	IP	R	UER	Err	UERA	W	L	ERA
Frank Tanana, Det	176.1	104	0	5	0.00	9	8	5.31
Dave Johnson, Bal	180.0	83	1	8	0.05	13	9	4.10
Les Lancaster, Cubs	109.0	57	1	4	0.08	9	5	4.62
Tom Browning, Cin	227.2	98	2	16	0.08	15	9	3.80
Tom Bolton, Bos	119.2	46	1	8	0.08	10	5	3.38

As we might have guessed, this is primarily a flyball-throwing contingent. And a group of pretty lucky hurlers, as well. Browning's Cincinnati mates committed 16 errors behind him, but they led to only two unearned runs. Despite some lackluster ERAs, all five pitchers turned in winning records.

If only Frank Tanana had pitched as well as his teammates fielded . . ..

A complete listing for this category can be found on page 291.

WHAT'S A SAVE-PLUS-HOLD PERCENTAGE?

One of the newer statistics appearing in baseball these days — and one we heartily endorse — is the "save percentage." This stat compares saves against save opportunities. The only problem is that it tends to underestimate the importance of middle relievers. Setup men often enter a game in a save opportunity, but leave without getting the actual save — whether they've pitched effectively or not. That's why we invented the "hold," a stat which rewards a reliever who enters a game with a save opportunity and exits with the opportunity still intact.

Even so, middle-men often look worse than they really are. The problem is that they miss out on chances to record saves (because the closer gets them), while their share of blown saves is as great as most closers. So we decided to examine relievers in a more complete way: by adding the holds (which are, after all, save opportunities passed on to the next reliever) to the save opportunities. That results in a saves-plus-holds percentage, and a truer look at which pitchers are actually holding off the opposition. Here are the 1990 leaders in hold-plus-save percentage; we begin by showing the traditional save percentage, so you can see the difference (note: Lee Smith's figures include his Boston totals):

American League	Save Pct.	Holds	Saves	H+S Opp.	H+S Pct.
Dennis Eckersley, Oak	96.0	0	48	50	96.0
Dave Righetti, Yanks	92.3	0	36	39	92.3
Rick Honeycutt, Oak	70.0	27	7	37	91.9
Rob Murphy, Bos	70.0	16	7	26	88.5
Gene Nelson, Oak	62.5	18	5	26	88.5
Mike Schooler, Sea	88.2	0	30	34	88.2
Gregg Olson, Bal	88.1	0	37	42	88.1
Bobby Thigpen, WSox	87.7	0	57	65	87.7
Jerry Don Gleaton, Det	81.3	7	13	23	87.0
Chuck Crim, Mil	68.9	19	11	35	85.7

National League	Save Pct.	Holds	Saves	H+S Opp.	H+S Pct.
John Franco, Mets	84.6	0	33	39	84.6
Jeff Brantley, SF	79.2	8	19	32	84.4
Lee Smith, Bos-SL	83.8	1	31	38	84.2
Tim Burke, Mon	80.0	6	20	31	83.9
Randy Myers, Cin	83.8	0	31	37	83.8
Juan Agosto, Hou	50.0	16	4	24	83.3

Rob Dibble, Cin	64.7	17	11	34	82.4
Dave Smith, Hou	82.1	0	23	28	82.1
Mitch Williams, Cubs	80.0	1	16	21	81.0
Joe Boever, Atl-Phi	73.7	5	14	24	79.2

Looked at this way, one can see that middle men get more of their due. Pitchers like Gene Nelson and Rob Dibble, with low save percentages because they're often lifted before they can log the save, are shown to be among the most effective relievers — which is exactly what they are.

You might wonder which pitchers fared **worst** in saves-plus-holds versus opportunities. Here they are:

American League	Save Pct.	Holds	Saves	H+S Opp.	H+S Pct.
Mike Jackson, Sea	25.0	13	3	25	64.0
Kenny Rogers, Tex	65.2	6	15	29	72.4
Dan Plesac, Mil	70.6	2	24	36	72.2
Jeff Montgomery, KC	70.6	7	24	41	75.6
Duane Ward, Tor	61.1	11	11	29	75.9

National League	Save Pct.	Holds	Saves	H+S Opp.	H+S Pct.
Paul Assenmacher, Cubs	50.0	10	10	30	66.7
Jay Howell, LA	66.7	1	16	25	68.0
Greg Harris, SD	56.3	10	9	26	73.0
Scott Ruskin, Pit-Mon	25.0	15	2	23	73.9
Ken Dayley, SL	28.6	14	2	21	76.2

Even these pitchers, most of them middle relievers, are revealed to be more effective than mere save percentage would indicate. Most of them pitched better than closers Dan Plesac and Jay Howell, both of whom struggled last year. Paul Assenmacher and Mike Jackson have both been auditioned as closers; one would have to say that each has flunked the audition thus far.

A complete listing for this category appears on page 292.

WHICH PITCHERS MAKE THE LEAST OF THEIR INHERITANCE?

The "inherited runner" stat is a useful one, and for sound reasons. When a reliever comes in with men on base and allows them to score, it's a blow to his team, but the damage won't show up in his ERA. As a result, lousy pitching often goes unnoticed, and good work — on the part of firemen who come in and set down the side — is ignored.

On average, major league relievers allow about a third of their inherited runners to score. As the graphic shows, the best pitchers are quite a bit better than that — and the worst a lot worse:

Minimum 30 inherited runners

BEST	Inherited runners	Inherited runners scored	PCT.	WORST			
Randy Myers	32	3	9.4%	Frank DiPino	37	21	56.8%
Joe Klink	31	4	12.9%	Greg Harris	42	21	50.0%
Juan Agosto	59	10	17.0%	Julio Machado	32	16	50.0%
Kevin Hickey	35	6	17.1%	Dennis Cook	35	17	48.6%
Lee Smith	34	6	17.7%	Mark Grant	52	25	48.1%
Bobby Thigpen	34	6	17.7%	Major Leagues	6312	2074	32.9%

The one repeater from 1989 was Randy Myers — fifth best in 1989, numero uno in 1990. Myers richly deserves his reputation as a top closer.

When we ran this study a year ago, we noted that the lists were dominated by middle relievers. That wasn't the case in 1990, as three of the six best were closers. It is true, however, as we note elsewhere, that middle men are much more likely to come in with men on base these days than closers are. Look at the pitchers who came in with the most men on base in 1990: Keith Comstock 80, Lee Guetterman 69, Mark Eichhorn 69, Paul Gibson 68 and Jeff Robinson, Don Carman, Rob Murphy, Don Pall and Mike Jackson 62 each. All middle relievers.

Among closers, only Doug Jones of the Indians came in with more than 40 inherited runners on base (48). More typical were Gregg Olson with 37, Thigpen and Lee Smith with 34, and John Franco and Dennis Eckersley with 29 each. Eckersley is often accused of getting a lot of cheap saves, but no one had an easier time of it last year than the Yanks' Dave Righetti. Rags recorded 36 saves while coming in with only 15 men on base all year.

Though he didn't come in with enough men on base to make the leaders list, Calvin Schiraldi of the Padres had a truly memorable season. Schiraldi inherited 19 runners last year — and all 19 scored!

We thought you might like to see how the teams rate in this category:

The Best	Runners Inherited	Runners Scored	Percent Scored
Astros	214	52	24.30
Reds	181	44	24.31
Athletics	192	47	24.48

The Worst	Runners Inherited	Runners Scored	Percent Scored
Braves	230	98	42.61
Padres	184	77	41.85
Red Sox	294	112	38.10

The surprise here is the Astros, a bad team with a good pen. Though both these teams ranked in the middle, there was a real contrast in how the White Sox and Mets handled their bullpens. The Sox came in with a total of 327 men on base last year, the Mets only 145 — less than half Chicago's total. Of course, it helped that New York's starting rotation was stronger.

A complete listing for this category can be found on page 293.

WHO KEEPS RUNNERS OFF BASE?

There are a number of stats which measure pitching effectiveness: earned run average, victories, winning percentage, and opponents' batting average among them. But one of the best systems is to rate hurlers by how good they are at keeping runners off base. Any pitcher who can keep the bases empty is giving himself a heck of a chance to win. So it's no surprise that the 1990 top ten in fewest baserunners per nine innings (minimum 162 IP) is a very impressive one:

Pitcher, Team	IP	H	BB	HB	Runners	Runners per 9
Danny Darwin, Hou	162.2	136	31	4	171	9.46
Nolan Ryan, Tex	204.0	137	74	7	218	9.62
Doug Drabek, Pit	231.1	190	56	3	249	9.69
Dennis Martinez, Mon	226.0	191	49	6	246	9.80
Roger Clemens, Bos	228.1	193	54	7	254	10.01
Ramon Martinez, LA	234.1	191	67	4	262	10.06
David Wells, Tor	189.0	165	45	2	212	10.10
Bruce Hurst, SD	223.2	188	63	1	252	10.14
Sid Fernandez, Mets	179.1	130	67	5	202	10.14
David Cone, Mets	211.2	177	65	1	243	10.33

A great list, all right — both ERA leaders (Darwin and Clemens), Mr. No Hit himself (Ryan) and the National League Cy Young winner (Drabek) make up four of the top five. But what's more interesting are these names, not among the leaders:

Pitcher, Team	Runners per 9
Ben McDonald, Bal	9.33
Bob Welch, Oak	11.19
Dwight Gooden, Mets	11.84

Ben McDonald, who pitched only 118.2 innings last year, didn't work enough to make our leaders list. But among pitchers who worked at least 100 innings, no one allowed fewer runners per nine. We think this is a pitcher to watch (and draft for your fantasy team, if you can) in 1991. As for Welch (27-6, AL Cy Young winner) and Gooden (19-7), you might be surprised by how many runners they put on last year. Both were under the major league average of 12.35 runners per nine, but not **that** much under it . . . especially Gooden. We point out elsewhere that both Welch and Gooden won so many games last year primarily because their clubs scored a lot of runs for them. Unless they continue to get that kind of support in '91 — an unlikely scenario — both will have to pitch a whole lot better if they want to be big winners again.

These guys will also have to pitch a lot better in 1991 — among ERA qualifiers, they allowed the most baserunners per nine innings last year:

Pitcher, Team	IP	H	BB	HB	Runners	Runners per 9
Mike Bielecki, Cubs	168.0	188	70	5	263	14.09
Jim Abbott, Cal	211.2	246	72	5	323	13.73
Tom Gordon, KC	195.1	192	99	3	294	13.55
Frank Tanana, Det	176.1	190	66	9	265	13.53
Dennis Rasmussen, SD	187.2	217	62	3	282	13.52

Bielecki, Tanana and Rasmussen, formerly very effective pitchers, fell on hard times last year, and there has to be some question about whether they can come back. They have age working against them, which is not the case for Jim Abbott and Tom Gordon. Talk about a sophomore jinx; both were among the top American League rookies in 1989, then slipped a long way in 1990. But a look at their figures for each year shows that we needn't have been too shocked by last year's problems:

	Gordon		Abbott	
	Hits per 9	Walks per 9	Hits per 9	Walks per 9
1989	6.7	4.7	9.4	3.7
1990	8.8	4.6	10.5	3.1

Gordon was extremely tough to hit as an '89 rookie, but his control was a big problem. He probably took a little off his pitches last year (his first pitches especially, as you'll see in another essay) in order to throw strikes, but it didn't work — his walk rate was only marginally better, and he gave up a lot more hits. Abbott gave up a lot of hits even in '89, and last year it was even worse, as opponents hammered him for a .295 average. He's an inspirational pitcher, but after two years there has to be a lot of doubt about whether Abbott can become a big winner.

A complete listing for this category appears on page 294.

WHO SHOULD NIBBLE MORE?

In the cat-and-mouse game between pitcher and hitter, everything is set up by the first pitch. The pitcher wants to get ahead in the count, so he's determined to throw a strike. But it has to be a **quality** strike; if he just lays the ball down the middle, the batter is liable to hit it a long way. It's a subtle game, and some pitchers are better at it than others.

Let's separate each pitcher's results according to whether the first pitch was a strike or a ball; if the batter puts the pitch in play, it counts in the strike column. Last year, when the first pitch was a strike, major league hitters batted only .242 for the plate appearance; when it was a ball, they batted .265. Thus the premium on throwing strikes — but remember, our admonition about **quality** strikes.

Now let's look at two groups of pitchers. The first believes in challenging the hitters (minimum 162 innings pitched):

| Pitcher, Team | 1 Strike | | 1 Ball | | |
	AB	Avg	AB	Avg	Diff
Tom Gordon, KC	424	.281	322	.227	.054
Jack Armstrong, Cin	371	.261	255	.212	.049
Tom Glavine, Atl	466	.300	361	.255	.045
Ron Robinson, Cin-Mil	413	.293	283	.258	.035
Brian Holman, Sea	417	.271	307	.244	.027
Tim Leary, Yanks	454	.269	331	.242	.027
Charlie Hough, Tex	419	.248	388	.222	.026
Matt Young, Sea	464	.248	372	.223	.025
Dennis Rasmussen, SD	428	.301	314	.280	.021
Melido Perez, WSox	421	.249	314	.229	.020

These guys do it backwards — they're actually more effective when the first pitch is a ball than they are when it's a strike. That would indicate that their strikes are a little too good to hit. That they have good stuff is indicated that they pitch very well when behind in the count. Thus they might be better off if they nibbled a little more, working the corners even on the first pitch. If they miss, they still have the ability to get the batter out. If they don't, the batter won't be getting as many juicy strikes to hit.

The second group already nibbles at the corners — probably a little too much:

Pitcher, Team	1 Strike		1 Ball		
	AB	Avg	AB	Avg	Diff
Joe Magrane, StL	438	.215	336	.327	−.112
Allan Anderson, Min	455	.251	286	.350	−.099
Frank Tanana, Det	389	.244	289	.329	−.085
Greg Harris, Bos	396	.230	307	.309	−.079
Zane Smith, Mon-Pit	490	.214	311	.293	−.079
Bud Black, Cle-Tor	488	.207	290	.276	−.069
Kevin Appier, KC	416	.224	294	.293	−.069
Mike Morgan, LA	471	.238	340	.306	−.068
Danny Darwin, Hou	410	.205	195	.267	−.062

These pitchers, finesse hurlers for the most part, are very dependent on getting ahead in the count. If they fall behind, they're more likely to get hurt than most pitchers — once the count is 1-and-0, the hitters bash them around at a plus-.300 pace in half the cases. Thus it's more vital for them to get the first pitch over than it was for the first group. At least some of them might be better off nibbling a little less on the first pitch, in order to make sure that they don't start falling behind.

Of course, it's not always quite that simple. When baseball men talk of pitchers like Frank Tanana or Greg Harris, they usually just say, "He has to throw strikes to be effective." What they mean is that, for pitchers of this ilk, working the corners is the only way they can survive. If they don't have that pinpoint location, chances are they're going to have an early shower. So while they may have a **little** margin for error — and maybe can nibble a little less on the first pitch — they don't have very much room to work with.

A complete listing for this category appears on page 295.

WHO WAS BETTER IN '90 — DWIGHT GOODEN OR JIM DESHAIES?

Those of you who read this book last year have smirks on your little faces, and have raised your hands in hopes that Teacher will call on you. For the rest of you, we'll let you in on a little secret: this is a trick question.

Last year Deshaies made 34 starts for the Astros, and Gooden recorded 34 starts for the Mets. Gooden's record was 19-7; Deshaies' record was 7-12, and that makes our question seem ridiculous. But look at their other stats. Deshaies allowed fewer hits per nine innings (8.0 to 8.9); he allowed fewer baserunners per nine (11.6 to 11.7 — intentional walks not included); and most tellingly, he had a lower ERA (3.78 to 3.83). The difference in their records was due almost entirely to run support. While Gooden was on the hill, the Mets were scoring 6.8 runs per nine innings for him. But when Deshaies was working for Houston, the Astros were managing a meager 3.5 runs per contest. We won't say that if the run support totals had been reversed, Gooden would have gone 7-12. (Dwight Gooden 7-12? Never!) But Doc certainly wouldn't have been 19-7.

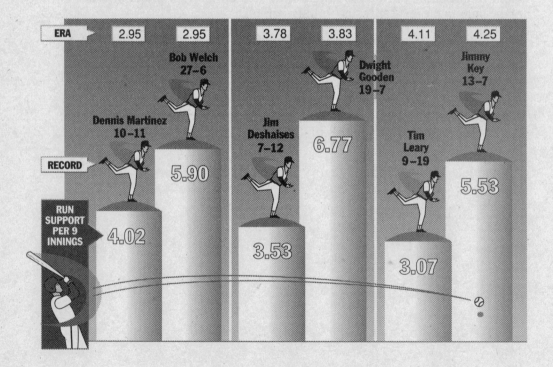

| ERA | 2.95 | 2.95 | 3.78 | 3.83 | 4.11 | 4.25 |

Bob Welch 27–6

Dennis Martinez 10–11

Dwight Gooden 19–7

Jimmy Key 13–7

Jim Deshaises 7–12

6.77

Tim Leary 9–19

RECORD

5.90

5.53

RUN SUPPORT PER 9 INNINGS

4.02

3.53

3.07

Though it seems so basic, the importance of run support to a pitcher's record is often seriously underestimated — even by people who should know better. Take the fair-haired boy of 1990, 27-game winner Bob Welch. There's no doubt that Welch pitched outstandingly last year. But as our graphic shows, Welch had the same ERA (2.95) as Montreal's Dennis Martinez, whose record was 10-11. Welch got 5.9 runs per nine innings of support from the A's; Martinez got 4.0 runs of support from the Expos.

Now compare Welch's support with those of his two main Cy Young rivals, Roger Clemens and Dave Stewart:

	W-L Record	ERA	Run Support per 9 Innings
Welch	27-6	2.95	5.90
Clemens	21-6	1.93	4.49
Stewart	22-11	2.56	5.02

We think Clemens and Stewart would have approached 27 wins, given Welch's kind of support.

The list of lucky pitchers who got the most run support in 1990 (minimum 20 starts) includes both Gooden and Welch. You'll note that, with one conspicuous exception, all had winning records despite a few hefty ERAs:

	W-L Record	ERA	Run Support per 9 Innings
Jeff Robinson, Det	10-9	5.96	7.08
Dwight Gooden, Mets	19-7	3.83	6.77
Doug Drabek, Pit	22-6	2.76	5.91
Ron Robinson, Cin-Mil	14-6	3.24	5.91
Bob Welch, Oak	27-6	2.95	5.90
Todd Stottlemyre, Tor	13-17	4.34	5.81
Pete Harnisch, Bal	11-11	4.34	5.77
Julio Navarro, Mil	8-7	4.99	5.77
John Burkett, SF	14-7	3.85	5.69
Storm Davis, KC	7-10	4.67	5.67

(Note: records are for pitchers' starting appearances only)

One of the two pitchers with a losing record was Storm Davis of the Royals. Poor, poor pitiful Storm. You might recall that when we discussed this subject a year ago, the first comparison we used was between Davis (19-7, 4.36 for the A's) and Doyle Alexander (6-18, 4.44 for the Tigers). We argued that Davis, given 6.5 runs a game to work with, hadn't pitched anywhere near as good as his 19-7 record indicated, and that he was a good candidate to flop in '90. Nonetheless, Davis signed a big-bucks contract with Kansas City (hey guys, we **warned** you), while Alexander couldn't find a job. Our hunch is that if the Royals had signed Alexander instead of Davis, they would have gotten pitching at least as good, and saved a lot of money besides.

The following pitchers got the worst run support in baseball last year (minimum 20 starts); it's practically a Cardinal-Yankee clubhouse meeting:

	W-L Record	ERA	Run Support per 9 Innings
Jose DeLeon, StL	7-19	4.43	2.96
Joe Magrane, StL	10-17	3.59	3.01
Andy Hawkins, Yanks	5-12	5.44	3.02
Tim Leary, Yanks	9-19	4.11	3.07
Mike Scott, Hou	9-13	3.81	3.11

The lousy-support Game of the Century could only be Hawkins' no-hitter against the White Sox last year, which he lost 4-0, on four unearned runs. Better luck in '91, Andy.

A complete listing for this category appears on page 296.

WHAT'S LASORDA DOING WITH RAMON MARTINEZ?

Ask anyone in baseball who the best young starting pitcher in baseball is, and one name is likely to come up: Ramon Martinez of the Dodgers. Last year, at the age of 22, Martinez won 20 games, lost only six, turned in a 2.92 earned run average, and struck out 223 batters in 234.1 innings. His performance helped make up for the Dodgers' loss of Orel Hershiser, and kept LA in the NL West race until the very end of the season. Remarkably, Martinez did all this in his first full major league season.

You'd think this was a portent of Cy Young Awards to come, and a long and successful career. A Cy Young Award in the very near future seems like a good bet for Martinez. And yet there are those who feel that Martinez faces an uncertain long-term future. It isn't that people doubt Martinez' talent; far from it. It's the way he's being used by Dodger manager Tom Lasorda. Lasorda loves to work his pitchers hard, and he made no exception of his newest young ace. Here's a list of the major league pitchers who threw the most pitches in 1990. We include their 1991 age (on 7/1/91) — for reasons we'll get into later — and the average number of pitches they threw per start:

Pitcher, Team	1991 Age	Starts	Innings	Total Pitches	Pitches per Start
Dave Stewart, Oak	34	36	267.0	3,977	110
Ramon Martinez, LA	23	33	234.1	3,802	115
Jack Morris, Det	36	36	249.2	3,753	104
Mark Langston, Cal	30	33	223.0	3,743	113
Eric Hanson, Sea	26	33	236.0	3,739	113
Randy Johnson, Sea	27	33	219.2	3,734	113
Bobby Witt, Tex	27	32	217.1	3,706	116
Dwight Gooden, Mets	26	34	232.2	3,690	109
Frank Viola, Mets	31	35	249.2	3,684	105
Chuck Finley, Cal	28	32	236.0	3,622	113

Martinez, by far the youngest hurler in the group, threw more pitches than anyone in the National League, and more than anyone in the majors except for Stewart. On a per-start basis, he again threw more pitches than anyone in the NL, and was second in the majors to Bobby Witt of Texas. Martinez threw 130 or more pitches in eight different starts, nearly a fourth of his starting assignments last year. He threw 148 pitches or more — an extremely heavy workload — three separate times.

What's wrong with that? The answer is simple: by using Martinez this way, Lasorda is taking a big risk of injuring him. Any pitcher's arm would be strained by the kind of usage Martinez is getting — but the strain is even worse for someone so young. STATS' Craig Wright has made an exhaustive study of pitchers' longevity, and Craig feels that it's very dangerous to overwork pitchers before the age of 25, when their arms are finally fully matured. In his excellent book, *The Diamond Appraised,* Wright offers this advice for the care and feeding of minor league pitchers: "For ages 20 to 22, (pitchers) should average no more than 105 pitches per start for the season. A single-game ceiling should be set at 130 pitches." Of course, Craig notes that at the major league level, managers cannot always afford to be that cautious. But he cites chapter and verse about pitchers who were overworked at a young age, but then faded out early. He also points out that the ones who survive are usually big and strong; Martinez, though 6-4, weighs only 172 pounds.

Many people will say that this theory of overwork is nonsense, and recall the sixties and early seventies, when pitchers routinely worked 300 innings or more per season. There are several things wrong with this argument:

1. Most of these pitchers were much older than Martinez, and their arms were fully developed when given the heavy workloads.

2. Even so, many of them came down with arm injuries or lost effectiveness at an early age.

3. With the complete game still an important goal, pitchers paced themselves much more than today's starters, who are expected to go all out until the bullpen takes over. As a result, the strain on the arms of today's pitchers can be just as great, if not greater, as it was in the days of the four-man rotation; current starters are not working 300 innings any more, but the strain per inning — and per start — is probably greater.

If you want some examples of the dangers of overworking starters, you need look no further than Martinez' Dodgers. In the sixties, Don Drysdale and Sandy Koufax pitched staggering totals of innings — than had to retire in their early thirties with arm problems. Andy Messersmith, the Dodgers' ace in the mid-seventies, was through as an effective pitcher at the age of 30. Since the early eighties, Lasorda has basically ridden three horses: first Fernando Valenzuela, who hasn't been a top pitcher since he was 25 (and worked 20 complete games for '86 Dodgers); then Hershiser, who went down last spring after he'd led the National League in innings pitched for three straight years; and now Martinez. Lasorda probably shouldn't be condemned for what happend to Hershiser; Orel was much older than Valenzuela or Martinez, and since he was an "economical" pitcher — not making a lot of pitches per inning — there was little reason to feel he was being overworked. But the younger arms of Valenzuela and Martinez are a different story.

Last year, in only his fourth start of the year, Martinez threw a staggering 152 pitches. He showed the effects: his next two outings were his worst of the year. You'd think that would have been a tipoff, wouldn't you? But Lasorda continued to take chances with his talented righthander — perhaps to the point of risking his future.

A complete listing for this category appears on page 297.

WHO WINS THE PITCHERS' "STAR WARS"?

One measure of a tough pitcher is how he performs against the best opponents. That can include the top teams; but it would also figure that he'd do well against the best of the best, the top hitters. For two years, we've kept track of which pitchers perform best against the top 15 batters in each league. The leaders list we compiled in 1989 was a little surprising; the one for 1990 is only slightly less so (minimum 60 opponents at bats):

Pitcher, Team	AB	H	HR	RBI	Avg	OBP	Slg
Matt Young, Sea	75	14	2	7	.187	.253	.280
Dennis Cook, Phi-LA	63	12	0	6	.190	.232	.254
Randy Johnson, Sea	91	18	1	9	.198	.282	.308
Jimmy Key, Tor	80	16	2	10	.200	.253	.338
Eric King, WSox	64	13	0	4	.203	.271	.234
Tom Browning, Cin	116	24	2	5	.207	.273	.293
Charlie Hough, Tex	72	15	1	4	.208	.374	.264
Chuck Finley, Cal	112	24	1	5	.214	.261	.321
Dennis Martinez, Mon	135	29	3	11	.215	.248	.326
Greg Hibbard, WSox	77	17	0	9	.221	.315	.312

Some good pitchers here — nothing wrong with a list which includes Matt Young, Randy Johnson, Jimmy Key, Tom Browning, Chuck Finley and Dennis Martinez, among others. It's a list of good pitchers . . . but it isn't a list of **great** pitchers. There's no Roger Clemens, Dave Stewart, Bob Welch; no Doug Drabek, Frank Viola, or Jose Rijo. What gives?

And then we remembered the leaders list from 1989, which was headed by the immortal Paul Kilgus, then of the Cubs. Unlike STATS, Inc., Kilgus did not ride his *Scoreboard* success to fame and fortune. He rode it to Toronto, where he promptly disappeared. (A savage business, baseball.) Which only deepens the mystery. That 1989 leaders list, like this one, was full of good-but-not great pitchers; Kilgus was almost certainly the worst of the bunch. In the article a year ago, we surmised that when a good hitter goes up against a top starting pitcher, he can psyche himself up, because that's his major challenge for the day. As a result, he may do better than expected. He may not psyche himself in quite the same way against pitchers of slightly lesser skills. So he has more trouble against them. It's one theory, anyway.

Is that a reasonable argument? Well, the top hitters of 1990 literally blasted the cream of the pitching crop. They hit Dwight Gooden at a .347 clip, Frank Viola at a .342 pace, Roger Clemens at .341. It goes on: Doug Drabek .327, Dave Stewart .315, Jose Rijo .307. In the confrontations between the very best pitchers and the very best hitters, the hitters won, convincingly, for the second year in a row. Strange . . . but true.

We'll offer one more possible explanation for the data. In this category, the leaders list in both 1989 and 1990 was dominated by lefthanded pitchers — four of the top five in 1989, the top four in '90. That may be because a disproportionate number of top hitters bat lefty. In last year's American League batting race, five of the top eight hitters batted lefty; in the NL, the top nine hitters included five lefties, three switch-hitters and only one righty. Against the very best hitters, throwing lefty is a needed edge. But, of course, it didn't help Frank Viola much, did it?

Who did **worst** against the top hitters? It increases the mystery of this category that the trailers list includes some respectable hurlers:

Pitcher, Team	AB	H	HR	RBI	Avg	OBP	Slg
Andy Hawkins, Yanks	68	30	2	11	.441	.513	.632
Mark Guthrie, Min	67	28	0	4	.418	.466	.537
Tom Candiotti, Cle	82	33	4	14	.402	.437	.622
Kevin Gross, Mon	85	34	4	19	.400	.460	.624
Terry Mulholland, Phi	93	37	5	15	.398	.434	.624

Not exactly a group of Cy Young candidates, but not bad either. Two of these guys (Hawkins and Mulholland) fashioned no-hitters last year. But we wouldn't like their chances if they were starting an All-Star game. Interestingly, Kevin Gross was in the bottom five in both 1989 and 1990. (Oooh, Gross!) If you can figure out exactly why, you're a lot smarter than we are.

The fair-haired boy in this category, Matt Young, ended the year by signing a hefty free-agent contract with the Red Sox. We hope you fare better than Paul Kilgus did in 1990, Matt.

A complete listing for this category can be found on page 298.

WHOSE HEATER IS THE HOTTEST?

When we were grade school kids back in the fifties, the hot game on the playgrounds of Chicago was called "fast-pitch." All you needed was two players, a bat, a rubber baseball, and a strike zone chalked onto the schoolyard wall. Each player would pitch to the other, and the game was strictly power-against-power. Hits or outs were recorded by how hard the batter hit the ball, but the idea was to avoid all that. Just strike the other guy out, and then run in for your turn at bat. Our heroes, logically enough, were the strikeout kings: Herb Score, Bob Turley, and more than anyone, the great — and scary — relief ace, Ryne Duren.

Looking at the playoffs and World Series last year, we could have sworn that "fast-pitch" had taken over the major leagues. What chance did the Pirates or A's have when the game went into the late innings, and the Reds trotted out Rob Dibble or Randy Myers? For that matter, why did Cincinnati even need fielders?

Pittsburgh and Oakland weren't the only clubs who were overmatched by the Nasty Boys last year. Looking at the 1990 leaders in strikeouts per nine innings, we find Dibble and Myers ranking first and fourth in the majors; the number-three man was a young fellow who probably played a little "fast-pitch" back in his own fifties childhood (though his was against the barn wall) — Nolan Ryan. The top ten:

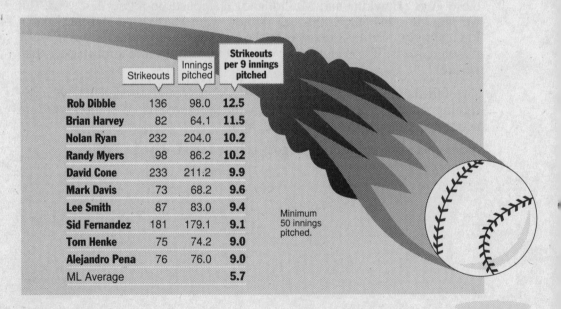

	Strikeouts	Innings pitched	Strikeouts per 9 innings pitched
Rob Dibble	136	98.0	12.5
Brian Harvey	82	64.1	11.5
Nolan Ryan	232	204.0	10.2
Randy Myers	98	86.2	10.2
David Cone	233	211.2	9.9
Mark Davis	73	68.2	9.6
Lee Smith	87	83.0	9.4
Sid Fernandez	181	179.1	9.1
Tom Henke	75	74.2	9.0
Alejandro Pena	76	76.0	9.0
ML Average			5.7

Minimum 50 innings pitched.

Ryan, at 43, was still getting the hang of things last year. He went into the season with a lifetime record of 9.55 strikeouts per nine innings . . . and proceeded to improve on it. The amazing Mr. Strikeout continued to outclass such young fireballers as David Cone, Dwight Gooden and his own teammate, Bobby Witt.

The question in our minds now is whether "fast-pitch" is going to take over the majors. In baseball, success breeds imitation, and every club in baseball was watching the Nasty Boys — and Jose Rijo, as well — overpower what was supposed to be an Oakland dynasty. During the Series, the Reds' pitchers' struck out more than three times as many batters as the A's moundsmen (28 to 9); compared to Cincinnati, the Oakland pitchers looked like a bunch of Chicago grade-school kids. Will we start to see a whole host of teams with two or three flamethrowers in their bullpen? We wouldn't be surprised.

Speaking of grade-school kids, you're probably wondering which pitchers recorded the **fewest** strikeouts per nine innings last year. Here they are:

Pitcher, Team	IP	SO	SO per 9
Billy Swift, Sea	128.0	42	2.95
Mark Knudson, Mil	168.1	56	2.99
Adam Peterson, WSox	85.0	29	3.07
Bob Tewksbury, StL	145.1	50	3.10
John Cerutti, Tor	140.0	49	3.15

With a name that belied his pitching style, Billy Swift offered proof last year that you don't need to blow hitters away in order to be an effective hurler. Despite ranking number last in the strikeout-per-nine category, Swift had a nifty ERA of 2.39.

No Oakland pitchers brought up the rear in this category, but Mike Moore, who fanned only 73 batters in 199.1 innings last year, was close, ranking number six. Once known for having an outstanding fastball, Moore's strikeout total dropped by nearly 100 from 1989 to 1990 — from 172 to 73. Will Moore spend the winter throwing fastballs against a playground wall? It might help.

A complete listing for this category appears on page 299.

WHAT IS THE "RED BARRETT TROPHY"?

Back in 1944, when most of the ballplayers were away fighting World War II, a Boston Braves pitcher named Red Barrett threw a complete game, according to legend, by tossing only 58 pitches in a game against the Reds. It's "according to legend" because no STATS reporter was present at Crosley Field that memorable day to record each pitch. A pity; where were you when we needed you, Dick Cramer?

The Red Barrett legend prompted us to wonder which pitchers were the most economical — they threw the fewest pitchers in a complete game (minimum eight innings in a losing effort, nine innings in a win) last year. Here they are:

Game & Score	Pitcher, Team	W/L	IP	H	R	ER	BB	K	# Pit.	
8/29 @Cin 9-1	Bob Tewksbury, SL	W	9	6	1	1	0	0	76	28
6/20 Min 8-0	Kevin Brown, Tex	W	9	4	0	0	0	4	79	34
8/17 Hou 5-0	Bob Tewksbury, SL	W	9	1	0	0	0	3	80	36.5
5/06 @ChN 8-3	Ed Whitson, SD	W	9	8	3	3	0	1	80	22.5
6/26 @Pit 0-1	Bruce Ruffin, Phi	L	8	6	1	1	0	2	80	15
9/30 @StL 2-0	Doug Drabek, Pit	W	9	3	0	0	0	2	80	34
4/20 SF 9-2	Ed Whitson, SD	W	9	9	2	2	0	3	85	24.5
7/18 NYN 1-0	Mike Scott, SD	W	9	4	0	0	0	4	85	34
5/10 @Min 2-3	Greg Swindell, Cle	L	8	7	3	3	2	3	86	8.5
7/21 ChA 2-0	Ben McDonald, Bal	W	9	4	0	0	1	5	86	33.5

We were mildly surprised to discover there were so many low-pitch outings; of course, that may be because we here at STATS are used to covering White Sox games. Tewksbury threw only three complete games all last year. He won them all while tossing 76, 80 and 93 pitches. Tewks is the unquestioned ruler of his category, but he's got some nice company. Despite the inclusion of Mike Scott and Ben McDonald, it's primarily a group of pitchers who don't walk or strike out many batters; they make the guy hit the ball. Nobody walked more than two, or struck out more than five, in his low-pitch effort.

As for Tewksbury's Red Barrett Award-winning game, it must have delighted anyone who prefers a fast-paced game. Tewks, the quickest worker in the majors last year, was matched against the Reds' Tom Browning, who has the same style: get it, throw it, don't mind if they hit it. The Cardinals did just that, pounding out nine runs and 14 hits (another unlikely occurrence). Nevertheless, the game was over in two hours. We wish we had been there.

We're not sure we would have liked to have been **here**, however — at the games where the starters threw the most pitches in a complete-game effort:

Game & Score		Pitcher, Team	W/L	IP	H	R	ER	BB	K	# Pit.	
4/28 ChN	5-4	Ramon Martinez, LA	W	9	7	4	3	1	10	152	26
8/26 ChN	4-3	John Smoltz, Atl	W	9	6	3	1	2	8	152	28
9/28 @ChA	13-4	Randy Johnson, Sea	W	9	10	4	3	2	11	151	22.5
6/12 @Det	7-3	Bud Black, Cle	W	9	8	3	3	3	4	151	21
9/14 @Cin	10-4	Fernando Valenzuela, LA	W	9	9	4	4	4	4	151	14
6/08 @Bos	3-4	John Farrell, Cle	L	8	6	4	4	4	6	149	4
6/16 SD	5-2	Ramon Martinez, LA	W	9	4	2	1	4	8	149	29
6/22 @ChN	7-0	Joe Magrane, SL	W	9	3	0	0	3	11	149	35.5
9/09 Cin	6-4	Ramon Martinez, LA	W	9	8	4	4	3	8	148	18
7/29 Phi	2-1	Doug Drabek, Pit	W	9	2	1	1	7	8	147	30

We comment in another essay on Tommy Lasorda's heavy-duty usage of his young ace, Ramon Martinez. You can see it here, with Martinez working three of the top nine "endurance tests." We'd give Martinez an award, also, but we're not sure he could lift his right arm to accept it.

Interestingly, Doug Drabek, who had an 80-pitch effort, also worked a complete game in which he threw 147 pitches while winning 2-1. Drabek will take either kind of win, but he'll remember the 80-pitch game on Sept. 30 for a long time. That was the win that clinched the NL East crown for the Pirates.

A complete listing for this category can be found on page 300.

WHO'S TOUGHEST TO HIT?

We warned you a year ago that Nolan Ryan was slipping, and as usual (we say modestly), we were right. In 1989 Ryan held his American League opponents to a .187 batting average; in 1990 they creamed him at a .188 clip. We were right on the mark (we say, even more modestly) in noting in our first book that American League hitters were catching up to Ryan at the rate of about one batting average point per year (.171 in 1972, .188 in 1990). Cheer up, Junior Circuiters. At this rate Ryan will be an average pitcher by the year 2061. He'll be 114 years old then; maybe you could try bunting on him.

Ryan is not the only current pitcher who, in this category, is "one for the ages." Here are 1990 leaders in lowest opponents' batting average (minimum 500 opponents' at bats) — and remember the number two man, Sid Fernandez:

Pitcher, Team	Avg	AB	H
Nolan Ryan, Tex	.188	729	137
Sid Fernandez, Mets	.200	650	130
Jose Rijo, Cin	.212	712	151
Randy Johnson, Sea	.216	806	174
Ramon Martinez, LA	.221	866	191
Doug Drabek, Pit	.225	846	190
John Tudor, StL	.225	534	120
Danny Darwin, Hou	.225	605	136
David Cone, Mets	.226	784	177

What's so special about Fernandez? People say that New York athletes are overrated, but often the opposite is true; with all those media eyes looking for the slightest flaw, a guy has to be pretty near perfect, and Fernandez, 78-59 lifetime, is hardly that. So you may not know that Sid is one of the toughest pitchers to hit of all time. According to the excellent book, the *Total Baseball 1990 Update,* the lifetime leaders in opponents' batting average were Ryan (.204) and Sandy Koufax (.205). Ryan's 1990 efforts lowered his lifetime mark a point to .203, but Fernandez is just behind him, and just ahead of Koufax, at .204. (Nice company.) With only 1212 career innings, Fernandez doesn't yet qualify for the lifetime leaders list, which requires 1500 minimum. But he'll be there soon, and hopefully he won't have to wait until then to gain a little more respect.

It's a little tough for **these** guys to get respect, based on their 1990 figures. Here are last season's trailers in opponents' batting average:

Pitcher, Team	Avg	AB	H
Roy Smith, Min	.313	611	191
Bert Blyleven, Cal	.303	538	163
John Cerutti, Tor	.297	546	162
Bruce Ruffin, Phi	.297	599	178
Jim Abbott, Cal	.295	833	246
Walt Terrell, Pit-Det	.293	629	184
Jaime Navarro, Mil	.293	600	176
Dennis Rasmussen, SD	.292	742	217
Dave LaPoint, Yanks	.292	617	180
Jeff Ballard, Bal	.290	525	152

When we looked at this subject a year ago, we noted that a number of the trailers were struggling to keep their major league careers. It may be an ominous sign that the struggle is now over for Jerry Reuss, Mike Smithson, Richard Dotson and Shane Rawley — those pension checks will be arriving before you know it, fellows. (And what ever became of Don August, who is not to be confused with Dan August, once played on TV by Burt Reynolds? Enjoying that "Evening Shade," Don? It just shows you what an unforgiving business baseball is. Not to mention the television business.) The 1990 trailers will, however, take heart from the fact that Dave Schmidt, Charlie Leibrandt, Mike Witt and Andy Hawkins, all among the worst in 1989, have rehabilitated their careers at least to some extent. Good luck in 1991, guys.

A complete listing of this category appears on page 301.

WHO'S EASIEST TO STEAL ON?

Stopping the running game is an important element in any club's defensive strategy. That's especially true in the National League, where the parks are bigger, the grass is plastic and the stolen base is king. Even so, some pitchers never seem to get the hang of preventing the stolen base. So who are these hapless bums, these dregs of pitching society? Frank Forgetful, maybe? Louie Lettemsteal? No, the list of pitchers who allowed the most stolen bases per nine innings last year includes some very famous names. The leaders (minimum 100 innings):

Pitcher, Team	Throws	SB	CS	Pick-offs	Stolen Base %	Stolen Bases per 9
Dwight Gooden, Mets	R	60	16	8	79.0	2.32
Mike Scott, Hou	R	53	7	0	88.3	2.32
Rob Dibble, Cin	R	20	3	0	87.0	1.84
Steve Avery, Atl	L	20	8	0	71.4	1.82
Ron Darling, Mets	R	24	4	15	85.7	1.71
Kevin Gross, Mon	R	31	5	4	86.1	1.71
Jack Morris, Det	R	45	6	4	88.2	1.62
Lee Smith, Bos-StL	R	14	5	0	73.7	1.52
Andy McGaffigan, SF-KC	R	14	0	0	100.0	1.51
Larry Andersen, Hou-Bos	R	16	3	0	84.2	1.51

You could fashion a pretty good pitching staff out of Gooden, Scott, Darling, Gross and Morris (starters), Avery (spot starter), McGaffigan and Andersen (middle relievers), Dibble (set-up man) and Smith (closer). Of course, your catcher's arm would fall off by Memorial Day, but you can't have everything.

How do these pitchers win despite being stolen blind? Primarily, by throwing hard and blowing the hitters away. Good fastballers usually have high leg kicks, which means that the anyone trying to steal is apt to get a good jump. When you have a high leg kick, even having a good pickoff move, as Gooden and Darling do, won't prevent the runners from going.

Now compare that list with this one, the **toughest** pitchers to steal on in 1990:

Pitcher, Team	Throws	SB	CS	Pick- offs	Stolen Base %	Stolen Bases per 9
Jeff Pico, Cubs	R	0	4	1	0.0	0.00
Mike Jeffcoat, Tex	L	0	6	0	0.0	0.00
Billy Swift, Sea	R	0	2	1	0.0	0.00
Dave Johnson, Bal	R	1	4	0	20.0	0.05
John Mitchell, Bal	R	1	2	1	33.3	0.08
Alex Fernandez, WSox	R	1	4	1	20.0	0.10
Greg Swindell, Cle	L	3	12	2	20.0	0.13
Bret Saberhagen, KC	R	2	5	10	28.6	0.13
Terry Mulholland, Phi	L	3	3	6	50.0	0.15
Bruce Ruffin, Phi	L	3	4	2	42.9	0.18

So who would you rather have, Dwight Gooden or Jeff Pico? Mike Scott or Mike Jeffcoat? Rob Dibble or Billy Swift? We think you catch our drift. The pitchers who are toughest to steal on are primarily finesse hurlers. They usually don't throw very hard, so a shorter leg kick or a slide step isn't going to harm them much. These guys usually allow a lot of baserunners, and they've learned to control the running game for a very good reason: they have to, in order to survive.

Of course, it's an oversimplification to say that anyone who throws hard is going to be helpless against the stolen base. Roger Clemens, who throws at least as hard as Gooden, allowed less than one fourth the steals Doc allowed per nine innings last year (0.55 for Clemens, 2.32 for Gooden). On the toughest-to-steal-against list, Saberhagen and Swindell have excellent fastballs. The guys who are easy to steal on probably won't change their styles until they stop winning. Which doesn't look like any time soon.

A complete listing for this category appears on page 302.

WHAT'S THE LONG AND THE SHORT OF IT FOR PITCHERS?

Three of the best young pitchers in the American League are Randy Johnson of the Mariners, Ben McDonald of the Orioles, and Tom Gordon of the Royals. In his first full season in the majors last year, Johnson won 14 games, recorded a 3.65 earned run average, and punctuated his efforts by throwing a no-hitter. McDonald, a rookie who was the first player chosen in the 1989 draft, got a later start — but in barely a half season, he was a very impressive 8-5 with a 2.43 ERA. Gordon's second season with the Royals was something of a disappointment after he'd won 17 games as a 1989 rookie. But Gordon still won a dozen contests, averaged nearly a strikeout an inning, and posted a decent 3.73 ERA.

There are lots of good young pitchers around, so what's so special about Johnson, McDonald and Gordon? Their height. Johnson, at 6-10, is the tallest pitcher in major league history. McDonald, at 6-7, is a little less of a curiosity, but his work last year indicated that he could become one of the best king-sized pitchers in major league history. Gordon, on the other hand, is just 5-9, and that makes him unusual as well — a winning pitcher who stands well under six feet.

One of the joys of baseball is that you don't have to a freak in order to succeed. That goes double for pitching, where muscular coordination counts much more than mere size. Walter Johnson, "the Big Train," was all of 6-1 and weighed 200 pounds. Christy Mathewson, known as "Big Six," was only 6-1½ and 195 pounds. Johnson and Mathewson were big for their day, but Bob Feller, the most feared strikeout pitcher of the thirties and forties, stood only six feet tall and weighed 185. As people have gotten bigger, so have pitchers. Nonetheless, such feared moderns as Sandy Koufax and Nolan Ryan were hardly huge — both stood 6-2, and weighed 210 and 220 pounds, respectively.

The success of guys like Randy Johnson and Ben McDonald suggests that things might be changing. But we'd venture that they're changing less than you think. We looked through our historical database to find seasons from pitchers who stood at least 6-7, won at least 15 games, and had ERAs less than 3.00. Not very imposing standards . . . but there were only a handful of such seasons, all from the recent past.

The Good Big Men (6-7 or Taller)

Name	Year	ERA	W	L	Pct	Height
Candelaria, John	1977	2.34	20	5	.800	6-7
Richard, J.R.	1979	2.71	18	13	.581	6-8
Richard, J.R.	1976	2.75	20	15	.571	6-8
Witt, Mike	1986	2.84	18	10	.643	6-7
Richard, J.R.	1977	2.97	18	12	.600	6-8

THE GOOD TALL MEN (6'7" or taller)	Year	W–L	Height
John Candelaria	1977	20–5	6'7"
J.R. Richard	1979	18–13	6'8"
J.R. Richard	1976	20–15	6'8"
Mike Witt	1986	18–10	6'7"
J.R. Richard	1977	18–12	6'8"

THE GOOD LITTLE MEN (5'9" or less)	Year	W–L	Height
Dolf Luque	1923	27–8	5'7"
Luis Arroyo	1961	15–5	5'8"
Bobby Shantz	1952	24–7	5'6"
Tom Phoebus	1968	15–15	5'8"
Ted Wilks	1944	17–4	5'9"
Lee Meadows	1920	16–14	5'9"

The Candy Man, John Candelaria, hangs on as the most durable big pitcher of all time. At 37, Candelaria has won 174 games, easily the most for a pitcher 6-7 or taller; Ron Reed, the number-two man, is next with only 146. Candelaria might have been challenged by the Astros' J.R. Richard, who was felled by a stroke at age 30 with 107 wins. For short-term brilliance, Richard was unmatched among the very tall pitchers. But in terms of career effectiveness, Candelaria outpaces the field. Rick Sutcliffe, a very good oversized pitcher (6-7), has only 133 career wins.

Good undersized pitchers, like Tom Gordon, were much more common in the early days of baseball, when people in general were much smaller. But if we restrict our study to the years since 1920, we find only a handful of pitchers who stood 5-9 or less, and had seasons in which they both won at least 15 games and had ERAs under 3.00:

The Good Little Men (5-9 or Less)

Name	Year	ERA	W	L	Pct	Height
Luque, Dolf	1923	1.93	27	8	.771	5-7
Arroyo, Luis	1961	2.19	15	5	.750	5-8
Shantz, Bobby	1952	2.47	24	7	.774	5-6
Phoebus, Tom	1968	2.61	15	15	.500	5-8
Wilks, Ted	1944	2.64	17	4	.810	5-9
Meadows, Lee	1920	2.84	16	14	.533	5-9

Not exactly a list of well-known names. Arroyo, the screwballing relief ace of the 1961 Yankees, is probably the most familiar to modern fans. Dolf Luque, probably the best pint-sized pitcher in the last 75 years, was one of the first Cuban players to appear in the major leagues. Luque won 194 games in a 20-year career; at only 5-7, he stood very tall.

The evidence indicates that, even now, it's difficult for a pitcher of unusual size to have a long and effective career. Randy Johnson, Ben McDonald and Tom Gordon will be bucking some very tough odds.

WHO ARE THE MOST EFFICIENT RELIEF PITCHERS?

The starting pitcher, like a long-distance truck driver, is in the game for the long haul. If he needs to fiddle with his gears against the first few hitters, there's plenty of time for him to recover. The relief pitcher, by contrast, is like a guy operating a drag racer: he needs everything in sync from the moment he hits the gas. Many a game has been lost when a reliever got belted for a crucial knock by the first batter he faced.

The following relievers emulated dragdom's Don (Big Daddy) Garletts last year — they zoomed down the straightaway from the moment they came into the game. Presenting the 1990 leaders in first batter efficiency (minimum 30 first batters faced in relief):

Player, Team	Avg	AB	H	HR	BB	SO
Danny Darwin, Hou	.000	28	0	0	2	9
Terry Leach, Min	.125	48	6	0	3	5
Gary Wayne, Min	.125	32	4	1	3	7
Bobby Thigpen, WSox	.127	63	8	2	9	12
Duane Ward, Tor	.129	70	9	1	3	22
Mike Schooler, Sea	.130	46	6	0	2	9
Darrel Akerfelds, Phi	.133	60	8	0	7	8
Stan Belinda, Pit	.146	48	7	1	6	16
Don Carman, Phi	.149	47	7	1	8	9
Willie Fraser, Cal	.154	39	6	1	5	4

As was the case when we studied the subject a year ago, the list is dominated by middle relievers rather than late men. The only true closers in the bunch are Bobby Thigpen and Mike Schooler. This points out the increasing specialization of the modern game. Until recently, the ace reliever was apt to appear whenever a late-inning jam developed. Now the vogue is to save the late man until the ninth inning whenever possible; more often than not, he'll come in to start the frame, with a little breathing room. If he lets the first guy get on, he usually has time to recover.

These days it's the middle relievers who usually come in during a jam. They do have one edge: since there are several middle men in every bullpen, they'll ordinarily be brought in with a platoon advantage, lefties to face lefties and righties to face righties. That's a good reason why southpaws like Gary Wayne and Don Carman were so high up on the leaders list. Both were ultra-tough against lefties — Wayne held them to a .174 average, Carman to a .175 mark — and the first batters they faced were usually lefties. Unfortunately, each had to face some righthanders eventually.

Interestingly, the guy who was numero uno in first-batter efficiency last year, Danny Darwin of the Astros, proved himself a little too efficient for a set-up role. Darwin was moved into the starting rotation in mid-season, and proceeded to lead the National League in ERA. Darwin proved he could do more than just retire the first batter.

Not so the following hurlers, the most **inefficient** relievers in 1990 against the first batter faced:

Player, Team	Avg	AB	H	HR	BB	SO
Bill Landrum, Pit	.423	52	22	2	1	5
Todd Burns, Oak	.400	35	14	2	5	8
Jim Acker, Tor	.382	55	21	2	4	5
Rob Murphy, Bos	.371	62	23	3	4	15
Rich Rodiguez, SD	.367	30	11	0	2	2

No wonder Pirates manager Jim Leyland lost faith in Landrum, who was his closer for much of the year. Landrum had some good overall stats, like a 2.13 ERA, but Leyland lost patience with the way he kept getting himself into trouble. Similarly, Todd Burns' first-batter woes may be one reason why the A's haven't given him a bigger role.

And then there's Paul Assenmacher, who finished the year as the Cubs' closer. Assenmacher allowed a major-league-leading four homers to first batters. That's probably why the Cubs didn't want to keep him as their late man.

A complete listing of this category appears on page 303.

WHO (STILL) THROWS TO FIRST?

A year ago, when we did this book for the first time, one of the most controversial essays was the one called, "Who Throws to First?" Some people, a few of whom actually read the book — but including several heavies in the world of Major League Baseball — attacked it. Our responses — we studied the subject because we try to find out something about baseball; we did it because we represent Jim Deshaies' agent; we did it because it was fun — didn't seem to satisfy people.

So you won't see any essays entitled "Who Throws to First?" in this book. Instead we present an entirely new-and-original essay called, "Who (Still) Throws to First?" For which we offer the following two justifications:

1. If pitchers' throws to first are a waste of time, why do even intelligent pitchers do it?

2. If pitchers' throws to first **aren't** a waste of time, why is it a waste of time to study the subject?

3. We represent Charlie Hough's agent.

With those caveats, here are the 1990 leaders in pitchers' throws to first:

Pitcher	Pickoff Throws		Pick-offs	Stolen Bases	
	Total	Per 9		Total	Per 9
Charlie Hough, Tex	368	15.2	3	33	1.36
Jim Deshaies, Hou	341	14.7	2	21	0.90
John Burkett, SF	280	12.4	1	18	0.79
Tom Glavine, Atl	272	11.4	0	22	0.92
Roger Clemens, Bos	269	10.6	1	14	0.55
Jeff Parrett, Phi-Atl	213	17.6	3	8	0.66
Don Robinson, SF	209	11.9	2	19	1.08
Jack McDowell, WSox	209	9.2	2	23	1.01
Kevin Brown, Tex	209	10.5	1	7	0.35
David Cone, Mets	208	8.8	3	23	0.98

What a tough break for Jim Deshaies, the feature of a Sports Illustrated article on the pitchers who threw to first the most in 1989. If Deshaies had known about Charlie Hough, maybe he would have thrown to first even with no one on base, in order to retain his title. As for Hough, he might end up with an Energizer endorsement contract: he keeps throwing and throwing and throwing to first . . .

The question, though, is whether all those throws were a waste of time. What can we say after looking at the 1990 leaders list?

1. "Mr. Throw to First" for 1990 might be either Hough (the most pickoff throws) or Jeff Parrett (the most on a throws-per-nine-innings basis. We'll leave it to you guys to decide who's the real champion.

2. Throwing to first didn't seem to help Hough a lot; he was still an easy pitcher to steal on. It didn't seem to help Dwight Gooden much, either. Gooden ranked 11th in most throws to first last year, but he still allowed 60 stolen bases — most in the majors. However, Parrett, the most prolific thrower to first on a per-nine basis, allowed only 0.66 steals per nine innings, which was well below the major league average of 0.79.

4. Before we conclude that throwing to first is just a waste of time, look at Roger Clemens. The Rocket, whose fast-balling, high leg-kicking style is pretty similar to Gooden's, not only throws to first a lot, but doesn't allow many stolen bases, either — a formidable accomplishment for a pitcher who throws so hard.

5. Perhaps the toughest pitcher to steal on in the majors is Dave Johnson of the Orioles. Johnson threw to first 104 times last year, about an average amount for a pitcher with his workload, but still allowed only one steal all year.

Throwing to first, as we show in another part of the book, does seem to help keep runners honest. But when it comes to throwing repeatedly, it's not how often you throw, but the strength of your legkick and the effectiveness of your move which determines whether runners will be will willing to go.

A complete listing for this category can be found on page 304.

DID THE LOCKOUT LOCK OUT THE PITCHERS?

Remember the fun spring of 1990 — owners locking out players, and dark talk of the season being cancelled? Eventually, the Cooler Heads prevailed (heck of a team, those Cooler Heads), an agreement was reached, and the season got under way a week late. The most serious consequence of the lockout was that spring training was shortened considerably. You'll recall that most clubs left camp warning that their pitchers would take a awhile to reach their usual form.

That's what we heard . . . but what actually happened? If the pitchers were off-form at the start of the year, you'd expect them to post poorer figures in April and possibly May as well. You'd also expect fewer complete games, and you'd expect the managers to use more relief pitchers per game. Let's look at the month-by-month data for the American League last year; we include data for starters (including complete games and innings pitched per game started) and relievers (including the number of relief pitchers per game):

		All Pitchers					Starters			Relievers	
Month	G	ERA	Avg	Slg	OBP	HR/G	CG	ERA	IP/GS	ERA	RP/G
April	132	3.90	.256	.388	.327	1.67	7	4.11	5.52	3.56	2.36
May	193	3.93	.256	.391	.323	1.74	40	4.22	6.03	3.33	2.01
June	196	3.96	.264	.398	.329	1.67	33	4.22	6.06	3.40	1.92
July	197	3.96	.261	.394	.329	1.70	48	3.99	6.09	3.88	1.88
August	200	3.93	.261	.382	.327	1.46	52	4.08	6.30	3.57	1.73
September	195	3.88	.258	.377	.330	1.38	43	3.83	6.15	4.00	2.04
October	20	3.24	.242	.343	.310	0.90	6	3.18	6.43	3.40	1.92

As you can see, the American League pitchers didn't seem to be bothered much by the lockout. The starters did work fewer innings per outing in April, and there was heavier use of relievers early in the year, but that was probably due more to managerial caution than anything. Certainly the overall results don't show many ill-effects. Opponents batting average showed the normal pattern (lower in the cool-weather months, higher in the summertime), and the league ERA varied little from month to month. The one figure that dropped over the course of the year was the home run rate, which dropped abruptly beginning in August. Were the pitchers finally in shape then? Frankly, we find it unlikely that it would take them until the 100-game mark to recover from missing a few weeks of spring training. Six weeks, perhaps, but not **that** long.

Here are the figures for the National League (note — opponents batting average, slugging and on-base percentage do not include pitchers' hitting):

National League											
	All Pitchers						Starters			Relievers	
Month	G	ERA	Avg	Slg	OBP	HR/G	CG	ERA	IP/GS	ERA	RP/G
April	114	3.66	.260	.381	.327	1.39	15	3.62	5.93	3.74	2.30
May	160	3.93	.272	.412	.336	1.69	30	4.00	6.02	3.77	2.15
June	168	4.10	.270	.416	.340	1.78	32	4.14	6.08	4.01	2.07
July	166	3.77	.261	.391	.326	1.49	31	3.87	6.17	3.56	1.90
August	173	3.58	.266	.391	.329	1.43	46	3.65	6.24	3.43	1.97
September	173	3.67	.255	.385	.325	1.47	43	3.94	5.92	3.16	2.11
October	18	4.18	.272	.415	.331	1.61	3	4.01	5.74	4.51	2.31

National League pitchers actually posted much better figures in April, when they were presumably out of shape, than they did in either May or June. However, they pitched much better — in almost every category, but especially in reducing the home run rate — after July 1. Once again we find it unlikely that it took them half a season to get into shape . . . if that were the case, why would they have pitched so well in April?

The only mystery, then, is why the home run rate dropped. Official baseball people keep assuring us that there's no such thing as a "lively" ball, that the baseball is identical to the one used in Babe Ruth's day. When the home run rate jumped to outrageous levels in 1987, turning guys like Larry Sheets into sluggers-for-a-year, we were assured that the problem was not the ball, but lousy pitching. When the pitchers reasserted themselves in 1988, we were assured the problem was lousy hitting. Could there have been a livelier ball in use for half of 1990? We can't say for sure, but we find that a more plausible explanation than blaming the lockout.

WHICH PITCHERS CAN REST IN PEACE?

Once upon a time, in the countries of the Left Coast, two rulers went to their final resting place (in this case, a hot shower). Both Lord Nelson — Lord "Gino" Nelson — of the North and Prince Andrew Benes of the South left generous bequests to their heirs. Lord Nelson's heirs — mainly the clever Richard of Honeycutt and the brilliantly precise Dennis of Eckersley — nurtured and cared for their bequest, and the House of Nelson prospered, to the tune of a 1.57 earned run average. But Prince Andrew's heirs — the immature Gregory of Harris, the frivolous Marcus of Grant (later exiled), and the self-doubting Calvin of Schiraldi (who had once squandered a similar bequest from a certain Duke Roger of Clemens) — foolishly lost almost all that Andrew had left them. As a result, people shook their heads when examining the House of Benes and said, "He haddeth a bad year (10-11, 3.60)."

This is not just a parable; it really happened. Last year middle reliever Gene Nelson of the A's had an outstanding ERA, but he could give a lot of credit to the great Oakland relievers who followed him; Nelson left — or bequeathed — 23 runners to the bullpen men who followed him, and the relievers allowed only one to score. That was a big factor in his nifty 1.57 ERA. Benes, meanwhile, left 21 runners to his shaky San Diego relievers, and 13 of those runners wound up crossing the plate; as an almost direct result, he turned in that mediocre 3.60 ERA. But reverse the situation. Say Nelson's relievers had allowed his runners to score the way Benes' relievers did, and vice versa. Nelson would have allowed 13 more earned runs, and his ERA would have been nearly twice as high (3.13 instead of 1.57). Benes would have allowed 12 fewer earned runs, and his ERA would have dropped from 3.60 to 3.04 — and people would have been a lot less inclined to say he had a bad year.

In the modern game, starters seldom go nine innings, and there's usually more than one reliever before the game is finished. Winning or losing depends on more than one pitcher, and the pitchers' stats are inter-dependent as well. Look at the following groups of 1990 pitchers. In the first group, the relievers allowed most of the bequeathed runners to score; in the second, the bullpen basically closed the door (minimum 20 runners left):

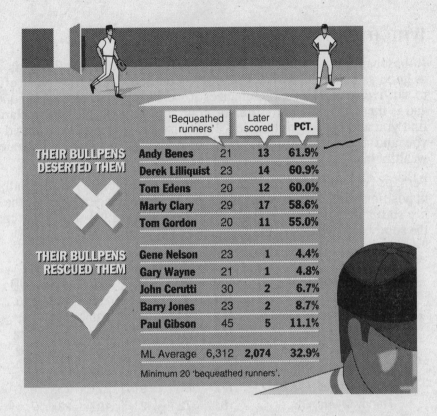

	'Bequeathed runners'	Later scored	PCT.
THEIR BULLPENS DESERTED THEM			
Andy Benes	21	13	**61.9%**
Derek Lilliquist	23	14	**60.9%**
Tom Edens	20	12	**60.0%**
Marty Clary	29	17	**58.6%**
Tom Gordon	20	11	**55.0%**
THEIR BULLPENS RESCUED THEM			
Gene Nelson	23	1	**4.4%**
Gary Wayne	21	1	**4.8%**
John Cerutti	30	2	**6.7%**
Barry Jones	23	2	**8.7%**
Paul Gibson	45	5	**11.1%**
ML Average	6,312	**2,074**	**32.9%**

Minimum 20 'bequeathed runners'.

As we've demonstrated with the Nelson/Benes comparison, how the subsequent relievers perform can have a huge effect on a pitcher's stats. Here's one more example. John Cerutti of the Blue Jays had a very mediocre year last year: nine wins, nine losses, a 4.76 ERA. But Cerutti was actually **helped** by his bullpen. If he'd gotten Andy Benes-type support from his relievers, his ERA would have been a hideous 5.85! No wonder the Blue Jays didn't offer him a contract.

The lesson from this is that even stats like ERA have to be looked at with a skeptical eye. As we show in another essay, the A's relievers allowed only 24 percent of their inherited runners to score last year. The relievers from the Padres and Braves, meanwhile, allowed over 40 percent of their inherited runners to cross the plate. A pitcher can bequeath a fortune to the hurlers who follow him; but how they perform — especialy if they're very bad or exceptionally good — will be a big factor in how **he** is perceived.

A complete listing for this category appears on page 305.

WHICH SOUTHPAWS EAT LEFTIES?

In baseball, being a left-handed pitcher, in particular a reliever, is almost as good as being the owner's nephew. You don't have to be very effective to survive, you'll get more chances to screw up than almost anyone else, and if the manager finally tires of your act . . . well, old Uncle Harry will find you another job right quick. How else can you explain a world where you and I have to struggle to make a living, but Dan Schatzeder is a wealthy man?

Perhaps we overstate the case a little. The ability to neutralize the opposition's left-handed guns is prized by any manager, whether the hurler is a starter or a reliever. A look at the 1990 leaders list shows that many of the southpaws were very tough against righties as well:

Player, Team	Vs. Lefties			Vs. Righties		
	Avg	AB	HR	Avg	AB	HR
Dan Plesac, Mil	.161	62	0	.286	199	5
Rick Honeycutt, Oak	.163	86	1	.230	139	1
Zane Smith, Pit	.164	116	1	.258	685	14
Bobby Ojeda, Mets	.168	113	1	.307	339	9
Don Carman, Phi	.175	103	7	.239	213	6
Scott Radinsky, WSox	.177	62	0	.271	133	1
Randy Myers, Cin	.181	72	2	.197	234	4
Wayne Edwards, WSox	.183	93	1	.253	253	5
Ken Patterson, WSox	.194	67	0	.260	173	6
Atlee Hammaker, SF-SD	.194	67	2	.276	261	6

(Minimum 60 AB by left-handed hitters)

Some of these names should be familiar to you from 1989. Smith, Honeycutt and Myers all ranked near the top in this category in 1989. Looking at their brilliant figures for the two years, one wonders why any manager would bother sending up a lefty — except maybe a Tony Gwynn or a Wade Boggs — to face them:

Player, Team	1989 vs. LHB			1990 vs. LHB			1989-90 vs. LHB		
	Avg	AB	HR	Avg	AB	HR	Avg	AB	HR
Smith	.143	140	1	.164	116	1	.152	256	2
Honeycutt	.156	90	1	.163	86	1	.159	176	2
Myers	.164	73	2	.181	72	2	.172	145	4

One reason Smith, Honeycutt and Myers had outstanding seasons last year was that in addition to being extremely effective against lefties, they were able to hold their own against righthanders. That wasn't the case among all the 1990 leaders, however. Plesac, Ojeda and Hammaker all had mediocre seasons because they had too many problems against righties. And while Don Carman had low opponents' batting averages against both kinds of hitters, he was plagued by the home run ball versus each.

Lest you think that all southpaws shine against lefty swingers, look at this list:

Player, Team	Vs. Lefties			Vs. Righties		
	Avg	AB	HR	Avg	AB	HR
Mark Guthrie, Min	.343	99	1	.262	458	7
Derek Lilliquist, Atl-SD	.326	92	3	.275	386	13
Neal Heaton, Pit	.311	90	4	.254	453	13
Dennis Cook, Phi-LA	.296	135	4	.252	456	16
Jeff Ballard, Bal	.294	136	4	.287	390	18

These five had the worst records against lefties last year — in fact, all of them were better against righties than against their own kind. Not surprisingly, almost all had rocky seasons. Lilliquist and Cook were traded in mid-season, Heaton faded after a hot start, and Ballard, an 18-game winner in 1989, was 2-11 in 1990. Rookie Mark Guthrie was one of the better pitchers on a lousy Twins staff, but he'll have to improve his work against lefties — or hope his uncle buys a ballclub — if he wants to have an effective career.

A complete listing for this category can be found on page 306.

WAS ECK THE BEST EVER?

It was a performance for the ages — not once, but twice. In 1989 Dennis Eckersley turned in one of the best pitching performances of all time: a 1.56 earned run average, 33 saves in 39 opportunities, only 32 hits and an unreal three walks allowed in 57.2 innings. Eckersley held his opponents to a .162 batting average and an amazing .175 on-base average. He averaged nearly a strikeout per inning, as well (55/57.2). Who could top that? Eckersley could. In 1990 Eck had an 0.61 ERA, 48 saves in 50 opportunities, 41 hits and only four walks — one of those intentional — in 73.1 innings. He lowered his opponents' batting average to .160, and his opponents' on-base average to .172. No mere control pitcher, he nudged his strikeout rate to just below one an inning (73/73.1).

Eckersley's numbers in 1989 and 1990 were so good that they deserve some perspective. Our historical database now goes back to 1920 (the beginning of the home run era), and we decided to compare Eckersley 1989-90 with all the pitchers who worked 50 or more innings in a season since that time. At times we'll be comparing Eck, a reliever who's worked a total of 131 innings over two years, with starters who toiled 300 innings or more in a year. But let's have some fun and do it anyway.

The first task was to find all pitchers since 1920 who met the following criteria: 50 or more innings, ERA below 2.50 and an opponents' on-base average (OOBA) of .230 or below. It's quite a distinguished group:

Pitchers with 50+ IP, ERA<2.50, OOBA<.230 (since 1920)

Name	Year	ERA	OOBA	W/9	H/9
Koufax, Sandy	1963	1.88	.230	1.68	6.19
Hall, Dick	1964	1.84	.226	1.64	5.93
Wilhelm, Hoyt	1965	1.81	.227	2.00	5.50
Koufax, Sandy	1965	2.04	.227	1.90	5.79
Wilhelm, Hoyt	1966	1.67	.226	1.89	5.56
Marichal, Juan	1966	2.23	.230	1.06	6.68
Eckersley, Dennis	1989	1.56	.175	0.47	4.99
Eckersley, Dennis	1990	0.61	.172	0.49	5.03

What a group — two Sandy Koufax seasons, two Hoyt Wilhelm seasons, a Juan Marichal season, the two Eckersley seasons . . . and of course the brilliant year turned in by Dick (Turkey) Hall of the 1964 Orioles. (That was the one we remembered best, too.) All the seasons are since 1963 — and except for Eckersley, all of them were in the high-mound, big-strike-zone period from 1963 through 1968. Which makes what Eckersley, who's performing in a period of much higher overall batting and on base averages, look all the better.

You're probably wondering about Bob Gibson, 1968 (1.12 ERA) — sorry, his opponents' on base average was a sky-high .233. Goose Gossage, 1981? He met the other criteria (ERA 0.77, OOBA .214), but only worked 47 innings. In the 1901-1920 ERA, where our data is not yet complete, we could find three years that qualified: Addie Joss 1908, Walter Johnson 1913, and Ferdie Schupp (the Turkey Hall of his time), 1916. We don't think there were any others, but we can't say that positively.

Can we really say that Eckersley in 1990 was better than Koufax in 1965? That's an apples/orange comparison. But no one's figures — starter or reliever — match Eckersley's 1990 numbers.

Now let's pick a simpler list — ERAs below 1.00 in 50 or more innings. Amazingly, there's only three, all modern-era relievers:

Pitchers with 50+ IP, ERA<1.00 (since 1920)

Name	Year	ERA	OOBA	W/9	H/9
Eckersley, Dennis	1990	0.61	.172	0.49	5.03
Murphy, Rob	1986	0.72	.245	3.75	4.65
Henry, Bill	1964	0.87	.231	2.08	5.37

Eckersley is once again the best. Gossage in 1981 (0.77) would have made it if he'd worked three more innings . . . but he wouldn't have topped Eckersley. Pre-1920? We could find that man Schupp again in 1916 (0.90 ERA) and, depending on what source you use, Dutch Leonard in 1914 (some say 0.96, others 1.00 or 1.01). Whatever, the point — that Eckersley had a year for the ages — is made.

How about opponents' on base averages below .220? There's only two seasons — Eckersley's 1989 and Eckersley's 1990:

Pitchers with 50+ IP, OOBA<.220 (since 1920)

Name	Year	ERA	OOBA	W/9	H/9
Eckersley, Dennis	1989	1.56	.175	0.47	4.99
Eckersley, Dennis	1990	0.61	.172	0.49	5.03

The 1901-1920 era? There's Johnson 1913 (.217) and Joss 1908 (.218). But that, we think, is all. Nice company.

How about pitchers who averaged below 0.5 walks per nine innings? Two years; you guessed it, both Eckersley. Not even the pre-1920 could do that (there were a number before 1900, when pitchers were working from shorter distance and often throwing underhanded):

Pitchers with 50+ IP, Walks per 9 <0.50 (since 1920)

Name	Year	ERA	OOBA	W/9	H/9
Eckersley, Dennis	1989	1.56	.175	0.47	4.99
Eckersley, Dennis	1990	0.61	.172	0.49	5.03

So was Eck the best ever? Certainly his 1990 was the best **relief** year ever, with no question. As we say, it's impossible to compare him to starters in any meaningful way. But this was one (no, two) of the great pitching performances of all time — of that there can be no doubt.

Good news to American League hitters: Eckersley is slipping. He gave up only three unintentional walks in both 1989 and 1990; but in 1990, Eck went to three balls on 21 hitters — five more than in '89! Here's his amazing ledger:

Dennis Eckersley going to 3 balls — 1989-90
1989 — 3-Ball Counts (16)

Date	Hitter	Count	Event
04/13/89	C. Washington	3-1	Line Out
04/22/89	M. McLemore	3-2	Strikeout
04/28/89	L. Whitaker	3-2	Walk
05/07/89	A. Trammell	3-2	Walk
07/13/89	G. Bell	3-2	Line Out
07/13/89	F. McGriff	3-2	Pop Out
07/26/89	B. Downing	3-2	Flied Out
08/01/89	C. Fisk	3-2	Flied Out
08/15/89	B. Jacoby	3-2	Walk
08/28/89	W. Tolleson	3-2	Hit by Pitch
09/06/89	W. Boggs	3-2	Double
09/17/89	M. Barrett	3-2	Flied Out
09/18/89	D. James	3-2	Flied Out
09/24/89	G. Larkin	3-0	Ground Out
09/26/89	R. Sierra	3-1	Ground Out
09/28/89	J. Daugherty	3-2	Ground Out

1990 — 3-Ball Counts (16)

Date	Hitter	Count	Event
04/14/90	P. O'brien	3-2	Strikeout
04/14/90	D. Coles	3-2	Strikeout
04/15/90	J. Leonard	3-2	Ground Out
05/25/90	S. Jefferson	3-2	Ground Out
06/01/90	K. Seitzer	3-1	Flied Out
06/05/90	J. Franco	3-2	Line Out

06/12/90	J. Daugherty	3-2	Strikeout
06/12/90	J. Franco	3-1	Walk
06/12/90	R. Sierra	3-2	Double
07/12/90	D. Sveum	3-2	Strikeout
07/24/90	L. Stevens	3-2	Flied Out
07/26/90	D. Bichette	3-2	Walk
07/30/90	H. Reynolds	3-2	Ground Out
08/09/90	C. Ripken	3-1	Flied Out
08/30/90	D. Tartabull	3-2	Strikeout
08/30/90	G. Perry	3-1	Triple
08/31/90	J. Daugherty	3-2	Flied Out
09/09/90	R. Kelly	3-2	Flied Out
09/16/90	K. Hrbek	3-0	Walk
09/21/90	T. Phillips	3-2	Line Out
09/21/90	A. Trammell	3-2	Single

WHO'S BEST AT HOLDING THE FORT?

Baseball is becoming more specialized than ever, especially in the relief pitching department. There are your long men, for when the starter gets knocked out early; there are the middle men, who come in during the fifth or sixth innings; there are the lefty specialists who come in to get out left-handed batters; there are the set-up men, who work the seventh and eighth and pave the way for the closers; and finally the closers themselves, the glamor guys who gets the saves.

The closers get the glory — and the big money — but what about the other pitchers who work so hard to protect a lead? For them we invented the "hold," which is nothing more than a save opportunity passed on to the next pitcher. It's a simple concept, really. Take Game 3 of last year's American League playoffs. Mike Moore worked six innings for the A's, leaving with a 4-1 lead. Gene Nelson worked the seventh, protecting the lead; then Rick Honeycutt came in during the eighth, and continued to protect the margin. Finally Dennis Eckersley pitched a scoreless ninth. We credit Eck with the save, of course. But we also give holds to both Nelson and Honeycutt, who did precisely what they were asked to do. Here are the major league leaders in holds for 1990:

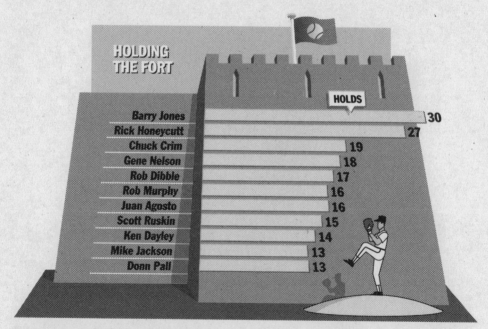

HOLDING THE FORT

HOLDS

Barry Jones	30
Rick Honeycutt	27
Chuck Crim	19
Gene Nelson	18
Rob Dibble	17
Rob Murphy	16
Juan Agosto	16
Scott Ruskin	15
Ken Dayley	14
Mike Jackson	13
Donn Pall	13

Talk about unsung heroes. Bobby Thigpen set a major league record last year with 57 saves, and Dennis Eckersley also eclipsed the old mark by recording 48. But where would they have been without Barry Jones, who set up Thigpen for the White Sox, and the Rick Honeycutt/Gene Nelson tandem, which did the same for Eckersley? A save is a save, of course, and we wouldn't denigrate the splendid work of Thigpen and Eckersley. But it's a lot easier on a closer when he has the luxury of entering a game in the ninth inning with no one on base. Jones, Honeycutt and Nelson took a lot of strain off their closers by setting them up so superbly.

Those of you who recall this study from a year ago will notice some familiar names. Jones was injured during most of '89, so he didn't appear on the leaders list a year ago. But Honeycutt, the number two man in 1990, led both leagues in holds with 24 in 1989. Chuck Crim of the Brewers, third in 1990, ranked fourth in '89. Rob Dibble had 23 holds in '89 — second only to Honeycutt — and probably would have had more than 17 last year if he hadn't been called on so frequently to finish games himself. Ken Dayley continued his strong set-up work last year. A lot of people didn't notice, but the Blue Jays did; they rewarded Dayley with a big free-agent contract. The same goes for ex-Houston pitcher Juan Agosto, who signed a big pact with the Cardinals.

We've only been keeping this stat for a couple of years, but Jones' 30 holds easily eclipsed Honeycutt's 1989 leading total of 24. Honeycutt himself bettered his old mark with 27. It's possible that this is a portent of a more aggressive use of set-up men — put them out there in more marginal games, rather than sticking with the starter. Curiously, Tony LaRussa used this philosophy all season long, then abandoned it in the crucial second game of the World Series. Rather than go to Nelson or Honeycutt, he sent Bob Welch out for the eighth inning, and ended up losing the game. No one will ever know how history would have been different had LaRussa — perhaps confused by the lack of the DH rule — followed his season-long pattern.

There is a segment of the baseball community which turns up its nose to anything new and says, "There are too many stats." In a way, we agree; there are a lot of dumb statistics out there, but we'd like to argue that **this** isn't one of them. If you look at the official major league statistics, you'll see that, for some reason, they still keep track of how many sacrifice hits and sacrifice flies each pitcher allows. Really meaningful stuff; does it help your understanding of baseball to know that Chuck Finley of the Angels allowed more sacrifice hits than any other American League pitcher in 1990? The only explanation for recording these stats is, "We keep these numbers because we've always kept them." Wouldn't it make a lot of sense — if there are indeed too many stats, a very debatable point with us — to deep-six those two, and substitute holds and save opportunities? We dare you to tell us that this doesn't make sense.

A complete listing for this category can be found on page 307.

WHO'S BEST ON SHORT REST?

Talk to any old-time baseball man about the modern game, and one subject bound to come up is how today's pitchers are pampered. In the good old days, the oldtimer will opine, men were men and pitchers worked every fourth day. Don Drysdale, in particular, constantly harps on this subject in his broadcasts.

People love to romanticize the past, and this is yet another case of it. It is simply **not** true that starting pitchers have traditionally worked on three days rest until recent times. For example, Lefty Grove, the prototype workhorse pitcher of the 1930s, made over 33 starts in a season only once in his entire career. Dizzy Dean, the National League counterpart of Grove in the thirties, made over 34 starts only once. Red Ruffing, the Yankees' ace during the same period, pitched 22 seasons — and made over 31 starts only once in all that time. And Ted Lyons, the White Sox Hall of Famer of that same era, pitched for 21 seasons, but made over 32 starts only once. (It is true, though, that Grove and Dean often pitched in relief between starts. Ruffing and Lyons worked only occasionally in relief.)

The real heyday of the four-man rotation was the 1960s and 70s, when hurlers like Sandy Koufax, Drysdale and Mickey Lolich frequently made over 40 starts and worked over 300 innings in a season. But even during that era, pitchers like Bob Gibson and Tom Seaver almost always worked on four days rest part of a five-man rotation. Since many of the workhorses came down with sore arms or had shortened careers, caution became the watchword, and almost every club adopted the five-man system.

These days working on three days rest is a seldom-used strategy. In 1990, no major league pitcher had more than six decisions or worked more than 48.1 innings on three days rest. Yet some pitchers were more effective on short rest than on the traditional four. The following were the best on short rest (minimum three starts and 20 innings on three days rest):

Better on Short Rest

Pitcher, Team	3 Days Rest				4 Days Rest				ERA Diff.
	ERA	IP	W	L	ERA	IP	W	L	
Shawn Boskie, Cubs	2.83	28.2	2	1	6.48	25.0	0	2	-3.65
Jaime Navarro, Mil	2.49	21.2	1	1	6.08	66.2	4	4	-3.58
Trevor Wilson, SF	2.78	45.1	3	2	6.32	31.1	3	3	-3.54
Allan Anderson, Min	3.24	25.0	3	0	6.22	81.0	1	11	-2.98
Greg Maddux, Cubs	1.30	48.1	5	1	4.01	128.0	7	11	-2.71
Dave Stewart, Oak	0.72	25.0	3	0	3.01	209.1	16	10	-2.29
Matt Young, Sea	1.74	20.2	0	2	3.29	147.2	6	9	-1.55
Norm Charlton, Cin	1.80	20.0	1	1	3.07	61.2	3	4	-1.27
John Mitchell, Bal	3.38	21.1	2	1	4.53	57.2	4	3	-1.15
Scott Garrelts, SF	3.47	49.1	3	2	4.48	80.1	5	5	-1.02

There's a scattering of teams and pitchers (most of them youthful) here. The best was the Cubs' Greg Maddux, who was 5-1 with a 1.30 on three days' rest. So would Maddux be better in a four-man rotation? There's no convincing evidence of this. In 1989, Cubs manager Don Zimmer also experimented with a four-man rotation. But that year Maddux proved much more effective on four days rest (11-6, 2.63 ERA) than on three (2-3, 4.69).

Just as many pitchers found short rest to be a disaster in 1990:

		Worse on Short Rest							
	3 Days Rest				**4 Days Rest**				**ERA**
Pitcher, Team	**ERA**	**IP**	**W**	**L**	**ERA**	**IP**	**W**	**L**	**Diff.**
Terry Mulholland, Phi	6.07	29.2	2	2	3.23	100.1	4	7	2.84
Tom Browning, Cin	5.60	37.0	4	2	3.17	150.1	9	5	2.43
Bob Ojeda, Mets	5.57	21.0	0	4	3.18	22.2	3	0	2.39
Mike Moore, Oak	6.92	27.1	1	1	4.54	113.0	9	9	2.38
Mike Harkey, Cubs	4.67	27.0	3	2	2.67	104.2	6	2	2.00
John Burkett, SF	4.56	49.1	3	2	3.34	116.0	8	3	1.23
Rick Mahler, Cin	5.06	26.2	2	1	4.11	46.0	2	4	0.95
Jack Morris, Det	4.94	27.1	2	0	4.23	178.2	11	14	0.71
John Smoltz, Atl	4.37	22.2	1	2	3.84	159.1	11	5	0.53
Bobby Witt, Tex	3.98	20.1	2	1	3.58	98.0	7	4	0.40

Most of the pitchers in this group are considered "strong-armed," and you'd think they wouldn't be bothered by pitching on short rest. Some of them, such as the Reds' Tom Browning, have been very effective on three days rest in the past. But we can find no evidence here for the Drysdale theory — that working in a four-man rotation helps a pitcher get into a groove.

It is true, however, that none of these pitchers was used extensively on short rest; one could argue that they'd find their rhythm if used regularly on three days rest, but of course that's all speculation. STATS' Craig Wright, for one, feels that pitchers would be more effective in a four-man rotation, and he presents evidence for this in *The Diamond Appraised*. However, in order to protect pitchers' arms, they'd have to be lifted earlier than they are now. This would put more pressure on the bullpen; a staff like Oakland's could probably handle it very well, but clubs without several good relievers would be struggling as much as ever. In baseball, the quest for consistently good pitching is endless, and often futile — whatever system is used.

A complete listing of this category appears on page 308.

WHO ARE THE QUALITY STARTERS?

The quality start, once ridiculed almost as much as the game-winning RBI, is beginning to earn a little respect. Some people still make the knee-jerk criticism that a quality start means nothing because a pitcher can get one for working six innings and allowing three earned runs — a 4.50 earned run average, for gosh sakes! Well, what if we told you that this "travesty" — the worst possible quality start — occurred only 136 times out of 2,202 quality starts last year, a mere six percent?

But forget all that. There's a simpler, stronger defense of the quality start: there's an extremely high correlation between a pitcher making a quality start and his team's winning the game. We recited this litany a year ago, but let's do it again based on the 1990 figures. Last year major league starters had a .744 winning percentage when they made a quality start. Their bullpens couldn't always hang on, but nonetheless their teams wound up winning the game 67 percent of the time, whether the starter got the win or not. In other words, if you made a quality start, the odds were two-to-one that your team would win the game. But that includes situations where **both** starters turned in a quality start. When one starter had a QS last year and the other didn't, the winning percentage was an overwhelming .956 (806-37). If that's not quality, what is?

We've argued the point enough. Here are the 1990 leaders in quality start percentage (minimum 20 starts):

Pitcher, Team	GS	QS	Pct
Roger Clemens, Bos	31	27	87.1
Ed Whitson, SD	32	27	84.4
Zane Smith, Mon-Pit	31	24	77.4
John Tudor, StL	22	17	77.3
Chuck Finley, Cal	32	24	75.0
Dave Stewart, Oak	36	27	75.0
Doug Drabek, Pit	33	24	72.7
Dave Stieb, Tor	33	24	72.7
David Wells, Tor	25	18	72.0
Mark Portugal, Hou	32	23	71.9

The model of consistency, Clemens made only four starts all season in which he didn't **both** work six innings and allow three earned runs or fewer. In his 27 quality starts, Clemens was 20-3 and the Red Sox were 21-6. Ed Whitson's Padres were only 75-87 overall, but when Whitson made a quality start, they were 18-9.

The quality start also points out pitchers who **aren't** consistent, and that includes some big names. Dwight Gooden was 19-7 last year, for example, but he only turned in a quality start 58.8% of the time. Also lacking in consistency were, among others, Nolan Ryan (56.7%) and Fernando Valenzuela (48.5%). And these guys, who had the worst percentage of quality starts last year:

Pitcher, Team	GS	QS	Pct
Curt Young, Oak	21	6	28.6
Steve Avery, Atl	20	6	30.0
John Cerutti, Tor	23	7	30.4
Andy Hawkins, Yanks	26	9	34.6
Dan Petry, Det	23	8	34.8

When these pitchers took the mound, their clubs had to get their hitting shoes on.

Which clubs turned in the most quality starts in 1990? Surprisingly, the Montreal Expos led the way with exactly 100, and the young and unheralded Seattle staff paced the AL with 96:

Most Quality Starts		Fewest Quality Starts	
Expos	100	Tigers	65
Reds	96	Brewers	73
Mariners	95	Yankees	74
Mets	95	Indians	75
Padres	94	Twins	75

As you might have guessed, the National League produced more quality starts on a per-team basis: the average NL team had 89 quality starts, the average AL team only 81. The DH rule had a lot to do with that.

A final note on the subject. The critics do have a point about those six-inning, three-earned-run efforts. We pointed out that there were only 136 of them last year; the starters' record in those 6IP-3ER outings was a terrible 33-63. Peter Gammons has started talking about "seven inning quality starts," and maybe that will become the new definition. Certainly 33-63 **ain't** quality.

A complete listing for this category appears on page 309.

WHICH STARTING STAFFS STAR, AND WHICH RELIEF STAFFS REEK?

One of the most crucial decisions facing a manager involves when to lift his starting pitcher. The choice becomes easier when you have a great bullpen, as Oakland's Tony LaRussa does, and tougher when your relief guys can't get anyone out, which is the dilemma facing Bobby Cox of the Braves. We like to analyze starting and relief crews as separate units. As our graphic shows, the best group in 1990 — by far — was the A's bullpen; the worst was the Braves pen. There's nothing like consistency, and the A's relief corps was also the top group in 1989.

LaRussa, the lucky fellow, is not just blessed with a great bullpen. He has one of the best starting staffs as well. Separating the staffs into starting and relief groups, here's how the 26 clubs ranked last year:

Starters	ERA	Relievers	ERA
1. Red Sox	3.32	1. Athletics	2.35
2. Expos	3.47	2. Reds	2.93
3. Athletics	3.51	3. Pirates	2.99
4. Mets	3.55	4. Mets	3.10
5. Pirates	3.60	5. Expos	3.14
6. Reds	3.61	6. White Sox	3.18
7. Mariners	3.67	7. Tigers	3.26
8. Astros	3.71	8. Dodgers	3.32
9. Padres	3.72	9. Astros	3.42
10. White Sox	3.83	10. Orioles	3.52
11. Cardinals	3.87	11. Rangers	3.52
12. Dodgers	3.92	12. Angels	3.55
13. Angels	3.92	13. Padres	3.61
14. Royals	3.93	14. Blue Jays	3.65
15. Blue Jays	3.93	15. Twins	3.67
16. Rangers	3.96	16. Yankees	3.77
17. Phillies	4.14	17. Indians	3.78
18. Brewers	4.20	18. Giants	3.81
19. Giants	4.21	19. Mariners	3.87
20. Orioles	4.35	20. Cardinals	3.91
21. Twins	4.38	21. Royals	3.93
22. Braves	4.39	22. Brewers	3.94
23. Yankees	4.47	23. Phillies	4.00
24. Cubs	4.48	24. Cubs	4.06
25. Indians	4.50	25. Red Sox	4.62
26. Tigers	5.00	26. Braves	5.01

In last year's World Series, LaRussa was criticized for sticking too long with Bob Welch in Game 2, and then again for staying with Dave Stewart in Game 4. Those were his two aces, and LaRussa's starting staff was one of the best in the majors. But his relief corp was **the** best. We wouldn't have hesitated too long about going to that solid-gold bullpen.

As the chart shows, Joe Morgan of the Red Sox has a different problem. His starters were the best in the majors last year; his relievers were the second worst. In the playoffs against Oakland, Morgan would go as far as he thought he could with his starting pitchers, and they kept him in every game. But when he turned two close games over to his bullpen, they quickly took the Bosox right out of each contest.

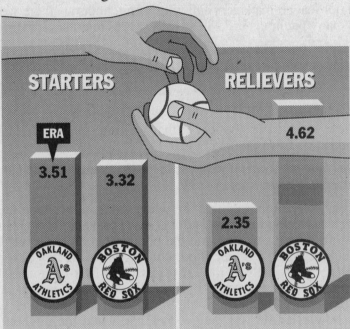

Was there a reason for Boston's terrible relief work last year? A lot of Boston pitchers will tell you privately, and some even stated publicly, that the blame rested squarely with Morgan. With a starting staff that was makeshift after Roger Clemens and Mike Boddicker, Morgan got his relievers up early and often. By the end of the season, some of them were complaining that they were worn out even before they can got into the game. Morgan seems to lack the knack that LaRussa, Detroit's Sparky Anderson and the White Sox' Jeff Torborg all seem to have. Each gives his relievers clearly defined roles, and is careful not to overwork them, or even warm them up too often without bringing them into a game. Managing a pitching staff is a tricky business indeed.

A staff to watch in 1991 could be the Seattle Mariners. The Mariner starting corps, with some great young arms, was one of the best in the American League last year. With better relief work — a healthy Mike Schooler would help — the whole staff could take off.

A complete listing for this category appears on page 310.

HOW EFFECTIVE ARE PITCHOUTS?

The pitchout remains a favorite weapon of major league managers, despite evidence that the strategy hardly ever works. We studied this question a year ago, with some surprising results. In case you missed it, here were the highlights:

- Major league managers call a lot of pitchouts — there were almost as many pitchouts in 1989 as there were stolen base attempts.

- Despite that, they seldom seem to guess right. The runner was actually going on only about seven percent of the pitchout calls.

- Even worse, the runner was often safe (45% of the time) even when the call was right.

- There was little evidence that calling pitchouts deterred the opposition from stealing.

- The Giants' Roger Craig, as expected, proved to be the best at calling pitchouts successfully.

This data basically suggested that the whole pitchout exercise was a waste of time. The call seldom works, and it doesn't prevent the opposition from running — all it seems to do is put the pitcher in a hole. So we decided to study the subject again, and see if our conclusions were any different. Here is pitchout data for each of the 26 teams. The first column shows how many pitchouts were attempted by each team — 149 in the case of the Orioles. The next columns show the results: how many times the runner stole, and how often he was caught stealing, when the pitchout call was right — for the Orioles, the runner was safe eight times out of ten, even when the pitchout was called correctly. Next we give the percentage that the pickoff call achieved its aim, which was to throw out the runner — for the O's, only 1.3 percent of the time (twice in 149 pitchouts). And finally, we add a new column — the total of stolen bases the opponents attempted against the team (147). This is an attempt to measure the deterrent effect.

Here's the 1990 data:

Team	Total Pitchouts	Pitchouts on SB Attempts			% of total Pitchouts with CS	Opp SB Att.
		SB	CS	%		
Baltimore	149	8	2	.800	1.3	147
Boston	180	4	6	.400	3.3	185
California	155	1	1	.500	0.6	160
Chicago	120	7	5	.583	4.2	149
Cleveland	115	1	4	.200	3.5	151
Detroit	192	8	6	.571	3.1	195
Kansas City	202	2	2	.500	1.0	143
Milwaukee	209	3	5	.375	2.4	156
Minnesota	130	2	7	.222	5.4	174
New York	186	2	8	.200	4.3	188
Oakland	158	5	13	.278	8.2	117
Seattle	156	4	1	.800	0.6	176
Texas	123	5	0	1.000	0.0	183
Toronto	182	6	5	.545	2.7	162
American League	2257	58	65	.472	2.9	2286
Atlanta	194	3	2	.600	1.0	243
Chicago	184	3	4	.429	2.2	154
Cincinnati	189	7	7	.500	3.7	195
Houston	189	9	6	.600	3.2	243
Los Angeles	167	4	2	.667	1.2	193
Montreal	198	9	4	.692	2.0	239
New York	213	3	2	.600	0.9	272
Philadelphia	128	8	4	.667	3.1	160
Pittsburgh	224	2	8	.200	3.6	203
St. Louis	166	6	3	.667	1.8	220
San Diego	189	3	3	.500	1.6	192
San Francisco	301	17	13	.567	4.3	200
National League	2342	74	58	.561	2.5	2514
Major Leagues	4599	132	123	.518	2.7	4800

There is, we will say right off, nothing in the 1990 data to change our conclusions from last year. Sometimes the numbers are almost laughable. The Rangers called 123 pitchouts last year; the runner was only going five times, and on all five occasions he stole the base anyway! The Mariners called 156 pitchouts to get one caught stealing, the Royals 202 to get two. The California Angels, at least, are improving. In 1989, they called 144 pitchouts and got no caught stealings; in 1990 they called 155 and got one. Overall, the 4,559 pitchouts resulted in only 123 caught stealings — a "success" rate of 2.7 percent. The runners were even more successful in 1990 when the call was made correctly — 52% of the time they were safe anyway, an increase of seven percent over '89.

Craig remains the most prolific caller of pitchouts, with 301 last year. But his reputation as the number one man is being challenged by Oakland's Tony LaRussa. Craig's catchers threw out 13 runners on pitchouts last year, the same number as LaRussa's. But Tony's catchers did it on only 18 attempts (the Giants needed 30), and they did it while calling only a little more than half as many pitchouts as Craig did. On a cost/efficiency basis, the A's were way ahead.

As for the deterrent effect, it's still hard to find it. A lot of teams which call numerous pitchouts seem to be doing it out of desperation. Their catchers can't throw anyone out, so they call pitchouts to give them more of a fighting chance. The Mets are a good example of this syndrome. Whereas a club like the Phillies, who could keep the running game under control, didn't feel the need to pitch out.

Of course, you could still argue that, without the pitchouts, the weak teams would be even worse: the opponents would run more often, and their success rate would be even higher. Perhaps that's true — about the only way to tell would be if some major league manager would volunteer his club as a "control" group, and offer not to call any pitchouts at all in 1991. (We'll be awaiting your call.) But given the nebulous advantages of the strategy, we still think it's being used way too often.

IV. QUESTIONS ON DEFENSE

WHO'S BEST IN THE INFIELD ZONE?

Few things in baseball will stir up a debate like the subject of who the best fielders are. Fielding stats are considered suspect, so people make evaluations on the basis of observation — or at least they say they do. You can easily see the flaw in doing it that way. To repeat an old Bill James argument: if there were no hitting stats that anyone trusted, we'd rate hitters on the smoothness of their swings, or on who recorded the most spectacular hits. Well, nobody had a prettier swing than Greg Walker of the 1980's White Sox, but Walker was hardly the best hitter in baseball. And no hitter provides more excitement than Bo Jackson — but if you had to rank the top 20 hitters in baseball, you'd have to strain to put Bo among the group. We would agree that observation has to play a role in evaluating fielders, but the name of this company isn't OBSERVATION, Inc.

So let's be upfront: we like fielding statistics, and our goal is to develop better ones. In truth, people criticize fielding stats, but they rely on them a lot more than they like to admit. Larry Bowa's reputation as a great shortstop dissolved when people started noticing how few assists he made; Ozzie Smith's reputation soared when his total chances rose. Baseball folks ridiculed James' "range factor" (total chances per games played), but they often rely on the same system — under a different name, of course. We like range factor, and have refined it so that it's now based on total chances per nine innings rather than games played.

But some fielders have the opportunity to make more chances than others do — infielders who play on groundball pitching staffs would be the obvious example. So we have a further refinement known as the Zone Rating. Our reporters record the location of every ball hit, and we can rate fielders on the basis of how many balls in their zone — an area about 50 feet around their normal position — they turn into outs. We'll be the first to admit the stat's limitations. Zone ratings don't differentiate between a ball hit right at the fielder and one on the fringe of his zone. And sometimes there's not that much difference between one fielder's rating and another's. But we think it's a very useful tool, and feel you'll find it's a step in the right direction. We feel it's the best statistic there is for evaluating fielding perfomance, and combined with fielding percentage and observation, can provide a good basis for evaluation.

Let's go through the infield positions. We'll rate the top fielders both by Zone Rating and Range Factor, along with the trailer at each position (minimum 700 innings played). Here are the first basemen, ranked only by zone rating; range factor doesn't work for first sackers, because they have so many automatic putouts:

Zone Ratings — First Basemen	
Dave Magadan, Mets	.928
Sid Bream, Pit	.926
Don Mattingly, Yanks	.926
Mark McGwire, Oak	.920
Kent Hrbek, Min	.909
Worst	
Pedro Guerrero, StL	.777

There's a lot of consistency in this list from 1989. Mattingly and McGwire (the 1990 AL Gold Glove winner) made the top five in '89, and Guerrero was the worst both years. Magadan, the 1990 leader, would have been first in '89 as well if he'd played enough innings; we'd have to say Dave is a very underrated glove man. Sid Bream was injured in 1989, and the Pirates credited his return with the improvement in their defense.

Second Basemen

Zone Ratings		Range Factors	
Julio Franco, Tex	.961	Lou Whitaker, Det	5.67
Bill Ripken, Bal	.960	Johnny Ray, Cal	5.60
Lou Whitaker, Det	.953	Robby Thompson, SF	5.58
Manny Lee, Tor	.947	Jose Lind, Pit	5.52
Jody Reed, Bos	.947	Jeff Treadway, Atl	5.46
Worst		**Worst**	
Nelson Liriano, Tor-Min	.877	Gregg Jefferies, Mets	4.44

The missing link — neither of the Gold Glove winners, Ryne Sandberg and Harold Reynolds, are represented in either of the rankings. Sandberg just missed in the zone rating; he was at .946, which was good enough to lead the National League. Reynolds was a little lower — .939 zone, 5.25 range — but very respectable in both categories. We don't claim our rating system is perfect, and we have enormous respect for both players. We will say, however, that Gregg Jefferies of the Mets has ranked very poorly both years in both categories. We don't think this is a statistical fluke.

Third Basemen

Zone Ratings		Range Factors	
Gary Gaetti, Min	.930	Charlie Hayes, Phi	3.24
Charlie Hayes, Phi	.923	Terry Pendleton, StL	3.02
Matt Williams, SF	.918	Tony Phillips, Det	3.02
Robin Ventura, WSox	.901	Gary Gaetti, Min	2.96
Terry Pendleton, StL	.884	Gary Sheffield, Mil	2.96
Worst		**Worst**	
Jim Presley, Atl	.756	Brook Jacoby, Cle	2.35

Perennial AL Gold Glove winner Gary Gaetti leads our zone ratings. In the National League, the award has bounced back and forth between Terry Pendleton and Tim Wallach in recent years. Wallach won the award last year, in good part because of Pendleton's poor hitting. Those astute Gold Glove voters, the major league managers and coaches, will almost never give the award to a guy who's struggling with the bat, no matter how well he's fielding. We're sure this makes as much sense to you as it does to us, but that's how they usually do it. They also seem to take a few years before noticing good glove work. The Phils' Charlie Hayes is now in that category. Hayes not only led our National League zone ratings, but had more assists, chances, double plays — and one fewer error — than Tim Wallach did last year, while playing in 15 fewer games. Unlike the Gold Glove voters, we won't wait until 1992 to recognize what Hayes is doing **now**.

Shortstops

Zone Ratings		Range Factors	
Dick Schofield, Cal	.962	Alvaro Espinoza, Yanks	5.34
Cal Ripken, Bal	.960	Dick Schofield, Cal	5.11
Ozzie Guillen, WSox	.959	Tony Fernandez, Tor	5.06
Alan Trammell, Det	.955	Barry Larkin, Cin	4.83
Ozzie Smith, StL	.944	Luis Rivera, Bos	4.81
		Felix Fermin, Cle	4.81
Worst		**Worst**	
Jeff Blauser, Atl	.853	Kurt Stillwell, KC	4.18

The remark we made about the Gold Glove voters factoring in a player's hitting applies to shortstops, but in a weird way. Dick Schofield's weak stick has kept him from serious Gold Glove consideration; we wouldn't consider him for a Gold Glove, either, based on last year — but only because injuries limited him to 99 games. Meanwhile Ozzie Guillen won his first award last year. Did people finally noticed him because he led the American League in hitting for two months?

On the other hand, Cal Ripken's bat has probably kept him from Gold Glove consideration, but for the opposite reason as Schofield — Ripken's is too potent. Ripken is big and strong and hits with home run power, and people automatically think guys like that have limited range. Oh yeah? Cal Rip has led American League shortstops in putouts four times, assists five times, and last year set a major league record for the position with only three errors. What's a guy got to do to win a little respect? So should we award a STATS Gold Glove for 1990 to Ripken, sort of like of like one of those "Lifetime Achievement Awards" Hollywood is always giving?

Well . . .

Without further ado, here are the STATS Gold Gloves for 1990 infielders, based on statistics and yes, observation as well:

- **First Base** — Mark McGwire AL, Sid Bream NL. Don Mattingly played in too few games to merit consideration, and we still want to see a little more of Dave Magadan.

- **Second Base** — Bill Ripken AL, Ryne Sandberg NL. The toughest choice. The AL award winner, Harold Reynolds, did not have good stats last year; Lou Whitaker was the best statistically, but we think he's helped a lot by the long Tiger Stadium grass. Anyway, we did say Ripken deserved a Gold Glove, we just didn't say which one. In the National League, Sandberg is now strongly challenged by the two Joses, Lind and Oquendo, but we'll stick with Ryno at least one more time.

- **Third Base** — Gary Gaetti AL, Charlie Hayes NL. We're very comfortable with these choices. All Charlie Hayes needs to win some official Gold Gloves is to start hitting a little better.

- **Shortstop** — Ozzie Guillen AL, Ozzie Smith NL. Sorry, Cal, but we think Guillen is a little better. In the NL, Barry Larkin was a close second. He'll get more consideration in 1991, especially if he changes his first name to Ozzie!

Technical Note: In this year's *Scoreboard,* we're using Bill James' original Range Factor, which subtracts errors from total chances, before adjusting on a per nine inning basis. Last year, we left in the errors with the argument that having the "range" to make an error should be considered; after all, the statistic is called "Range" Factor, and the fielder is penalized for the error by having a lower fielding percentage. However, the Original Range Factor takes into account those failed chances by subtracting errors; if two players have the same number of chances, the player with fewer errors will have a better range factor. In essence, Range Factor takes into account both range and success; fielding percentage only measures success. So, Range Factor = Putouts+Assists per 9 Defensive Innings. Happy, Bill?

A complete listing for this category can be found on page 311.

WHO ARE THE BEST-THROWING CATCHERS?

We made this argument a year ago, and since nobody noticed, we think we'll make it again: why aren't Stolen Bases Allowed and Caught Stealings — for both pitchers and catchers, but especially catchers — found in the list of official statistics? We have trouble fathoming the argument which says "there are too many statistics already." When it comes to defense, the problem is that there aren't nearly enough. Look at the record books. The leagues keep track of 21 batting stats, 24 pitching stats, but only seven or eight defensive stats (depending on the position). Hey, guys, aren't you always telling us how important defense is?

Be that as it may, **we** keep track of stolen bases allowed, and we'd venture to say it's one of the reasons you buy this book. So once again, sample some Forbidden Fruit — the leading 1990 catchers in caught stealing percentage (minimum 60 games caught):

Catcher, Team	SB	CS	%	Pick-offs	SB/9	Without Pitcher CS Pit. CS	CS%
Ron Karkovice, WSox	18	18	50.0	2	0.34	0	50.0
Lance Parrish, Cal	62	55	47.0	2	0.51	5	44.6
Tom Pagnozzi, StL	40	33	45.2	0	0.69	5	41.2
Bob Geren, Yanks	55	42	43.3	1	0.66	6	39.6
Charlie O'Brien, Mil-Mets	40	30	42.9	1	0.61	4	39.4
Pat Borders, Tor	54	40	42.6	2	0.61	6	38.6
Junior Ortiz, Min	21	15	41.7	3	0.44	3	36.4
Joe Oliver, Cin	64	43	40.2	2	0.61	9	34.7
Carlton Fisk, WSox	71	42	37.2	1	0.66	7	33.0
Darren Daulton, Phi	78	42	35.0	3	0.63	1	34.5

You'll notice that there are two different percentages. If a runner takes off for second on a pitcher's pickoff attempt but is retired, it's scored a caught stealing. But since the catcher didn't throw him out, many teams don't credit the catcher's caught stealing total. Those are the "Without Pitcher CS" figures on the right. However, there are a few problems with doing it that way. One is that if the runner takes off on a pickoff attempt and is safe (as happens with some frequency), the catcher **will** get charged with the steal; most teams have no way of differentiating that particular kind of stolen base. Second, the catcher will often not bother with a throw to second because, due to the pitcher's inattentiveness, the runner gets a good lead; once again the catcher gets charged with the steal. The third problem is that, if you subtract the pitchers' caught stealings from the catchers' totals, the team caught stealing totals for all the catchers won't balance with the total runners caught by the team. So we normally include the pitcher caught stealings; you'll note that this whole thing only affects the rankings in ninth and tenth place, where Fisk and Daulton would switch.

As for the leaders list, it's completely different from last year — none of the 1989 leaders made the leaders list again in 1990. What happened? Injuries, more than anything. Damon Berryhill, Bob Boone, Dave Valle and Benito Santiago, the top four in 1989, all missed considerable time in 1990. At the same time, younger catchers like Karkovice, Pagnozzi and Oliver have begun asserting themselves. This could signal a changing of the guard in the catching ranks.

The following receivers had the poorest percentage against opposing runners in 1990:

Catcher, Team	SB	CS	%	Pick-offs	SB/9	Without Pitcher CS Pit. CS	CS%
Mike MacFarlane, KC	68	14	17.1	0	0.67	1	16.0
Jeff Reed, Cin	67	15	18.6	0	1.23	3	15.2
Mike Fitzgerald, Mon	103	26	20.2	0	1.19	3	18.3
Mike Stanley, Tex	41	12	22.6	0	1.02	5	14.6
Greg Olson, Atl	75	23	23.5	0	0.94	6	18.5

Among the weaker throwers, subtracting the pitcher caught stealings makes a bigger difference, as Stanley would move to the head (or is it the back?) of the pack. Stanley, who's had to catch the easy-to-run-on Nolan Ryan, Bobby Witt and Charlie Hough, gets some sympathy from us.

Anyone who says "they always steal on the pitcher" should compare the caught-stealing records of Cincinnati's two receivers, Joe Oliver and Jeff Reed. On a percentage basis, Oliver threw out more than twice as many runners.

A complete listing for this category can be found on page 313.

WHICH OUTFIELDERS HAVE THE CANNONS?

Before STATS entered the picture, assists was the only statistic we had for rating outfielders' throwing arms. For years, people have argued that outfield assist totals were misleading because "runners don't challenge the great throwing arms." That really isn't true; runners will challenge anyone in certain situations. Bill James once pointed out that Roberto Clemente won more outfield assist crowns (five) than batting titles (four). And among current players, Jesse Barfield has led American outfielders in assists five of the last six years.

Even so, it's not a good idea to rely on assists alone to rate an outfielder's arm. Look at the 1990 assist leaders by position:

Outfield Assist Leaders, 1990

Right Field		Center Field		Left Field	
Barfield, Yanks	17	McGee, StL-Oak	12	Bonds, Pit	14
Deer, Mil	14	White, Cal	11	McReynolds, Mets	14
Sosa, WSox	14	Carter, SF	9	Daniels, LA	13
		Griffey Jr, Sea	9		

There are some fine arms among the leaders, but also guys like Kal Daniels, who is near the top of everyone's "Future DH" list, and Willie McGee, who had a miserable time in center last year with 17 errors. Did Daniels and McGee record those assists because runners felt free to challenge them? And does Barfield's mere presence keep runners from advancing? The numbers alone can't tell us.

Fortunately, we have a stat which can begin to clarify the situation: the "outfielder hold percentage." What it does is to compare the total chances runners had to take an extra base on each fielder with the extra bases they actually took. (For purposes of this hold percentage, two bases on a single and scoring on a double qualify as taking an extra base.) If an outfielder's arm has an intimidation factor, it should show up here; if he got a lot of assists because more runners were taking chances on him, we should see that, too. The graphic shows the 1990 leaders at each position (minimum 80 opportunities).

Does an outfielder's arm force runners to put on the brakes? We thought so last year, and we feel ever more strongly about it after looking at another year's worth of data. Dave Henderson, Joe Carter, and Jesse Barfield all made the top three at their positions in both 1989 and 1990. Ken Griffey Jr. ranked fourth in center field in '89, first in 1990. George Bell, the leader in left field in '89, was fourth in 1990. We noted last year that

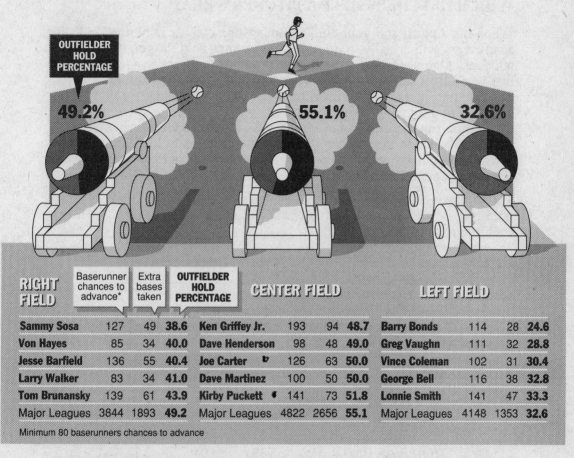

RIGHT FIELD	Baserunner chances to advance*	Extra bases taken	**OUTFIELDER HOLD PERCENTAGE**	**CENTER FIELD**				**LEFT FIELD**			
Sammy Sosa	127	49	**38.6**	Ken Griffey Jr.	193	94	**48.7**	Barry Bonds	114	28	**24.6**
Von Hayes	85	34	**40.0**	Dave Henderson	98	48	**49.0**	Greg Vaughn	111	32	**28.8**
Jesse Barfield	136	55	**40.4**	Joe Carter	126	63	**50.0**	Vince Coleman	102	31	**30.4**
Larry Walker	83	34	**41.0**	Dave Martinez	100	50	**50.0**	George Bell	116	38	**32.8**
Tom Brunansky	139	61	**43.9**	Kirby Puckett	141	73	**51.8**	Lonnie Smith	141	47	**33.3**
Major Leagues	3844	1893	**49.2**	Major Leagues	4822	2656	**55.1**	Major Leagues	4148	1353	**32.6**

Minimum 80 baserunners chances to advance

Hubie Brooks was the easiest right fielder to run in 1989; Brooks was the worst again in '90.

And what of Kal Daniels and Willie McGee? Daniels was better than expected, but ranked only in the middle of the pack among left fielders (34.6%). McGee, a little below average in 1989 (54.7%), was in the same spot in 1990 (55.3%). The assists totals for both were indeed misleading.

One cannon silenced in 1990 was Dave Winfield. Our stats rated him the easiest right fielder in the majors to run on (68.8%). Maybe it was just the year's layoff; more likely, it was age rearing its ugly head.

A complete listing for this category appears on page 314.

WHICH CATCHERS HELP A PITCHER'S ERA?

When it's August and your club's number-one catcher is hitting .211, the announcers will usually start pointing out that he's "a good handler of pitchers." One needs to be cautious that sort of faint praise — it's kind of like when they start telling you your blind date has a "great personality." But the truth is that some receivers seem to have a knack for getting the most out of a pitching staff. The stat known as "catcher's ERA" compiles the earned run averages of a club's moundsmen under each individual catcher. Thanks to the catcher's ERA stats compiled by Bill James, Craig Wright and others, we've seen that some receivers can consistently coax better work out of their pitchers.

The following catchers produced the greatest benefit in ERA for their pitchers last year, in comparison with the other catchers on their teams (minimum 300 innings caught):

Catcher, Team	Own ERA	Others ERA	Diff.
Lance Parrish, Cal	3.47	4.88	− 1.41
Junior Ortiz, Min	3.50	4.41	− 0.91
Gary Carter, SF	3.64	4.33	− 0.69
Bob Geren, Yanks	3.92	4.56	− 0.64
Joe Girardi, Cubs	4.19	4.76	− 0.57
Bob Boone, KC	3.57	4.05	− 0.48
Charlie O'Brien, Mil-Mets	3.71	4.14	− 0.43
Ron Hassey, Oak	2.89	3.32	− 0.43
Mike Scioscia, LA	3.63	4.05	− 0.42
Tony Pena, Bos	3.65	4.04	− 0.39

Except for the presence of Junior Ortiz of the Twins (and maybe Bob Geren of the Yankees), there are no real surprises on this list. The players primarily are veterans who have long been known for their ability to handle a mound staff. That's one reason why the Royals brought in Boone for a couple of years, the Giants wanted Carter (at least for one year), the Mets went after O'Brien and the Red Sox picked up Pena. It really is true, our stats show, that a heady veteran can get the maximum out of a pitcher.

But those of you who have been studying catcher's ERA stats for several years are probably wondering, "Where's Fisk?" Carlton Fisk of the White Sox was usually one of the leaders in this category, but not in 1990. The problem isn't that Fisk is slipping; it's that Ron Karkovice is improving:

| | 1989 | | | 1990 | | |
Catcher, Team	Own ERA	Others ERA	Diff.	Own ERA	Others ERA	Diff.
Carlton Fisk, WSox	3.80	4.72	− 0.92	3.70	3.44	+ 0.26
Ron Karkovice, WSox	4.75	3.97	+ 0.78	3.44	3.70	− 0.26

In previous years, Karkovice had been known for his great throwing arm, but his ability to work with pitchers was a little suspect. Not any more — thanks in good part to his mentor, Fisk. The Fisk/Karkovice stats point out that you can't just look at the differences between one catcher on a team and another. Sometimes **both** are good — or bad.

How about the catcher's with the worst ERA differences? Here they are (again, 300 innings minimum):

Catcher, Team	Own ERA	Others ERA	Diff.
Brian Harper, Min	4.46	3.42	+ 1.04
Ernie Whitt, Atl	5.04	4.38	+ 0.66
Rick Dempsey, LA	4.23	3.60	+ 0.63
Mickey Tettleton, Bal	4.29	3.83	+ 0.46
Darren Daulton, Phi	4.20	3.75	+ 0.45
Matt Nokes, Det-Yanks	4.79	4.36	+ 0.43
Joe Oliver, Cin	3.53	3.14	+ 0.39
Mackey Sasser, Mets	3.66	3.27	+ 0.39
Mike Stanley, Tex	4.09	3.74	+ 0.35
Dave Valle, Sea	3.85	3.54	+ 0.31

Sometimes the differences are hard to explain. Harper, Dempsey and Nokes, for example, were among the catchers whose mound staffs **improved** with them behind the plate in 1989. That's why it's best to study these stats over several years before drawing any sweeping conclusions.

Think managers don't notice stats like this? Ernie Whitt was brought into Atlanta to work with the young Braves pitchers; when they did worse instead of better with Whitt behind the plate, Ernie was sent packing. And Tettleton's problems handling the Orioles pitching staff have sent him packing to Detroit.

A complete listing for this category appears on page 315.

WHEN IS AN ERROR NOT AN ERROR?

Some hitters, whatever their batting averages, have a reputation for coming through with a key hit at just the right moment. Others might rank higher in the batting race, but somehow their hits don't seem to mean much. Does that work with fielders, also? The idea has a certain appeal. You sometimes here about a shortstop, "Sure, he makes a lot of errors, but they're not crucial errors. They never lead to any runs." Whereas you could swear that the kid who's only committed three boots all year has cost your club three wins.

Okay, let's consider the notion. When a fielder commits an error, it sometimes turns out to do no damage at all, and no runs score. Other times it opens the floodgates and leads to a whole bunch of markers. You could argue that it's unfair to blame a fielder for one little two-out error that might eventually result in six runs. Okay, we'll buy that . . . except that we absolve the pitcher from all blame when those "unearned" runs score, even if his poor pitching might make him at least partially culpable. Here are the players in each league whose errors led to the most unearned runs in 1990:

American League	Err	Runs	National League	Err	Runs
Kurt Stillwell, KC	24	30	Jim Presley, Atl	26	30
Greg Gagne, Min	14	20	Alfredo Griffin, LA	26	24
Edgar Martinez, Sea	27	19	Rafael Ramirez, Hou	25	20
Gary Sheffield, Mil	25	19	Garry Templeton, SD	26	19
Carlos Quintana, Bos	17	19	Jeff Blauser, Atl	16	19
Julio Franco, Tex	19	18	Charlie Hayes, Phi	20	18
Robin Ventura, WSox	25	16	Shawon Dunston, Cubs	20	18
Kevin Seitzer, KC	19	16	Terry Pendleton, SL	19	18
Edgar Diaz, Mil	17	16	Jay Bell, Pit	22	17
Mike Blowers, Yanks	10	15	Howard Johnson, Mets	28	16

Remember how those friendly fellows on WTBS used to tell us that Rafael Ramirez' errors didn't really do any damage? Now they're probably telling us the same thing about Jim Presley and Jeff Blauser; if you believe them, you believe the dentist when he says, "This isn't going to hurt a bit." Presley's errors cost Braves pitchers 30 unearned runs last year, which is enough to cost the team three victories. Kurt Stillwell did the same amount of damage to the Royals. No wonder their teams were so lousy.

You see a lot of your old favorites here, the Alfredo Griffins and Garry Templetons who have been booting 'em for years. But how about young Mike Blowers of the Yanks? Ten errors leading to 15 runs!

The following players all committed at least 15 errors, but their miscues did a minimum amount of damage:

American League	Err	Runs	National League	Err	Runs
Kelly Gruber, Tor	19	7	Bobby Bonilla, Pit	15	5
Dick Schofield, Cal	17	7	Kevin Elster, Mets	17	6
Carlos Baerga, Cle	17	8	Gregg Jefferies, Mets	16	6
Alvaro Espinoza, Yanks	17	9	Mike Sharperson, LA	15	7
Jeff Huson, Tex	19	10	Todd Zeile, SL	15	7
Craig Worthington, Bal	18	10	Roberto Alomar, SD	19	7
Jack Howell, Cal	18	11	Barry Larkin, Cin	17	8
Ozzie Guillen, WSox	17	11	Eric Yelding, Hou	17	8
Felix Fermin, Cle	16	11	Ken Caminiti, Hou	21	9
Jody Reed, Bos	16	11	Mariano Duncan, Cin	18	9

Admittedly, there was a good deal of luck at work here . . . teammates, especially pitchers, who helped keep the damage to a minimum. (And maybe the players themselves at times.) We can't say these players will be on the same list next year. But we can say that, in 1990, their miscues did not cost their teams as much as you'd think from their error totals.

A complete listing for this category can be found on page 316.

WHO BOOTS 'EM, AND WHO TOSSES 'EM AWAY?

When you see the errors listed in most box scores, you don't know whether the player committed a fielding or a throwing error. That can be more than a little annoying. If your club's young shortstop is making a lot of miscues, we think you ought be able to know whether he's been booting the ball or tossing it into the seats. Maybe he just can't make the long throw from the hole, and would cut down on the errors if shifted to second base. But without that basic information, how would you know?

Fortunately, the STATS box scores carried in *USA Today* correct the oversight; they not only list each miscue as a fielding or throwing error, they even tell you when it happened. (If you haven't checked out these boxscores yet, do it this season. You'll find a wealth of information every day that you'll never see anywhere else.) Unfortunately, boxscores won't help you at the end of the year, when you're checking the official stats and find only "errors" listed, not what kind.

Once again STATS comes to the rescue. Here are the 1990 leaders in total errors, with a breakdown of whether they were fielding or throwing:

Fielder, Team	Position	Errors	Throwing	Fielding
Howard Johnson, Mets	3b/ss	28	16	12
Edgar Martinez, Sea	3b	27	6	21
Alfred Griffin, LA	ss	26	7	19
Garry Templeton, SD	ss	26	8	18
Jim Presley, Atl	3b	26	7	19
Gary Sheffield, Mil	3b	25	9	16
Robin Ventura, WSox	3b	25	14	11
Dickie Thon, Phi	ss	25	8	17
Rafael Ramirez, Hou	ss	25	7	18
Kurt Stillwell, KC	ss	24	6	18

Not surprisingly, all the leaders are shortstops and third basemen; those are the positions which produce the most errors. But you can see there's a difference in the kind of errors they make. Edgar Martinez of the Mariners committed 21 fielding errors, but only six throwing errors — a sign that his hands are suspect. Rookie Robin Ventura of the White Sox had the opposite problem — 14 of his 25 miscues came on throws. No wonder the Sox brass was forgiving toward Ventura's high error total; they felt he often made a fine play and then threw the ball away, which is a problem that can be corrected with more experience. The Mets seem to feel the same way about Howard Johnson at shortstop.

Some observations about errors by position:

1. Catchers' errors are usually throwing errors on steals, which should be no great surprise. Sandy Alomar, Jr., the most error-prone catcher last year, committed 11 of his 14 errors on throws. By contrast, the accurate-armed Tony Pena of the Red Sox had only three throwing errors all year (out of five total).

2. First basemen usually commit fielding errors, the most common being a dropped throw. The error leader at first last year was Carlos Quintana, who made only two of his 19 errors on throws. Detroit's Cecil Fielder had four throwing errors, a high total for a first sacker.

3. Second basemen usually make more fielding than throwing errors, but some have a surprising amount of problems with the short throw. Harold Reynolds of the Mariners, now a perennial Gold Glover, committed eight throwing errors (out of 19 total) last year.

4. At shortstop and third, the Johnson/Ventura type is the exception. Most players at these two positions commit more fielding errors. We were a little surprised by that.

5. Outfielders make more fielding than throwing errors as well. Of Willie McGee's major-league leading 17 errors in center field last year, 12 were of the fielding variety.

6. Pitchers don't make many errors. But Matt Young, discussed elsewhere in this section, made eight of his nine errors on throws last year. No other major league pitcher committed more than five errors.

A complete listing for this category can be found on page 317.

WHO LED THE LEAGUE IN FUMBLES?

In baseball, it doesn't matter whether you're young or old — if you can boot an easy grounder, there'll always be a place in the lineup for you. We couldn't help noticing the way the "Stone Hands" side of our second annual "Hands of Stone/Soft Hands" matchup has such a nice blend of youth and experience. Gets you all misty for the traditions of the game, doesn't it?

HANDS OF STONE		GAMES PER ERROR*	SOFT HANDS		GAMES PER ERROR*
P	Matt Young	2.8	P	Dave Stewart	0 in 29.7
C	Sandy Alomar Jr.	8.4	C	Tony Pena	26.4
1B	Carlos Quintana	7.9	1B	Kent Hrbek	37.8
2B	Julio Franco	7.7	2B	Jose Oquendo	44.5
3B	Gary Sheffield	4.8	3B	Carney Lansford	12.7
SS	Rafael Ramirez	4.7	SS	Cal Ripken	52.0
LF	Kevin Mitchell	14.6	LF	Kevin McReynolds	45.9
CF	Willie McGee	8.3	CF	Ellis Burks	70.4
RF	Sammy Sosa	10.7	RF	Paul O'Neill	64.7

*A 'game' is eqivalent to 9 defensive innings played; minimum 1,000 defensive innings (162 for pitchers).

Take first base, for example. In 1989, the most error-prone first baseman was Jack Clark of the Padres. But last year, Clark, along with everyone else, was outdistanced by rookie Carlos Quintana of the BoSox. Quintana showed his great promise by managing to make an error every 7.9 games, no mean feat for a first baseman. Now — to give our story a nice rosy glow — Clark will be Quintana's teammate in 1991. We can just see Jack showing Carlos how, if you keep your gloved hand closed, there's no way you can catch the ball. All season long he'll be giving Quintana the benefit of his fumble-fingered wisdom. It couldn't be more perfect if Boston had brought in "Dr. Strangeglove" himself, Dick Stuart, as a fielding coach.

Or how about that catching spot? In 1990, nobody booted 'em behind the plate like Benito Santiago of the Padres. Those lessons must have rubbed off on Santiago's young substitute, Sandy Alomar Jr. Last year Sandy got his own chance to play regularly when he was dealt to the Indians. And wouldn't you know it, Alomar succeeded the injured Benito as the number one error man among catchers. What a story.

We could go on and on. Bobby Bonilla, the former "Mr. E-5," gets moved off third base . . . but now we have Gary Sheffield, with all that potential to excite the souvenir hunters in the stands behind first base. The Pirates moved Bonilla to right, and Bobby made a great effort to win the error crown at his new position. But Bonilla couldn't beat out young Sammy Sosa of the White Sox, another player with great "potential."

Of course, a club like this needs some stumbling veterans as well, and the "Hands of Stone" team has it. Isn't it exciting to think what Willie McGee (17 errors last year) will do in 1991, now that he has the winds at Candlestick to make his life even more interesting? Or what Julio Franco can accomplish, now that he's an experienced hand at second? And you have to love that Kevin Mitchell. In 1989, he was on highlight shows all season long for his nifty bare-handed catch. But who would have guessed he'd play the entire '90 season without a glove?

Our very favorite defensive player, though, is Matt Young, who will bring his very special style of play to Fenway Park this year. Matt has had some truly wonderful defensive seasons before. Like 1986 — 17 chances, four errors, a .765 fielding average. Or 1987 — six chances, two errors, a .667 fielding average. But because he was in the bullpen then, he never really had a chance to show America what he could do. Then came 1990, when the Mariners finally put Matt in their starting rotation all season. He didn't let us down. 52 chances, nine (!) errors, an .827 fielding average. Young now has a lifetime fielding average of .891; he's gaining on the legendary Mitch Williams (.871), who was once thought to be beyond reach when it came to defensive ineptitude. Don't look back (and get yourself hit in the eye), Mitch; someone's gaining on you.

Rafael Ramirez — the legend, the king, the man they all look up to. Hands of Stone Hall of Fame, first ballot. He'll probably drop the plaque.

Compared to that, the "Soft Hands" team is dull, dull, dull. Except maybe for Carney Lansford's snowmobile accident. (Exciting thought: Matt Young, behind a snowmobile! Gives us the chills.) Hey, Jose Oquendo, if we wanted to watch someone vacuuming a carpet, we'd go find a cleaning lady. And Cal Ripken — never misses a game, never makes an error. Cal, baby, you're putting us to sleep!

A complete listing for this category can be found on page 318.

WHO ARE THE PRIME PIVOT MEN?

We love good defensive statistics, and this is one of our favorites. It measures ability to turn the double play in simple terms — opportunities for the second baseman to get a DP on a toss from another fielder versus double plays actually turned. You might think that there would be no consistency from one year to another. Guess again. Here are the 1990 leaders in percentage of double plays turned (minimum 20 DPs completed):

Fielder, Team	DP Opp.	Turned	%
Fred Manrique, Min	35	28	.800
Frank White, KC	45	33	.733
Tommy Herr, Phi-Mets	79	57	.722
Tony Phillips, Det	38	27	.711
Scott Fletcher, WSox	98	69	.704
Willie Randolph, LA-Oak	60	41	.683
Al Newman, Min	40	27	.675
Bill Ripken, Bal	78	52	.667
Mike Gallego, Oak	41	27	.659
Jody Reed, Bos	59	38	.644

We'd be the first to admit that this stat is not perfect — it doesn't measure, among other things, how hard the ball was hit, or how quick the shortstop was at getting the ball to the second baseman. And yet Reed, Newman, Fletcher, Randolph and Ripken all made the leaders list in both 1989 and 1990. We think there's something to these stats, and something to the idea that some second baseman are simply quicker on the pivot than others are.

We felt this even more strongly when we looked at the 1990 trailers in percentage of DPs turned:

Fielder, Team	DP Opp.	Turned	%
Gregg Jefferies, Mets	53	20	.377
Jerry Browne, Cle	80	36	.450
Manny Lee, Tor	62	28	.452
Paul Molitor, Mil	41	19	.463
Bill Doran, Hou-Cin	48	23	.479

The key names here are Gregg Jefferies and Jerry Browne. Each made the trailers list in both 1989 and 1990, and we think that's no coincidence. Both are offensive second baseman, in the game primarily for their bats. The question is whether their teams can afford that, and whether the players' bats can overcome their defensive limitations. Jefferies is probably the worse of the two, and at this point it seems as though the Mets have given up on him — they've said that they have to move this guy off second base. Interestingly, the Mets were previously managed by Davey Johnson, no slouch on defense but a second baseman known primarily for his bat. Now the New Yorkers are managed by Bud Harrelson, a great-fielding shortstop but not much of a hitter. The Mets go for defense at second, with Tommy Herr, which makes you think they're committed to good glovework. But at the same time they have — curiously enough — apparently opted for a slugging shortstop in Howard Johnson. They've made the same choice — let's go for the hitter — except at a different position. And probably a more important one.

This is an age-old argument, and one that's hard to settle, even by an organization like ours which prides itself on supplying the cogent statistics. The general sabermetric argument is that, given the choice, you go for the hitter — as the cliche goes, shake a tree and a thousand gloves will drop out. And yet another cliche, the one about "strength up the middle," continues its hold on the central decision-makers in baseball. You'll seldom find a championship club that doesn't have good defense at short and second. We wonder how low the Mets will go with strictly a bat (HoJo) at shortstop, now that they appear to have given up on Jefferies at second.

A complete listing for this category can be found on page 319.

WHICH SHORTSTOPS ARE BEST AT GOING INTO THE HOLE?

The ultimate test of shortstopping is the ground ball "in the hole," the area deep to his right. To record an out, the shortstop must not only get in front of the ball, but must then reverse his momentum and make a strong and accurate throw to first base, or a long flip to second.

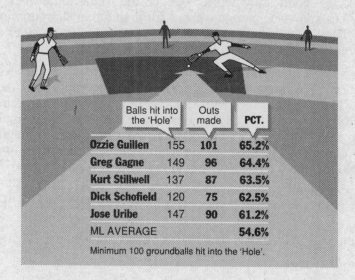

	Balls hit into the 'Hole'	Outs made	PCT.
Ozzie Guillen	155	101	65.2%
Greg Gagne	149	96	64.4%
Kurt Stillwell	137	87	63.5%
Dick Schofield	120	75	62.5%
Jose Uribe	147	90	61.2%
ML AVERAGE			54.6%

Minimum 100 groundballs hit into the 'Hole'.

The STATS Reporters are required to record the direction of each batted ball. We thought it would be interesting to ask our computer to count up all ground balls into the hole during 1989 and 1990, and see which shortstops most often meet this fielding challenge. Here's what we found for all shortstops who confronted at least 100 ground balls hit into the hole during either 1989 or 1990, sorted by their 1990 success rate. The overall major league success rate for 1990 was .546.

	American League					
	During 1989			During 1990		
Player, 1990 Team	Hit to Hole	Out Made	Success Rate	Hit to Hole	Out Made	Success Rate
Ozzie Guillen, WSox	195	125	.641	155	101	.652
Greg Gagne, Min	160	95	.594	149	96	.644
Kurt Stillwell, KC	118	73	.619	137	87	.635

Player	Hit to Hole	Out Made	Success Rate	Hit to Hole	Out Made	Success Rate
Dick Schofield, Cal	79	50	.633	120	75	.625
Cal Ripken, Bal	162	105	.648	140	84	.600
Alvaro Espinoza, Yanks	170	99	.582	130	77	.592
Walt Weiss, Oak	60	35	.583	130	77	.592
Jeff Huson, Tex	22	10	.455	110	65	.591
Alan Trammell, Det	125	83	.664	148	87	.588
Tony Fernandez, Tor	164	101	.616	162	94	.580
Omar Vizquel, Sea	109	70	.642	77	43	.558
Felix Fermin, Cle	167	112	.671	182	98	.538
Bill Spiers, Mil	97	59	.608	131	70	.534
Luis Rivera, Bos	84	46	.548	109	58	.532

	National League					
	During 1989			During 1990		
Player, 1990 Team	Hit to Hole	Out Made	Success Rate	Hit to Hole	Out Made	Success Rate
Jose Uribe, SF	119	78	.655	147	90	.612
Kevin Elster, Mets	120	68	.567	97	57	.588
Alfredo Griffin, LA	120	64	.533	155	88	.568
Shawon Dunston, Cubs	126	69	.548	103	57	.553
Jay Bell, Pit	58	31	.534	167	88	.527
Rafael Ramirez, Hou	118	68	.576	104	53	.510
Barry Larkin, Cin	82	52	.634	147	70	.476
Spike Owen, Mon	128	77	.602	131	62	.473
Ozzie Smith, StL	139	66	.475	140	66	.471
Andres Thomas, Atl	128	70	.547	60	27	.450
Dickie Thon, Phi	136	76	.559	137	58	.423
Garry Templeton, SD	144	74	.514	131	53	.405
Jeff Blauser, Atl	25	11	.440	117	33	.282

A shortstop is challenged about once per game. Notice how consistent a skill the play from the hole is — mostly the shortstops at the top or bottom of the 1990 list were in about the same place in 1989. The few larger changes, all declines of a hundred points, are mostly players whose age or limited experience make them bargains in most Rotisserie Leagues — specifically Fermin (-.133), Owen (-.129), Thon (-.137), and Templeton (-.109). However the biggest drop of all was by Barry Larkin (-.158) — perhaps his arm is not yet recovered from his 1989 injury.

The biggest surprise, at least for those who do not often see him play, is the low ranking of Ozzie Smith. Sadly, Ozzie's arm, never outstanding, now prevents any play to first at all on a ground ball hit to his right that he cannot get in front of. His grace afield remains a delight to watch. The younger Ozzie, Guillen of the White Sox, by leading in outs in both 1989 and 1990 as well as in success rate in 1990, must be considered the best shortstop in baseball. A pity that he does not have the older Ozzie's patience at bat.

One obvious question is whether there is an advantage in the study to shortstops who play on grass fields. This makes intuitive sense, since turf shortstops have to play deeper, and thus face a longer throw from the hole. However, two of three best in the American League for 1990 played their home games on turf. And while the top four in the NL for '90 played on grass fields, the 1989 data showed no obvious bias: three of the top four, and four of the top six, played their home games on turf.

A complete listing for this category can be found on page 320.

WHO'S BEST IN THE OUTFIELD ZONE?

By now, we hope you are familiar with the stats we use to measure defensive performance. The "zone rating" measures the number of outs recorded per number of balls hit in the fielder's fielding zone — that is, the percentage of outs he records on chances he could be expected to reach. The "range factor" is simpler — total chances handled cleanly per nine innings. Both are attempts to measure fielders' range statistically, rather than by reputation alone. And we think both are pretty good, though not perfect. Here are the five best — and single worst — left fielders in 1990, according to each system (minimum 700 innings played):

Left Fielders

Zone Ratings		Range Factors	
Rickey Henderson, Oak	.895	Rickey Henderson, Oak	2.68
Phil Bradley, Bal-WSox	.845	Barry Bonds, Pit	2.45
Tim Raines, Mon	.839	Dan Gladden, Min	2.42
Dan Gladden, Min	.825	Kevin Mitchell, SF	2.34
Vince Coleman, StL	.823	Phil Bradley, Bal-WSox	2.34
Worst		**Worst**	
Kevin McReynolds, Mets	.739	Kevin McReynolds, Mets	1.82

As we observed last season, speed is the key to being a good left fielder. Among the leaders in each category, only Kevin Mitchell would not be considered speedy. We can't see, for one thing, why Rickey Henderson doesn't have a better defensive reputation — could it be because the New York writers still don't like him? The trailer, Kevin McReynolds, is known as a "smart baserunner," as opposed to a fast one. McReynolds also has a reputation as a good outfielder; we agree that he's a smart one, but the ratings show his speed limitations.

Center Fielders

Zone Ratings		Range Factors	
Mitch Webster, Cle	.888	Mitch Webster, Cle	3.35
Mike Devereaux, Bal	.869	Lenny Dykstra, Phi	3.12
Mookie Wilson, Tor	.866	Mike Devereaux, Bal	3.01
Lance Johnson, WSox	.865	Dave Henderson, Oak	3.00
Dave Henderson, Oak	.853	Willie McGee, StL-Oak	2.93
Worst		**Worst**	
Ellis Burks, Bos	.778	Daryl Boston, WSox-Mets	2.28

Mitch Webster, center fielder supreme? You probably weren't ready for this, and the truth is that neither were we. Well, playing for the Indians, Mitch probably got a lot of practice running down long flyballs. The other players are more logical candidates for their lofty rankings — and let us put in a plug for Baltimore's Mike Devereaux, a fine flychaser not many people know about. Dykstra led the National in both zone rating (84.5) and range factor; we think he deserves more recognition.

Right Fielders

Zone Ratings		Range Factors	
Milt Thompson, StL	.876	Rob Deer, Mil	2.52
Tony Gwynn, SD	.854	Chet Lemon, Det	2.48
Darryl Strawberry, Mets	.849	Tony Gwynn, SD	2.40
Sammy Sosa, WSox	.843	Jesse Barfield, Yanks	2.38
Ruben Sierra, Tex	.838	Sammy Sosa, WSox	2.35
Worst		**Worst,**	
Andre Dawson, Cubs	.755	Dave Winfield, Yanks-Cal	1.67

Among right fielders, the big news is the man who ranked number last in range factor (worst in the AL in zone rating), Dave Winfield. Winfield showed last year that he's still a fine hitter, but his fielding woes — he also ranked at the bottom of our throwing rankings — suggest a nice, safe role for a fellow who's 39 years old — designated hitter.

We thought you'd like to see the STATS choices for outfield Gold Gloves, based on both stats and observation. We pick them by position, rather than choosing three outfielders, the way the official voters nonsensically do:

- **Left Field** — AL Rickey Henderson, NL Barry Bonds. Fairly easy choices; we'd have picked both even if they weren't the respective MVPs.

- **Center Field** — AL Gary Pettis, NL Lenny Dykstra. Andy Van Slyke is usually considered one of the best in the National League, but he continues to rank well down in our stats. We do like Andy, but we're going with Dykstra. In the American League, we just don't think Webster is the best, despite those great stats last year. How can you go wrong with Gary Pettis?

- **Right Field** — AL Jesse Barfield, NL Tony Gwynn. Gwynn is pretty automatic in the National League, and Barfield earns the nod over Cory Snyder and Ruben Sierra, both of whom slumped with the glove as well the bat last year, in the American. Sierra had good range stats, but made too many careless mistakes. Sammy Sosa also had outstanding range stats last year, but his 13 errors were way too many. Anyway, the White Sox seem about to hand his job to Snyder.

A complete listing for this category can be found on page 321.

APPENDIX

DANGER! DANGER! VOLUMES OF STATISTICS BEYOND THIS POINT!

Welcome to the Appendix! There are 80 pages of data in the following section, corresponding to Essays in the body of the book. For some of the Essays, (23, to be exact) all of the figures used for that particular study appear in the essay itself. In such cases, there is no additional data back here. In general, we've attempted to give you all the data which we used for the Essay — and then some.

Each Appendix is keyed twice. The "Title" key serves as a reminder as to what topic is being covered, and corrersponds to a title in the Table of Contents. The "Page" key refers you to the page where you'll find the appropriate essay.

Many fans of last year's Scoreboard were helpful in their comments concerning the organization of the charts, and we've made every effort to incorporate the best of their suggestions. Each Appendix is accompanied by a label — describing how the list has been ordered — a "minimum requirement" — telling you how much of what a player needed to make the list — and a key for deciphering any obscure abbreviations.

There are really two reasons for providing the detailed Appendices that follow. Reason #1 is so that if your favorite player (or pitcher) failed to make both the Top (alas!) and Bottom (whew!) of any category, there is still a place where you can find out where he stood. That's why most of the Appendices have been ordered alphabetically; it makes it easier to find your favorite player. Reason #2 is so that, if you like, you can pursue your own investigations.

Also note: there were lonesome, mournful cries in the letters we received on last year's book, many of them bemoaning the lack of an Index. The constant wailing kept many of us up nights, and we're pleased to say that an Index appears at the end of the book, after this section. Happy to oblige.

The team abbreviation following a player's name refers to the team with which he finished the season. Here are the abbreviations:

American League Teams		National League Teams	
Bal	Baltimore Orioles	Atl	Atlanta Braves
Bos	Boston Red Sox	ChN	Chicago Cubs
Cal	California Angels	Cin	Cincinnati Reds
ChA	Chicago White Sox	Hou	Houston Astros
Cle	Cleveland Indians	LA	Los Angeles Dodgers
Det	Detroit Tigers	Mon	Montreal Expos
KC	Kansas City Royals	NYN	New York Mets
Mil	Milwaukee Brewers	Phi	Philadelphia Phillies
Min	Minnesota Twins	Pit	Pittsburgh Pirates
NYA	New York Yankees	StL	St. Louis Cardinals
Oak	Oakland Athletics	SD	San Diego Padres
Sea	Seattle Mariners	SF	San Francisco Giants
Tex	Texas Rangers		
Tor	Toronto Blue Jays		

See you in Chicago (South Side, of course) for the 1991 World Series!

WHO'S REALLY OUT IN LEFT FIELD? (p. 16)

The first number at each position indicates the number of different players who started at that position. The second number indicates the number of players who played at that position in 1990.

Team	C	1B	2B	3B	SS	LF	CF	RF	DH/PH
Bal	3-3	7-8	4-5	5-5	1-4	8 -8	5-6	8 -9	21-23
Bos	3-3	6-7	3-6	3-5	3-3	2 -5	3-4	6 -6	13-21
Cal	4-4	6-7	8-8	6-6	5-6	5 -5	4-4	5 -5	7-20
ChA	2-3	5-7	3-3	2-3	2-3	4 -8	4-6	4 -9	14-21
Cle	2-2	7-7	4-5	6-6	5-5	5 -6	5-6	5 -6	10-18
Det	4-4	2-4	3-3	4-5	3-4	9 -10	6-7	8 -11	18 22
KC	4-4	6-7	5-5	4-7	3-3	9 -10	5-6	7 -11	12 20
Mil	3-3	6-7	5-7	6-8	3-4	4 -4	2-3	4 -4	9-16
Min	3-3	6-7	4-6	2-6	3-6	8 -9	3-5	7 -8	15-18
NYA	5-5	3-3	4-5	3-5	3-4	9 -10	3-3	6 -6	17-21
Oak	4-4	6-9	3-5	5-7	3-3	7 -10	5-7	8 -12	20 25
Sea	3-4	5-7	2-4	6-7	4-5	6 -7	3-5	5 -5	13-19
Tex	4-5	4-4	5-7	6-7	3-3	5 -9	5-7	6 -10	15 22
Tor	2-4	2-3	3-4	5-5	2-3	7 -8	4-4	5 -5	14-18
Atl	5-6	7-7	4-5	4-6	4-5	4 -7	2-3	5 -6	0-23
ChN	4-5	3-3	3-4	3-3	3-4	7 -10	3-4	5 -5	0-18
Cin	4-5	4-5	5-5	4-4	3-3	8 -9	3-4	3 -5	0-22
Hou	5-5	7-9	5-5	4-6	4-5	11-13	7-8	8 -11	0 26
LA	3-5	4-5	5-5	5-5	4-5	6 -7	5-7	5 -6	0-25
Mon	4-4	4-5	4-4	2-4	2-4	6 -8	4-5	7 -8	0-22
NYN	6-7	5-6	4-5	5-5	5-5	7 -10	4-6	6 -7	0-27
Phi	4-4	5-5	5-5	3-3	2-2	8 -9	4-5	6 -9	0-24
Pit	4-5	4-5	3-3	3-4	2-3	7 -9	5-6	3 -6	0-21
StL	3-3	7-7	5-5	5-6	3-4	8 -9	5-8	9 -10	0 21
SD	4-5	4-4	4-4	4-4	5-5	6 -7	5-5	6 -6	0-21
SF	5-6	5-5	4-6	3-5	5-8	6 -7	2-4	6 -7	0-23

IS THE SKYDOME HOME RUN HEAVEN? (p. 18)

Blue Jays players with 100+ AB or 25+ IP at SkyDome

Dome Open	G	AB	R	H	2B	3B	HR	RBI	BB	K	SB	AVG	SLG	OBP
Tony FERNANDEZ	36	143	18	41	9	7	1	20	14	12	2	.287	.469	.358
Fred McGRIFF	35	126	24	36	6	0	8	21	23	15	1	.286	.524	.393
John OLERUD	28	89	12	25	2	0	6	9	15	20	0	.281	.506	.387
Pat BORDERS	26	54	8	15	3	0	3	12	7	6	0	.278	.500	.355
Mookie WILSON	31	119	10	32	8	1	0	7	4	26	4	.269	.353	.293
George BELL	27	106	12	26	4	0	3	10	5	16	0	.245	.368	.283
Junior FELIX	25	87	12	21	6	3	0	6	8	19	3	.241	.379	.299
Glenallen HILL	23	64	13	15	4	0	4	7	4	16	1	.234	.484	.279
Manny LEE	28	95	9	21	2	0	0	10	7	23	2	.221	.242	.275
Greg MYERS	24	70	6	16	1	0	1	6	8	13	0	.229	.286	.304
Kelly GRUBER	34	136	14	28	4	0	6	18	7	24	2	.206	.368	.252
Team Totals	36	1214	151	300	55	11	33	140	118	219	19	.247	.392	.315

Dome Closed	G	AB	R	H	2B	3B	HR	RBI	BB	K	SB	AVG	SLG	OBP
Kelly GRUBER	43	169	34	61	9	4	17	44	10	23	3	.361	.763	.395
Tony FERNANDEZ	45	178	28	58	8	5	1	18	17	24	10	.326	.444	.390
Manny LEE	30	95	12	29	2	2	2	9	4	22	1	.305	.432	.330
Pat BORDERS	37	110	16	30	10	1	7	16	5	17	0	.273	.573	.299
Fred McGRIFF	42	138	18	37	4	0	6	17	32	22	0	.268	.428	.405
John OLERUD	30	98	13	26	5	1	5	17	14	23	0	.265	.490	.357
George BELL	43	168	24	44	8	0	8	31	11	25	0	.262	.452	.309,
Greg MYERS	19	52	9	13	1	0	2	7	5	6	0	.250	.385	.310
Junior FELIX	42	149	23	37	7	3	7	23	16	31	3	.248	.477	.325
Glenallen HILL	25	76	12	18	4	0	3	10	7	13	0	.237	.408	.301
Mookie WILSON	38	152	21	35	8	1	0	13	8	24	6	.230	.296	.269
Team Totals	45	1526	234	424	75	18	60	227	148	250	27	.278	.469	.342

Dome Open	W	L	IP	ERA	AVG	SLG	OBP	H	HR	BB	K
David WELLS	3	2	45.2	2.56	.235	.388	.288	40	4	13	28
Tom HENKE	1	0	13.2	2.63	.208	.415	.263	11	2	4	13
Todd STOTTLEMYRE	3	4	45.2	3.35	.271	.345	.337	48	1	15	31
Frank WILLS	0	1	26.1	3.42	.253	.414	.288	25	3	5	12
Dave STIEB	4	3	49.2	3.44	.237	.332	.308	45	3	17	30
Jimmy KEY	2	2	37.1	3.62	.293	.447	.301	44	4	2	23
Duane WARD	0	3	28.1	3.81	.229	.333	.264	24	2	5	18
John CERUTTI	2	1	32.2	4.13	.313	.508	.348	40	4	8	16
Jim ACKER	1	3	25.1	5.33	.327	.433	.386	34	1	10	14
Willie BLAIR	0	1	8.2	12.46	.359	.564	.444	14	1	6	5
Team Totals	16	20	333.0	3.68	.270	.400	.319	348	26	92	201

Dome Closed	W	L	IP	ERA	AVG	SLG	OBP	H	HR	BB	K
Willie BLAIR	3	1	23.2	0.76	.138	.175	.217	11	0	9	16
Tom HENKE	1	0	24.0	2.25	.222	.378	.278	20	4	7	27
Jim ACKER	1	0	27.1	2.30	.276	.419	.350	29	2	10	13
Duane WARD	0	1	37.1	2.41	.183	.260	.241	24	2	9	35
David WELLS	0	0	37.0	2.68	.235	.386	.279	31	5	7	20
Dave STIEB	5	2	53.1	2.87	.273	.383	.333	57	3	18	34
Todd STOTTLEMYRE	4	4	57.1	5.02	.281	.452	.341	64	8	20	31
Jimmy KEY	5	1	51.1	5.08	.265	.430	.302	53	8	11	29
Frank WILLS	3	3	35.2	5.30	.259	.430	.315	35	7	11	28
John CERUTTI	3	4	38.1	6.34	.288	.527	.356	42	10	12	11
Team Totals	28	17	416.0	4.00	.261	.414	.318	413	49	125	254

WHICH TEAMS HAVE NIGHT VISION? (p. 30)

Both Leagues — Listed Alphabetically (500+ Plate Appearances)

Player, Team	Day	Ngt	Dff	Player, Team	Day	Ngt	Dff	Player, Team	Day	Ngt	Dff
Alomar R, SD	.329	.270	-60	Griffin Alf, LA	.172	.226	55	Puckett, Min	.346	.279	-68
Barfield Je, NYA	.241	.247	6	Gruber, Tor	.236	.290	54	Quintana, Bos	.300	.282	-18
Bell Geo, Tor	.309	.247	-62	Guerrero, StL	.321	.265	-56	Raines, Mon	.273	.292	20
Bell Jay, Pit	.281	.244	-37	Guillen, ChA	.282	.278	-5	Reed Jd, Bos	.328	.273	-55
Biggio, Hou	.390	.239	-151	Gwynn T, SD	.260	.329	69	Reynolds H, Sea	.241	.256	15
Boggs W, Bos	.328	.289	-39	Harper B, Min	.310	.290	-20	Ripken C, Bal	.290	.235	-55
Bonds, Pit	.283	.307	24	Hatcher B, Cin	.228	.291	64	Roberts Bip, SD	.274	.323	49
Bonilla B, Pit	.289	.277	-12	Hayes C, Phi	.207	.276	70	Sabo, Cin	.232	.282	50
Brett, KC	.307	.337	29	Hayes V, Phi	.292	.251	-41	Samuel, LA	.226	.248	22
Brooks, LA	.271	.264	-7	HendersonR,Oak	.287	.346	59	Sandberg,ChN	.319	.292	-27
Browne J, Cle	.247	.275	29	Herr, NYN	.245	.267	23	Sax S, NYA	.322	.234	-88
Brunansky, Bos	.280	.245	-35	Hrbek, Min	.286	.287	1	Seitzer, KC	.245	.284	39
Burks, Bos	.293	.297	4	Incaviglia, Tex	.161	.247	86	Sheffield, Mil	.275	.302	28
Butler, SF	.294	.318	24	Jacoby, Cle	.263	.305	42	Sierra, Tex	.259	.284	25
Calderon, ChA	.266	.276	10	James C, Cle	.331	.288	-43	Smith Lo, Atl	.333	.294	-39
Caminiti, Hou	.252	.239	-13	Jefferies, NYN	.317	.265	-52	Smith O, StL	.236	.262	26
Canseco, Oak	.277	.273	-4	Johnson H,NYN	.267	.231	-37	Sosa, ChA	.188	.248	60
Carter J, SD	.207	.242	35	Johnson L, ChA	.298	.280	-18	Stillwell, KC	.306	.228	-77
Clark W, SF	.268	.313	45	Justice, Atl	.231	.299	68	Strawberry, NYN	.302	.264	-37
Coleman, StL	.285	.294	10	Kelly, NYA	.306	.278	-28	Stubbs, Hou	.224	.276	52
Daniels, LA	.277	.302	25	Kruk, Phi	.296	.290	-7	Surhoff BJ, Mil	.250	.288	38
Daulton, Phi	.296	.259	-37	Lansford, Oak	.279	.262	-16	Templeton, SD	.276	.238	-38
Davis A, Sea	.281	.284	3	Larkin B, Cin	.293	.304	12	Tettleton, Bal	.230	.220	-10
Davis E, Cin	.288	.250	-38	Leonard J, Sea	.236	.256	20	Thompson R, SF	.256	.237	-19
Dawson, ChN	.326	.293	-32	Lind, Pit	.307	.245	-62	Thon, Phi	.180	.281	101
Deer, Mil	.161	.231	70	Magadan,NYN	.305	.339	34	Trammell, Det	.331	.292	-39
Deshields, Mon	.284	.290	7	Maldonado, Cle	.337	.248	-90	Treadway, Atl	.301	.277	-24
Dunston, ChN	.271	.253	-18	Martinez E, Sea	.280	.309	29	Van Slyke, Pit	.277	.287	10
Dykstra, Phi	.359	.315	-44	McGee, Oak	.373	.306	-68	Ventura, ChA	.240	.253	12
Eisenreich, KC	.345	.261	-84	McGriff F, Tor	.293	.303	10	Wallach, Mon	.335	.280	-56
Evans Dw, Bos	.305	.224	-81	McGwire, Oak	.229	.240	11	Weiss, Oak	.281	.253	-28
Felix, Tor	.263	.264	1	McReynolds,NYN	.298	.254	-44	Whitaker, Det	.220	.245	25
Fernandez , Tor	.290	.269	-21	Mitchell K, SF	.296	.286	-10	White D, Cal	.230	.213	-16
Fielder, Det	.212	.304	92	Murphy Dl, Phi	.225	.251	26	Williams MD, SF	.292	.267	-25
Finley S, Bal	.234	.265	31	Murray E, LA	.318	.334	16	Wilson M, Tor	.236	.278	42
Fisk, ChA	.266	.290	24	O'Neill, Cin	.243	.282	38	Winfield, Cal	.233	.280	48
Fletcher S, ChA	.266	.234	-32	Oquendo, StL	.201	.274	72	Worthington, Bal	.256	.214	-42
Franco Ju, Tex	.266	.301	35	Owen S, Mon	.242	.231	-11	Yelding, Hou	.248	.257	9
Gaetti, Min	.208	.236	27	Palmeiro, Tex	.315	.320	6	Yount, Mil	.197	.271	74
Galarraga, Mon	.207	.275	67	Parker D, Mil	.259	.302	43	Zeile, StL	.255	.242	-13
Gant, Atl	.294	.306	12	Parrish Ln, Cal	.208	.279	71				
Gladden, Min	.311	.264	-47	Pena T, Bos	.234	.273	38	AL Total	.259	.259	0
Grace, ChN	.322	.295	-27	Perry G, KC	.308	.236	-72	NL Total	.270	.261	-9
Greenwell, Bos	.341	.278	-62	Phillips, Det	.235	.258	23				
Griffey Jr, Sea	.338	.287	-51	Presley, Atl	.226	.247	21				

WHICH TEAMS ARE BEST IN THE CLUTCH? (p. 36)

1990 Team Batting and Pitching — Late & Close Situations

American League Batting

Team	AVG	OBP	SLG	AB	R	H	2B	3B	HR	BB	K
Baltimore	.245	.340	.385	902	123	221	29	2	31	129	170
Boston	.283	.358	.396	938	122	265	44	7	16	110	158
California	.248	.327	.381	939	123	233	36	4	27	111	179
Chicago	.245	.320	.345	826	105	202	34	5	13	89	161
Cleveland	.249	.318	.354	830	107	207	39	3	14	84	151
Detroit	.228	.323	.331	797	93	182	37	3	13	107	159
Kansas City	.258	.314	.383	841	101	217	32	8	19	67	154
Milwaukee	.237	.304	.318	817	112	194	29	2	11	77	137
Minnesota	.252	.316	.347	853	98	215	33	6	12	76	126
New York	.237	.304	.378	966	121	229	42	5	28	90	190
Oakland	.269	.360	.374	733	106	197	30	4	13	103	149
Seattle	.248	.327	.347	925	117	229	36	7	14	104	148
Texas	.261	.337	.389	936	111	244	45	3	23	107	190
Toronto	.254	.313	.377	917	123	233	37	8	20	80	172

American League Pitching

Team	AVG	OBP	SLG	AB	R	H	2B	3B	HR	BB	K
Baltimore	.250	.334	.378	864	88	216	28	4	25	112	149
Boston	.249	.319	.365	943	109	235	40	3	21	94	173
California	.260	.324	.361	928	93	241	34	3	18	89	188
Chicago	.215	.305	.307	997	105	214	36	7	14	126	196
Cleveland	.247	.324	.347	740	59	183	34	2	12	81	128
Detroit	.263	.347	.382	778	59	205	30	4	18	98	112
Kansas City	.280	.354	.404	797	90	223	41	2	18	86	173
Milwaukee	.267	.325	.390	884	84	236	40	9	17	76	143
Minnesota	.271	.338	.391	808	69	219	38	4	17	79	150
New York	.251	.345	.379	949	74	238	27	13	23	134	139
Oakland	.190	.250	.263	830	61	158	25	1	11	65	166
Seattle	.258	.335	.374	899	78	232	37	2	21	101	182
Texas	.257	.342	.384	913	83	235	56	6	16	120	165
Toronto	.262	.321	.397	890	69	233	37	7	23	73	180
AL Total	**.251**	**.326**	**.362**								

National League Batting

Team	AVG	OBP	SLG	AB	R	H	2B	3B	HR	BB	K
Atlanta	.216	.282	.342	804	107	174	29	3	22	72	174
Chicago	.278	.338	.403	910	134	253	33	9	21	83	156
Cincinnati	.246	.313	.363	879	97	216	38	7	17	82	142
Houston	.247	.329	.351	949	121	234	30	9	17	117	186
Los Angeles	.257	.342	.373	764	103	196	32	3	17	96	155
Montreal	.258	.333	.352	1141	149	294	41	8	17	127	217
New York	.255	.318	.383	945	122	241	42	2	25	86	158
Philadelphia	.285	.371	.390	904	123	258	31	5	18	118	159
Pittsburgh	.252	.332	.355	805	97	203	38	3	13	99	142
St. Louis	.250	.334	.327	897	97	224	41	2	8	114	151
San Diego	.246	.328	.353	994	105	245	32	7	20	118	177
San Francisco	.267	.331	.391	906	126	242	28	3	26	86	165

National League Pitching

Team	AVG	OBP	SLG	AB	R	H	2B	3B	HR	BB	K
Atlanta	.276	.370	.390	815	95	225	28	4	19	119	168
Chicago	.270	.346	.372	922	79	249	37	3	17	106	172
Cincinnati	.233	.309	.344	928	74	216	37	6	18	100	235
Houston	.250	.323	.350	964	77	241	37	4	17	102	174
Los Angeles	.262	.336	.378	798	73	209	29	2	20	83	137
Montreal	.263	.335	.396	1109	93	292	36	3	35	119	174
New York	.233	.296	.331	842	80	196	27	7	14	75	161
Philadelphia	.252	.335	.343	866	83	218	32	4	13	107	129
Pittsburgh	.237	.310	.335	849	90	201	35	3	14	92	168
St. Louis	.289	.349	.425	849	67	245	45	13	15	85	138
San Diego	.259	.332	.375	983	88	255	33	6	23	107	172
San Francisco	.239	.313	.340	976	75	233	39	6	16	103	156
NL Total	**.254**	**.328**	**.362**								

WHY THROW TO FIRST? (p. 38)

Both Leagues — Listed Alphabetically (25+ Stolen Base Attempts)

Runner, Team	No Throws Made			Throws Made		
	SB	CS	%	SB	CS	%
Alomar R, SD	10	2	83	11	5	69
Biggio, Hou	13	3	81	8	7	53
Bonds, Pit	15	1	94	25	9	74
Boston, NYN	12	3	80	6	4	60
Butler, SF	21	8	72	28	10	74
Calderon, ChA	17	7	71	9	8	53
Canseco, Oak	8	4	67	9	3	75
Carter J, SD	9	2	82	9	3	75
Cole, Cle	6	0	100	25	9	74
Coleman, StL	25	5	83	33	11	75
Deshields, Mon	13	5	72	22	15	59
Devereaux, Bal	2	3	40	9	8	53
Doran, Cin	15	3	83	5	5	50
Dunston, ChN	6	1	86	13	1	93
Dykstra, Phi	12	1	92	16	4	80
Eisenreich, KC	6	3	67	5	8	38
Felder, Mil	6	2	75	13	3	81
Fernandez T, Tor	15	3	83	9	10	47
Finley S, Bal	7	3	70	12	6	67
Franco Ju, Tex	18	3	86	11	5	69
Gant, Atl	13	7	65	17	9	65
Gibson K, LA	7	2	78	10	0	100
Gladden, Min	12	5	71	9	4	69
Griffey Jr, Sea	5	3	62	8	7	53
Guillen, ChA	7	7	50	3	9	25
Gwynn T, SD	7	5	58	4	3	57
Harris L, LA	5	6	45	7	4	64
Hatcher B, Cin	7	3	70	15	4	79
Henderson R, Oak	19	2	90	29	6	83
Hudler, StL	5	1	83	10	7	59
Johnson H, NYN	13	4	76	19	2	90
Johnson L, ChA	13	3	81	18	13	58
Kelly, NYA	11	3	79	24	11	69
Lansford, Oak	5	9	36	5	1	83
Larkin B, Cin	9	1	90	9	4	69
McGee, Oak	12	3	80	18	4	82
Nixon O, Mon	16	2	89	21	9	70
Pettis, Tex	10	1	91	26	12	68
Phillips, Det	7	4	64	8	5	62
Polonia, Cal	10	4	71	7	7	50
Raines, Mon	24	7	77	14	6	70
Reynolds H, Sea	11	7	61	17	8	68
Roberts Bip, SD	12	2	86	27	6	82
Sabo, Cin	8	1	89	11	6	65
Samuel, LA	12	5	71	20	11	65
Sandberg, ChN	19	1	95	5	6	45
Sax S, NYA	15	3	83	17	6	74
Sheffield, Mil	14	2	87	6	7	46
Smith O, StL	13	2	87	12	4	75
Sosa, ChA	11	5	69	15	8	65
Stubbs, Hou	14	1	93	5	4	56
Surhoff BJ, Mil	14	3	82	4	3	57
Thompson M, StL	15	2	88	9	2	82
Walker L, Mon	8	2	80	10	4	71
Webster M, Cle	13	2	87	5	3	62
White D, Cal	6	3	67	8	2	80
Wilson M, Tor	9	1	90	14	3	82
Wilson W, KC	12	2	86	9	4	69
Yelding, Hou	15	0	100	39	20	66

Note: Steals of second with second base open only

WHICH TEAMS HAVE LEAD FEET? (p. 42)

1990 Team Baserunning — Ranked By Extra Base%

American League

Team	Runs Scored Rank	%	Opportunities	Extra Bases Taken	Outs on the Bases
Chicago	9	45.8	1046	479	28
Milwaukee	5	45.2	1131	511	27
Oakland	3	44.2	1088	481	27
Toronto	1	44.2	1112	492	27
Texas	10	44.0	1067	470	27
Kansas City	6	43.1	1196	515	32
Cleveland	5	43.0	1150	494	45
Baltimore	11	42.6	1068	455	29
California	8	42.4	1042	442	35
Minnesota	12	41.8	1079	451	49
Detroit	2	40.6	1039	422	35
Seattle	13	39.4	1094	431	27
New York	14	38.8	987	383	27
Boston	7	38.0	1193	453	31

National League

Team	Runs Scored Rank	%	Opportunities	Extra Bases Taken	Outs on the Bases
Los Angeles	3	47.2	1081	510	32
New York	1	46.2	1082	500	48
Cincinnati	5	45.0	1067	480	28
Montreal	9	44.9	1028	462	36
San Diego	8	43.6	1060	462	39
Pittsburgh	2	43.1	1025	442	35
San Francisco	4	42.7	1118	477	23
Houston	12	42.2	1012	427	36
Chicago	6	42.0	1101	462	33
St. Louis	11	41.1	1138	468	27
Philadelphia	10	40.3	1148	463	31
Atlanta	7	38.7	1003	388	38

WHICH UMPIRES ARE OFFENSIVE? (p. 44)

Home Plate Umpires — Listed Alphabetically

American League Umpires: 1990

Umpire	G	Count 0-0 C%	3-0 C%	3-2 C%	R/G	W/G	AVG
Barnett, L	37	40.1	55.4	20.2	8.6	6.1	.254
Brinkman, J	36	35.2	61.8	18.3	8.4	7.3	.265
Cedarstrom	11	35.6	61.9	13.5	8.0	6.5	.268
Clark, A	34	37.1	60.7	8.8	7.7	6.4	.248
Coble, D	37	36.2	63.6	16.4	8.9	6.3	.252
Cooney, T	36	35.2	60.5	14.2	9.8	7.6	.272
Cousins, D	33	33.5	52.0	12.5	9.0	7.9	.270
Craft, T	15	38.8	56.9	14.3	7.9	6.3	.247
Denkinger, D	33	34.2	49.6	23.0	7.9	6.8	.248
Evans, J	37	37.3	60.7	15.7	8.1	6.8	.258
Ford, D	36	35.2	58.3	12.2	9.0	7.6	.263
Garcia, R	37	36.5	56.3	10.8	8.4	6.7	.252
Hendry, T	26	38.3	61.5	14.0	8.6	6.3	.263
Hickox, D	12	36.5	54.1	24.2	10.2	5.5	.288
Hirschbeck, J	38	36.9	64.8	16.5	8.5	7.2	.253
Johnson, M	32	37.8	69.5	15.8	8.0	6.9	.246
Joyce, J	28	39.1	52.9	12.9	9.1	6.4	.268
Kaiser, K	18	35.7	55.4	15.4	8.6	6.2	.264
Kosc, G	37	41.4	58.2	16.3	7.8	5.9	.260
McClelland, T	37	32.9	55.6	12.4	9.1	7.2	.260
McCoy, L	36	41.9	60.9	18.9	7.7	5.3	.251
McKean, J	35	38.3	52.4	16.5	8.0	5.8	.257
Meriwether, C	20	35.5	65.7	7.2	10.4	6.8	.299
Merrill, D	36	37.0	53.4	16.8	9.4	7.0	.263
Morrison, D	37	33.3	63.7	11.8	8.2	6.9	.254
Palermo, S	25	38.8	60.2	10.2	8.8	8.0	.262
Phillips, D	36	37.6	60.9	16.4	9.0	6.6	.267
Reed, R	35	36.1	59.8	17.0	9.3	6.7	.270
Reilly, M	36	35.8	64.1	12.9	7.9	7.0	.249
Roe, R	36	31.6	57.9	9.2	9.5	7.8	.269
Scott, D	30	37.0	52.9	13.0	8.7	6.3	.240
Shulock, J	36	36.1	54.8	19.0	9.6	7.3	.274
Tschida, T	28	36.2	53.5	21.7	7.1	6.5	.247
Voltaggio, V	30	38.3	57.1	19.6	7.9	6.6	.245
Welke, T	36	38.0	58.5	23.8	9.0	5.9	.259
Young, L	31	34.6	57.4	15.7	8.1	6.4	.251
AL Average		**36.7**	**57.8**	**15.3**	**8.6**	**6.7**	**.259**

C% = Percentage of pitches taken by batters at that count which were called strikes

G = Games; R/G = Runs per Game; W/G = Walks per Game; AVG = Batting Average

National League Umpires: 1990

Umpire	G	Count 0-0 C%	3-0 C%	3-2 C%	R/G	W/G	AVG
Barnes, R	11	35.1	80.0	10.7	7.0	5.4	.252
Bonin, G	35	38.3	64.4	17.4	7.4	5.6	.254
Brocklander, F	24	37.3	50.7	11.7	8.3	6.8	.255
Crawford, J	37	34.0	53.9	20.8	9.0	7.0	.261
Darling, G	37	37.3	57.1	17.1	8.7	6.5	.253
Davidson, B	35	39.7	66.7	26.8	8.6	5.2	.250
Davis, G	37	35.7	59.2	22.6	7.7	5.6	.245
DeMuth, D	38	34.0	57.9	14.2	8.4	6.6	.262
Engel, B	4	30.9	73.7	16.7	15.0	7.5	.305
Froemming, B	38	33.5	65.5	13.4	7.7	6.4	.252
Gregg, E	25	38.8	76.6	9.6	7.8	5.5	.247
Hallion, T	35	37.1	57.1	12.1	9.4	6.7	.264
Harvey, D	37	34.3	56.2	13.6	8.7	6.3	.256
Hirschbeck, M	31	36.1	61.7	24.7	8.4	5.2	.258
Hohn, B	29	37.0	51.7	13.8	8.8	5.4	.265
Layne, J	33	36.6	53.0	15.2	8.2	7.6	.262
Marsh, R	36	34.1	59.4	11.2	8.8	6.6	.256
McSherry, J	35	34.0	55.2	17.7	9.0	7.3	.261
Montague, E	34	35.4	55.8	20.9	7.1	6.1	.251
Pulli, F	36	36.5	54.1	13.6	7.2	5.8	.256
Quick, J	35	35.5	59.0	17.0	9.4	6.6	.259
Rapuano, E	16	35.2	66.0	32.5	8.6	5.0	.275
Reliford, C	16	30.5	60.3	27.3	10.0	7.7	.275
Rennert, D	32	36.2	68.0	19.8	8.5	6.6	.254
Rippley, S	38	34.3	60.0	11.5	9.1	7.2	.254
Runge, P	32	37.2	61.7	17.2	7.7	7.1	.245
Tata, T	35	36.9	53.6	16.3	8.6	6.5	.254
Wendelstedt, H	34	40.2	54.3	19.0	7.4	6.0	.247
West, J	36	34.9	50.4	14.1	9.3	7.8	.260
Wickham, D	1	30.3	60.0	0.0	31.0	4.0	.442
Williams, C	36	34.5	60.3	16.7	8.1	6.2	.257
Winters, M	34	34.2	62.4	21.2	7.8	6.5	.251
NL Average		**35.9**	**58.0**	**17.0**	**8.4**	**6.4**	**.256**

C% = Percentage of pitches taken by batters at that count which were called strikes

G = Games; R/G = Runs per Game; W/G = Walks per Game; AVG = Batting Average

WHEN CAN A MONTH SEEM LIKE A YEAR? (p. 46)

The Top 25 Batting and Pitching Months of 1990

Batting (75 or more Plate Appearances)

Player	Month	AVG	SLG	OBP	AB	R	H	2B	3B	HR	RBI	SB	BB
Dykstra, Phi	May	.431	.569	.512	102	24	44	9	1	1	12	5	16
Morris H, Cin	July	.427	.640	.438	75	17	32	3	2	3	13	3	3
Mack, Min	September	.427	.573	.482	75	10	32	3	1	2	15	6	7
Magadan, NYN	June	.402	.598	.485	87	23	35	5	3	2	17	0	14
Polonia, Cal	September	.402	.471	.448	87	12	35	2	2	0	7	4	8
Grace, ChN	August	.398	.583	.451	108	14	43	8	0	4	26	3	10
Jacoby, Cle	June	.394	.625	.452	104	17	41	4	1	6	21	1	11
McGee, Oak	July	.392	.495	.427	97	12	38	7	0	1	15	4	5
Sabo, Cin	April	.391	.719	.487	64	16	25	6	0	5	12	4	12
Murray E, LA	September	.390	.620	.483	100	21	39	5	0	6	15	2	19
Thomas F, ChA	September	.389	.600	.513	90	20	35	4	0	5	17	0	23
Brett, KC	September	.389	.644	.433	90	12	35	7	2	4	16	2	7
Brett, KC	July	.388	.716	.442	116	27	45	18	1	6	24	2	12
Griffey Jr, Sea	April	.387	.625	.419	80	10	31	2	1	5	17	1	5
Larkin B, Cin	April	.385	.446	.461	65	12	25	2	1	0	12	4	8
Javier, LA	September	.385	.462	.459	65	13	25	2	0	1	3	2	9
Guillen, ChA	May	.383	.457	.410	94	10	36	3	2	0	8	5	5
Puckett, Min	May	.382	.706	.457	102	23	39	13	1	6	21	0	13
Hudler, StL	August	.378	.689	.395	74	10	28	7	2	4	15	4	1
Harper B, Min	July	.378	.520	.415	98	12	37	11	0	1	13	2	5
Samuel, LA	September	.377	.662	.424	77	14	29	8	1	4	15	3	7
Harris L, LA	September	.377	.481	.435	77	14	29	5	0	1	4	2	8
Sandberg, ChN	June	.377	.789	.438	114	32	43	3	1	14	25	6	13
Strawberry, NYN	June	.376	.731	.477	93	22	35	3	0	10	27	3	17
Sandberg, ChN	May	.373	.686	.427	118	22	44	10	0	9	21	6	12

Pitching (25 or more Innings Pitched)

Pitcher	Month	ERA	W	L	S	IP	H	R	ER	BB	K
Boyd, Mon	May	0.55	2	0	0	33.0	26	3	2	9	24
Cook D, LA	April	0.66	3	0	0	27.1	15	2	2	6	6
Smith Z, Pit	September	0.66	3	1	0	41.0	26	9	3	4	30
Whitson, SD	August	0.86	3	0	0	42.0	41	4	4	6	24
Stieb, Tor	July	0.94	3	0	0	28.2	16	3	3	13	17
Finley C, Cal	April	0.96	3	1	0	28.0	19	6	3	7	13
Tudor, StL	April	0.96	4	0	0	28.0	19	3	3	7	8
Clemens, Bos	July	1.00	2	2	0	45.0	38	8	5	9	38
Bolton, Bos	July	1.04	4	1	0	34.2	21	4	4	16	20
Darwin, Hou	July	1.04	4	0	0	43.1	28	5	5	7	28
Welch, Oak	April	1.06	3	1	0	34.0	23	5	4	7	13
McCaskill, Cal	April	1.07	2	0	0	25.1	22	3	3	13	13
Clemens, Bos	August	1.09	6	0	0	49.1	43	6	6	5	48
Boddicker, Bos	August	1.11	2	2	0	40.2	33	9	5	12	25
Charlton, Cin	August	1.22	2	1	0	44.1	30	9	6	18	25
Rijo, Cin	September	1.26	4	2	0	57.0	35	11	8	19	51
Portugal, Hou	August	1.27	4	0	0	35.1	33	7	5	12	29
Viola, NYN	April	1.32	4	0	0	27.1	18	4	4	2	29
Stewart D, Oak	April	1.32	5	0	0	34.0	26	5	5	12	14
Hurst, SD	September	1.33	3	0	0	47.1	35	7	7	8	33
Stewart D, Oak	September	1.35	5	0	0	40.0	30	9	6	14	24
Gardner M, Mon	July	1.35	2	1	0	40.0	19	6	6	11	40
Farr, KC	August	1.35	2	0	1	26.2	21	4	4	3	17
Erickson S, Min	September	1.35	5	0	0	46.2	27	10	7	21	21
McDonald, Bal	July	1.39	3	0	0	32.1	25	6	5	6	19

WHO ARE THE SLOWEST-STARTING BATTERIES (p. 50)

Average game time for starting pitchers (15+ starts) and catchers (54+ starts).

Both Leagues — Listed Alphabetically

Pitcher, Team	GS	Time	Pitcher, Team	GS	Time	Pitcher, Team	GS	Time
Abbott, Cal	33	2:56	Hough, Tex	32	2:59	Tapani, Min	28	2:37
Anderson A, Min	31	2:39	Howell K, Phi	18	2:45	Tudor, StL	22	2:49
Appier, KC	24	2:47	Hurst, SD	33	2:52	Valenzuela, LA	33	2:57
Armstrong, Cin	27	2:44	Jackson Dan, Cin	21	2:49	Viola, NYN	35	2:40
Avery, Atl	20	2:45	Johnson D, Bal	29	3:01	Walk, Pit	24	2:56
Ballard, Bal	17	3:02	Johnson R, Sea	33	3:00	Welch, Oak	35	2:45
Belcher, LA	24	2:44	Key, Tor	27	2:56	Wells, Tor	25	3:06
Benes, SD	31	2:54	Kiecker, Bos	25	2:55	West, Min	27	2:44
Bielecki, ChN	29	2:50	King E, ChA	25	3:03	Whitson, SD	32	2:34
Black, Tor	31	2:44	Knudson, Mil	27	2:59	Wilson S, ChN	15	2:50
Blyleven, Cal	23	2:58	Krueger, Mil	17	3:03	Wilson Tr, SF	17	2:41
Boddicker, Bos	34	2:55	LaPoint, NYA	27	2:58	Witt B, Tex	32	2:59
Bolton, Bos	16	2:59	Langston, Cal	33	3:04	Witt M, NYA	16	2:56
Bosio, Mil	20	2:57	Leary, NYA	31	2:55	Young C, Oak	21	3:01
Boskie, ChN	15	2:44	Leibrandt, Atl	24	2:46	Young Mt, Sea	33	2:52
Boyd, Mon	31	2:56	Lilliquist, SD	18	2:42			
Brown Kev, Tex	26	2:56	Maddux G, ChN	35	2:34			
Browning, Cin	35	2:39	Magrane, StL	31	2:39	Catcher, Team	GS	Time
Burkett, SF	32	2:55	Mahler R, Cin	16	2:41	Alomar S, Cle	118	2:48
Candiotti, Cle	29	2:42	Martinez De, Mon	32	3:02	Biggio, Hou	101	2:48
Cary, NYA	27	2:58	Martinez R, LA	33	2:59	Borders, Tor	83	2:53
Cerutti, Tor	23	2:58	McCaskill, Cal	29	2:57	Carter G, SF	58	2:54
Charlton, Cin	16	2:37	McDonald, Bal	15	2:59	Daulton, Phi	123	2:52
Clemens, Bos	31	2:58	McDowell J, ChA	33	3:09	Fisk, ChA	112	3:03
Combs, Phi	31	2:55	Milacki, Bal	24	3:07	Fitzgerald, Mon	84	2:58
Cone, NYN	30	2:52	Mitchell J, Bal	17	2:57	Geren, NYA	81	2:55
Cook D, LA	16	3:02	Moore M, Oak	33	2:58	Girardi, ChN	120	2:44
Darling, NYN	18	2:49	Morgan M, LA	33	2:43	Harper B, Min	116	2:42
Darwin, Hou	17	2:52	Morris Jk, Det	36	2:52	Hassey, Oak	57	2:49
Davis Storm, KC	20	2:43	Mulholland, Phi	26	2:45	Heath, Det	99	2:59
DeJesus J, Phi	22	2:52	Navarro, Mil	22	2:56	Kennedy, SF	84	2:47
DeLeon J, StL	32	2:55	Perez M, ChA	35	2:56	Lavalliere, Pit	87	2:53
Deshaies, Hou	34	2:54	Petry, Det	23	3:00	Macfarlane, KC	103	2:48
Drabek, Pit	33	2:46	Portugal, Hou	32	2:48	Melvin, Bal	70	3:03
Erickson S, Min	17	2:42	Rasmussen D, SD	32	2:48	Myers G, Tor	79	2:58
Farrell, Cle	17	2:50	Rijo, Cin	29	2:41	Oliver, Cin	107	2:43
Fernandez S, NYN	30	3:02	Robinson D, SF	25	2:44	Olson Greg, Atl	78	2:52
Finley C, Cal	32	2:50	Robinson JM, Det	27	3:07	Pagnozzi, StL	59	2:43
Gardner M, Mon	26	2:50	Robinson R, Mil	22	3:00	Parent, SD	55	2:50
Garrelts, SF	31	2:49	Ruffin, Phi	25	2:45	Parrish Ln, Cal	125	2:59
Glavine, Atl	33	2:57	Ryan, Tex	30	2:58	Pena T, Bos	133	2:57
Gooden, NYN	34	3:01	Saberhagen, KC	20	2:49	Petralli, Tex	98	2:56
Gordon, KC	32	2:52	Sanderson, Oak	34	2:55	Santiago, SD	89	2:45
Gross K, Mon	26	2:57	Scott M, Hou	32	2:43	Sasser, NYN	67	2:57
Gubicza, KC	16	2:54	Smiley, Pit	25	2:46	Scioscia, LA	124	2:51
Gullickson, Hou	32	2:45	Smith B, StL	25	2:46	Slaught, Pit	61	2:43
Guthrie, Min	21	2:42	Smith Roy, Min	23	2:47	Steinbach, Oak	77	2:56
Hanson, Sea	33	2:49	Smith Z, Pit	31	2:43	Surhoff BJ, Mil	119	2:54
Harkey, ChN	27	2:49	Smoltz, Atl	34	2:44	Tettleton, Bal	85	3:04
Harnisch, Bal	31	3:09	Stewart D, Oak	36	2:52	Valle, Sea	98	2:53
Harris GA, Bos	30	3:00	Stieb, Tor	33	2:55	Whitt, Atl	54	2:45
Hawkins, NYA	26	2:55	Stottlemyre, Tor	33	2:48	Zeile, StL	98	2:50
Heaton, Pit	24	2:48	Swindell, Cle	34	2:46			
Hibbard, ChA	33	2:51	Tanana, Det	29	3:06	AL Avg—2:51	NL Avg—2:48	
Higuera, Mil	27	2:47	Terrell, Det	16	2:54			
Holman B, Sea	28	2:46	Tewksbury, StL	20	2:29			

DO FREE AGENTS BUST OUT WITH THEIR NEW CLUBS? (p. 52)

Batters Signed as Free Agents

Year	When?	Avg	AB	R	H	HR	RBI	SB
1975-76		No Free Agents Signed						
1977	Before	.265	6523	896	1728	160	832	219
	After	.278	6826	1025	1896	221	913	161
1978	Before	.276	3106	447	856	137	528	50
	After	.266	3470	489	923	108	477	31
1979	Before	.263	2301	272	606	46	245	40
	After	.283	2217	268	627	53	271	46
1980	Before	.257	3791	437	976	64	439	68
	After	.269	4653	576	1253	89	561	73
1981	Before	.266	6477	827	1720	153	798	200
	After	.257	3181	366	818	60	398	82
1982	Before	.239	2540	291	606	58	298	37
	After	.257	2916	375	749	113	392	32
1983	Before	.261	3339	382	872	63	384	88
	After	.266	2782	362	741	74	363	93
1984	Before	.264	4481	631	1183	98	542	100
	After	.261	3962	491	1036	62	431	67
1985	Before	.261	3687	457	961	119	483	53
	After	.257	3133	390	804	94	420	44
1986	Before	.266	1673	205	445	35	196	44
	After	.280	1123	148	315	25	137	21
1987	Before	.265	3142	406	834	108	440	30
	After	.245	3140	364	770	127	442	22
1988	Before	.267	3957	624	1058	143	512	111
	After	.262	3616	531	949	97	449	108
1989	Before	.255	4164	453	1062	93	478	92
	After	.265	3722	434	986	74	416	75
1990	Before	.253	6575	773	1661	148	785	109
	After	.258	5508	686	1419	132	671	99

Pitchers Signed as Free Agents

Year	When?	ERA	W	L	S	IP
1975	Before	2.49	25	12	0	318.0
	After	2.58	23	14	0	328.0
1976	Before	2.29	19	14	1	322.0
	After	3.04	11	11	1	207.0
1977	Before	3.01	77	41	42	937.0
	After	3.62	80	64	66	1157.0
1978	Before	3.73	77	65	40	1162.0
	After	3.33	75	59	52	1107.0
1979	Before	3.64	84	69	22	1366.0
	After	3.59	91	66	24	1385.0
1980	Before	3.64	110	80	52	1512.0
	After	3.59	70	62	29	1341.0
1981	Before	3.72	65	77	12	1276.0
	After	3.79	41	42	0	732.0
1982	Before	4.05	15	34	8	496.0
	After	3.93	40	56	8	777.2
1983	Before	3.52	53	52	10	953.2
	After	3.62	51	44	28	786.0
1984	Before	4.16	63	60	53	995.2
	After	4.07	42	37	36	719.1
1985	Before	4.07	61	64	27	1094.1
	After	4.10	54	64	28	1052.2
1986	Before	4.23	13	26	14	334.0
	After	3.73	17	16	10	309.0
1987	Before	3.92	8	17	14	280.1
	After	3.93	21	11	6	327.2
1988	Before	5.30	14	12	0	263.0
	After	4.05	24	21	3	402.2
1989	Before	3.66	98	96	36	1806.2
	After	3.65	102	93	4	1689.2
1990	Before	3.90	131	147	99	2286.2
	After	3.90	105	120	73	1857.0

DO THEY STEAL BETTER ON TURF? (p. 54)

Both Leagues — Listed Alphabetically
(players with 25+ stolen base attempts in 1990; totals exclude pitchers)

Player, Team	1990 Grass			1990 Turf			1987-1990 Grass			1987-1990 Turf		
	SB	CS	Pct	SB	CS	Pct	SB	CS	Pct	SB	CS	Pct
Alomar R, SD	19	4	82.6	5	3	62.5	58	22	72.5	5	3	62.5
Biggio, Hou	7	3	70.0	18	8	69.2	13	5	72.2	18	8	69.2
Bonds, Pit	12	4	75.0	40	9	81.6	31	16	66.0	40	9	81.6
Boston, NYN	13	6	68.4	6	1	85.7	38	16	70.4	6	1	85.7
Butler, SF	39	15	72.2	12	4	75.0	123	51	70.7	12	4	75.0
Calderon, ChA	29	14	67.4	3	2	60.0	50	22	69.4	3	2	60.0
Canseco, Oak	17	9	65.4	2	1	66.7	67	28	70.5	2	1	66.7
Carter J, SD	16	5	76.2	6	1	85.7	72	19	79.1	6	1	85.7
Cole, Cle	37	6	86.0	3	3	50.0	37	6	86.0	3	3	50.0
Coleman, StL	14	7	66.7	63	10	86.3	66	20	76.7	63	10	86.3
Deshields, Mon	8	6	57.1	34	16	68.0	8	6	57.1	34	16	68.0
Devereaux, Bal	11	10	52.4	2	2	50.0	33	22	60.0	2	2	50.0
Doran, Cin	8	4	66.7	15	5	75.0	25	7	78.1	15	5	75.0
Dunston, ChN	17	4	81.0	8	1	88.9	64	22	74.4	8	1	88.9
Dykstra, Phi	8	3	72.7	25	2	92.6	56	18	75.7	25	2	92.6
Eisenreich, KC	4	7	36.4	8	7	53.3	23	11	67.6	8	7	53.3
Felder, Mil	16	6	72.7	4	3	57.1	73	17	81.1	4	3	57.1
Fernandez T, Tor	11	4	73.3	15	9	62.5	33	16	67.3	15	9	62.5
Finley S, Bal	21	9	70.0	1	0	100.0	34	11	75.6	1	0	100.0
Franco Ju, Tex	26	6	81.3	5	4	55.6	93	26	78.2	5	4	55.6
Gant, Atl	22	10	68.8	11	6	64.7	46	24	65.7	11	6	64.7
Gibson K, LA	21	2	91.3	5	0	100.0	72	11	86.7	5	0	100.0
Gladden, Min	11	3	78.6	14	6	70.0	35	13	72.9	14	6	70.0
Griffey Jr, Sea	4	6	40.0	12	5	70.6	9	7	56.3	12	5	70.6
Guillen, ChA	12	15	44.4	1	2	33.3	84	45	65.1	1	2	33.3
Gwynn T, SD	13	4	76.5	4	4	50.0	98	28	77.8	4	4	50.0
Harris L, LA	14	8	63.6	1	2	33.3	20	12	62.5	1	2	33.3
Hatcher B, Cin	10	2	83.3	20	8	71.4	36	11	76.6	20	8	71.4
Henderson R, Ok	53	9	85.5	12	1	92.3	209	34	86.0	12	1	92.3
Hudler, StL	8	7	53.3	10	3	76.9	12	9	57.1	10	3	76.9
Johnson H, NYN	20	5	80.0	14	3	82.4	86	23	78.9	14	3	82.4
Johnson L, ChA	32	16	66.7	4	6	40.0	50	20	71.4	4	6	40.0
Kelly, NYA	40	16	71.4	2	1	66.7	80	27	74.8	2	1	66.7
Lansford, Oak	12	13	48.0	4	1	80.0	87	35	71.3	4	1	80.0
Larkin B, Cin	10	1	90.9	20	4	83.3	22	6	78.6	20	4	83.3
McGee, Oak	7	2	77.8	24	7	77.4	18	8	69.2	24	7	77.4
Nixon O, Mon	11	2	84.6	39	11	78.0	29	10	74.4	39	11	78.0
Pettis, Tex	31	15	67.4	7	0	100.0	128	40	76.2	7	0	100.0
Phillips, Det	15	8	65.2	4	1	80.0	23	21	52.3	4	1	80.0
Polonia, Cal	18	10	64.3	3	4	42.9	85	31	73.3	3	4	42.9
Raines, Mon	12	4	75.0	37	12	75.5	35	11	76.1	37	12	75.5
Reynolds H, Sea	8	10	44.4	23	6	79.3	54	36	60.0	23	6	79.3
Roberts Bip, SD	34	8	81.0	12	4	75.0	47	19	71.2	12	4	75.0
Sabo, Cin	5	4	55.6	20	6	76.9	16	11	59.3	20	6	76.9
Samuel, LA	25	18	58.1	13	2	86.7	59	34	63.4	13	2	86.7
Sandberg, ChN	18	6	75.0	7	1	87.5	58	19	75.3	7	1	87.5
Sax S, NYA	38	7	84.4	5	2	71.4	126	40	75.9	5	2	71.4
Sheffield, Mil	22	9	71.0	3	1	75.0	30	15	66.7	3	1	75.0
Smith O, StL	3	2	60.0	29	4	87.9	20	7	74.1	29	4	87.9
Sosa, ChA	23	12	65.7	9	4	69.2	28	16	63.6	9	4	69.2
Stubbs, Hou	1	3	25.0	18	3	85.7	16	8	66.7	18	3	85.7
Surhoff BJ, Mil	15	6	71.4	3	1	75.0	55	32	63.2	3	1	75.0
Thompson, StL	3	1	75.0	22	4	84.6	20	13	60.6	22	4	84.6
Walker L, Mon	7	0	100.0	14	7	66.7	7	0	100.0	14	7	66.7
Webster M, Cle	19	4	82.6	3	2	60.0	46	12	79.3	3	2	60.0
White D, Cal	18	4	81.8	3	2	60.0	101	31	76.5	3	2	60.0
Wilson M, Tor	12	0	100.0	11	4	73.3	44	11	80.0	11	4	73.3
Wilson W, KC	7	2	77.8	17	4	81.0	46	12	79.3	17	4	81.0
Yelding, Hou	19	7	73.1	45	18	71.4	24	8	75.0	45	18	71.4
MLB Average	**1888**	**936**	**66.9**	**1396**	**573**	**70.9**	**7419**	**3642**	**67.1**	**5862**	**2250**	**72.3**

WHAT'S THE OPPOSITE OF A GRAND SLAM HOME RUN? (p. 62)

1990 Batters and Pitchers with 2 or more Grand Slam Double Plays

Batters Hitting Grand Slam HRs or DPs			Pitchers Allowing Grand Slam HRs or DPs		
Player	GS HR	GS DP	Player	GS HR	GS DP
Backman, Pit	0	2	Brown Kev, Tex	1	2
Burks, Bos	0	2	Browning, Cin	0	2
Candaele, Hou	0	2	Charlton, Cin	1	2
Clark Jk, SD	0	3	Combs, Phi	0	2
Coleman, StL	0	2	Crews, LA	1	2
Davis A, Sea	3	2	Edens, Mil	0	2
Downing, Cal	0	3	Edwards, ChA	0	2
Fermin, Cle	0	2	Gardner M, Mon	0	2
Gallego, Oak	0	3	Garrelts, SF	0	2
Girardi, ChN	0	2	Glavine, Atl	0	3
Greenwell, Bos	1	3	Gordon, KC	0	2
Gruber, Tor	1	2	Gullickson, Hou	0	2
Gwynn T, SD	0	2	Higuera, Mil	0	3
Harper B, Min	1	2	Horton, StL	0	2
Jackson B, KC	0	2	Hough, Tex	1	2
Jacoby, Cle	0	3	Jackson M, Sea	0	2
Johnson L, ChA	0	2	Jeffcoat, Tex	0	2
Joyner, Cal	1	2	Johnson R, Sea	0	2
Larkin B, Cin	0	2	Klink, Oak	0	4
Marshall, Bos	1	2	Knudson, Mil	0	3
McGriff F, Tor	0	2	LaCoss, SF	0	3
Milligan, Bal	0	3	Lancaster, ChN	1	3
Morris H, Cin	0	2	Landrum B, Pit	0	2
Murphy Dl, Phi	0	2	Layana, Cin	2	2
Palmeiro, Tex	0	2	Leach T, Min	0	2
Portugal, Hou	0	2	Maddux G, ChN	0	2
Ramos D, ChN	0	2	Martinez De, Mon	0	2
Reed Jd, Bos	0	2	Mielke, Tex	0	2
Ripken C, Bal	0	2	Milacki, Bal	0	2
Rivera L, Bos	1	2	Morgan M, LA	1	2
Sabo, Cin	0	2	Olin, Cle	0	3
Tartabull, KC	0	2	Perez M, ChA	0	3
Tettleton, Bal	0	3	Petry, Det	0	2
Thon, Phi	1	2	Pico, ChN	0	2
Valle, Sea	0	3	Plesac, Mil	1	2
Wallach, Mon	1	2	Show, SD	0	2
Winfield, Cal	0	2	Smith Z, Pit	2	3
			Swift, Sea	0	3
MLB Totals	72	162	Terrell, Det	0	2
			Walker MC, Cle	0	2
			Young Mt, Sea	1	3

WHO TAKES 'EM, WHO SWINGS AT 'EM, WHO FOULS 'EM OFF? (p. 64)

The tables below show how hitters react to pitches thrown based on the count in 1990.

Listed by League — All Teams Included

American League

Count	Total	Ball	Taken Strike	Swing -ing Strike	Foul	In Play
0-0	86225	37800	21886	4957	9545	12037
Pct	100	44	25	6	11	14
0-1	36236	16244	3906	3425	5646	7015
Pct	100	45	11	9	16	19
0-2	15616	7727	723	1648	2622	2896
Pct	100	49	5	11	17	19
1-0	37743	13409	8126	2816	5724	7668
Pct	100	36	22	7	15	20
1-1	32649	12047	3702	3149	6058	7693
Pct	100	37	11	10	19	24
1-2	25723	9632	1235	3250	5272	6334
Pct	100	37	5	13	20	25
2-0	13356	4411	3393	841	1992	2719
Pct	100	33	25	6	15	20
2-1	18171	5317	1938	1767	3988	5161
Pct	100	29	11	10	22	28
2-2	22732	6641	1104	2849	5596	6542
Pct	100	29	5	13	25	29
3-0	4399	1678	2301	85	154	181
Pct	100	38	52	2	4	4
3-1	7781	2292	1143	557	1597	2192
Pct	100	29	15	7	21	28
3-2	13496	3180	575	1373	3664	4704
Pct	100	24	4	10	27	35

National League

Count	Total	Ball	Taken Strike	Swing -ing Strike	Foul	In Play
0-0	73741	31610	17695	4727	8760	10949
Pct	100	43	24	6	12	15
0-1	31066	13213	3362	3167	5091	6233
Pct	100	43	11	10	16	20
0-2	14004	6594	811	1615	2384	2600
Pct	100	47	6	12	17	19
1-0	31640	11190	6293	2605	5085	6467
Pct	100	35	20	8	16	20
1-1	26956	9493	2877	2904	5203	6479
Pct	100	35	11	11	19	24
1-2	22231	7902	1118	2894	4822	5495
Pct	100	36	5	13	22	25
2-0	11119	3635	2822	671	1640	2351
Pct	100	33	25	6	15	21
2-1	14556	4143	1443	1398	3308	4264
Pct	100	28	10	10	23	29
2-2	18523	5373	889	2232	4591	5438
Pct	100	29	5	12	25	29
3-0	3639	1359	1880	57	140	203
Pct	100	37	52	2	4	6
3-1	6155	1803	935	407	1201	1809
Pct	100	29	15	7	20	29
3-2	10980	2359	483	1112	3116	3910
Pct	100	21	4	10	28	36

WHO'S BEST WITH DUCKS ON THE POND? (p. 68)

Team Batting and Pitching — Runners In Scoring Position

American League Batting

Team	AVG	OBP	SLG	AB	H	2B	3B	HR	BB	K
Baltimore	.243	.350	.354	1360	330	53	7	28	232	269
Boston	.271	.358	.392	1438	390	71	11	27	213	226
California	.248	.332	.382	1324	329	51	9	36	183	270
Chicago	.278	.352	.413	1328	369	69	16	26	166	233
Cleveland	.278	.341	.389	1376	383	69	7	23	160	214
Detroit	.248	.345	.402	1369	339	55	11	45	214	269
Kansas City	.262	.342	.385	1479	387	83	12	25	198	251
Milwaukee	.258	.340	.389	1387	358	70	11	30	200	233
Minnesota	.262	.336	.380	1354	355	65	8	26	161	207
New York	.234	.309	.343	1239	290	43	7	26	136	232
Oakland	.251	.347	.347	1356	340	45	5	25	208	283
Seattle	.261	.345	.372	1385	361	58	6	28	190	209
Texas	.259	.347	.371	1357	352	69	8	22	196	260
Toronto	.270	.339	.429	1390	375	72	15	40	167	234

American League Pitching

Team	AVG	OBP	SLG	AB	H	2B	3B	HR	BB	K
Baltimore	.255	.332	.397	1329	339	62	5	39	180	209
Boston	.276	.352	.372	1472	407	66	9	19	181	307
California	.268	.351	.380	1397	375	58	16	22	191	246
Chicago	.250	.337	.374	1246	311	66	13	21	180	220
Cleveland	.273	.350	.385	1387	378	60	9	26	178	243
Detroit	.243	.349	.388	1435	349	66	2	46	249	246
Kansas City	.251	.342	.375	1473	370	59	11	34	209	299
Milwaukee	.272	.340	.376	1450	395	61	7	25	171	213
Minnesota	.279	.346	.408	1391	388	70	11	29	163	226
New York	.253	.348	.401	1371	347	67	11	38	216	256
Oakland	.239	.314	.370	1215	290	50	13	28	149	184
Seattle	.241	.332	.354	1364	329	65	7	25	196	282
Texas	.255	.353	.365	1355	345	52	10	26	221	254
Toronto	.267	.336	.407	1257	335	71	9	29	140	205
AL Total	**.259**	**.342**	**.381**							

National League Batting

Team	AVG	OBP	SLG	AB	H	2B	3B	HR	BB	K
Atlanta	.255	.336	.391	1320	336	63	6	35	170	266
Chicago	.258	.331	.381	1385	357	64	11	28	167	241
Cincinnati	.252	.331	.370	1447	365	76	10	25	178	269
Houston	.243	.334	.349	1340	325	43	9	27	195	279
Los Angeles	.267	.359	.385	1362	363	48	9	32	211	256
Montreal	.238	.337	.363	1400	333	63	11	30	222	298
New York	.273	.351	.434	1365	373	69	9	44	187	238
Philadelphia	.262	.351	.366	1448	380	60	9	24	215	247
Pittsburgh	.275	.360	.422	1371	377	67	15	35	211	250
St. Louis	.242	.322	.339	1473	357	84	8	14	189	250
San Diego	.255	.345	.383	1354	345	56	11	32	200	227
San Francisco	.261	.338	.380	1386	362	58	7	31	174	254

National League Pitching

Team	AVG	OBP	SLG	AB	H	2B	3B	HR	BB	K
Atlanta	.286	.370	.425	1533	439	76	7	41	231	289
Chicago	.277	.370	.418	1470	407	80	20	29	234	250
Cincinnati	.230	.325	.328	1367	315	61	8	19	194	306
Houston	.252	.334	.383	1362	343	64	9	32	185	232
Los Angeles	.251	.338	.386	1286	323	61	10	31	183	253
Montreal	.239	.331	.348	1373	328	49	7	29	194	255
New York	.231	.297	.338	1363	315	51	10	25	137	332
Philadelphia	.253	.349	.389	1449	366	68	12	35	224	238
Pittsburgh	.248	.322	.370	1264	313	48	7	31	150	207
St. Louis	.276	.350	.383	1427	394	75	12	18	187	240
San Diego	.255	.341	.382	1358	346	65	9	30	195	253
San Francisco	.274	.358	.397	1401	384	53	4	37	205	222
NL Total	**.257**	**.341**	**.377**							

WHO'S BEST IN THE PINCH? (p. 72)

Both Leagues — 1990 Pinch Hitters Listed Alphabetically

Player, Team	Avg	AB	H	HR
Abner, SD	.185	27	5	0
Aldrete, Mon	.270	37	10	1
Anderson B, Bal	.333	18	6	0
Backman, Pit	.200	15	3	0
Baerga, Cle	.355	31	11	1
Baines, Oak	.308	13	4	0
Balboni, NYA	.200	40	8	2
Barfield Je, NYA	.231	13	3	1
Bathe, SF	.231	39	9	2
Benzinger, Cin	0.000	15	0	0
Bergman, Det	.182	33	6	0
Booker R, Phi	.154	13	2	0
Borders, Tor	.208	24	5	0
Bosley, Tex	.158	19	3	1
Boston, NYN	.167	18	3	0
Bradley S, Sea	.286	35	10	0
Braggs, Cin	.286	14	4	0
Bream, Pit	.143	14	2	0
Briley, Sea	.222	18	4	0
Bush, Min	.167	12	2	0
Cabrera, Atl	.286	21	6	1
Campusano, Phi	.125	16	2	0
Candaele, Hou	.333	30	10	1
Cangelosi, Pit	.231	39	9	0
Carreon, NYN	.167	24	4	1
Carter G, SF	.211	19	4	1
Castillo C, Min	.227	22	5	0
Clark D, ChN	.262	42	11	0
Clark Je, SD	.286	28	8	0
Coles, Det	.296	27	8	0
Collins, StL	.240	25	6	0
Cotto, Sea	.276	29	8	0
Daugherty, Tex	.222	45	10	0
Dempsey, LA	.059	17	1	0
Doran, Cin	.182	11	2	0
Dwyer, Min	.400	15	6	0
Ford C, Phi	.118	17	2	0
Gonzalez Jo, LA	.143	21	3	0
Gregg, Atl	.340	53	18	4
Griffey, Sea	.182	33	6	0
Grissom, Mon	.286	21	6	0
Gwynn C, LA	.228	57	13	1
Hall M, NYA	.200	15	3	1
Harris L, LA	.130	23	3	0
Hassey, Oak	.300	20	6	0
Hatcher M, LA	.298	47	14	0
Heep, Bos	.111	18	2	0
Hollins, Phi	.216	37	8	3
Hudler, StL	.190	21	4	2
Huson, Tex	.167	18	3	0
Jackson Dar, SD	.222	18	4	1
James D, Cle	.214	14	3	0
Javier, LA	.258	31	8	0
Jennings, Oak	.143	14	2	0
Johnson L, ChA	.235	17	4	0
Johnson W, Mon	.114	35	4	1
Jones Tim, StL	.286	14	4	0
Jones Tr, Sea	.167	18	3	0
King J, Pit	.238	21	5	1
Kingery, SF	.412	17	7	0
Kittle, Bal	.286	14	4	1
Komminsk, Bal	.167	12	2	0
Kruk, Phi	.357	14	5	1
Leach R, SF	.350	20	7	0
Lemke, Atl	.133	15	2	0
Litton, SF	.143	35	5	0
Lynn, SD	.344	32	11	1
Lyons S, ChA	.143	21	3	0
Mack, Min	.438	16	7	0
Magadan, NYN	.391	23	9	0
Martinez Crm, Pit	.235	17	4	0
Martinez Da, Mon	.250	16	4	0
McClendon, Pit	.125	16	2	1
McDowell O, Atl	.206	34	7	0
Meadows, Phi	0.000	16	0	0
Merced, Pit	.208	24	5	0
Miller K, NYN	.250	16	4	0
Morris H, Cin	.318	22	7	0
Moses, Min	.269	26	7	0
Mulliniks, Tor	.364	22	8	0
Newman A, Min	.167	12	2	0
Nixon O, Mon	.214	28	6	0
Noboa, Mon	.297	37	11	0
Nokes, NYA	.235	34	8	2
O'Malley, NYN	.175	40	7	1
Oberkfell, Hou	.133	30	4	0
Orsulak, Bal	.214	14	3	0
Pagliarulo, SD	.250	16	4	1
Parker R, SF	.211	19	4	0
Pasqua, ChA	.222	18	4	0
Petralli, Tex	.208	24	5	0
Phelps, Cle	.235	17	4	1
Polonia, Cal	.316	19	6	0
Puhl, Hou	.400	20	8	0
Quinones L, Cin	.351	37	13	1
Ramos D, ChN	.111	18	2	0
Ready, Phi	.267	45	12	0
Redus, Pit	.158	19	3	0
Reimer, Tex	.300	40	12	0
Reynolds RJ, Pit	.231	39	9	0
Riles, SF	.286	42	12	4
Rohde, Hou	.136	22	3	0
Roomes, Mon	.286	14	4	0
Russell Jn, Tex	.235	17	4	0
Salas, Det	.118	17	2	0
Sasser, NYN	.240	25	6	0
Sharperson, LA	.368	19	7	0
Sheets, Det	.190	21	4	1
Shelby, Det	.259	27	7	1
Slaught, Pit	.313	16	5	1
Smith Dw, ChN	.235	34	8	0
Smith Lo, Atl	.263	19	5	0
Stanley M, Tex	.259	27	7	1
Stephenson, SD	.200	35	7	0
Tabler, NYN	.222	18	4	0
Teufel, NYN	.276	29	8	2
Thompson M, StL	.190	21	4	0
Trevino, Cin	.318	22	7	1
Varsho, ChN	.256	43	11	0
Vatcher, Atl	.333	33	11	0
Venable, Cal	.188	16	3	0
Villanueva, ChN	.167	18	3	1
Vizcaino, LA	.133	15	2	0
Walling, StL	.239	46	11	0
Ward G, Det	.357	14	5	0
Williams K, Tor	.111	18	2	0
Wilson C, StL	.391	23	9	0
Wilson G, Hou	.200	15	3	1
Winningham, Cin	.286	21	6	0
Wynne, ChN	.160	25	4	0

WHO CREATED THE MOST RUNS? (p. 74)

Both Leagues — Listed Alphabetically (500+ Plate Appearances)

Player, Team	RC	OW%	Player, Team	RC	OW%	Player, Team	RC	OW%
Alomar R, SD	76.5	.549	Gruber, Tor	101.2	.645	Puckett, Min	87.8	.643
Barfield Je, NYA	83.6	.675	Guerrero, StL	69.4	.598	Reed Jd, Bos	86.8	.592
Bell Geo, Tor	69.5	.484	Guillen, ChA	52.1	.411	Reynolds H, Sea	79.7	.512
Bell Jay, Pit	72.5	.468	Gwynn T, SD	82.8	.612	Ripken C, Bal	87.9	.588
Biggio, Hou	67.9	.554	Harper B, Min	61.8	.531	Roberts Bip, SD	97.1	.697
Boggs W, Bos	102.5	.679	Hatcher B, Cin	65.4	.576	Sabo, Cin	94.4	.683
Bonds, Pit	128.0	.819	Hayes C, Phi	55.2	.391	Samuel, LA	59.6	.446
Bonilla B, Pit	103.7	.662	Hayes V, Phi	78.0	.640	Sandberg, ChN	123.7	.729
Brett, KC	106.0	.736	Henderson R,Oak	137.1	.869	Sax S, NYA	67.9	.446
Brooks, LA	71.1	.493	Herr, NYN	63.4	.475	Seitzer, KC	81.7	.532
Browne J, Cle	71.8	.511	Hrbek, Min	88.5	.681	Sheffield, Mil	73.1	.563
Brunansky, Bos	72.2	.551	Incaviglia, Tex	62.9	.463	Sierra, Tex	85.4	.583
Burks, Bos	92.1	.636	Jacoby, Cle	83.0	.579	Smith Lo, Atl	86.2	.682
Butler, SF	108.1	.669	James C, Cle	77.8	.585	Smith O, StL	59.5	.486
Calderon, ChA	76.1	.515	Jefferies, NYN	89.2	.608	Sosa, ChA	57.9	.432
Caminiti, Hou	49.9	.399	Johnson H, NYN	86.9	.576	Stillwell, KC	54.2	.407
Canseco, Oak	98.3	.758	Johnson L, ChA	59.4	.454	Strawberry, NYN	104.2	.720
Carter J, SD	72.1	.455	Justice, Atl	91.7	.731	Stubbs, Hou	74.2	.702
Clark W, SF	101.2	.660	Kelly, NYA	86.7	.568	Surhoff BJ, Mil	60.9	.479
Coleman, StL	74.0	.633	Kruk, Phi	74.8	.671	Templeton, SD	45.9	.343
Daniels, LA	95.6	.758	Lansford, Oak	53.7	.447	Tettleton, Bal	71.3	.616
Daulton, Phi	75.7	.654	Larkin B, Cin	90.7	.642	Thompson R, SF	59.2	.451
Davis A, Sea	87.4	.706	Leonard J, Sea	48.5	.408	Thon, Phi	56.8	.411
Davis E, Cin	81.1	.714	Lind, Pit	50.6	.388	Trammell, Det	95.2	.636
Dawson, ChN	100.7	.707	Magadan, NYN	91.3	.754	Treadway, Atl	59.2	.474
Deer, Mil	64.1	.530	Maldonado, Cle	85.1	.555	Van Slyke, Pit	89.2	.709
Deshields, Mon	75.4	.643	Martinez E, Sea	85.6	.712	Ventura, ChA	54.1	.454
Dunston, ChN	65.3	.456	McGee, Oak	97.0	.689	Wallach, Mon	95.7	.668
Dykstra, Phi	121.1	.777	McGriff F, Tor	123.8	.778	Weiss, Oak	51.5	.498
Eisenreich, KC	64.1	.515	McGwire, Oak	100.9	.719	Whitaker, Det	68.3	.525
Evans Dw, Bos	60.0	.531	McReynolds, NYN	88.0	.659	White D, Cal	47.0	.386
Felix, Tor	68.8	.578	Mitchell K, SF	101.3	.715	Williams MD, SF	92.4	.592
Fernandez T, Tor	88.1	.540	Murphy Dl, Phi	70.7	.451	Wilson M, Tor	64.4	.428
Fielder, Det	128.5	.747	Murray E, LA	117.7	.767	Winfield, Cal	70.5	.583
Finley S, Bal	47.5	.394	O'Neill, Cin	69.3	.585	Worthington, Bal	46.8	.417
Fisk, ChA	78.6	.705	Oquendo, StL	56.9	.519	Yelding, Hou	47.5	.387
Fletcher S, ChA	49.5	.386	Owen S, Mon	55.2	.519	Yount, Mil	80.6	.504
Franco Ju, Tex	95.4	.661	Palmeiro, Tex	94.2	.647	Zeile, StL	67.0	.567
Gaetti, Min	55.6	.348	Parker D, Mil	85.9	.531			
Galarraga, Mon	71.6	.549	Parrish Ln, Cal	70.5	.601			
Gant, Atl	109.3	.686	Pena T, Bos	50.2	.399			
Gladden, Min	60.1	.449	Perry G, KC	52.5	.435			
Grace, ChN	94.1	.629	Phillips, Det	80.8	.512			
Greenwell, Bos	93.8	.633	Presley, Atl	61.9	.418			
Griffey Jr, Sea	103.3	.703	Quintana, Bos	67.2	.548			
Griffin Alf, LA	31.2	.204	Raines, Mon	75.0	.678			

WHO'S NO. 1 AT NO. 1? (p. 80)

Both Leagues — Listed Alphabetically
(Players with 100+ Plate Appearances batting Leadoff in 1990)

Player, Team	OBP	AB	R	H	BB	HBP	SB
Backman, Pit	.371	297	56	88	37	0	6
Boggs W, Bos	.402	353	52	106	61	1	0
Boston, NYN	.250	96	11	18	8	0	6
Bradley P, ChA	.353	311	38	80	37	9	13
Browne J, Cle	.313	293	42	75	26	1	7
Butler, SF	.398	621	108	192	90	6	51
Cole, Cle	.379	227	42	68	28	1	40
Coleman, StL	.346	479	71	143	33	2	77
Dascenzo, ChN	.336	134	18	38	11	0	10
Deshields, Mon	.380	401	57	118	54	2	34
Downing, Cal	.382	128	24	35	20	3	0
Dykstra, Phi	.419	588	106	192	89	7	33
Felder, Mil	.308	132	18	34	10	0	7
Felix, Tor	.288	198	30	47	15	0	7
Fernandez T, Tor	.338	202	22	51	23	3	7
Finley S, Bal	.323	244	22	70	14	1	12
Gantner, Mil	.317	91	14	20	12	1	5
Gladden, Min	.318	487	59	137	23	5	24
Harris L, LA	.359	321	55	101	21	1	8
Hatcher B, Cin	.328	212	28	58	14	3	14
Henderson R, Oak	.439	485	119	158	95	4	63
Huson, Tex	.271	226	33	45	21	2	4
Javier, LA	.447	111	26	39	20	0	8
Jefferies, NYN	.329	208	35	58	14	2	5
Johnson H, NYN	.313	165	29	41	16	0	13
Johnson L, ChA	.274	261	35	61	15	0	12
Kelly, NYA	.328	395	54	115	20	3	26
Larkin B, Cin	.398	93	10	31	9	1	1
McDowell O, Atl	.299	267	41	66	18	2	13
Miller K, NYN	.344	112	18	29	14	1	6
Molitor, Mil	.348	373	58	108	33	1	16
Nixon O, Mon	.342	101	20	25	15	0	24
Pettis, Tex	.319	325	45	76	40	2	31
Phillips, Det	.349	386	60	94	59	4	13
Polonia, Cal	.377	346	48	116	24	1	18
Redus, Pit	.359	134	17	36	20	0	6
Reed Jd, Bos	.363	263	30	69	39	3	3
Reynolds H, Sea	.336	642	100	162	81	3	31
Roberts Bip, SD	.377	503	92	158	47	6	43
Sabo, Cin	.366	289	53	81	36	3	17
Samuel, LA	.249	158	15	29	14	0	18
Sax S, NYA	.318	205	27	53	18	0	16
Seitzer, KC	.346	469	74	129	50	2	7
Smith Lo, Atl	.419	315	53	107	41	4	5
Sosa, ChA	.296	258	33	65	17	1	15
Walton, ChN	.347	387	62	101	48	4	14
Whitaker, Det	.362	249	51	66	39	0	7
White D, Cal	.178	97	6	15	3	0	5
Wilson M, Tor	.305	237	33	67	8	0	7
Yelding, Hou	.305	463	60	118	35	0	55
Young G, Hou	.261	106	7	21	9	0	3
AL Team Avg	.333	671	97	177	68	4	31
NL Team Avg	.356	669	106	191	71	4	44

WHO SOARED TO THE SKIES — AND WHO CRASHED AND BURNED — IN 1990? (p. 86)

Both Leagues — Listed Alphabetically (300 PA in 1989 and 1990)

Player, Team	1989	1990	+/-	Player, Team	1989	1990	+/-	Player, Team	1989	1990	+/-
Alomar R, SD	.295	.287	-8	Guillen, ChA	.253	.279	26	Pettis, Tex	.257	.239	-18
Baines, Oak	.309	.284	-25	Gwynn T, SD	.336	.309	-27	Phillips, Det	.262	.251	-11
Barfield Je, NYA	.234	.246	12	Hall M, NYA	.260	.258	-2	Polonia, Cal	.300	.335	35
Bell Geo, Tor	.297	.265	-32	Harper B, Min	.325	.294	-31	Presley, Atl	.236	.242	6
Benzinger, Cin	.245	.253	8	Harris L, LA	.236	.304	68	Puckett, Min	.339	.298	-41
Biggio, Hou	.257	.276	19	Hatcher B, Cin	.231	.276	45	Raines, Mon	.286	.287	1
Blauser, Atl	.270	.269	0	Hayes C, Phi	.257	.258	1	Ramirez R, Hou	.246	.261	15
Boggs W, Bos	.330	.302	-28	Hayes V, Phi	.259	.261	2	Randolph, Oak	.282	.260	-22
Bonds, Pit	.248	.301	53	Heath, Det	.263	.270	7	Ray, Cal	.289	.277	-12
Bonilla B, Pit	.281	.280	-1	Henderson D, Oak	.250	.271	21	Reed Jd, Bos	.288	.289	1
Bradley P, ChA	.277	.256	-21	Henderson R, Oak	.274	.325	51	Reynolds H, Sea	.300	.252	-48
Braggs, Cin	.247	.280	33	Herr, NYN	.287	.261	-26	Ripken B, Bal	.239	.291	52
Brett, KC	.282	.329	47	Howell Jk, Cal	.228	.228	0	Ripken C, Bal	.257	.250	-7
Briley, Sea	.266	.246	-20	Hrbek, Min	.272	.287	15	Rivera L, Bos	.257	.225	-32
Brock, Mil	.265	.248	-17	Incaviglia, Tex	.236	.233	-3	Roberts Bip, SD	.301	.309	8
Brooks, LA	.268	.266	-2	Jackson B, KC	.256	.272	16	Sabo, Cin	.260	.270	10
Browne J, Cle	.299	.267	-32	Jacoby, Cle	.272	.293	21	Salazar L, ChN	.282	.254	-28
Brunansky, Bos	.239	.255	16	James C, Cle	.243	.299	56	Samuel, LA	.235	.242	7
Burks, Bos	.303	.296	-7	Javier, LA	.248	.298	50	Sandberg, ChN	.290	.306	14
Butler, SF	.283	.309	26	Jefferies, NYN	.258	.283	25	Santiago, SD	.236	.270	34
Calderon, ChA	.286	.273	-13	Johnson H, NYN	.287	.244	-43	Sax S, NYA	.315	.260	-55
Caminiti, Hou	.255	.242	-13	Jordan, Phi	.285	.241	-44	Schofield, Cal	.228	.255	27
Carter J, SD	.243	.232	-11	Joyner, Cal	.282	.268	-14	Scioscia, LA	.250	.264	14
Clark Jk, SD	.242	.266	24	Kelly, NYA	.302	.285	-17	Seitzer, KC	.281	.275	-6
Clark W, SF	.333	.295	-38	Kennedy, SF	.239	.277	38	Sheets, Det	.243	.261	18
Coleman, StL	.254	.292	38	Kruk, Phi	.300	.291	-9	Sheffield, Mil	.247	.294	47
Daulton, Phi	.201	.268	67	Lansford, Oak	.336	.268	-68	Sierra, Tex	.306	.280	-26
Davis A, Sea	.305	.283	-22	Larkin B, Cin	.342	.301	-41	Smith Lo, Atl	.315	.305	-10
Davis C, Cal	.271	.265	-6	Larkin G, Min	.267	.269	2	Smith O, StL	.273	.254	-19
Davis E, Cin	.281	.260	-21	Lee M, Tor	.260	.243	-17	Snyder C, Cle	.215	.233	18
Davis G, Hou	.269	.251	-18	Lemon, Det	.237	.258	21	Spiers, Mil	.255	.242	-13
Dawson, ChN	.252	.310	58	Leonard J, Sea	.254	.251	-3	Steinbach, Oak	.273	.251	-22
Deer, Mil	.210	.209	-1	Lind, Pit	.232	.261	29	Stillwell, KC	.261	.249	-12
Devereaux, Bal	.266	.240	-26	Liriano, Min	.263	.234	-29	Strawberry, NYN	.225	.277	52
Doran, Cin	.219	.300	81	Magadan, NYN	.286	.328	42	Surhoff BJ, Mil	.248	.276	28
Downing, Cal	.283	.273	-10	Maldonado, Cle	.217	.273	56	Tartabull, KC	.268	.268	0
Dunston, ChN	.278	.262	-16	Martinez Da, Mon	.274	.279	5	Templeton, SD	.255	.248	-7
Dykstra, Phi	.237	.325	88	Mattingly, NYA	.303	.256	-47	Tettleton, Bal	.258	.223	-35
Eisenreich, KC	.293	.280	-13	McDowell O, Atl	.266	.243	-23	Thompson M, StL	.290	.218	-72
Elster, NYN	.231	.207	-24	McGriff F, Tor	.269	.300	31	Thompson Ro, SF	.241	.245	4
Espinoza, NYA	.282	.224	-58	McGwire, Oak	.231	.235	4	Thon, Phi	.271	.255	-16
Evans Dw, Bos	.285	.249	-36	McReynolds, NYN	.272	.269	-3	Trammell, Det	.243	.304	61
Felix, Tor	.258	.263	5	Milligan, Bal	.268	.265	-3	Treadway, Atl	.277	.283	6
Fermin, Cle	.238	.256	18	Mitchell K, SF	.291	.290	-1	Uribe, SF	.221	.248	27
Fernandez T, Tor	.257	.276	19	Molitor, Mil	.315	.285	-30	Valle, Sea	.237	.214	-23
Fisk, ChA	.293	.285	-8	Moseby, Det	.221	.248	27	Van Slyke, Pit	.237	.284	47
Fletcher S, ChA	.253	.242	-11	Murphy Dl, Phi	.228	.245	17	Wallach, Mon	.277	.296	19
Franco Ju, Tex	.316	.296	-20	Murray E, LA	.247	.330	83	Walton, ChN	.293	.263	-30
Gaetti, Min	.251	.229	-22	Newman A, Min	.253	.242	-11	Whitaker, Det	.251	.237	-14
Gagne, Min	.272	.235	-37	O'Brien P, Sea	.260	.224	-36	White D, Cal	.245	.217	-28
Galarraga, Mon	.257	.256	-1	O'Neill, Cin	.276	.270	-4	Wilson G, Hou	.266	.245	-21
Gallego, Oak	.252	.206	-46	Oquendo, StL	.291	.252	-39	Wilson M, Tor	.251	.265	14
Gantner, Mil	.274	.263	-11	Orsulak, Bal	.285	.269	-16	Wilson W, KC	.253	.290	37
Gladden, Min	.295	.275	-20	Owen S, Mon	.233	.234	1	Worthington, Bal	.247	.226	-21
Grace, ChN	.314	.309	-5	Pagliarulo, SD	.197	.254	57	Yount, Mil	.318	.247	-71
Greenwell, Bos	.308	.297	-11	Palmeiro, Tex	.275	.319	44				
Griffey Jr, Sea	.264	.300	36	Parker D, Mil	.264	.289	25	American League	.261	.259	-2
Griffin Alf, LA	.247	.210	-37	Parrish Ln, Cal	.238	.268	30	National League	.246	.256	10
Gruber, Tor	.290	.274	-16	Pena T, Bos	.259	.263	4				
Guerrero, StL	.311	.281	-30	Pendleton, StL	.264	.230	-34				

WHO HAS THE BEST "KNOCKOUT PUNCH"? (p. 88)

Both Leagues — Listed Alphabetically (10+ Home runs)

Player, Team	HR	RBI	RBI/HR
Anthony, Hou	10	15	1.50
Baines, Oak	16	19	1.19
Balboni, NYA	17	20	1.18
Barfield Je, NYA	25	39	1.56
Bell Geo, Tor	21	34	1.62
Bichette, Cal	15	25	1.67
Bonds, Pit	33	52	1.58
Bonilla B, Pit	32	52	1.63
Borders, Tor	15	23	1.53
Boston, NYN	12	19	1.58
Bream, Pit	15	26	1.73
Brett, KC	14	20	1.43
Brooks, LA	20	32	1.60
Brunansky, Bos	16	29	1.81
Burks, Bos	21	34	1.62
Calderon, ChA	14	26	1.86
Canseco, Oak	37	61	1.65
Carreon, NYN	10	14	1.40
Carter J, SD	24	44	1.83
Clark Jk, SD	25	39	1.56
Clark W, SF	19	31	1.63
Daniels, LA	27	54	2.00
Daulton, Phi	12	17	1.42
Davis A, Sea	17	29	1.71
Davis C, Cal	12	24	2.00
Davis E, Cin	24	38	1.58
Davis G, Hou	22	37	1.68
Dawson, ChN	27	40	1.48
Deer, Mil	27	44	1.63
Devereaux, Bal	12	20	1.67
Downing, Cal	14	24	1.71
Duncan, Cin	10	15	1.50
Dunston, ChN	17	29	1.71
Evans Dw, Bos	13	22	1.69
Felix, Tor	15	23	1.53
Fielder, Det	51	84	1.65
Fisk, ChA	18	24	1.33
Franco Ju, Tex	11	23	2.09
Gaetti, Min	16	31	1.94
Galarraga, Mon	20	36	1.80
Gant, Atl	32	44	1.38
Greenwell, Bos	14	21	1.50
Griffey Jr, Sea	22	34	1.55
Gruber, Tor	31	55	1.77
Guerrero, StL	13	22	1.69
Hall M, NYA	12	18	1.50
Hayes C, Phi	10	16	1.60
Hayes V, Phi	17	26	1.53
Henderson D, Oak	20	29	1.45
Henderson R, Oak	28	38	1.36
Hill G, Tor	12	18	1.50
Horn, Bal	14	26	1.86
Hrbek, Min	22	35	1.59
Incaviglia, Tex	24	39	1.63
Jackson B, KC	28	52	1.86
Jacoby, Cle	14	19	1.36
James C, Cle	12	16	1.33
Jefferies, NYN	15	19	1.27
Johnson H, NYN	23	37	1.61
Jose, StL	11	21	1.91
Justice, Atl	28	43	1.54
Kelly, NYA	15	18	1.20
King J, Pit	14	23	1.64
Kittle, Bal	18	24	1.33
Leonard J, Sea	10	19	1.90
Maas, NYA	21	28	1.33
Maldonado, Cle	22	35	1.59
Marshall, Bos	10	16	1.60
Martinez Crm, Pit	10	18	1.80
Martinez Da, Mon	11	15	1.36
Martinez E, Sea	11	18	1.64
McGriff F, Tor	35	48	1.37
McGwire, Oak	39	63	1.62
McReynolds, NYN	24	41	1.71
Milligan, Bal	20	25	1.25
Mitchell K, SF	35	47	1.34
Molitor, Mil	12	18	1.50
Moseby, Det	14	21	1.50
Murphy Dl, Phi	24	44	1.83
Murray E, LA	26	43	1.65
Nokes, NYA	11	16	1.45
O'Neill, Cin	16	28	1.75
Olerud, Tor	14	21	1.50
Orsulak, Bal	11	20	1.82
Palmeiro, Tex	14	20	1.43
Parker D, Mil	21	31	1.48
Parrish Ln, Cal	24	41	1.71
Pasqua, ChA	13	22	1.69
Presley, Atl	19	23	1.21
Puckett, Min	12	22	1.83
Ripken C, Bal	21	27	1.29
Sabo, Cin	25	35	1.40
Salazar L, ChN	12	20	1.67
Samuel, LA	13	20	1.54
Sandberg, ChN	40	61	1.52
Santiago, SD	11	24	2.18
Scioscia, LA	12	14	1.17
Sheets, Det	10	19	1.90
Sheffield, Mil	10	14	1.40
Sierra, Tex	16	28	1.75
Snyder C, Cle	14	24	1.71
Sosa, ChA	15	23	1.53
Strawberry, NYN	37	64	1.73
Stubbs, Hou	23	38	1.65
Tartabull, KC	15	25	1.67
Tettleton, Bal	15	24	1.60
Teufel, NYN	10	14	1.40
Thompson Ro, SF	15	22	1.47
Trammell, Det	14	24	1.71
Treadway, Atl	11	18	1.64
Van Slyke, Pit	17	27	1.59
Vaughn G, Mil	17	27	1.59
Walker L, Mon	19	28	1.47
Wallach, Mon	21	39	1.86
Webster M, Cle	12	22	1.83
Whitaker, Det	18	35	1.94
White D, Cal	11	18	1.64
Williams MD, SF	33	59	1.79
Wilson G, Hou	10	16	1.60
Winfield, Cal	21	33	1.57
Yount, Mil	17	31	1.82
Zeile, StL	15	21	1.40
MLB Total	**3,317**	**5,225**	**1.58**

WHO HITS FLYBALLS? (p. 90)

Grd stands for total groundballs (hits and outs). Fly includes for all flyballs hit (hits and outs). G/F is the groundball/flyball ratio.

Both Leagues — Listed Alphabetically (500+ Plate Appearances)

Player, Team	Grd Fly G/F	Player, Team	Grd Fly G/F	Player, Team	Grd Fly G/F
Alomar R, SD	258 134 1.93	Griffey Jr, Sea	215 166 1.30	Phillips, Det	210 148 1.42
Barfield Je, NYA	121 141 0.86	Griffin Alf, LA	163 151 1.08	Presley, Atl	175 170 1.03
Bell Geo, Tor	168 221 0.76	Gruber, Tor	206 213 0.97	Puckett, Min	267 112 2.38
Bell Jay, Pit	203 172 1.18	Guerrero, StL	171 177 0.97	Quintana, Bos	232 114 2.04
Biggio, Hou	209 144 1.45	Guillen, ChA	221 145 1.52	Raines, Mon	197 125 1.58
Boggs W, Bos	250 158 1.58	Gwynn T, SD	263 125 2.10	Reed Jd, Bos	210 189 1.11
Bonds, Pit	160 193 0.83	Harper B, Min	197 157 1.25	Reynolds H, Sea	243 202 1.20
Bonilla B, Pit	192 245 0.78	Hatcher B, Cin	202 145 1.39	Ripken C, Bal	243 200 1.22
Brett, KC	223 153 1.46	Hayes C, Phi	219 156 1.40	Roberts Bip, SD	247 122 2.02
Brooks, LA	227 165 1.38	Hayes V, Phi	144 146 0.99	Sabo, Cin	194 225 0.86
Browne J, Cle	223 157 1.42	Henderson R, Oak	166 176 0.94	Samuel, LA	162 124 1.31
Brunansky, Bos	130 183 0.71	Herr, NYN	242 135 1.79	Sandberg, ChN	219 204 1.07
Burks, Bos	199 202 0.99	Hrbek, Min	189 171 1.11	Sax S, NYA	343 121 2.83
Butler, SF	289 132 2.19	Incaviglia, Tex	165 140 1.18	Seitzer, KC	258 179 1.44
Calderon, ChA	249 176 1.41	Jacoby, Cle	203 188 1.08	Sheffield, Mil	172 179 0.96
Caminiti, Hou	185 156 1.19	James C, Cle	211 157 1.34	Sierra, Tex	247 172 1.44
Canseco, Oak	122 143 0.85	Jefferies, NYN	211 224 0.94	Smith Lo, Atl	147 160 0.92
Carter J, SD	202 228 0.89	Johnson H, NYN	142 234 0.61	Smith O, StL	263 124 2.12
Clark W, SF	210 192 1.09	Johnson L, ChA	262 116 2.26	Sosa, ChA	176 128 1.38
Coleman, StL	191 117 1.63	Justice, Atl	107 138 0.78	Stillwell, KC	195 167 1.17
Daniels, LA	166 109 1.52	Kelly, NYA	196 178 1.10	Strawberry, NYN	177 175 1.01
Daulton, Phi	162 152 1.07	Kruk, Phi	184 96 1.92	Stubbs, Hou	118 130 0.91
Davis A, Sea	148 177 0.84	Lansford, Oak	229 139 1.65	Surhoff BJ, Mil	194 133 1.46
Davis E, Cin	170 129 1.32	Larkin B, Cin	286 174 1.64	Templeton, SD	199 155 1.28
Dawson, ChN	200 167 1.20	Leonard J, Sea	145 146 0.99	Tettleton, Bal	113 114 0.99
Deer, Mil	84 155 0.54	Lind, Pit	231 141 1.64	Thompson Ro, SF	172 157 1.10
Deshields, Mon	206 96 2.15	Magadan, NYN	154 102 1.51	Thon, Phi	214 163 1.31
Dunston, ChN	176 185 0.95	Maldonado, Cle	197 170 1.16	Trammell, Det	185 180 1.03
Dykstra, Phi	246 165 1.49	Martinez E, Sea	173 161 1.07	Treadway, Atl	166 159 1.04
Eisenreich, KC	229 129 1.78	McGee, Oak	322 90 3.58	Van Slyke, Pit	167 155 1.08
Evans Dw, Bos	154 145 1.06	McGriff F, Tor	181 170 1.06	Ventura, ChA	207 137 1.51
Felix, Tor	188 108 1.74	McGwire, Oak	118 219 0.54	Wallach, Mon	204 223 0.91
Fernandez T, Tor	272 167 1.63	McReynolds, NYN	154 214 0.72	Weiss, Oak	193 107 1.80
Fielder, Det	148 161 0.92	Mitchell K, SF	155 211 0.73	Whitaker, Det	141 161 0.88
Finley S, Bal	216 105 2.06	Murphy Dl, Phi	196 163 1.20	White D, Cal	155 114 1.36
Fisk, ChA	166 144 1.15	Murray E, LA	204 176 1.16	Williams MD, SF	189 204 0.93
Fletcher S, ChA	183 158 1.16	O'Neill, Cin	166 149 1.11	Wilson M, Tor	265 121 2.19
Franco Ju, Tex	247 128 1.93	Oquendo, StL	162 166 0.98	Winfield, Cal	192 133 1.44
Gaetti, Min	198 187 1.06	Owen S, Mon	185 139 1.33	Worthington, Bal	153 107 1.43
Galarraga, Mon	181 133 1.36	Palmeiro, Tex	221 175 1.26	Yelding, Hou	198 112 1.77
Gant, Atl	189 198 0.95	Parker D, Mil	225 175 1.29	Yount, Mil	193 216 0.89
Gladden, Min	191 163 1.17	Parrish Ln, Cal	148 136 1.09	Zeile, StL	189 155 1.22
Grace, ChN	240 151 1.59	Pena T, Bos	247 99 2.49		
Greenwell, Bos	271 183 1.48	Perry G, KC	197 136 1.45	**MLB Avg.**	1.28

IF LINEOUTS WERE HITS . . . ? (p. 94)

The table below shows the number of Lineouts (LO) a player hit into, the hypothetical increase in his batting average (Inc) if all the lineouts had been hits, and his new batting average (New Avg)

Both Leagues — Listed Alphabetically (500+ Plate Appearances)

Player, Team	LO	Inc	New Avg	Player, Team	LO	Inc	New Avg	Player, Team	LO	Inc	New Avg
Alomar R, SD	31	.053	.340	Gruber, Tor	18	.030	.304	Raines, Mon	26	.057	.344
Barfield Je, NYA	12	.025	.271	Guerrero, StL	19	.038	.319	Reed Jd, Bos	43	.072	.361
Bell Geo, Tor	29	.052	.317	Guillen, ChA	31	.060	.339	Reynolds H, Sea	35	.055	.307
Bell Jay, Pit	22	.038	.292	Gwynn T, SD	59	.103	.412	Ripken C, Bal	33	.055	.305
Biggio, Hou	34	.061	.337	Harper B, Min	25	.052	.347	Roberts Bip, SD	31	.056	.365
Boggs W, Bos	48	.078	.380	Hatcher B, Cin	34	.067	.343	Sabo, Cin	21	.037	.307
Bonds, Pit	20	.039	.339	Hayes C, Phi	30	.053	.312	Samuel, LA	20	.041	.283
Bonilla B, Pit	30	.048	.328	Hayes V, Phi	36	.077	.338	Sandberg, ChN	34	.055	.361
Brett, KC	18	.033	.362	Henderson R,Oak	18	.037	.362	Sax S, NYA	36	.059	.319
Brooks, LA	14	.025	.290	Herr, NYN	34	.062	.324	Seitzer, KC	26	.042	.317
Browne J, Cle	33	.064	.331	Hrbek, Min	26	.053	.339	Sheffield, Mil	19	.039	.333
Brunansky, Bos	20	.039	.293	Incaviglia, Tex	18	.034	.267	Sierra, Tex	24	.039	.319
Burks, Bos	25	.043	.338	Jacoby, Cle	30	.054	.347	Smith Lo, Atl	22	.047	.352
Butler, SF	29	.047	.355	James C, Cle	20	.038	.337	Smith O, StL	27	.053	.307
Calderon, ChA	32	.053	.326	Jefferies, NYN	37	.061	.344	Sosa, ChA	24	.045	.278
Caminiti, Hou	27	.050	.292	Johnson H, NYN	37	.063	.307	Stillwell, KC	27	.053	.302
Canseco, Oak	10	.021	.295	Johnson L, ChA	27	.050	.335	Strawberry, NYN	18	.033	.310
Carter J, SD	35	.055	.287	Justice, Atl	25	.057	.339	Stubbs, Hou	17	.038	.299
Clark W, SF	25	.042	.337	Kelly, NYA	28	.044	.329	Surhoff BJ, Mil	27	.057	.333
Coleman, StL	23	.046	.338	Kruk, Phi	23	.052	.343	Templeton, SD	32	.063	.311
Daniels, LA	20	.044	.340	Lansford, Oak	21	.041	.310	Tettleton, Bal	9	.020	.243
Daulton, Phi	21	.046	.314	Larkin B, Cin	34	.055	.357	Thompson R, SF	16	.032	.277
Davis A, Sea	22	.045	.328	Leonard J, Sea	28	.059	.310	Thon, Phi	32	.058	.313
Davis E, Cin	16	.035	.296	Lind, Pit	39	.076	.337	Trammell, Det	45	.081	.385
Dawson, ChN	21	.040	.350	Magadan, NYN	40	.089	.417	Treadway, Atl	35	.074	.357
Deer, Mil	11	.025	.234	Maldonado, Cle	26	.044	.317	Van Slyke, Pit	16	.032	.316
Deshields, Mon	17	.034	.323	Martinez E, Sea	21	.043	.345	Ventura, ChA	28	.057	.306
Dunston, ChN	23	.042	.305	McGee, Oak	23	.037	.362	Wallach, Mon	30	.048	.343
Dykstra, Phi	34	.058	.383	McGriff F, Tor	14	.025	.325	Weiss, Oak	18	.040	.306
Eisenreich, KC	16	.032	.313	McGwire, Oak	14	.027	.262	Whitaker, Det	28	.059	.297
Evans Dw, Bos	18	.040	.290	McReynolds, NYN	29	.056	.324	White D, Cal	8	.018	.235
Felix, Tor	12	.026	.289	Mitchell K, SF	18	.034	.324	Williams MD, SF	16	.026	.303
Fernandez T, Tor	35	.055	.331	Murphy Dl, Phi	21	.037	.282	Wilson M, Tor	20	.034	.299
Fielder, Det	19	.033	.311	Murray E, LA	29	.052	.382	Winfield, Cal	14	.029	.297
Finley S, Bal	18	.039	.295	O'Neill, Cin	24	.048	.318	Worthington, Bal	14	.033	.259
Fisk, ChA	20	.044	.330	Oquendo, StL	32	.068	.320	Yelding, Hou	26	.051	.305
Fletcher S, ChA	34	.067	.308	Owen S, Mon	18	.040	.274	Yount, Mil	20	.034	.281
Franco Ju, Tex	37	.064	.359	Palmeiro, Tex	36	.060	.380	Zeile, StL	21	.042	.287
Gaetti, Min	20	.035	.263	Parker D, Mil	27	.044	.333	**MLB Average**		.046	.304
Galarraga, Mon	23	.040	.295	Parrish Ln, Cal	15	.032	.300				
Gant, Atl	23	.040	.343	Pena T, Bos	21	.043	.305				
Gladden, Min	31	.058	.333	Perry G, KC	20	.043	.297				
Grace, ChN	39	.066	.375	Phillips, Det	36	.063	.314				
Greenwell, Bos	28	.046	.343	Presley, Atl	11	.020	.262				
Griffey Jr, Sea	32	.054	.353	Puckett, Min	20	.036	.334				
Griffin Alf, LA	23	.050	.260	Quintana, Bos	20	.039	.326				

WHO SHOULD BE PLATOONED (p. 100)

Both Leagues — Listed Alphabetically (500+ Total PA in 1990)

Player, Team	LHP	RHP	Diff	Player, Team	LHP	RHP	Diff	Player, Team	LHP	RHP	Diff
Alomar R, SD	.260	.301	-41	Griffin Alf, LA	.207	.212	-5	Puckett, Min	.299	.297	2
Barfield Je, NYA	.259	.239	20	Gruber, Tor	.295	.265	30	Quintana, Bos	.352	.252	100
Bell Geo, Tor	.248	.271	-23	Guerrero, StL	.274	.285	-11	Raines, Mon	.289	.285	4
Bell Jay, Pit	.275	.238	37	Guillen, ChA	.267	.287	-20	Reed Jd, Bos	.299	.285	14
Biggio, Hou	.229	.306	-76	Gwynn T, SD	.281	.328	-47	Reynolds H, Sea	.285	.237	48
Boggs W, Bos	.274	.319	-45	Harper B, Min	.315	.285	30	Ripken C, Bal	.264	.244	20
Bonds, Pit	.304	.297	7	Hatcher B, Cin	.246	.296	-50	Roberts Bip, SD	.294	.319	-25
Bonilla B, Pit	.261	.296	-35	Hayes C, Phi	.295	.239	56	Sabo, Cin	.327	.235	92
Brett, KC	.316	.336	-21	Hayes V, Phi	.274	.253	20	Samuel, LA	.289	.213	76
Brooks, LA	.240	.282	-42	HendersonR,Oak	.313	.330	-16	Sandberg, ChN	.252	.334	-82
Browne J, Cle	.281	.262	19	Herr, NYN	.264	.260	5	Sax S, NYA	.249	.265	-16
Brunansky, Bos	.285	.239	46	Hrbek, Min	.287	.287	0	Seitzer, KC	.278	.274	4
Burks, Bos	.298	.295	3	Incaviglia, Tex	.249	.225	24	Sheffield, Mil	.274	.301	-27
Butler, SF	.302	.313	-11	Jacoby, Cle	.316	.284	33	Sierra, Tex	.324	.255	69
Calderon, ChA	.295	.261	35	James C, Cle	.302	.298	5	Smith Lo, Atl	.294	.312	-18
Caminiti, Hou	.246	.239	7	Jefferies, NYN	.266	.293	-27	Smith O, StL	.289	.232	57
Canseco, Oak	.276	.274	3	Johnson H, NYN	.208	.266	-57	Sosa, ChA	.262	.211	51
Carter J, SD	.197	.248	-51	Johnson L, ChA	.321	.270	50	Stillwell, KC	.211	.262	-51
Clark W, SF	.317	.279	38	Justice, Atl	.366	.247	120	Strawberry, NYN	.244	.298	-54
Coleman, StL	.262	.310	-49	Kelly, NYA	.304	.278	26	Stubbs, Hou	.258	.263	-5
Daniels, LA	.285	.301	-16	Kruk, Phi	.222	.316	-94	Surhoff BJ, Mil	.317	.265	52
Daulton, Phi	.257	.272	-15	Lansford, Oak	.345	.245	100	Templeton, SD	.254	.244	10
Davis A, Sea	.256	.298	-42	Larkin B, Cin	.266	.319	-53	Tettleton, Bal	.234	.218	16
Davis E, Cin	.287	.248	39	Leonard J, Sea	.309	.218	91	Thompson R, SF	.273	.229	45
Dawson, ChN	.298	.316	-18	Lind, Pit	.231	.282	-50	Thon, Phi	.262	.251	11
Deer, Mil	.293	.170	123	Magadan, NYN	.256	.371	-115	Trammell, Det	.289	.311	-22
Deshields, Mon	.264	.304	-40	Maldonado, Cle	.331	.248	83	Treadway, Atl	.303	.276	26
Dunston, ChN	.287	.249	38	Martinez E, Sea	.308	.299	9	Van Slyke, Pit	.261	.298	-38
Dykstra, Phi	.290	.344	-54	McGee, Oak	.324	.324	1	Ventura, ChA	.221	.263	-42
Eisenreich, KC	.224	.306	-82	McGriff F, Tor	.257	.324	-67	Wallach, Mon	.289	.299	-9
Evans Dw, Bos	.265	.242	24	McGwire, Oak	.258	.228	30	Weiss, Oak	.261	.267	-6
Felix, Tor	.211	.289	-79	McRynlds, NYN	.232	.291	-59	Whitaker, Det	.162	.257	-96
Fernandez , Tor	.238	.293	-56	Mitchell K, SF	.306	.282	23	White D, Cal	.246	.204	42
Fielder, Det	.371	.235	135	Murphy Dl, Phi	.311	.214	97	Williams MD, SF	.284	.274	10
Finley S, Bal	.193	.277	-84	Murray E, LA	.316	.338	-23	Wilson M, Tor	.245	.275	-30
Fisk, ChA	.315	.268	47	O'Neill, Cin	.259	.275	-16	Winfield, Cal	.288	.257	31
Fletcher S, ChA	.283	.220	63	Oquendo, StL	.220	.269	-49	Worthington, Bal	.254	.214	40
Franco Ju, Tex	.296	.295	1	Owen S, Mon	.259	.214	44	Yelding, Hou	.281	.232	49
Gaetti, Min	.223	.231	-8	Palmeiro, Tex	.339	.311	28	Yount, Mil	.269	.239	30
Galarraga, Mon	.226	.273	-48	Parker D, Mil	.259	.301	-42	Zeile, StL	.266	.233	33
Gant, Atl	.299	.305	-6	Parrish Ln, Cal	.304	.255	49	AL Average	.265	.256	9
Gladden, Min	.270	.278	-8	Pena T, Bos	.290	.250	40	NL Average	.265	.252	13
Grace, ChN	.308	.309	-1	Perry G, KC	.209	.272	-63				
Greenwell, Bos	.257	.316	-59	Phillips, Det	.248	.253	-6				
Griffey Jr, Sea	.306	.296	10	Presley, Atl	.267	.230	37				

CAN HITTERS CAUSE ERRORS? (p. 102)

Player	AB	Safe on Error	%	Player	AB	Safe on Error	%
Alomar R, SD	586	8	.014	Kruk, Phi	443	6	.014
Barfield Je, NYA	476	5	.011	Lansford, Oak	507	8	.016
Bell Geo, Tor	562	10	.018	Larkin B, Cin	614	8	.013
Bell Jay, Pit	583	12	.021	Leonard J, Sea	478	1	.002
Biggio, Hou	555	7	.013	Lind, Pit	514	2	.004
Boggs W, Bos	619	8	.013	Magadan, NYN	451	3	.007
Bonds, Pit	519	4	.008	Maldonado, Cle	590	10	.017
Bonilla B, Pit	625	9	.014	Martinez E, Sea	487	3	.006
Brett, KC	544	2	.004	McGee, Oak	614	10	.016
Brooks, LA	568	11	.019	McGriff F, Tor	557	6	.011
Browne J, Cle	513	11	.021	McGwire, Oak	523	5	.010
Brunansky, Bos	518	3	.006	McReynolds, NYN	521	10	.019
Burks, Bos	588	8	.014	Mitchell K, SF	524	7	.013
Butler, SF	622	11	.018	Murphy Dl, Phi	563	10	.018
Calderon, ChA	607	4	.007	Murray E, LA	558	3	.005
Caminiti, Hou	541	5	.009	O'Neill, Cin	503	1	.002
Canseco, Oak	481	7	.015	Oquendo, StL	469	2	.004
Carter J, SD	634	15	.024	Owen S, Mon	453	9	.020
Clark W, SF	600	8	.013	Palmeiro, Tex	598	5	.008
Coleman, StL	497	5	.010	Parker D, Mil	610	8	.013
Daniels, LA	450	8	.018	Parrish Ln, Cal	470	5	.011
Daulton, Phi	459	2	.004	Pena T, Bos	491	9	.018
Davis A, Sea	494	4	.008	Perry G, KC	465	5	.011
Davis E, Cin	453	7	.015	Phillips, Det	573	10	.017
Dawson, ChN	529	12	.023	Presley, Atl	541	8	.015
Deer, Mil	440	3	.007	Puckett, Min	551	10	.018
Deshields, Mon	499	3	.006	Quintana, Bos	512	8	.016
Dunston, ChN	545	16	.029	Raines, Mon	457	8	.018
Dykstra, Phi	590	4	.007	Reed Jd, Bos	598	9	.015
Eisenreich, KC	496	9	.018	Reynolds H, Sea	642	9	.014
Evans Dw, Bos	445	8	.018	Ripken C, Bal	600	12	.020
Felix, Tor	463	6	.013	Roberts Bip, SD	556	14	.025
Fernandez T, Tor	635	6	.009	Sabo, Cin	567	8	.014
Fielder, Det	573	9	.016	Samuel, LA	492	7	.014
Finley S, Bal	464	7	.015	Sandberg, ChN	615	15	.024
Fisk, ChA	452	3	.007	Sax S, NYA	615	5	.008
Fletcher S, ChA	509	6	.012	Seitzer, KC	622	9	.014
Franco Ju, Tex	582	10	.017	Sheffield, Mil	487	7	.014
Gaetti, Min	577	14	.024	Sierra, Tex	608	5	.008
Galarraga, Mon	579	7	.012	Smith Lo, Atl	466	8	.017
Gant, Atl	575	10	.017	Smith O, StL	512	8	.016
Gladden, Min	534	7	.013	Sosa, ChA	532	6	.011
Grace, ChN	589	11	.019	Stillwell, KC	506	6	.012
Greenwell, Bos	610	10	.016	Strawberry, NYN	542	7	.013
Griffey Jr, Sea	597	3	.005	Stubbs, Hou	448	7	.016
Griffin Alf, LA	461	9	.020	Surhoff BJ, Mil	474	10	.021
Gruber, Tor	592	7	.012	Templeton, SD	505	3	.006
Guerrero, StL	498	5	.010	Tettleton, Bal	444	4	.009
Guillen, ChA	516	6	.012	Thompson Ro, SF	498	10	.020
Gwynn T, SD	573	6	.010	Thon, Phi	552	8	.014
Harper B, Min	479	8	.017	Trammell, Det	559	7	.013
Hatcher B, Cin	504	12	.024	Treadway, Atl	474	4	.008
Hayes C, Phi	561	15	.027	Van Slyke, Pit	493	8	.016
Hayes V, Phi	467	5	.011	Ventura, ChA	493	6	.012
Henderson R, Oak	489	6	.012	Wallach, Mon	626	10	.016
Herr, NYN	547	6	.011	Weiss, Oak	445	6	.013
Hrbek, Min	492	3	.006	Whitaker, Det	472	4	.008
Incaviglia, Tex	529	6	.011	White D, Cal	443	12	.027
Jacoby, Cle	553	7	.013	Williams MD, SF	617	7	.011
James C, Cle	528	9	.017	Wilson M, Tor	588	5	.009
Jefferies, NYN	604	12	.020	Winfield, Cal	475	9	.019
Johnson H, NYN	590	5	.008	Worthington, Bal	425	5	.012
Johnson L, ChA	541	11	.020	Yelding, Hou	511	6	.012
Justice, Atl	439	2	.005	Yount, Mil	587	8	.014
Kelly, NYA	641	5	.008	Zeile, StL	495	2	.004

WHO ARE THE "HUMAN AIR CONDITIONERS"? (p. 104)

The table below shows swings missed (Sw) as a % of total pitches swung at (Pit).

Both Leagues — Listed Alphabetically (500+ Plate Appearances)

Player, Team	Sw	Pit	%	Player, Team	Sw	Pit	%	Player, Team	Sw	Pit	%
Alomar R, SD	142	1094	13.0	Gruber, Tor	276	1221	22.6	Perry G, KC	160	859	18.6
Alomar S, Cle	140	855	16.4	Guerrero, StL	182	961	18.9	Presley, Atl	354	1098	32.2
Baines, Oak	142	763	18.6	Guillen, ChA	101	990	10.2	Puckett, Min	161	997	16.1
Barfield Je, NYA	302	989	30.5	Gwynn T, SD	59	913	6.5	Quintana, Bos	118	871	13.5
Bell Geo, Tor	204	1072	19.0	Harper B, Min	106	874	12.1	Raines, Mon	108	845	12.8
Bell Jay, Pit	163	1126	14.5	Harris L, LA	83	716	11.6	Ramirez R, Hou	124	788	15.7
Biggio, Hou	149	979	15.2	Hatcher B, Cin	111	905	12.3	Reed Jd, Bos	66	944	7.0
Boggs W, Bos	84	1147	7.3	Hayes C, Phi	222	1098	20.2	Reynolds , Sea	98	1087	9.0
Bonds, Pit	135	901	15.0	Hayes V, Phi	150	906	16.6	Ripken B, Bal	97	706	13.7
Bonilla B, Pit	262	1322	19.8	HendersonD,Oak	214	941	22.7	Ripken C, Bal	146	1069	13.7
Bradley P, ChA	159	897	17.7	HendersonR,Oak	121	909	13.3	Roberts B, SD	145	1037	14.0
Brett, KC	166	999	16.6	Herr, NYN	86	965	8.9	Sabo, Cin	142	1097	12.9
Brooks, LA	241	1131	21.3	Hrbek, Min	144	950	15.2	Samuel, LA	292	1077	27.1
Browne J, Cle	101	901	11.2	Huson, Tex	86	702	12.3	Sandberg,ChN	207	1106	18.7
Brunansky, Bos	196	957	20.5	Incaviglia, Tex	397	1058	37.5	Sax S, NYA	97	1045	9.3
Burks, Bos	168	1108	15.2	Jackson B, KC	343	918	37.4	Scioscia, LA	67	715	9.4
Butler, SF	108	1268	8.5	Jacoby, Cle	117	919	12.7	Seitzer, KC	104	1084	9.6
Calderon, ChA	206	1186	17.4	James C, Cle	143	939	15.2	Sheffield, Mil	106	852	12.4
Caminiti, Hou	172	961	17.9	Jefferies, NYN	99	1028	9.6	Sierra, Tex	218	1110	19.6
Canseco, Oak	343	1021	33.6	Johnson H,NYN	217	1118	19.4	Smith Lo, Atl	220	966	22.8
Carter J, SD	273	1406	19.4	Johnson L,ChA	84	857	9.8	Smith O, StL	59	837	7.0
Clark W, SF	244	1238	19.7	Jose, StL	186	835	22.3	Snyder C, Cle	271	947	28.6
Coleman, StL	137	913	15.0	Justice, Atl	234	923	25.4	Sosa, ChA	402	1172	34.3
Daniels, LA	204	844	24.2	Kelly, NYA	334	1310	25.5	Stillwell, KC	116	846	13.7
Daulton, Phi	112	829	13.5	Kruk, Phi	185	874	21.2	Strawberry,NYN	226	1079	20.9
Davis A, Sea	97	812	11.9	Lansford, Oak	86	847	10.2	Stubbs, Hou	230	889	25.9
Davis C, Cal	195	849	23.0	Larkin B, Cin	104	1094	9.5	Surhoff BJ, Mil	76	770	9.9
Davis E, Cin	211	847	24.9	Larkin G, Min	110	698	15.8	Templeton, SD	174	1020	17.1
Dawson, ChN	254	1047	24.3	Leonard J, Sea	276	995	27.7	Tettleton, Bal	268	848	31.6
Deer, Mil	303	919	33.0	Lind, Pit	103	928	11.1	ThompsonM,StL	121	751	16.1
Deshields, Mon	182	908	20.0	Magadan,NYN	64	734	8.7	Thompson R,SF	204	1006	20.3
Doran, Cin	134	761	17.6	Maldonado,Cle	310	1215	25.5	Thon, Phi	199	971	20.5
Duncan, Cin	189	836	22.6	Martinez E, Sea	67	808	8.3	Trammell, Det	107	897	11.9
Dunston, ChN	243	1098	22.1	McGee, Oak	275	1319	20.8	Treadway, Atl	83	876	9.5
Dykstra, Phi	62	1055	5.9	McGriff F, Tor	242	1060	22.8	Van Slyke, Pit	157	925	17.0
Eisenreich, KC	121	875	13.8	McGwire, Oak	265	941	28.2	Ventura, ChA	84	820	10.2
Espinoza, NYA	120	863	13.9	McRynlds,NYN	136	915	14.9	Walker L, Mon	245	853	28.7
Evans Dw, Bos	132	759	17.4	Milligan, Bal	138	755	18.3	Wallach, Mon	266	1256	21.2
Felix, Tor	212	860	24.7	Mitchell K, SF	220	1004	21.9	Webster M, Cle	113	773	14.6
Fermin, Cle	51	682	7.5	Molitor, Mil	112	772	14.5	Weiss, Oak	98	786	12.5
Fernandez, Tor	145	1209	12.0	Moseby, Det	178	875	20.3	Whitaker, Det	145	880	16.5
Fielder, Det	465	1273	36.5	Murphy Dl, Phi	320	1084	29.5	White D, Cal	252	928	27.2
Finley S, Bal	114	801	14.2	Murray E, LA	231	1127	20.5	Williams M, SF	378	1286	29.4
Fisk, ChA	152	851	17.9	O'Neill, Cin	256	1007	25.4	Wilson M, Tor	230	1223	18.8
Fletcher S, ChA	99	879	11.3	Oquendo, StL	87	824	10.6	Winfield, Cal	202	863	23.4
Franco Ju, Tex	153	1015	15.1	Orsulak, Bal	106	803	13.2	Worthington, Bal	169	817	20.7
Gaetti, Min	307	1219	25.2	Owen S, Mon	105	792	13.3	Yelding, Hou	118	877	13.5
Galarraga, Mon	364	1210	30.1	Palmeiro, Tex	125	1017	12.3	Yount, Mil	197	1108	17.8
Gant, Atl	236	1099	21.5	Parker D, Mil	282	1249	22.6	Zeile, StL	134	810	16.5
Gladden, Min	135	939	14.4	Parrish Ln, Cal	204	861	23.7	MLB Average			18.8
Grace, ChN	124	1041	11.9	Pena T, Bos	139	973	14.3				
Greenwell, Bos	100	1051	9.5	Pendleton, StL	150	849	17.7				
Griffey Jr, Sea	184	1100	16.7	Pettis, Tex	212	818	25.9				
Griffin Alf, LA	134	872	15.4	Phillips, Det	145	1043	13.9				

WHO LEADS THE LEAGUE IN LOOKING? (p. 106)

Both leagues — Listed Alphabetically (300+ Plate Appearances)

Player, Team	P/PA	Player, Team	P/PA	Player, Team	P/PA	Player, Team	P/PA
Alomar R, SD	3.78	Fielder, Det	4.08	Lee M, Tor	3.97	Rivera L, Bos	3.35
Alomar S, Cle	3.36	Finley S, Bal	3.48	Lemon, Det	3.88	Roberts B, SD	3.66
Backman, Pit	3.74	Fisk, ChA	3.64	Leonard J, Sea	3.60	Sabo, Cin	3.54
Baerga, Cle	3.43	Fitzgerald, Mon	3.91	Leyritz, NYA	3.76	Salazar L, ChN	3.77
Baines, Oak	3.63	Fletcher S, ChA	3.44	Lind, Pit	3.26	Samuel, LA	3.85
Balboni, NYA	3.95	Franco Ju, Tex	3.82	Liriano, Min	3.62	Sandberg, ChN	3.52
Barfield Je, NYA	4.16	Gaetti, Min	3.46	Maas, NYA	3.98	Santiago, SD	3.32
Bell Geo, Tor	3.71	Gagne, Min	3.29	Macfarlane, KC	3.38	Sax S, NYA	3.59
Bell Jay, Pit	3.84	Galarraga, Mon	3.74	Mack, Min	3.44	Schofield, Cal	3.85
Benzinger, Cin	3.41	Gallego, Oak	3.51	Magadan,NYN	4.07	Scioscia, LA	3.50
Bichette, Cal	3.81	Gant, Atl	3.68	Maldonado, Cle	3.75	Seitzer, KC	3.60
Biggio, Hou	3.69	Gantner, Mil	3.20	Martinez D, Mon	3.49	Sharperson, LA	3.48
Blauser, Atl	3.53	Geren, NYA	3.71	Martinez E, Sea	4.09	Sheets, Det	3.54
Boggs W, Bos	4.30	Gibson K, LA	3.62	Mattingly, NYA	3.16	Sheffield, Mil	3.37
Bonds, Pit	3.72	Girardi, ChN	2.68	McDowell O, Atl	3.48	Sierra, Tex	3.53
Bonilla B, Pit	3.59	Gladden, Min	3.50	McGee, Oak	3.70	Smith Dw, ChN	3.62
Borders, Tor	3.45	Grace, ChN	3.40	McGriff F, Tor	3.81	Smith Lo, Atl	3.64
Boston, NYN	3.85	Greenwell, Bos	3.22	McGwire, Oak	3.65	Smith O, StL	3.53
Bradley P, ChA	3.83	Griffey Jr, Sea	3.59	McReynolds,NYN	3.70	Snyder C, Cle	3.53
Braggs, Cin	3.81	Griffin Alf, LA	3.15	Melvin, Bal	3.23	Sosa, ChA	3.64
Bream, Pit	3.88	Grissom, Mon	3.72	Milligan, Bal	4.23	Spiers, Mil	3.31
Brett, KC	3.45	Gruber, Tor	3.35	Mitchell K, SF	3.48	Steinbach, Oak	3.58
Briley, Sea	3.69	Guerrero, StL	3.54	Molitor, Mil	3.50	Stillwell, KC	3.49
Brock, Mil	3.68	Guillen, ChA	2.85	Morris H, Cin	3.35	Strawberry, NYN	3.83
Brooks, LA	3.50	Gwynn T, SD	3.37	Moseby, Det	3.97	Stubbs, Hou	3.64
Browne J, Cle	3.65	Hall M, NYA	3.30	Murphy Dl, Phi	3.53	Surhoff BJ, Mil	3.40
Brunansky, Bos	3.89	Harper B, Min	3.26	Murray E, LA	3.50	Tartabull, KC	3.99
Burks, Bos	3.73	Harris L, LA	3.11	Newman A, Min	3.25	Templeton, SD	3.19
Butler, SF	3.96	Hatcher B, Cin	3.31	Nokes, NYA	3.35	Tettleton, Bal	4.44
Calderon, ChA	3.30	Hayes C, Phi	3.42	O'Brien P, Sea	3.41	Thompson,StL	3.51
Caminiti, Hou	3.49	Hayes V, Phi	3.92	O'Neill, Cin	3.76	ThompsonR,SF	3.72
Canseco, Oak	4.12	Heath, Det	3.76	Olerud, Tor	4.09	Thon, Phi	3.10
Carter J, SD	3.63	HendersonD,Oak	3.84	Oliver, Cin	3.37	Trammell, Det	3.56
Clark Jk, SD	4.23	HendersonR,Oak	4.28	Olson Greg, Atl	3.59	Treadway, Atl	3.23
Clark W, SF	3.66	Herr, NYN	3.64	Oquendo, StL	3.75	Uribe, SF	3.01
Coleman, StL	3.55	Hill D, Cal	3.76	Orsulak, Bal	3.53	Valle, Sea	3.81
Cotto, Sea	3.34	Howell Jk, Cal	3.84	Owen S, Mon	3.92	Van Slyke, Pit	3.74
Daniels, LA	4.09	Hrbek, Min	3.33	Pagliarulo, SD	3.50	Vaughn G, Mil	3.64
Daugherty, Tex	3.63	Huson, Tex	3.88	Palmeiro, Tex	3.47	Ventura, ChA	3.76
Daulton, Phi	3.69	Incaviglia, Tex	3.57	Parker D, Mil	3.30	Walker L, Mon	3.53
Davis A, Sea	3.98	Jackson B, KC	3.77	Parrish Ln, Cal	3.77	Wallach, Mon	3.60
Davis C, Cal	3.81	Jacoby, Cle	3.18	Pasqua, ChA	3.94	Walton, ChN	3.70
Davis E, Cin	3.79	James C, Cle	3.38	Pena T, Bos	3.67	Ward D, Det	3.71
Davis G, Hou	3.54	Javier, LA	3.85	Pendleton, StL	3.26	Webster M, Cle	3.29
Dawson, ChN	3.25	Jefferies, NYN	3.54	Perry G, KC	3.53	Weiss, Oak	3.58
Deer, Mil	4.12	Johnson H, NYN	3.53	Petralli, Tex	3.83	Whitaker, Det	3.87
Deshields, Mon	4.01	Johnson L, ChA	3.01	Pettis, Tex	4.01	White D, Cal	3.97
Devereaux, Bal	3.38	Jordan, Phi	3.14	Phillips, Det	4.05	Williams M, SF	3.23
Doran, Cin	3.83	Jose, StL	3.42	Polonia, Cal	3.38	Wilson G, Hou	3.60
Downing, Cal	4.16	Joyner, Cal	3.71	Presley, Atl	3.53	Wilson M, Tor	3.59
Duncan, Cin	3.34	Justice, Atl	3.94	Puckett, Min	3.17	Wilson W, KC	3.60
Dunston, ChN	3.19	Kelly, NYA	3.70	Quintana, Bos	3.54	Winfield, Cal	3.66
Dykstra, Phi	3.69	Kennedy, SF	3.55	Raines, Mon	3.67	Worthington,Bal	4.18
Eisenreich, KC	3.32	King J, Pit	3.48	Ramirez R, Hou	3.40	Yelding, Hou	3.62
Elster, NYN	3.80	Kittle, Bal	3.70	Randolph, Oak	3.47	Yount, Mil	3.64
Espinoza, NYA	3.13	Kruk, Phi	3.62	Ray, Cal	3.59	Zeile, StL	3.97
Evans Dw, Bos	3.74	Lansford, Oak	3.19	Reed Jd, Bos	3.86	**MLB Average**	**3.60**
Felix, Tor	3.59	Larkin B, Cin	3.57	Reynolds H, Sea	3.64		
Fermin, Cle	3.07	Larkin G, Min	3.54	Ripken B, Bal	3.47		
Fernandez T, Tor	3.58	Lavalliere, Pit	3.46	Ripken C, Bal	3.69		

IS "GIVING YOURSELF UP" A GIVE-UP PLAY? (p. 108)

The first table details the number of times the batter hit a groundball in the "give-up play" situation (man on second and no one out). The second table details the number of times the batter was not able to produce a groundball to the right of 2b in this situation. In the second table, groundballs to the right side fielded by the pitcher have been excluded from the number of failures (RSF).
Opp=# of times man on second and none out; Grd=# of times a groundball was hit; RS=# of times a groundball was hit to the right side; R->3B=# of times the runner on 2nd advanced to 3rd; B->1B=# of times the batter reached first base; RS/Opp=# of times a groundball was hit to the right side of second base (RS) per opportunity (Opp)

Team	Opp	Grd	RS	R->3B	B->1B	RS/Opp
Baltimore	95	32	15	15	3	.158
Boston	97	29	14	14	6	.144
California	103	27	16	15	7	.155
Chicago	121	37	21	20	2	.174
Cleveland	111	30	17	17	6	.153
Detroit	109	33	19	19	6	.174
Kansas City	140	52	32	31	7	.229
Milwaukee	101	23	14	14	2	.139
Minnesota	116	37	23	22	8	.198
New York	105	31	13	13	2	.124
Oakland	103	36	22	21	5	.214
Seattle	111	36	21	21	2	.189
Texas	102	28	15	15	7	.147
Toronto	116	41	26	26	9	.224
AL Totals	1530	472	268	263	72	.175
Atlanta	129	50	17	16	4	.132
Chicago	120	37	14	12	2	.117
Cincinnati	127	49	33	33	7	.260
Houston	107	28	14	14	0	.131
Los Angeles	129	45	33	32	9	.256
Montreal	125	33	20	20	6	.160
New York	119	33	19	19	8	.160
Philadelphia	103	33	20	18	5	.194
Pittsburgh	134	40	27	27	12	.202
St. Louis	139	55	26	26	7	.187
San Diego	93	27	14	14	3	.150
San Francisco	106	34	18	18	6	.170
NL Totals	1431	464	255	249	69	.178

Team	Opp	RSF	R->3B	B->1B	RS/Opp
Baltimore	95	73	44	28	.463
Boston	97	79	33	16	.340
California	103	76	45	27	.437
Chicago	121	96	58	39	.479
Cleveland	111	84	41	28	.369
Detroit	109	84	41	28	.376
Kansas City	140	102	54	35	.386
Milwaukee	101	79	44	27	.436
Minnesota	116	83	45	30	.388
New York	105	85	45	28	.429
Oakland	103	70	34	22	.330
Seattle	111	85	55	39	.496
Texas	102	81	42	26	.412
Toronto	116	83	37	25	.319
AL Totals	1530	160	618	398	.758
Atlanta	129	106	43	23	.333
Chicago	120	97	51	32	.425
Cincinnati	127	84	53	30	.417
Houston	107	82	36	26	.336
Los Angeles	129	87	56	33	.434
Montreal	125	87	47	32	.376
New York	119	89	38	27	.319
Philadelphia	103	78	37	22	.359
Pittsburgh	134	101	65	42	.485
St. Louis	139	104	55	36	.396
San Diego	93	74	43	30	.462
San Francisco	106	81	42	28	.396
NL Totals	1431	1070	566	361	.748

WHAT'S AN AVERAGE LINEUP? (p. 110)

1990 Composite League Statistics — Per 600 Plate Appearances

American League

Pos	AVG	OBP	SLG	AB	R	H	2B	3B	HR	RBI	BB	K	SB
Batting #1	.265	.334	.374	534	78	141	23	6	8	47	54	76	25
Batting #2	.265	.332	.371	532	72	141	25	4	8	58	52	68	16
Batting #3	.271	.343	.420	531	71	144	27	3	15	74	58	80	10
Batting #4	.263	.338	.442	529	71	139	26	2	22	85	60	106	4
Batting #5	.265	.336	.427	533	71	141	27	3	18	69	56	98	7
Batting #6	.252	.326	.386	534	65	135	23	3	14	63	56	97	7
Batting #7	.261	.325	.385	538	59	141	24	3	12	67	49	90	6
Batting #8	.242	.307	.342	537	61	130	23	3	8	58	48	94	7
Batting #9	.243	.299	.331	538	59	131	23	3	6	51	42	88	10

National League

Pos	AVG	OBP	SLG	AB	R	H	2B	3B	HR	RBI	BB	K	SB
Batting #1	.286	.357	.401	534	85	153	27	5	8	44	57	71	36
Batting #2	.279	.342	.402	534	79	149	27	4	10	56	51	69	19
Batting #3	.283	.351	.426	532	74	150	25	4	15	76	57	80	19
Batting #4	.272	.340	.467	536	76	146	27	3	24	90	55	94	9
Batting #5	.258	.323	.413	539	68	139	24	3	18	80	52	89	13
Batting #6	.255	.317	.381	541	59	138	26	3	12	64	49	89	11
Batting #7	.251	.317	.371	538	57	135	25	2	12	58	51	86	9
Batting #8	.239	.303	.330	539	51	129	22	4	6	50	49	81	5
Batting #9	.223	.292	.320	533	59	119	17	4	9	57	51	135	8

DOES THE COLISEUM HURT MARK McGWIRE? (p. 113)

All Players with 150 Career Home Runs since 1950

Player	Hm HR	Rd HR	Player	Hm HR	Rd HR	Player	Hm HR	Rd HR	Player	Hm HR	Rd HR
Aaron H	385	370	Doby L	107	108	Mathews E	238	274	Singleton K	117	129
Adcock J	137	199	Downing B	126	122	Matthews G	127	107	Skowron W	86	125
Allen R	183	168	Driessen D	86	67	Mattingly D	102	67	Smalley R	84	79
Allison W	123	133	Dropo W	91	61	May L	179	175	Smith A	81	83
Alou F	105	101	Ennis D	112	92	Mayberry J	116	139	Smith C	158	156
Armas A	119	132	Evans Da	219	195	Mays W	335	325	Snider E	215	164
Bailey L	95	60	Evans Dw	199	180	McAuliffe R	110	87	Stargell W	221	254
Bailey R	83	106	Fairly R	112	103	McCovey W	264	257	Staub D	144	148
Baines H	97	108	Fisk C	177	177	McGwire M	60	96	Strawberry D	123	129
Baker J	121	121	Foster G	184	164	McMullen K	80	76	Stuart R	115	113
Balboni S	75	106	Freehan W	100	100	McRae H	87	104	Tenace F	94	107
Bando S	119	123	Fregosi J	68	83	McReynolds	87	80	Thomas F	126	160
Banks E	290	222	Furillo C	94	65	Melton W	93	67	Thomas J	131	137
Barfield J	117	105	Gaetti G	95	106	Mincher D	108	92	Thompson J	109	99
Bauer H	68	85	Gamble O	112	88	Minoso S	84	101	Thomson R	88	102
Baylor D	156	182	Garvey S	151	121	Monday R	125	116	Thornton A	138	115
Bell B	99	102	Gentile J	76	103	Money D	94	82	Torre J	116	136
Bell G	117	89	Gibson K	94	98	Morgan J	122	146	Trammell A	77	75
Bell J	88	114	Grich R	109	115	Moseby L	85	78	Tresh T	81	72
Bench J	195	194	Griffey G	86	65	Murcer B	142	110	Triandos G	80	87
Berra L	179	132	Guerrero P	85	121	Murphy Da	206	172	Wagner L	100	111
Bonds B	173	159	Harrah C	105	90	Murphy Dw	73	93	Wallach T	71	111
Boyer C	69	93	Hart J	72	98	Murray E	176	203	Washington C	90	74
Boyer K	148	134	Hebner R	115	88	Musial S	188	141	Watson R	67	117
Brett G	125	156	Held W	81	98	Nettles G	216	174	Wertz V	113	120
Brunansky T	103	121	Henderson R	74	92	Northrup J	87	66	Whitaker L	96	71
Buckner W	83	91	Hendrick G	134	133	Oglivie B	107	128	White F	75	85
Burroughs J	119	121	Hernandez K	74	88	Oliva P	95	125	White R	86	74
Callison J	110	116	Hickman J	92	67	Oliver A	101	118	White W	120	82
Campanella	120	91	Hisle L	84	82	Otis A	85	108	Williams B	245	181
Canseco J	76	89	Hodges G	186	149	Parker D	164	164	Williams T	124	132
Carter G	157	156	Horner J	142	76	Parrish Lan	136	149	Winfield D	174	204
Carter J	81	94	Horton W	154	171	Parrish Lar	112	144	Wynn J	137	154
Carty R	132	72	Howard E	54	113	Pepitone J	116	103	Yastrzemski	237	215
Cash N	213	164	Howard F	186	196	Perez A	182	197	Yount R	112	113
Cedeno C	87	112	Hrbek K	119	104	Petrocelli A	134	76	Zernial G	123	109
Cepeda O	182	197	Jackson R	280	283	Pinson V	151	105	Zisk R	101	106
Cey R	166	150	Jensen J	91	108	Porter D	77	111			
Chambliss C	104	81	Johnson C	103	93	Post W	119	91			
Clark J	137	170	Johnson D	131	114	Powell J	150	189			
Clemente R	102	138	Johnson H	71	88	Rader D	75	80			
Clendenon D	58	101	Jones W	85	84	Rice J	207	175			
Colavito R	193	181	Kaline A	226	173	Ripken C	113	112			
Colbert N	77	96	Killebrew H	291	282	Robinson B	137	131			
Conigliaro A	89	77	Kiner R	114	87	Robinson F	321	265			
Cooper C	112	129	Kingman D	217	225	Robinson W	88	78			
Crandall D	77	98	Kittle R	81	93	Rose P	85	75			
Cruz J	59	106	Kluszewski T	148	111	Rosen A	103	89			
Davis C	70	86	Lemon C	119	96	Rudi J	88	91			
Davis E	75	91	Lemon J	100	64	Sandberg R	104	75			
Davis G	72	94	Lopes D	81	74	Santo R	216	126			
Davis H	76	77	Luzinski G	179	128	Sauer H	120	95			
Davis W	70	112	Lynn F	177	129	Schmidt M	265	283			
Dawson A	154	192	Madlock B	88	75	Scott G	150	121			
Decinces D	133	104	Mantle M	266	270	Sievers R	144	158			
Demeter D	79	84	Maris R	122	153	Simmons T	116	132			

WHO BUNTS THE BEST? (p. 116)

The following table shows how batters fared in two aspects of bunting. Sacrificing (SH=Sac Hits; FSH=Failed Sac Hits), and Bunting for a Hit (BH=Bunt Hits; FBH=Failed Bunt Hits).

Both Leagues — Listed Alphabetically (10+ Bunts In Play)

Batter, Team	SH	FSH	%	BH	FBH	%	Batter, Team	SH	FSH	%	BH	FBH	%
Alomar R, SD	5	0	100	6	1	86	Liriano, Min	4	4	50	0	3	0
Anderson B, Bal	4	1	80	3	4	43	Magrane, StL	9	1	90	0	0	0
Armstrong, Cin	13	1	93	1	1	50	Martinez De, Mon	12	3	80	0	0	0
Backman, Pit	0	0	0	7	7	50	Martinez R, LA	9	4	69	1	3	25
Barrett M, Bos	11	0	100	1	2	33	McDowell O, Atl	0	0	0	15	11	58
Belcher, LA	9	1	90	1	1	50	Mcrae B, KC	3	0	100	4	6	40
Bell Jay, Pit	39	8	83	3	0	100	Newman A, Min	8	0	100	4	3	57
Bielecki, ChN	10	1	91	2	2	50	Nixon O, Mon	3	0	100	8	14	36
Biggio, Hou	9	1	90	13	7	65	O'Brien C, NYN	10	1	91	0	1	0
Boyd, Mon	12	0	100	0	0	0	Pettis, Tex	11	0	100	5	8	38
Bradley P, ChA	11	0	100	4	0	100	Phillips, Det	9	0	100	8	5	62
Browne J, Cle	12	0	100	3	2	60	Polonia, Cal	3	1	75	10	5	67
Browning, Cin	9	2	82	0	0	0	Ramirez R, Hou	9	2	82	0	0	0
Buechele, Tex	7	1	88	2	0	100	Randolph, Oak	10	2	83	4	2	67
Butler, SF	7	0	100	24	22	52	Reed Jd, Bos	11	0	100	2	0	100
Cole, Cle	0	0	0	4	7	36	Reynolds H, Sea	5	0	100	5	10	33
Coleman, StL	4	2	67	10	11	48	Rijo, Cin	11	1	92	3	1	75
Cone, NYN	9	3	75	0	0	0	Ripken B, Bal	17	5	77	5	4	56
Dascenzo, ChN	5	1	83	3	6	33	Rivera L, Bos	12	3	80	1	3	25
Deshields, Mon	1	3	25	8	7	53	Roberts Bip, SD	8	1	89	2	6	25
Espinoza, NYA	11	0	100	2	3	40	Samuel, LA	5	0	100	2	3	40
Felder, Mil	8	0	100	8	6	57	Sax S, NYA	6	3	67	1	2	33
Fermin, Cle	13	1	93	1	1	50	Schofield, Cal	13	0	100	4	1	80
Fernandez S, NYN	5	5	50	0	0	0	Sharperson, LA	8	1	89	5	2	71
Finley S, Bal	10	2	83	5	14	26	Sheffield, Mil	4	0	100	5	3	63
Fletcher S, ChA	11	2	85	11	4	73	Smith B, StL	11	0	100	0	0	0
Gagne, Min	8	0	100	2	4	33	Smith O, StL	7	2	78	3	7	30
Gallego, Oak	17	0	100	2	1	67	Smith Z, Pit	8	1	89	0	1	0
Gardner M, Mon	8	2	80	0	0	0	Spiers, Mil	6	3	67	3	2	60
Glavine, Atl	7	2	78	1	0	100	Surhoff BJ, Mil	7	1	88	4	2	67
Gooden, NYN	14	4	78	1	0	100	Tewksbury, StL	9	1	90	0	1	0
Griffin Alf, LA	6	0	100	7	9	44	Thompson R, SF	8	0	100	7	3	70
Gross K, Mon	7	3	70	0	0	0	Tudor, StL	7	1	88	0	2	0
Guillen, ChA	15	2	88	7	0	100	Vaughn G, Mil	7	0	100	2	3	40
Gullickson, Hou	7	2	78	0	1	0	Venable, Cal	7	1	88	3	2	60
Gwynn T, SD	7	2	78	4	1	80	Ventura, ChA	13	2	87	3	4	43
Harkey, ChN	8	1	89	1	0	100	Vizquel, Sea	10	2	83	3	0	100
Harris L, LA	3	0	100	3	5	38	Walk, Pit	10	1	91	0	0	0
Hatcher B, Cin	1	0	100	10	6	63	Walton, ChN	1	1	50	6	7	46
Herr, NYN	6	1	86	2	3	40	Webster M, Cle	11	1	92	8	9	47
Howell K, Phi	8	3	73	0	0	0	White D, Cal	10	0	100	5	3	63
Hudler, StL	2	1	67	8	5	62	Whitson, SD	13	1	93	0	0	0
Huson, Tex	7	2	78	0	3	0	Wilson M, Tor	6	1	86	1	2	33
Javier, LA	6	0	100	3	4	43	Yelding, Hou	4	3	57	12	8	60
Johnson L, ChA	8	0	100	4	10	29	**ML Average**	1559	264	86	559	499	53
Karkovice, ChA	7	3	70	6	2	75							
Larkin B, Cin	7	2	78	2	0	100							

WHO SWINGS AT THE FIRST PITCH? (p. 118)

The first column shows the percentage of times the batter swung at the first pitch (S%); the second column how often he put his first swings in play (IP%); the third how successful he was (in terms of batting average).

Listed Alphabetically — Players with 500 Plate Appearances

Player, Team	S% IP% Avg	Player, Team	S% IP% Avg	Player, Team	S% IP% Avg
Alomar R, SD	18.7 41.7 .362	Gruber, Tor	46.2 44.0 .331	Puckett, Min	46.8 50.9 .357
Barfield Je, NYA	30.8 27.9 .417	Guerrero, StL	42.8 42.6 .409	Quintana, Bos	31.5 54.4 .400
Bell Geo, Tor	15.1 48.9 .273	Guillen, ChA	50.2 49.8 .346	Raines, Mon	28.9 53.7 .313
Bell Jay, Pit	29.7 40.8 .288	Gwynn T, SD	21.6 67.4 .262	Reed Jd, Bos	14.2 53.1 .327
Biggio, Hou	23.8 44.2 .311	Harper B, Min	30.5 49.0 .360	Reynolds H, Sea	19.7 55.3 .229
Boggs W, Bos	3.9 44.4 .167	Hatcher B, Cin	37.1 47.1 .340	Ripken C, Bal	18.6 60.5 .338
Bonds, Pit	22.7 46.7 .333	Hayes C, Phi	43.6 45.5 .304	Roberts Bip, SD	27.0 49.2 .391
Bonilla B, Pit	42.2 42.6 .359	Hayes V, Phi	23.2 41.7 .235	Sabo, Cin	29.9 42.6 .291
Brett, KC	34.6 44.2 .422	Henderson R, Oak	10.4 31.9 .227	Samuel, LA	28.2 30.2 .275
Brooks, LA	25.8 36.9 .351	Herr, NYN	22.7 52.6 .375	Sandberg, ChN	25.1 44.2 .427
Browne J, Cle	21.5 55.4 .290	Hrbek, Min	45.4 45.6 .368	Sax S, NYA	17.9 53.2 .288
Brunansky, Bos	26.0 47.1 .324	Incaviglia, Tex	46.4 34.9 .309	Seitzer, KC	25.9 57.0 .350
Burks, Bos	23.7 43.2 .333	Jacoby, Cle	42.1 57.7 .304	Sheffield, Mil	33.1 52.5 .323
Butler, SF	23.8 48.4 .318	James C, Cle	28.5 45.0 .352	Sierra, Tex	23.6 50.6 .282
Calderon, ChA	46.7 38.1 .287	Jefferies, NYN	19.4 51.9 .231	Smith Lo, Atl	48.2 38.9 .382
Caminiti, Hou	35.1 45.0 .270	Johnson H, NYN	31.0 50.2 .363	Smith O, StL	25.2 53.5 .353
Canseco, Oak	26.7 31.3 .356	Johnson L, ChA	40.0 64.8 .363	Sosa, ChA	43.0 33.0 .361
Carter J, SD	33.2 31.9 .366	Justice, Atl	35.9 32.0 .404	Stillwell, KC	23.7 53.1 .299
Clark W, SF	38.0 42.9 .365	Kelly, NYA	31.1 41.0 .360	Strawberry, NYN	30.3 37.4 .324
Coleman, StL	29.8 47.3 .429	Kruk, Phi	35.7 41.8 .257	Stubbs, Hou	33.5 47.1 .421
Daniels, LA	24.8 40.8 .451	Lansford, Oak	40.8 56.5 .232	Surhoff BJ, Mil	20.9 61.6 .339
Daulton, Phi	24.4 53.1 .369	Larkin B, Cin	21.0 52.5 .333	Templeton, SD	42.2 48.4 .388
Davis A, Sea	10.6 65.0 .342	Leonard J, Sea	43.8 37.6 .298	Tettleton, Bal	16.3 36.7 .406
Davis E, Cin	30.3 38.1 .323	Lind, Pit	20.8 50.4 .315	Thompson R, SF	29.9 41.5 .344
Dawson, ChN	29.8 47.4 .360	Magadan, NYN	15.4 58.8 .432	Thon, Phi	40.8 49.4 .254
Deer, Mil	27.7 31.2 .156	Maldonado, Cle	35.3 36.7 .405	Trammell, Det	19.8 59.2 .366
Deshields, Mon	20.8 48.8 .317	Martinez E, Sea	13.0 45.8 .433	Treadway, Atl	42.9 51.1 .358
Dunston, ChN	39.3 41.3 .376	McGee, Oak	44.5 33.6 .389	Van Slyke, Pit	29.8 50.9 .378
Dykstra, Phi	24.9 59.0 .365	McGriff F, Tor	31.0 41.0 .422	Ventura, ChA	21.6 56.0 .322
Eisenreich, KC	37.0 51.0 .304	McGwire, Oak	37.4 38.5 .384	Wallach, Mon	35.9 40.3 .352
Evans Dw, Bos	19.7 50.5 .255	McReynolds, NYN	20.7 49.2 .224	Weiss, Oak	27.7 56.4 .395
Felix, Tor	37.5 41.8 .407	Mitchell K, SF	36.8 42.3 .211	Whitaker, Det	30.0 42.9 .284
Fernandez T, Tor	33.6 46.0 .330	Murphy Dl, Phi	39.2 42.1 .327	White D, Cal	26.6 30.4 .278
Fielder, Det	33.8 29.5 .431	Murray E, LA	42.9 39.3 .429	Williams MD, SF	50.2 38.0 .341
Finley S, Bal	26.1 54.0 .279	O'Neill, Cin	31.4 39.3 .456	Wilson M, Tor	40.1 40.9 .310
Fisk, ChA	28.0 41.8 .373	Oquendo, StL	26.3 51.8 .309	Winfield, Cal	21.9 45.7 .373
Fletcher S, ChA	26.4 56.1 .299	Owen S, Mon	16.2 50.6 .308	Worthington, Bal	20.1 40.4 .324
Franco Ju, Tex	14.3 48.0 .319	Palmeiro, Tex	25.3 54.7 .353	Yelding, Hou	27.7 49.1 .294
Gaetti, Min	47.6 35.9 .286	Parker D, Mil	47.8 46.0 .324	Yount, Mil	24.2 53.4 .313
Galarraga, Mon	34.9 36.0 .307	Parrish Ln, Cal	30.0 45.5 .324	Zeile, StL	15.6 50.0 .286
Gant, Atl	34.1 38.6 .349	Pena T, Bos	35.4 40.8 .397	Major League Avg	31.9 45.1 .315
Gladden, Min	32.3 54.2 .347	Perry G, KC	33.2 34.1 .279		
Grace, ChN	39.6 55.5 .329	Phillips, Det	24.3 51.2 .357		
Greenwell, Bos	37.9 56.8 .340	Presley, Atl	42.4 36.5 .341		
Griffey Jr, Sea	32.0 42.1 .416				
Griffin Alf, LA	45.2 50.7 .308				

WHO'S HOT WHEN IT'S COLD? (p. 120)

**1987-1990 Performance, 50 degrees or lower
(Players with 50 or more plate appearances)**

Player, Team	Avg	AB	H	HR	RBI	Player, Team	Avg	AB	H	HR	RBI
Allanson, Tex	.216	74	16	0	7	Murray E, LA	.111	90	10	0	2
Baines, Oak	.253	79	20	0	7	Nokes, NYA	.277	83	23	4	9
Barfield Je, NYA	.219	105	23	2	14	O'Brien P, Sea	.250	68	17	3	8
Barrett M, Bos	.309	94	29	1	13	Owen S, Mon	.237	80	19	1	5
Bell Geo, Tor	.333	120	40	4	16	Palmeiro, Tex	.296	81	24	3	11
Bell Jay, Pit	.214	70	15	1	6	Parker D, Mil	.286	70	20	1	9
Boggs W, Bos	.357	112	40	0	15	Pena T, Bos	.342	76	26	4	9
Bonds, Pit	.250	104	26	4	12	Phillips, Det	.269	67	18	0	7
Bonilla B, Pit	.236	106	25	3	16	Raines, Mon	.267	75	20	2	13
Braggs, Cin	.233	103	24	6	15	Randolph, Oak	.240	75	18	0	6
Brett, KC	.250	88	22	2	11	Reed Jd, Bos	.212	66	14	0	2
Brock, Mil	.265	68	18	0	8	Ripken C, Bal	.152	79	12	3	12
Brookens, Cle	.229	70	16	2	8	Sandberg, ChN	.268	138	37	1	12
Brooks, LA	.288	66	19	1	9	Sax S, NYA	.306	85	26	0	7
Browne J, Cle	.319	91	29	0	6	Seitzer, KC	.306	98	30	0	8
Brunansky, Bos	.221	68	15	3	8	Sheets, Det	.320	75	24	3	11
Burks, Bos	.365	96	35	3	20	Sheffield, Mil	.278	72	20	1	5
Calderon, ChA	.282	103	29	3	10	Slaught, Pit	.271	70	19	2	11
Carter J, SD	.289	142	41	5	24	Snyder C, Cle	.273	139	38	6	23
Coleman, StL	.203	74	15	1	2	Stillwell, KC	.164	73	12	0	6
Dawson, ChN	.294	119	35	5	20	Surhoff BJ, Mil	.245	102	25	2	10
Deer, Mil	.286	112	32	7	13	Tabler, NYN	.289	90	26	2	10
Dunston, ChN	.178	101	18	2	6	Tartabull, KC	.244	78	19	3	13
Evans Dw, Bos	.269	104	28	0	14	Trammell, Det	.257	113	29	2	16
Franco Ju, Tex	.268	112	30	3	17	Van Slyke, Pit	.310	71	22	2	11
Galarraga, Mon	.378	90	34	3	22	Wallach, Mon	.407	86	35	3	16
Gantner, Mil	.247	81	20	0	5	Webster M, Cle	.352	71	25	1	6
Grace, ChN	.282	71	20	1	8	Whitaker, Det	.279	104	29	6	14
Greenwell, Bos	.229	109	25	2	10	White F, KC	.188	80	15	1	10
Gruber, Tor	.348	92	32	2	13	Wilson W, KC	.229	83	19	0	9
Guillen, ChA	.286	112	32	0	4	Winfield, Cal	.348	66	23	7	16
Hall M, NYA	.185	92	17	0	9	Yount, Mil	.303	122	37	5	16
Hayes V, Phi	.324	68	22	7	21						
Henderson R, Oak	.286	119	34	4	17	**MLB Avg**	**.249**				
Herr, NYN	.363	91	33	1	8						
Jackson B, KC	.255	98	25	7	16						
Jacoby, Cle	.329	140	46	3	14						
Kelly, NYA	.312	77	24	0	11						
Lee M, Tor	.247	73	18	0	7						
Lemon, Det	.221	104	23	3	10						
Lind, Pit	.310	100	31	1	9						
Liriano, Min	.286	70	20	0	6						
Lynn, SD	.159	82	13	1	9						
Martinez Da, Mon	.203	64	13	2	5						
Mattingly, NYA	.273	132	36	1	16						
McGriff F, Tor	.250	84	21	5	14						
McGwire, Oak	.233	73	17	7	12						
Molitor, Mil	.330	97	32	1	3						
Moseby, Det	.218	124	27	2	8						

WHO BRINGS 'EM HOME? (p. 122)

Both Leagues — Listed Alphabetically(125+ RBI Opportunities)

Player, Team	RBI	Op	%	Player, Team	RBI	Op	%	Player, Team	RBI	Op	%
Alomar R, SD	48	179	26.8	Griffin Alf, LA	32	170	18.8	Phillips, Det	42	163	25.8
Alomar S, Cle	50	176	28.4	Gruber, Tor	69	215	32.1	Presley, Atl	45	200	22.5
Baines, Oak	45	191	23.6	Guerrero, StL	57	227	25.1	Puckett, Min	53	182	29.1
Barfield Je, NYA	40	166	24.1	Guillen, ChA	53	188	28.2	Quintana, Bos	49	175	28.0
Bell Geo, Tor	55	202	27.2	Gwynn T, SD	56	208	26.9	Raines, Mon	48	195	24.6
Bell Jay, Pit	38	169	22.5	Harper B, Min	40	157	25.5	Ramirez R, Hou	30	132	22.7
Benzinger, Cin	37	157	23.6	Hatcher B, Cin	18	132	13.6	Randolph, Oak	26	137	19.0
Biggio, Hou	34	183	18.6	Hayes C, Phi	42	188	22.3	Reed Jd, Bos	42	189	22.2
Boggs W, Bos	52	214	24.3	Hayes V, Phi	43	201	21.4	Reynolds H, Sea	41	169	24.3
Bonds, Pit	66	212	31.1	Henderson D,Oak	33	159	20.8	Ripken C, Bal	52	268	19.4
Bonilla B, Pit	72	272	26.5	Henderson R,Oak	26	142	18.3	Rivera L, Bos	34	138	24.6
Boston, NYN	27	131	20.6	Herr, NYN	43	190	22.6	Roberts Bip, SD	29	132	22.0
Bradley P, ChA	22	130	16.9	Hrbek, Min	47	188	25.0	Sabo, Cin	39	181	21.5
Bream, Pit	41	163	25.2	Incaviglia, Tex	44	201	21.9	Salazar L, ChN	29	144	20.1
Brett, KC	59	199	29.6	Jackson B, KC	37	166	22.3	Samuel, LA	33	186	17.7
Brock, Mil	39	157	24.8	Jacoby, Cle	52	197	26.4	Sandberg, ChN	41	175	23.4
Brooks, LA	61	218	28.0	James C, Cle	53	194	27.3	Santiago, SD	35	130	26.9
Browne J, Cle	40	157	25.5	Jefferies, NYN	43	176	24.4	Sax S, NYA	32	179	17.9
Brunansky, Bos	48	230	20.9	Johnson H, NYN	52	199	26.1	Scioscia, LA	50	183	27.3
Burks, Bos	59	227	26.0	Johnson L, ChA	46	153	30.1	Seitzer, KC	24	164	14.6
Butler, SF	36	154	23.4	Jordan, Phi	30	131	22.9	Sharperson, LA	30	139	21.6
Calderon, ChA	50	180	27.8	Jose, StL	36	133	27.1	Sheets, Det	35	135	25.9
Caminiti, Hou	41	197	20.8	Justice, Atl	39	151	25.8	Sheffield, Mil	50	170	29.4
Canseco, Oak	46	183	25.1	Kelly, NYA	38	154	24.7	Sierra, Tex	69	226	30.5
Carter J, SD	75	289	26.0	King J, Pit	31	154	20.1	Smith Lo, Atl	28	135	20.7
Clark Jk, SD	29	164	17.7	Kruk, Phi	48	196	24.5	Smith O, StL	48	201	23.9
Clark W, SF	65	234	27.8	Lansford, Oak	47	191	24.6	Snyder C, Cle	29	139	20.9
Coleman, StL	32	148	21.6	Larkin B, Cin	56	223	25.1	Sosa, ChA	44	186	23.7
Daniels, LA	47	179	26.3	Larkin G, Min	33	147	22.4	Steinbach, Oak	41	136	30.1
Daulton, Phi	36	172	20.9	Leonard J, Sea	56	197	28.4	Stillwell, KC	41	173	23.7
Davis A, Sea	45	197	22.8	Lind, Pit	43	184	23.4	Strawberry, NYN	55	209	26.3
Davis C, Cal	37	158	23.4	Macfarlane, KC	43	169	25.4	Stubbs, Hou	34	159	21.4
Davis E, Cin	46	188	24.5	Magadan, NYN	59	159	37.1	Surhoff BJ, Mil	45	171	26.3
Davis G, Hou	30	143	21.0	Maldonado, Cle	63	231	27.3	Tartabull, KC	35	135	25.9
Dawson, ChN	59	208	28.4	Martinez E, Sea	32	186	17.2	Templeton, SD	42	169	24.9
Deer, Mil	32	173	18.5	Mattingly, NYA	32	132	24.2	Tettleton, Bal	28	190	14.7
Deshields, Mon	37	155	23.9	McGee, Oak	65	242	26.9	Thompson R, SF	33	172	19.2
Doran, Cin	23	133	17.3	McGriff F, Tor	40	191	20.9	Thon, Phi	36	197	18.3
Duncan, Cin	36	138	26.1	McGwire, Oak	51	215	23.7	Trammell, Det	64	210	30.5
Dunston, ChN	37	157	23.6	McReynolds,NYN	46	199	23.1	Treadway, Atl	42	154	27.3
Dykstra, Phi	45	173	26.0	Milligan, Bal	32	148	21.6	Uribe, SF	19	143	13.3
Eisenreich, KC	45	185	24.3	Mitchell K, SF	43	207	20.8	Van Slyke, Pit	47	196	24.0
Evans Dw, Bos	42	192	21.9	Moseby, Det	29	161	18.0	Vaughn G, Mil	36	136	26.5
Felix, Tor	41	144	28.5	Murphy Dl, Phi	41	193	21.2	Ventura, ChA	43	178	24.2
Fermin, Cle	33	142	23.2	Murray E, LA	59	221	26.7	Walker L, Mon	26	151	17.2
Fernandez T, Tor	53	211	25.1	Newman A, Min	29	148	19.6	Wallach, Mon	58	236	24.6
Fielder, Det	58	249	23.3	O'Brien P, Sea	20	138	14.5	Weiss, Oak	31	138	22.5
Finley S, Bal	34	145	23.4	O'Neill, Cin	54	204	26.5	Whitaker, Det	30	158	19.0
Fisk, ChA	40	186	21.5	Oliver, Cin	33	143	23.1	White D, Cal	28	163	17.2
Fletcher S, ChA	44	178	24.7	Oquendo, StL	33	176	18.8	Williams MD, SF	67	211	31.8
Franco Ju, Tex	49	201	24.4	Orsulak, Bal	40	166	24.1	Wilson G, Hou	40	136	29.4
Gaetti, Min	55	209	26.3	Owen S, Mon	27	154	17.5	Wilson M, Tor	43	174	24.7
Galarraga, Mon	56	226	24.8	Palmeiro, Tex	59	203	29.1	Wilson W, KC	38	144	26.4
Gant, Atl	40	184	21.7	Parker D, Mil	59	221	26.7	Winfield, Cal	46	185	24.9
Girardi, ChN	32	140	22.9	Parrish Ln, Cal	33	155	21.3	Worthington, Bal	35	163	21.5
Gladden, Min	31	150	20.7	Pasqua, ChA	36	140	25.7	Yelding, Hou	25	133	18.8
Grace, ChN	69	238	29.0	Pena T, Bos	46	167	27.5	Yount, Mil	50	222	22.5
Greenwell, Bos	49	250	19.6	Pendleton, StL	45	177	25.4	Zeile, StL	32	199	16.1
Griffey Jr, Sea	44	191	23.0	Perry G, KC	45	177	25.4	**MLB Avg**			**22.6**

WHO PULLS? (p. 126)

The table below shows the percentgae of batted balls pulled (Pl) vs. those hit the opposite way (Op). The batting side (B) is also shown for each player.

Both Leagues — Listed Alphabetically (500+ Plate Appearances)

Player, Team	B	Op	Pl	Player, Team	B	Op	Pl	Player, Team	B	Op	Pl
Alomar R, SD	S	48	52	Griffin Alf, LA	S	46	54	Puckett, Min	R	57	43
Barfield Je, NYA	R	32	68	Gruber, Tor	R	37	63	Quintana, Bos	R	49	51
Bell Geo, Tor	R	42	58	Guerrero, StL	R	42	58	Raines, Mon	S	44	56
Bell Jay, Pit	R	50	50	Guillen, ChA	L	56	44	Reed Jd, Bos	R	35	65
Biggio, Hou	R	35	65	Gwynn T, SD	L	49	51	Reynolds H, Sea	S	35	65
Boggs W, Bos	L	63	37	Harper B, Min	R	40	60	Ripken C, Bal	R	35	65
Bonds, Pit	L	41	59	Hatcher B, Cin	R	41	59	Roberts Bip, SD	S	45	55
Bonilla B, Pit	S	42	58	Hayes C, Phi	R	45	55	Sabo, Cin	R	22	78
Brett, KC	L	36	64	Hayes V, Phi	L	33	67	Samuel, LA	R	44	56
Brooks, LA	R	43	57	Henderson R, Oak	R	35	65	Sandberg, ChN	R	34	66
Browne J, Cle	S	38	62	Herr, NYN	S	49	51	Sax S, NYA	R	48	52
Brunansky, Bos	R	31	69	Hrbek, Min	L	38	62	Seitzer, KC	R	53	47
Burks, Bos	R	36	64	Incaviglia, Tex	R	41	59	Sheffield, Mil	R	31	69
Butler, SF	L	55	45	Jacoby, Cle	R	41	59	Sierra, Tex	S	33	67
Calderon, ChA	R	47	53	James C, Cle	R	42	58	Smith Lo, Atl	R	37	63
Caminiti, Hou	S	39	61	Jefferies, NYN	S	40	60	Smith O, StL	S	46	54
Canseco, Oak	R	34	66	Johnson H, NYN	S	38	62	Sosa, ChA	R	42	58
Carter J, SD	R	37	63	Johnson L, ChA	L	41	59	Stillwell, KC	S	47	53
Clark W, SF	L	43	57	Justice, Atl	L	34	66	Strawberry, NYN	L	37	63
Coleman, StL	S	50	50	Kelly, NYA	R	43	57	Stubbs, Hou	L	28	72
Daniels, LA	L	46	54	Kruk, Phi	L	57	43	Surhoff BJ, Mil	L	45	55
Daulton, Phi	L	30	70	Lansford, Oak	R	45	55	Templeton, SD	S	47	53
Davis A, Sea	L	32	68	Larkin B, Cin	R	44	56	Tettleton, Bal	S	32	68
Davis E, Cin	R	35	65	Leonard J, Sea	R	44	56	Thompson R, SF	R	34	66
Dawson, ChN	R	32	68	Lind, Pit	R	56	44	Thon, Phi	R	38	62
Deer, Mil	R	31	69	Magadan, NYN	L	45	55	Trammell, Det	R	41	59
Deshields, Mon	L	49	51	Maldonado, Cle	R	37	63	Treadway, Atl	L	44	56
Dunston, ChN	R	38	62	Martinez E, Sea	R	50	50	Van Slyke, Pit	L	35	65
Dykstra, Phi	L	44	56	McGee, Oak	S	51	49	Ventura, ChA	L	47	53
Eisenreich, KC	L	53	47	McGriff F, Tor	L	38	62	Wallach, Mon	R	43	57
Evans Dw, Bos	R	39	61	McGwire, Oak	R	41	59	Weiss, Oak	S	39	61
Felix, Tor	S	44	56	McReynolds, NYN	R	37	63	Whitaker, Det	L	38	63
Fernandez T, Tor	S	44	56	Mitchell K, SF	R	34	66	White D, Cal	S	43	57
Fielder, Det	R	30	70	Murphy Dl, Phi	R	34	66	Williams MD, SF	R	37	63
Finley S, Bal	L	37	63	Murray E, LA	S	37	63	Wilson M, Tor	S	50	50
Fisk, ChA	R	37	63	O'Neill, Cin	L	43	57	Winfield, Cal	R	40	60
Fletcher S, ChA	R	43	57	Oquendo, StL	S	45	55	Worthington, Bal	R	38	62
Franco Ju, Tex	R	53	47	Owen S, Mon	S	43	57	Yelding, Hou	R	45	55
Gaetti, Min	R	25	75	Palmeiro, Tex	L	39	61	Yount, Mil	R	50	50
Galarraga, Mon	R	42	58	Parker D, Mil	L	40	60	Zeile, StL	R	35	65
Gant, Atl	R	30	70	Parrish Ln, Cal	R	30	70				
Gladden, Min	R	44	56	Pena T, Bos	R	53	47	MLB Avg		41	59
Grace, ChN	L	48	52	Perry G, KC	L	44	56				
Greenwell, Bos	L	45	55	Phillips, Det	S	46	54				
Griffey Jr, Sea	L	40	60	Presley, Atl	R	33	67				

WHICH HITTERS ARE AT HOME ON THE ROAD? (p. 128)

Both League—Listed Alphabetically (500+ Plate Appearances)

Player, Team	Hm	Rd	Dff	Player, Team	Hm	Rd	Dff	Player, Team	Hm	Rd	Dff
Alomar R, SD	.285	.288	3	Griffey Jr, Sea	.292	.308	16	Phillips, Det	.241	.261	20
Barfield Je, NYA	.218	.274	57	Griffin Alf, LA	.220	.202	-19	Presley, Atl	.260	.221	-39
Bell Geo, Tor	.255	.274	19	Gruber, Tor	.292	.254	-37	Puckett, Min	.344	.252	-93
Bell Jay, Pit	.261	.247	-15	Guerrero, StL	.276	.287	11	Quintana, Bos	.299	.276	-23
Biggio, Hou	.274	.277	3	Guillen, ChA	.279	.279	-1	Raines, Mon	.307	.271	-36
Boggs W, Bos	.359	.245	-114	Gwynn T, SD	.310	.307	-3	Reed Jd, Bos	.293	.286	-7
Bonds, Pit	.276	.321	45	Harper B, Min	.283	.305	23	Reynolds H, Sea	.253	.252	-1
Bonilla B, Pit	.261	.298	37	Hatcher B, Cin	.264	.287	23	Ripken C, Bal	.213	.287	73
Brett, KC	.319	.340	20	Hayes C, Phi	.245	.272	28	Roberts Bip, SD	.282	.338	56
Brooks, LA	.251	.280	29	Hayes V, Phi	.276	.250	-26	Sabo, Cin	.280	.260	-20
Browne J, Cle	.272	.262	-10	Henderson R, Oak	.305	.342	37	Samuel, LA	.246	.239	-7
Brunansky, Bos	.333	.180	-153	Herr, NYN	.272	.252	-20	Sandberg, ChN	.357	.255	-103
Burks, Bos	.306	.285	-21	Hrbek, Min	.279	.294	15	Sax S, NYA	.259	.262	3
Butler, SF	.337	.281	-56	Incaviglia, Tex	.247	.220	-27	Seitzer, KC	.312	.239	-73
Calderon, ChA	.306	.245	-62	Jacoby, Cle	.287	.298	11	Sheffield, Mil	.272	.315	43
Caminiti, Hou	.288	.191	-96	James C, Cle	.286	.310	23	Sierra, Tex	.266	.293	27
Canseco, Oak	.258	.288	30	Jefferies, NYN	.318	.246	-73	Smith Lo, Atl	.312	.298	-14
Carter J, SD	.220	.244	23	Johnson H, NYN	.234	.254	21	Smith O, StL	.266	.242	-23
Clark W, SF	.318	.273	-45	Johnson L, ChA	.302	.268	-34	Sosa, ChA	.256	.211	-45
Coleman, StL	.297	.286	-12	Justice, Atl	.320	.243	-77	Stillwell, KC	.268	.230	-38
Daniels, LA	.290	.301	11	Kelly, NYA	.305	.267	-38	Strawberry, NYN	.254	.299	46
Daulton, Phi	.250	.285	35	Kruk, Phi	.318	.265	-54	Stubbs, Hou	.253	.269	16
Davis A, Sea	.278	.289	11	Lansford, Oak	.298	.247	-51	Surhoff BJ, Mil	.306	.247	-60
Davis E, Cin	.233	.281	48	Larkin B, Cin	.273	.326	53	Templeton, SD	.247	.248	1
Dawson, ChN	.316	.304	-12	Leonard J, Sea	.222	.279	56	Tettleton, Bal	.237	.210	-28
Deer, Mil	.187	.230	43	Lind, Pit	.261	.260	-1	Thompson R, SF	.266	.224	-42
Deshields, Mon	.314	.267	-47	Magadan, NYN	.278	.372	94	Thon, Phi	.248	.262	14
Dunston, ChN	.250	.274	24	Maldonado, Cle	.268	.277	9	Trammell, Det	.339	.271	-69
Dykstra, Phi	.339	.313	-26	Martinez E, Sea	.299	.305	5	Treadway, Atl	.301	.267	-35
Eisenreich, KC	.258	.300	42	McGee, Oak	.335	.311	-24	Van Slyke, Pit	.288	.281	-7
Evans Dw, Bos	.252	.247	-6	McGriff F, Tor	.277	.321	44	Ventura, ChA	.273	.227	-46
Felix, Tor	.246	.282	36	McGwire, Oak	.224	.245	20	Wallach, Mon	.276	.314	38
Fernandez , Tor	.308	.242	-66	McRynlds, NYN	.258	.278	20	Weiss, Oak	.247	.286	39
Fielder, Det	.280	.275	-6	Mitchell K, SF	.278	.300	22	Whitaker, Det	.215	.257	42
Finley S, Bal	.231	.286	55	Murphy Dl, Phi	.229	.261	31	White D, Cal	.215	.219	4
Fisk, ChA	.288	.283	-4	Murray E, LA	.343	.317	-26	Williams MD, SF	.271	.283	13
Fletcher S, ChA	.242	.242	0	O'Neill, Cin	.290	.252	-39	Wilson M, Tor	.247	.281	34
Franco Ju, Tex	.317	.272	-44	Oquendo, StL	.239	.264	25	Winfield, Cal	.261	.274	14
Gaetti, Min	.238	.220	-18	Owen S, Mon	.228	.239	12	Worthington, Bal	.234	.218	-17
Galarraga, Mon	.266	.246	-20	Palmeiro, Tex	.288	.350	62	Yelding, Hou	.253	.256	3
Gant, Atl	.313	.293	-20	Parker D, Mil	.273	.303	30	Yount, Mil	.222	.272	50
Gladden, Min	.300	.251	-49	Parrish Ln, Cal	.277	.260	-17	Zeile, StL	.262	.229	-33
Grace, ChN	.331	.285	-46	Pena T, Bos	.275	.250	-25	**AL Avg**	**.263**	**.256**	**-7**
Greenwell, Bos	.310	.283	-28	Perry G, KC	.286	.220	-65	**NL Avg**	**.267**	**.262**	**-5**

WHO HAS OPPOSITE FIELD POWER? (p. 134)

Op stands for the number of opposite field homers. HR is the total Homeruns hit.

Both Leagues — Listed Alphabetically (9 or more Homeruns)

Player, Team	Op	HR	%	Player, Team	Op	HR	%	Player, Team	Op	HR	%
Alomar S, Cle	0	9	0	Gant, Atl	0	32	0	Palmeiro, Tex	3	14	21
Anthony, Hou	1	10	10	Grace, ChN	0	9	0	Pasqua, ChA	4	13	31
Baines, Oak	8	16	50	Greenwell, Bos	0	14	0	Presley, Atl	2	19	11
Balboni, NYA	0	17	0	Griffey Jr, Sea	6	22	27	Puckett, Min	4	12	33
Barfield Je, NYA	7	25	28	Gruber, Tor	5	31	16	Raines, Mon	0	9	0
Bell Geo, Tor	0	21	0	Guerrero, StL	0	13	0	Ripken C, Bal	0	21	0
Bichette, Cal	2	15	13	Hall M, NYA	0	12	0	Roberts Bip, SD	1	9	11
Bonds, Pit	4	33	12	Hayes C, Phi	2	10	20	Sabo, Cin	0	25	0
Bonilla B, Pit	8	32	25	Hayes V, Phi	0	17	0	Salas, Det	0	9	0
Borders, Tor	0	15	0	Henderson D, Oak	3	20	15	Salazar L, ChN	1	12	8
Boston, NYN	1	12	8	Henderson R, Oak	1	28	4	Samuel, LA	3	13	23
Braggs, Cin	0	9	0	Hill G, Tor	1	12	8	Sandberg, ChN	1	40	3
Bream, Pit	2	15	13	Horn, Bal	4	14	29	Santiago, SD	0	11	0
Brett, KC	2	14	14	Hrbek, Min	0	22	0	Scioscia, LA	0	12	0
Brooks, LA	3	20	15	Incaviglia, Tex	11	24	46	Sheets, Det	1	10	10
Brunansky, Bos	1	16	6	Jackson B, KC	13	28	46	Sheffield, Mil	0	10	0
Burks, Bos	1	21	5	Jacoby, Cle	2	14	14	Sierra, Tex	3	16	19
Calderon, ChA	1	14	7	James C, Cle	1	12	8	Smith Lo, Atl	1	9	11
Canseco, Oak	6	37	16	Jefferies, NYN	1	15	7	Snyder C, Cle	0	14	0
Carreon, NYN	0	10	0	Johnson H, NYN	0	23	0	Sosa, ChA	1	15	7
Carter G, SF	0	9	0	Jose, StL	0	11	0	Steinbach, Oak	1	9	11
Carter J, SD	5	24	21	Justice, Atl	3	28	11	Strawberry, NYN	7	37	19
Clark Jk, SD	4	25	16	Kelly, NYA	8	15	53	Stubbs, Hou	1	23	4
Clark W, SF	6	19	32	King J, Pit	0	14	0	Tartabull, KC	5	15	33
Daniels, LA	15	27	56	Kittle, Bal	1	18	6	Templeton, SD	0	9	0
Daulton, Phi	0	12	0	Leonard J, Sea	1	10	10	Tettleton, Bal	4	15	27
Davis A, Sea	0	17	0	Maas, NYA	2	21	10	Teufel, NYN	0	10	0
Davis C, Cal	2	12	17	Maldonado, Cle	3	22	14	Thompson Ro, SF	0	15	0
Davis E, Cin	8	24	33	Marshall, Bos	3	10	30	Trammell, Det	0	14	0
Davis G, Hou	3	22	14	Martinez Crm, Pit	0	10	0	Treadway, Atl	0	11	0
Dawson, ChN	1	27	4	Martinez Da, Mon	0	11	0	Van Slyke, Pit	3	17	18
Deer, Mil	2	27	7	Martinez E, Sea	0	11	0	Vaughn G, Mil	1	17	6
Devereaux, Bal	1	12	8	McGriff F, Tor	10	35	29	Walker L, Mon	2	19	11
Downing, Cal	1	14	7	McGwire, Oak	9	39	23	Wallach, Mon	2	21	10
Duncan, Cin	2	10	20	McReynolds, NYN	0	24	0	Ward G, Det	1	9	11
Dunston, ChN	0	17	0	Milligan, Bal	3	20	15	Webster M, Cle	0	12	0
Dykstra, Phi	0	9	0	Mitchell K, SF	8	35	23	Whitaker, Det	0	18	0
Elster, NYN	1	9	11	Molitor, Mil	0	12	0	White D, Cal	1	11	9
Evans Dw, Bos	0	13	0	Moseby, Det	0	14	0	Williams MD, SF	7	33	21
Felix, Tor	3	15	20	Murphy Dl, Phi	7	24	29	Wilson G, Hou	4	10	40
Fielder, Det	7	51	14	Murray E, LA	4	26	15	Winfield, Cal	5	21	24
Fisk, ChA	0	18	0	Nokes, NYA	0	11	0	Yount, Mil	10	17	59
Fitzgerald, Mon	1	9	11	O'Neill, Cin	3	16	19	Zeile, StL	0	15	0
Franco Ju, Tex	3	11	27	Olerud, Tor	3	14	21				
Fryman T, Det	1	9	11	Orsulak, Bal	0	11	0	**MLB Avg**			12
Gaetti, Min	1	16	6	Parker D, Mil	0	21	0				
Galarraga, Mon	6	20	30	Parrish Ln, Cal	5	24	21				

WHAT'S AN AVERAGE FIRST BASEMAN? (p. 136)

1990 Composite League Statistics — Per 600 Plate Appearances

American League

Pos	AVG	OBP	SLG	AB	H	2B	3B	HR	RBI	BB	K
C	.260	.321	.380	539	140	24	2	12	64	47	89
1B	.271	.353	.438	524	142	25	2	19	73	66	85
2B	.253	.320	.346	533	135	25	4	6	51	52	64
3B	.259	.333	.375	530	137	25	3	10	58	57	83
SS	.252	.314	.342	535	135	23	4	6	52	48	69
LF	.268	.329	.406	541	145	26	3	14	65	47	86
CF	.270	.330	.408	540	146	25	6	12	63	47	95
RF	.254	.321	.409	536	136	25	4	17	72	52	111
DH	.251	.326	.395	529	133	25	2	16	70	58	102
PH	.225	.311	.313	519	115	16	3	8	78	65	123

National League

Pos	AVG	OBP	SLG	AB	H	2B	3B	HR	RBI	BB	K
P	.138	.172	.169	516	71	9	1	2	27	20	181
C	.246	.319	.358	533	131	26	2	10	58	56	82
1B	.276	.347	.438	532	147	28	3	17	79	57	90
2B	.274	.337	.393	538	147	27	4	10	56	50	73
3B	.261	.315	.393	546	142	26	2	14	66	43	82
SS	.250	.307	.347	542	135	23	4	7	51	44	74
LF	.274	.351	.433	528	145	24	4	18	68	62	84
CF	.277	.345	.403	536	149	27	5	11	55	54	79
RF	.269	.335	.435	537	145	23	4	19	78	52	91
PH	.227	.301	.322	529	120	18	3	8	71	56	131

WHO'S PRIMARY IN SECONDARY AVERAGE? (p. 138)

Both Leagues — Listed Alphabetically (250 Plate Appearances)

Player, Team	SA	Player, Team	SA	Player, Team	SA	Player, Team	SA
Alomar R, SD	.205	Fermin, Cle	.111	Larkin B, Cin	.215	Ripken C, Bal	.305
Alomar S, Cle	.191	Fernandez T, Tor	.247	Larkin G, Min	.232	Rivera L, Bos	.194
Backman, Pit	.248	Fielder, Det	.469	Lee M, Tor	.169	Roberts Bip, SD	.284
Baines, Oak	.311	Finley S, Bal	.168	Lemon, Det	.273	Sabo, Cin	.340
Barfield Je, NYA	.384	Fisk, ChA	.312	Leonard J, Sea	.186	Salazar L, ChN	.185
Bell Geo, Tor	.215	Fitzgerald, Mon	.364	Lind, Pit	.163	Samuel, LA	.280
Bell Jay, Pit	.226	Fletcher S, ChA	.155	Liriano, Min	.203	Sandberg, ChN	.364
Benzinger, Cin	.136	Franco Ju, Tex	.284	Macfarlane, KC	.190	Santiago, SD	.227
Bichette, Cal	.232	Gaetti, Min	.218	Mack, Min	.256	Sax S, NYA	.200
Biggio, Hou	.193	Gagne, Min	.188	Magadan, NYN	.295	Schofield, Cal	.206
Blauser, Atl	.225	Galarraga, Mon	.238	Maldonado, Cle	.253	Scioscia, LA	.274
Boggs W, Bos	.257	Gallego, Oak	.157	Martinez Da, Mon	.210	Seitzer, KC	.206
Bonds, Pit	.518	Gant, Atl	.353	Martinez E, Sea	.277	Sharperson, LA	.230
Bonilla B, Pit	.312	Gantner, Mil	.192	Mattingly, NYA	.152	Sheets, Det	.203
Borders, Tor	.260	Gibson K, LA	.340	McGee, Oak	.208	Sheffield, Mil	.248
Boston, NYN	.275	Girardi, ChN	.126	McGriff F, Tor	.402	Sierra, Tex	.242
Bradley P, ChA	.213	Gladden, Min	.180	McGwire, Oak	.467	Smith Lo, Atl	.279
Braggs, Cin	.261	Grace, ChN	.219	McReynolds,NYN	.336	Smith O, StL	.221
Bream, Pit	.319	Greenwell, Bos	.246	Milligan, Bal	.478	Snyder C, Cle	.212
Brett, KC	.301	Griffey Jr, Sea	.295	Mitchell K, SF	.359	Sosa, ChA	.263
Briley, Sea	.255	Griffin Alf, LA	.113	Molitor, Mil	.304	Spiers, Mil	.132
Brock, Mil	.243	Gruber, Tor	.340	Moseby, Det	.297	Steinbach, Oak	.169
Brooks, LA	.211	Guerrero, StL	.233	Murphy Dl, Phi	.291	Stillwell, KC	.176
Browne J, Cle	.255	Guillen, ChA	.105	Murray E, LA	.342	Strawberry, NYN	.384
Brunansky, Bos	.282	Gwynn T, SD	.199	Newman A, Min	.139	Stubbs, Hou	.350
Burks, Bos	.269	Hall M, NYA	.192	Nokes, NYA	.194	Surhoff BJ, Mil	.209
Butler, SF	.272	Harper B, Min	.180	O'Brien P, Sea	.210	Tartabull, KC	.319
Calderon, ChA	.259	Harris L, LA	.148	O'Neill, Cin	.260	Templeton, SD	.156
Caminiti, Hou	.165	Hatcher B, Cin	.210	Olerud, Tor	.318	Tettleton, Bal	.392
Canseco, Oak	.437	Hayes C, Phi	.139	Oliver, Cin	.231	Thompson M, StL	.251
Carter J, SD	.260	Hayes V, Phi	.358	Oquendo, StL	.222	Thompson R, SF	.235
Clark Jk, SD	.581	Heath, Det	.170	Orsulak, Bal	.235	Thon, Phi	.174
Clark W, SF	.267	HendersonD,Oak	.289	Owen S, Mon	.267	Trammell, Det	.270
Coleman, StL	.300	HendersonR,Oak	.562	Pagliarulo, SD	.214	Treadway, Atl	.171
Cotto, Sea	.203	Herr, NYN	.188	Palmeiro, Tex	.216	Uribe, SF	.116
Daniels, LA	.389	Hill D, Cal	.168	Parker D, Mil	.225	Valle, Sea	.260
Daulton, Phi	.318	Howell Jk, Cal	.297	Parrish Ln, Cal	.281	Van Slyke, Pit	.335
Davis A, Sea	.314	Hrbek, Min	.333	Pasqua, ChA	.335	Vaughn G, Mil	.306
Davis C, Cal	.279	Huson, Tex	.177	Pena T, Bos	.177	Ventura, ChA	.174
Davis E, Cin	.397	Incaviglia, Tex	.270	Pendleton, StL	.166	Walker L, Mon	.344
Davis G, Hou	.428	Jackson B, KC	.375	Perry G, KC	.219	Wallach, Mon	.238
Dawson, ChN	.331	Jacoby, Cle	.242	Petralli, Tex	.194	Walton, ChN	.212
Deer, Mil	.366	James C, Cle	.205	Pettis, Tex	.286	Webster M, Cle	.238
Deshields, Mon	.277	Javier, LA	.252	Phillips, Det	.290	Weiss, Oak	.173
Devereaux, Bal	.232	Jefferies, NYN	.242	Polonia, Cal	.156	Whitaker, Det	.339
Doran, Cin	.365	Johnson H, NYN	.351	Presley, Atl	.226	White D, Cal	.260
Downing, Cal	.345	Johnson L, ChA	.159	Puckett, Min	.254	Williams MD, SF	.269
Duncan, Cin	.239	Jose, StL	.190	Quintana, Bos	.195	Wilson G, Hou	.182
Dunston, ChN	.228	Joyner, Cal	.261	Raines, Mon	.330	Wilson M, Tor	.175
Dykstra, Phi	.314	Justice, Atl	.410	Ramirez R, Hou	.135	Winfield, Cal	.293
Eisenreich, KC	.198	Kelly, NYA	.223	Randolph, Oak	.196	Worthington, Bal	.242
Elster, NYN	.258	King J, Pit	.221	Ray, Cal	.139	Yelding, Hou	.196
Espinoza, NYA	.084	Kittle, Bal	.284	Reed Jd, Bos	.226	Yount, Mil	.278
Evans Dw, Bos	.290	Kruk, Phi	.307	Reynolds H, Sea	.245	Zeile, StL	.285
Felix, Tor	.285	Lansford, Oak	.144	Ripken B, Bal	.172	**ML Average**	.237

WHO'S BEST WITH TWO STRIKES? (p. 140)

Player, Team	Avg	AB	H	HR	Player, Team	Avg	AB	H	HR
Alomar R, SD	.248	266	66	4	Kruk, Phi	.209	177	37	1
Barfield Je, NYA	.144	278	40	11	Lansford, Oak	.200	145	29	0
Bell Geo, Tor	.227	251	57	5	Larkin B, Cin	.244	234	57	3
Bell Jay, Pit	.188	292	55	5	Leonard J, Sea	.198	227	45	2
Biggio, Hou	.172	239	41	1	Lind, Pit	.239	188	45	0
Boggs W, Bos	.256	328	84	2	Magadan, NYN	.309	204	63	0
Bonds, Pit	.216	199	43	5	Maldonado, Cle	.156	270	42	6
Bonilla B, Pit	.184	267	49	12	Martinez E, Sea	.270	226	61	3
Brett, KC	.190	189	36	3	McGee, Oak	.247	275	68	0
Brooks, LA	.184	267	49	7	McGriff F, Tor	.176	255	45	10
Browne J, Cle	.195	195	38	2	McGwire, Oak	.140	215	30	9
Brunansky, Bos	.191	251	48	6	McReynolds, NYN	.273	220	60	11
Burks, Bos	.249	257	64	8	Mitchell K, SF	.188	207	39	10
Butler, SF	.275	284	78	2	Murphy Dl, Phi	.150	246	37	3
Calderon, ChA	.237	232	55	4	Murray E, LA	.273	216	59	4
Caminiti, Hou	.227	216	49	2	O'Neill, Cin	.185	243	45	3
Canseco, Oak	.149	281	42	8	Oquendo, StL	.210	200	42	0
Carter J, SD	.208	289	60	9	Owen S, Mon	.194	206	40	2
Clark W, SF	.230	261	60	7	Palmeiro, Tex	.241	220	53	1
Coleman, StL	.211	223	47	4	Parker D, Mil	.190	242	46	6
Daniels, LA	.221	226	50	8	Parrish Ln, Cal	.188	223	42	11
Daulton, Phi	.162	197	32	1	Pena T, Bos	.178	225	40	1
Davis A, Sea	.236	216	51	4	Perry G, KC	.180	189	34	2
Davis E, Cin	.165	188	31	6	Phillips, Det	.206	281	58	3
Dawson, ChN	.250	212	53	5	Presley, Atl	.156	262	41	5
Deer, Mil	.154	254	39	9	Puckett, Min	.189	190	36	1
Deshields, Mon	.180	228	41	0	Quintana, Bos	.184	206	38	0
Dunston, ChN	.183	218	40	3	Raines, Mon	.235	153	36	4
Dykstra, Phi	.253	233	59	2	Reed Jd, Bos	.256	254	65	0
Eisenreich, KC	.194	155	30	0	Reynolds H, Sea	.170	241	41	1
Evans Dw, Bos	.153	177	27	4	Ripken C, Bal	.208	250	52	2
Felix, Tor	.155	206	32	3	Roberts Bip, SD	.229	245	56	4
Fernandez T, Tor	.207	241	50	1	Sabo, Cin	.229	210	48	7
Fielder, Det	.148	305	45	14	Samuel, LA	.167	264	44	2
Finley S, Bal	.191	188	36	1	Sandberg, ChN	.224	246	55	11
Fisk, ChA	.179	190	34	4	Sax S, NYA	.218	243	53	2
Fletcher S, ChA	.149	194	29	2	Seitzer, KC	.189	222	42	1
Franco Ju, Tex	.221	263	58	2	Sheffield, Mil	.229	170	39	2
Gaetti, Min	.165	249	41	3	Sierra, Tex	.172	239	41	5
Galarraga, Mon	.176	284	50	7	Smith Lo, Atl	.254	189	48	0
Gant, Atl	.200	255	51	8	Smith O, StL	.174	172	30	0
Gladden, Min	.212	212	45	2	Sosa, ChA	.159	270	43	2
Grace, ChN	.230	191	44	0	Stillwell, KC	.163	190	31	0
Greenwell, Bos	.254	185	47	2	Strawberry, NYN	.196	270	53	10
Griffey Jr, Sea	.226	261	59	7	Stubbs, Hou	.165	206	34	6
Griffin Alf, LA	.146	185	27	0	Surhoff BJ, Mil	.238	172	41	0
Gruber, Tor	.188	245	46	7	Templeton, SD	.167	210	35	1
Guerrero, StL	.180	217	39	4	Tettleton, Bal	.146	254	37	7
Guillen, ChA	.238	181	43	0	Thompson Ro, SF	.159	226	36	6
Gwynn T, SD	.282	181	51	1	Thon, Phi	.193	197	38	1
Harper B, Min	.212	165	35	1	Trammell, Det	.260	219	57	4
Hatcher B, Cin	.205	176	36	0	Treadway, Atl	.160	156	25	3
Hayes C, Phi	.196	235	46	2	Van Slyke, Pit	.179	201	36	5
Hayes V, Phi	.179	229	41	3	Ventura, ChA	.191	199	38	2
Henderson R, Oak	.310	252	78	7	Wallach, Mon	.205	273	56	6
Herr, NYN	.198	212	42	0	Weiss, Oak	.186	172	32	1
Hrbek, Min	.221	149	33	3	Whitaker, Det	.180	222	40	6
Incaviglia, Tex	.126	262	33	8	White D, Cal	.143	252	36	2
Jacoby, Cle	.214	168	36	1	Williams MD, SF	.186	263	49	10
James C, Cle	.214	206	44	1	Wilson M, Tor	.231	273	63	1
Jefferies, NYN	.269	234	63	5	Winfield, Cal	.194	206	40	5
Johnson H, NYN	.140	228	32	7	Worthington, Bal	.166	241	40	3
Johnson L, ChA	.235	179	42	0	Yelding, Hou	.219	256	56	0
Justice, Atl	.159	201	32	6	Yount, Mil	.174	235	41	7
Kelly, NYA	.216	329	71	6	Zeile, StL	.172	227	39	6

WHO TAKES THE EXTRA BASE? (p. 142)

Both Leagues — Listed Alphabetically
(30 or more Opportunities to Advance as a Baserunner)

Runner	Op	XB	%	Runner	Op	XB	%	Runner	Op	XB	%
Alomar R, SD	52	28	53.8	Grace, ChN	53	23	43.4	Parker D, Mil	39	12	30.8
Alomar S, Cle	40	22	55.0	Greenwell, Bos	59	23	39.0	Perry G, KC	37	20	54.1
Backman, Pit	35	17	48.6	Griffey Jr, Sea	54	31	57.4	Pettis, Tex	42	23	54.8
Baerga, Cle	34	14	41.2	Griffin Alf, LA	32	22	68.8	Phillips, Det	55	29	52.7
Baines, Oak	42	17	40.5	Gruber, Tor	49	31	63.3	Polonia, Cal	36	23	63.9
Barfield Je, NYA	39	24	61.5	Guerrero, StL	30	8	26.7	Presley, Atl	33	9	27.3
Bell Geo, Tor	37	18	48.6	Guillen, ChA	41	24	58.5	Puckett, Min	59	31	52.5
Bell Jay, Pit	54	29	53.7	Gwynn T, SD	35	15	42.9	Quintana, Bos	56	16	28.6
Benzinger, Cin	35	13	37.1	Harper B, Min	44	21	47.7	Raines, Mon	35	19	54.3
Biggio, Hou	32	17	53.1	Harris L, LA	42	31	73.8	Randolph, Oak	44	23	52.3
Blauser, Atl	31	15	48.4	Hatcher B, Cin	44	21	47.7	Reed Jd, Bos	60	31	51.7
Boggs W, Bos	76	27	35.5	Hayes C, Phi	44	25	56.8	Reynolds H, Sea	48	28	58.3
Bonds, Pit	43	27	62.8	Hayes V, Phi	52	34	65.4	Ripken B, Bal	41	20	48.8
Bonilla B, Pit	40	24	60.0	Heath, Det	30	15	50.0	Ripken C, Bal	46	28	60.9
Boston, NYN	37	29	78.4	Henderson D,Oak	36	21	58.3	Roberts B, SD	70	47	67.1
Bradley P, ChA	30	18	60.0	Henderson R,Oak	65	35	53.8	Sabo, Cin	52	32	61.5
Bream, Pit	32	8	25.0	Herr, NYN	41	15	36.6	Sandberg, ChN	56	38	67.9
Brett, KC	46	19	41.3	Hrbek, Min	37	12	32.4	Santiago, SD	30	12	40.0
Briley, Sea	33	18	54.5	Huson, Tex	43	28	65.1	Sax S, NYA	57	26	45.6
Brooks, LA	41	19	46.3	Incaviglia, Tex	34	21	61.8	Scioscia, LA	33	14	42.4
Browne J, Cle	60	40	66.7	Jackson B, KC	30	22	73.3	Seitzer, KC	62	32	51.6
Burks, Bos	54	29	53.7	Jacoby, Cle	60	24	40.0	Sharperson, LA	34	25	73.5
Butler, SF	70	43	61.4	James C, Cle	48	16	33.3	Sheffield, Mil	31	18	58.1
Calderon, ChA	41	28	68.3	Javier, LA	38	23	60.5	Sierra, Tex	55	26	47.3
Caminiti, Hou	49	28	57.1	Jefferies, NYN	51	29	56.9	Smith Lo, Atl	41	24	58.5
Canseco, Oak	31	18	58.1	Johnson H,NYN	47	32	68.1	Smith O, StL	61	33	54.1
Carter J, SD	41	29	70.7	Johnson L, ChA	48	39	81.3	Sosa, ChA	33	19	57.6
Clark Jk, SD	40	10	25.0	Jose, StL	32	20	62.5	Stillwell, KC	37	24	64.9
Clark W, SF	55	32	58.2	Justice, Atl	47	21	44.7	Strawberry, NYN	40	19	47.5
Coleman, StL	37	23	62.2	Kelly, NYA	41	22	53.7	Stubbs, Hou	41	20	48.8
Daniels, LA	51	17	33.3	Kruk, Phi	49	21	42.9	Surhoff BJ, Mil	46	19	41.3
Daulton, Phi	45	16	35.6	Lansford, Oak	30	14	46.7	Tettleton, Bal	47	22	46.8
Davis A, Sea	44	15	34.1	Larkin B, Cin	47	31	66.0	Thompson R, SF	46	22	47.8
Davis C, Cal	37	18	48.6	Lee M, Tor	30	17	56.7	Thon, Phi	44	18	40.9
Davis E, Cin	44	25	56.8	Leonard J, Sea	30	11	36.7	Trammell, Det	51	28	54.9
Dawson, ChN	46	24	52.2	Mack, Min	33	15	45.5	Treadway, Atl	39	16	41.0
Deshields, Mon	40	16	40.0	Magadan, NYN	53	25	47.2	Van Slyke, Pit	35	18	51.4
Doran, Cin	36	19	52.8	Maldonado, Cle	49	18	36.7	Ventura, ChA	35	18	51.4
Downing, Cal	31	10	32.3	Martinez Da, Mon	35	24	68.6	Wallach, Mon	33	19	57.6
Duncan, Cin	37	21	56.8	Martinez E, Sea	52	22	42.3	Walton, ChN	40	20	50.0
Dunston, ChN	38	24	63.2	Mattingly, NYA	31	12	38.7	Weiss, Oak	35	28	80.0
Dykstra, Phi	73	43	58.9	McGee, Oak	67	46	68.7	Whitaker, Det	48	29	60.4
Eisenreich, KC	47	18	38.3	McGriff F, Tor	50	22	44.0	Williams M, SF	49	29	59.2
Espinoza, NYA	31	17	54.8	McGwire, Oak	52	22	42.3	Wilson G, Hou	33	14	42.4
Evans Dw, Bos	47	23	48.9	McReynolds,NYN	50	30	60.0	Wilson M, Tor	50	35	70.0
Felix, Tor	33	24	72.7	Milligan, Bal	38	25	65.8	Wilson W, KC	32	27	84.4
Fermin, Cle	45	21	46.7	Mitchell K, SF	43	20	46.5	Winfield, Cal	31	17	54.8
Fernandez T, Tor	52	26	50.0	Morris H, Cin	31	15	48.4	Worthington, Bal	36	13	36.1
Fielder, Det	40	17	42.5	Moseby, Det	32	23	71.9	Yelding, Hou	38	28	73.7
Finley S, Bal	32	15	46.9	Murray E, LA	58	25	43.1	Yount, Mil	54	34	63.0
Fisk, ChA	39	14	35.9	Myers G, Tor	30	10	33.3	Zeile, StL	40	17	42.5
Fletcher S, ChA	48	27	56.3	O'Neill, Cin	37	12	32.4				
Franco Ju, Tex	69	53	76.8	Olson Greg, Atl	31	16	51.6	**MLB Avg**			**51.1**
Gaetti, Min	37	13	35.1	Oquendo, StL	39	14	35.9				
Galarraga, Mon	41	23	56.1	Orsulak, Bal	37	23	62.2				
Gant, Atl	50	37	74.0	Palmeiro, Tex	51	28	54.9				
Gantner, Mil	36	19	52.8	Parrish Ln, Cal	30	8	26.7				
Gladden, Min	38	24	63.2	Pena T, Bos	45	21	46.7				

WHO'S TOPS IN GO-AHEAD RBI? (p. 144)

Both Leagues — Listed Alphabetically (55+ RBI Total)

Player, Team	Go-Ahead RBI	Occ	All RBI	%	Player, Team	Go-Ahead RBI	Occ	All RBI	%
Alomar R, SD	14	53	60	26	Kruk, Phi	19	52	67	37
Alomar S, Cle	10	58	66	17	Lansford, Oak	12	46	50	26
Baines, Oak	18	57	65	32	Larkin B, Cin	23	56	67	41
Barfield Je, NYA	16	57	78	28	Leonard J, Sea	20	57	75	35
Bell Geo, Tor	26	70	86	37	Macfarlane, KC	8	46	58	17
Boggs W, Bos	12	52	63	23	Magadan, NYN	16	57	72	28
Bonds, Pit	18	86	114	21	Maldonado, Cle	16	76	95	21
Bonilla B, Pit	22	96	120	23	McGee, Oak	20	64	77	31
Bream, Pit	15	52	67	29	McGriff F, Tor	16	72	88	22
Brett, KC	22	74	87	30	McGwire, Oak	23	77	108	30
Brooks, LA	22	71	91	31	McReynolds, NYN	16	63	82	25
Brunansky, Bos	15	55	73	27	Milligan, Bal	16	48	60	33
Burks, Bos	27	65	89	42	Mitchell K, SF	20	76	93	26
Calderon, ChA	24	59	74	41	Murphy Dl, Phi	17	58	83	29
Canseco, Oak	27	70	101	39	Murray E, LA	28	72	95	39
Carter J, SD	36	84	115	43	O'Neill, Cin	16	57	78	28
Clark Jk, SD	14	44	62	32	Orsulak, Bal	14	42	57	33
Clark W, SF	27	76	95	36	Palmeiro, Tex	20	71	89	28
Daniels, LA	28	59	94	47	Parker D, Mil	24	75	92	32
Daulton, Phi	13	46	57	28	Parrish Ln, Cal	16	50	70	32
Davis A, Sea	13	54	68	24	Pasqua, ChA	19	44	58	43
Davis C, Cal	12	40	58	30	Pena T, Bos	8	49	56	16
Davis E, Cin	23	64	86	36	Pendleton, StL	19	45	58	42
Davis G, Hou	13	42	64	31	Perry G, KC	12	49	57	24
Dawson, ChN	25	78	100	32	Phillips, Det	7	43	55	16
Deer, Mil	14	49	69	29	Presley, Atl	21	62	72	34
Duncan, Cin	9	46	55	20	Puckett, Min	22	65	80	34
Dunston, ChN	11	48	66	23	Quintana, Bos	17	53	67	32
Dykstra, Phi	10	53	60	19	Raines, Mon	16	51	62	31
Evans Dw, Bos	24	48	63	50	Reynolds H, Sea	11	45	55	24
Felix, Tor	10	50	65	20	Ripken C, Bal	28	69	84	41
Fernandez T, Tor	9	52	66	17	Sabo, Cin	15	58	71	26
Fielder, Det	30	93	132	32	Sandberg, ChN	23	76	100	30
Fisk, ChA	22	54	65	41	Scioscia, LA	11	52	66	21
Fletcher S, ChA	9	43	56	21	Sheffield, Mil	14	60	67	23
Franco Ju, Tex	17	53	69	32	Sierra, Tex	26	76	96	34
Gaetti, Min	28	65	85	43	Snyder C, Cle	16	42	55	38
Galarraga, Mon	27	68	87	40	Sosa, ChA	19	55	70	35
Gant, Atl	16	68	84	24	Steinbach, Oak	13	39	57	33
Grace, ChN	25	77	82	32	Strawberry, NYN	21	79	108	27
Greenwell, Bos	14	59	73	24	Stubbs, Hou	17	53	71	32
Griffey Jr, Sea	24	63	80	38	Surhoff BJ, Mil	10	45	59	22
Gruber, Tor	29	83	118	35	Tartabull, KC	8	43	60	19
Guerrero, StL	23	64	80	36	Templeton, SD	12	45	59	27
Guillen, ChA	10	52	58	19	Thompson R, SF	11	43	56	26
Gwynn T, SD	17	60	72	28	Trammell, Det	23	69	89	33
Hayes C, Phi	9	47	57	19	Treadway, Atl	9	50	59	18
Hayes V, Phi	21	60	73	35	Van Slyke, Pit	22	63	77	35
Henderson D, Oak	16	49	63	33	Vaughn G, Mil	9	47	61	19
Henderson R, Oak	16	48	61	33	Wallach, Mon	23	72	98	32
Herr, NYN	13	50	60	26	Webster M, Cle	10	42	55	24
Hrbek, Min	16	62	79	26	Whitaker, Det	10	41	60	24
Incaviglia, Tex	24	63	85	38	Williams MD, SF	33	88	122	38
Jackson B, KC	24	54	78	44	Wilson G, Hou	9	46	55	20
Jacoby, Cle	13	66	75	20	Winfield, Cal	19	60	78	32
James C, Cle	15	58	70	26	Yount, Mil	22	58	77	38
Jefferies, NYN	12	60	68	20	Zeile, StL	14	48	57	29
Johnson H, NYN	15	66	90	23					
Justice, Atl	17	61	78	28					
Kelly, NYA	19	54	61	35					

WHO HAS THE BEST "HEART OF THE ORDER"? (p. 146)

Team	Avg	HR	RBI	Slg	Main 3-4-5 Hitters
Pittsburgh	.284	86	333	.502	Van Slyke, Bonilla, Bonds
San Francisco	.281	88	330	.474	Clark, Mitchell, Williams
Los Angeles	.288	80	321	.464	Daniels, Murray, Brooks
Oakland	.254	97	310	.458	Canseco, McGwire, D.Henderson
Toronto	.276	95	310	.481	Gruber, Bell, McGriff
San Diego	.262	61	309	.419	Gwynn, Carter, Clark
New York Mets	.268	86	307	.457	Jefferies, Strawberry, McReynolds
Detroit	.266	85	294	.460	Trammell, Fielder, Sheets
Texas	.285	53	282	.433	Palmeiro, Sierra, Incaviglia
Kansas City	.285	60	280	.462	Brett, Jackson, Tartabulll
Cincinnati	.281	60	280	.438	O'Neill, Davis, Morris
Atlanta	.257	79	280	.450	Gant, Justice, Presley
Philadelphia	.268	49	272	.406	V.Hayes, Murphy, Kruk
Montreal	.264	57	270	.408	Raines, Wallach, Galarraga
California	.259	63	269	.414	Downing, Winfield, Parrish
Chicago Cubs	.280	55	265	.422	Grace, Dawson, Smith
Milwaukee	.261	53	262	.402	Yount, Parker, Vaughn
Minnesota	.266	50	261	.422	Puckett, Gaetti, Hrbek
Seattle	.281	55	259	.428	Griffey Jr., Davis, Leonard
Chicago WSox	.272	64	254	.445	Calderon, Thomas, Fisk
St. Louis	.269	41	254	.396	McGee, Guerrero, Zeile
Boston	.283	43	247	.422	Boggs, Burks, Greenwell
Cleveland	.265	46	246	.398	C. James, Maldonado, Alomar
Baltimore	.234	63	235	.395	C. Ripken, Milligan, Tettleton
Houston	.249	54	234	.388	Caminiti, Davis, Stubbs
New York Yanks	.239	72	231	.397	Mattingly, Hall, Maas
AL Avg Team	**.266**	**64**	**267**	**.430**	
NL Avg Team	**.271**	**66**	**288**	**.435**	

WHO CAN POP IN THE CLUTCH? (p. 148)

Both Leagues — Listed Alphabetically
(85 Plate Apperances in Late Innings of Close Games)

Player, Team	AVG	AB	H	HR	RBI	Player, Team	AVG	AB	H	HR	RBI
Alomar R, SD	.229	105	24	0	12	Maldonado, Cle	.293	82	24	2	14
Alomar S, Cle	.314	86	27	3	15	Martinez E, Sea	.311	90	28	4	15
Barfield Je, NYA	.211	90	19	3	11	McGee, Oak	.376	93	35	1	17
Bell Geo, Tor	.191	89	17	5	14	McGriff F, Tor	.230	87	20	4	11
Bell Jay, Pit	.308	78	24	0	9	McGwire, Oak	.339	62	21	5	16
Biggio, Hou	.193	109	21	0	5	McReynolds, NYN	.289	97	28	4	18
Boggs W, Bos	.291	103	30	0	7	Mitchell K, SF	.352	88	31	8	17
Bonds, Pit	.293	82	24	3	9	Murphy Dl, Phi	.129	85	11	0	6
Bonilla B, Pit	.241	79	19	2	13	Murray E, LA	.321	78	25	1	9
Brooks, LA	.301	83	25	4	16	O'Neill, Cin	.267	86	23	2	9
Browne J, Cle	.244	82	20	1	7	Oquendo, StL	.279	86	24	0	5
Brunansky, Bos	.233	86	20	0	4	Owen S, Mon	.242	91	22	3	11
Burks, Bos	.280	93	26	1	9	Palmeiro, Tex	.288	111	32	3	14
Butler, SF	.265	98	26	1	9	Parker D, Mil	.232	82	19	0	6
Calderon, ChA	.216	88	19	1	6	Parrish Ln, Cal	.235	85	20	5	12
Caminiti, Hou	.280	100	28	0	9	Pena T, Bos	.293	99	29	0	10
Carter J, SD	.220	123	27	4	22	Pendleton, StL	.200	85	17	0	10
Clark Jk, SD	.200	60	12	4	6	Phillips, Det	.263	76	20	1	4
Clark W, SF	.266	94	25	4	16	Presley, Atl	.179	84	15	3	11
Daulton, Phi	.259	85	22	3	13	Puckett, Min	.225	89	20	2	13
Davis A, Sea	.271	85	23	3	10	Quintana, Bos	.305	82	25	1	9
Dawson, ChN	.310	87	27	4	13	Raines, Mon	.319	91	29	2	15
Deer, Mil	.233	73	17	4	11	Ramirez R, Hou	.269	78	21	0	9
Deshields, Mon	.228	101	23	0	7	Reed Jd, Bos	.297	91	27	1	13
Dunston, ChN	.272	92	25	3	14	Reynolds H, Sea	.295	105	31	1	26
Dykstra, Phi	.361	83	30	1	17	Ripken C, Bal	.276	98	27	4	13
Eisenreich, KC	.268	82	22	2	11	Roberts Bip, SD	.266	94	25	1	10
Evans Dw, Bos	.294	85	25	8	24	Sabo, Cin	.247	89	22	5	11
Fernandez T, Tor	.329	85	28	0	5	Sandberg, ChN	.323	96	31	6	19
Fielder, Det	.224	85	19	3	9	Sax S, NYA	.330	94	31	1	13
Fitzgerald, Mon	.216	88	19	0	11	Seitzer, KC	.214	84	18	0	3
Fletcher S, ChA	.229	83	19	1	8	Sierra, Tex	.296	98	29	5	21
Franco Ju, Tex	.340	97	33	2	9	Smith O, StL	.185	81	15	0	9
Gaetti, Min	.227	88	20	3	12	Sosa, ChA	.183	82	15	0	3
Galarraga, Mon	.261	119	31	2	17	Stillwell, KC	.247	81	20	1	4
Gant, Atl	.234	77	18	4	8	Strawberry, NYN	.239	88	21	5	11
Gladden, Min	.183	82	15	0	6	Stubbs, Hou	.360	86	31	7	18
Grace, ChN	.316	98	31	1	13	Templeton, SD	.240	104	25	2	16
Greenwell, Bos	.232	99	23	3	13	Tettleton, Bal	.179	78	14	6	13
Griffey Jr, Sea	.221	95	21	2	9	Thompson M, StL	.224	76	17	1	10
Gruber, Tor	.258	97	25	3	24	Thompson R, SF	.239	88	21	3	13
Guerrero, StL	.250	72	18	1	8	Thon, Phi	.320	97	31	0	5
Guillen, ChA	.300	90	27	0	14	Trammell, Det	.301	73	22	1	12
Gwynn T, SD	.283	106	30	1	7	Van Slyke, Pit	.234	77	18	3	13
Hatcher B, Cin	.224	76	17	0	1	Walker L, Mon	.241	87	21	2	7
Hayes C, Phi	.274	95	26	2	11	Wallach, Mon	.287	129	37	3	16
Hayes V, Phi	.306	72	22	3	9	White D, Cal	.195	87	17	3	8
Herr, NYN	.211	90	19	1	9	Williams MD, SF	.230	100	23	3	13
Hrbek, Min	.299	77	23	1	8	Wilson M, Tor	.309	97	30	1	12
Incaviglia, Tex	.178	101	18	4	18	Winfield, Cal	.305	82	25	4	14
Jacoby, Cle	.253	87	22	2	10	Worthington, Bal	.256	82	21	4	8
Jefferies, NYN	.286	98	28	0	11	Yelding, Hou	.244	78	19	0	4
Johnson H, NYN	.252	111	28	4	20	Yount, Mil	.233	86	20	1	16
Johnson L, ChA	.271	85	23	0	8	Zeile, StL	.205	88	18	1	6
Kelly, NYA	.261	111	29	4	15						
Kruk, Phi	.268	71	19	2	14	AL Avg	.252				
Larkin B, Cin	.309	94	29	1	15	NL Avg	.254				
Leonard J, Sea	.141	78	11	0	10						
Lind, Pit	.319	94	30	0	8						

WHICH PLAYERS HAVE THE BIGGEST "IMPACT"? (p. 150)

Both Leagues — Alphabetical (350 Plate Appearances)

Player, Team	Im-pact	Player, Team	Im-pact	Player, Team	Im-pact	Player, Team	Im-pact
Alomar R, SD	.266	Fitzgerald, Mon	.295	Magadan, NYN	.339	Sheets, Det	.245
Alomar S, Cle	.271	Fletcher S, ChA	.220	Maldonado, Cle	.279	Sheffield, Mil	.287
Backman, Pit	.295	Franco Ju, Tex	.301	Martinez Da, Mon	.260	Sierra, Tex	.272
Baines, Oak	.291	Gaetti, Min	.223			Smith Lo, Atl	.321
Barfield Je, NYA	.307	Gagne, Min	.226	Martinez E, Sea	.311	Smith O, StL	.246
Bell Geo, Tor	.255	Galarraga, Mon	.255	Mattingly, NYA	.214	Snyder C, Cle	.229
Bell Jay, Pit	.253	Gallego, Oak	.185	McGee, Oak	.296	Sosa, ChA	.242
Benzinger, Cin	.226	Gant, Atl	.329	McGriff F, Tor	.349	Spiers, Mil	.199
Bichette, Cal	.256	Gantner, Mil	.240	McGwire, Oak	.318	Steinbach, Oak	.231
Biggio, Hou	.255	Gibson K, LA	.298	McReynolds, NYN	.300	Stillwell, KC	.235
Blauser, Atl	.276	Girardi, ChN	.214			Strawberry, NYN	.321
Boggs W, Bos	.297	Gladden, Min	.244	Milligan, Bal	.338	Stubbs, Hou	.303
Bonds, Pit	.364	Grace, ChN	.297	Mitchell K, SF	.324	Surhoff BJ, Mil	.260
Bonilla B, Pit	.304	Greenwell, Bos	.285	Molitor, Mil	.302	Tartabull, KC	.295
Borders, Tor	.276	Griffey Jr, Sea	.305	Moseby, Det	.264	Templeton, SD	.211
Boston, NYN	.279	Griffin Alf, LA	.170	Murphy Dl, Phi	.252	Tettleton, Bal	.292
Bradley P, ChA	.249	Gruber, Tor	.309	Murray E, LA	.335	Thompson M, StL	.233
Braggs, Cin	.291	Guerrero, StL	.267	Newman A, Min	.211		
Bream, Pit	.298	Guillen, ChA	.222	Nokes, NYA	.232	Thompson Ro, SF	.253
Brett, KC	.327	Gwynn T, SD	.273	O'Brien P, Sea	.222		
Briley, Sea	.256	Hall M, NYA	.248	O'Neill, Cin	.265	Thon, Phi	.227
Brock, Mil	.251	Harper B, Min	.263	Olerud, Tor	.297	Trammell, Det	.304
Brooks, LA	.255	Harris L, LA	.261	Oliver, Cin	.228	Treadway, Atl	.259
Browne J, Cle	.272	Hatcher B, Cin	.265	Oquendo, StL	.251	Uribe, SF	.192
Brunansky, Bos	.268	Hayes C, Phi	.224	Orsulak, Bal	.262	Valle, Sea	.237
Burks, Bos	.292	Hayes V, Phi	.292	Owen S, Mon	.246	Van Slyke, Pit	.317
Butler, SF	.313	Heath, Det	.242	Pagliarulo, SD	.246	Vaughn G, Mil	.249
Calderon, ChA	.256	Henderson D, Oak	.297	Palmeiro, Tex	.293	Ventura, ChA	.238
Caminiti, Hou	.213			Parker D, Mil	.272	Walker L, Mon	.279
Canseco, Oak	.332	Henderson R, Oak	.394	Parrish Ln, Cal	.283	Wallach, Mon	.287
Carter J, SD	.239	Herr, NYN	.247	Pasqua, ChA	.309	Walton, ChN	.260
Clark Jk, SD	.357	Hill D, Cal	.238	Pena T, Bos	.226	Webster M, Cle	.256
Clark W, SF	.304	Howell Jk, Cal	.262	Pendleton, StL	.201	Weiss, Oak	.244
Coleman, StL	.291	Hrbek, Min	.310	Perry G, KC	.241	Whitaker, Det	.275
Cotto, Sea	.236	Huson, Tex	.224	Petralli, Tex	.238	White D, Cal	.233
Daniels, LA	.342	Incaviglia, Tex	.249	Pettis, Tex	.255	Williams MD, SF	.286
Daulton, Phi	.298	Jackson B, KC	.309	Phillips, Det	.275		
Davis A, Sea	.308	Jacoby, Cle	.282	Polonia, Cal	.284	Wilson G, Hou	.219
Davis C, Cal	.273	James C, Cle	.284	Presley, Atl	.249	Wilson M, Tor	.243
Davis E, Cin	.313	Javier, LA	.290	Puckett, Min	.291	Winfield, Cal	.281
Davis G, Hou	.311	Jefferies, NYN	.285	Quintana, Bos	.265	Worthington, Bal	.236
Dawson, ChN	.320	Johnson H, NYN	.280	Raines, Mon	.296		
Deer, Mil	.278			Ramirez R, Hou	.216	Yelding, Hou	.218
Deshields, Mon	.284	Johnson L, ChA	.239	Randolph, Oak	.241	Yount, Mil	.269
Devereaux, Bal	.233	Jose, StL	.251	Ray, Cal	.237	Zeile, StL	.267
Doran, Cin	.335	Joyner, Cal	.270	Reed Jd, Bos	.278		
Downing, Cal	.310	Justice, Atl	.340	Reynolds H, Sea	.255	**MLB Avg**	**.257**
Duncan, Cin	.295	Kelly, NYA	.275	Ripken B, Bal	.269		
Dunston, ChN	.259	King J, Pit	.239	Ripken C, Bal	.274		
Dykstra, Phi	.340	Kittle, Bal	.262	Rivera L, Bos	.215		
Eisenreich, KC	.263	Kruk, Phi	.296	Roberts Bip, SD	.314		
Elster, NYN	.233	Lansford, Oak	.231	Sabo, Cin	.301		
Espinoza, NYA	.175	Larkin B, Cin	.285	Salazar L, ChN	.247		
Evans Dw, Bos	.263	Larkin G, Min	.274	Samuel, LA	.251		
Felix, Tor	.286	Lee M, Tor	.224	Sandberg, ChN	.337		
Fermin, Cle	.207	Lemon, Det	.274	Santiago, SD	.272		
Fernandez T, Tor	.271	Leonard J, Sea	.224	Sax S, NYA	.241		
Fielder, Det	.347	Lind, Pit	.213	Schofield, Cal	.253		
Finley S, Bal	.228	Liriano, Min	.226	Scioscia, LA	.270		
Fisk, ChA	.306	Macfarlane, KC	.248	Seitzer, KC	.266		
		Mack, Min	.322	Sharperson, LA	.284		

WHO WENT TO THE MOON IN 1990? (p. 152)

Both Leagues — 1990 Home Runs Listed by Distance (440+ Feet)

Dis	Batter	Pitcher	When?	Where?
510	Fielder, Det	Stewart D, Oak	08/25	Det
500	Strawberry, NYN	Hernandez X, Hou	07/03	NYN
480	Canseco, Oak	Wills, Tor	05/22	Tor
470	Galarraga, Mon	Hartley, LA	09/01	Mon
470	Clark Jk, SD	Jackson Dan, Cin	09/28	Cin
460	Canseco, Oak	Candiotti, Cle	07/08	Cle
460	Jose, StL	Combs, Phi	09/19	StL
460	Jackson B, KC	Morris Jk, Det	07/01	KC
460	Strawberry, NYN	Combs, Phi	06/23	NYN
460	Jackson B, KC	Hawkins, NYA	07/17	NYA
460	Barfield Je, NYA	Young C, Oak	09/07	NYA
460	Strawberry, NYN	Morgan M, LA	05/21	LA
450	Canseco, Oak	Tanana, Det	08/25	Det
450	Mitchell K, SF	Martinez R, LA	08/03	SF
450	Strawberry, NYN	Carman, Phi	07/25	Phi
450	Mitchell K, SF	Benes, SD	09/04	SD
450	Mitchell K, SF	Fernandez S, NYN	05/08	NYN
450	Bathe, SF	Hammaker, SD	09/04	SD
450	Puckett, Min	Milacki, Bal	07/15	Bal
450	Bell Geo, Tor	Morris Jk, Det	05/13	Det
450	Canseco, Oak	Anderson A, Min	05/14	Min
450	Kittle, Bal	Murphy R, Bos	04/17	ChA
450	Fielder, Det	Finley C, Cal	06/17	Det
450	Deer, Mil	Gibson P, Det	08/14	Det
450	Fielder, Det	Candelaria, Tor	04/24	Min
450	Clark W, SF	Fernandez S, NYN	05/14	SF
450	Strawberry, NYN	Terrell, Det	06/15	Pit
450	Hrbek, Min	Valdez, Cle	05/09	Min
450	Murphy Dl, Phi	Combs, Phi	07/04	Phi
450	Kittle, Bal	Cary, NYA	06/29	ChA
450	Fielder, Det	Mitchell J, Bal	07/24	Det
450	Mitchell K, SF	Kipper, Pit	05/25	Pit
440	Fielder, Det	Stewart D, Oak	08/25	Det
440	Jackson B, KC	Johnson R, Sea	08/26	KC
440	Jackson B, KC	Guetterman, NYA	07/04	KC
440	Fielder, Det	Swindell, Cle	06/06	Cle
440	Tartabull, KC	Drummond, Min	06/24	Min
440	Calderon, ChA	Cummings, Tor	05/09	Tor
440	Mitchell K, SF	Greene, Phi	06/15	SF
440	Jackson B, KC	Stottlemyre, Tor	09/12	KC
440	Gant, Atl	Olivares, StL	08/30	Atl
440	Maas, NYA	Hanson, Sea	08/07	Sea
440	Canseco, Oak	Ryan, Tex	06/06	Tex
440	Sorrento, Min	Davis Storm, KC	06/24	Min
440	Davis E, Cin	Deshaies, Hou	06/16	Cin
440	Maas, NYA	Weston, Bal	09/25	NYA
440	Fielder, Det	Higuera, Mil	09/07	Mil
440	Brooks, LA	Gooden, NYN	08/14	NYN
440	Puckett, Min	Price, Bal	05/28	Min
440	Murphy Dl, Phi	Cone, NYN	07/19	NYN
440	McGriff F, Tor	Clemens, Bos	06/28	Bos
440	Bonilla B, Pit	Bielecki, ChN	04/20	ChN
440	Puckett, Min	Murphy R, Bos	05/26	Min
440	Hall M, NYA	Drummond, Min	05/23	Min
440	Tartabull, KC	Guthrie, Min	06/16	KC
440	Sierra, Tex	Codiroli, KC	09/06	Tex
440	Kittle, Bal	Berenguer, Min	06/08	Min
440	Walker L, Mon	Terrell, Det	06/22	Mon
440	Strawberry, NYN	Walk, Pit	06/08	NYN
440	Horn, Bal	Perez M, ChA	07/22	Bal
440	Buhner, Sea	Morris Jk, Det	06/01	Sea

WHO CLEANS 'EM UP? (p. 154)

Both Leagues — Listed Alphabetically
(Players with 100+ Plate Appearances batting Cleanup)

Player, Team	Slg	AB	H	2B	3B	HR	RBI	AB/RBI
Baines, Oak	.415	106	27	5	0	4	17	6.2
Balboni, NYA	.367	177	29	3	0	11	22	8.0
Bell Geo, Tor	.425	489	128	20	0	20	76	6.4
Benzinger, Cin	.375	112	32	6	2	0	17	6.6
Bonilla B, Pit	.519	624	175	39	7	32	120	5.2
Brunansky, Bos	.457	245	70	16	4	6	38	6.4
Burks, Bos	.449	285	80	12	3	10	42	6.8
Carter J, SD	.386	337	74	12	1	14	59	5.7
Clark Jk, SD	.558	215	60	10	1	16	41	5.2
Davis A, Sea	.443	201	56	9	0	8	34	5.9
Davis C, Cal	.410	188	47	10	1	6	25	7.5
Davis E, Cin	.488	387	102	23	2	20	75	5.2
Davis G, Hou	.521	326	81	15	4	22	63	5.2
Dawson, ChN	.541	501	156	26	4	27	95	5.3
Fielder, Det	.585	424	120	18	1	36	96	4.4
Gaetti, Min	.338	228	47	10	1	6	28	8.1
Galarraga, Mon	.397	184	49	9	0	5	29	6.3
Guerrero, StL	.437	444	127	31	0	12	75	5.9
Hall M, NYA	.422	251	68	16	2	6	34	7.4
Horn, Bal	.394	127	28	10	0	4	18	7.1
Hrbek, Min	.480	325	89	19	0	16	56	5.8
Jackson B, KC	.516	285	73	9	1	21	62	4.6
Jordan, Phi	.375	192	48	12	0	4	28	6.9
Justice, Atl	.565	147	42	7	2	10	31	4.7
Kittle, Bal	.453	192	45	9	0	11	27	7.1
Leonard J, Sea	.368	386	99	13	0	10	66	5.8
Maldonado, Cle	.419	496	132	27	2	15	75	6.6
McGriff F, Tor	.496	139	44	4	0	7	17	8.2
McGwire, Oak	.544	349	86	11	0	31	84	4.2
McReynolds, NYN	.362	94	21	4	0	3	10	9.4
Mitchell K, SF	.544	522	151	24	2	35	93	5.6
Murphy Dl, Phi	.425	228	61	10	1	8	32	7.1
Murray E, LA	.523	554	184	22	3	26	95	5.8
Parker D, Mil	.445	589	166	27	3	21	88	6.7
Pasqua, ChA	.506	269	74	22	2	12	50	5.4
Presley, Atl	.447	418	102	29	1	18	63	6.6
Sierra, Tex	.436	569	160	36	2	16	92	6.2
Snyder C, Cle	.396	101	25	6	0	3	14	7.2
Strawberry, NYN	.530	477	132	17	1	34	98	4.9
Stubbs, Hou	.453	150	41	9	0	6	24	6.3
Tartabull, KC	.488	207	57	14	0	10	40	5.2
Tettleton, Bal	.333	243	48	8	2	7	28	8.7
Thomas F, ChA	.581	93	34	6	1	4	14	6.6
Wallach, Mon	.420	441	125	21	3	11	59	7.5
Wilson G, Hou	.481	104	32	6	0	4	18	5.8
Winfield, Cal	.458	288	82	13	2	11	51	5.6
Zeile, StL	.408	98	24	4	0	4	10	9.8
AL Composite	.437	620	162	30	2	25	99	6.3
NL Composite	.464	627	170	31	3	28	105	6.0

WHO GETS THOSE CHEAP SAVES? (p. 157)

Listed Alphabetically — 1990 Relievers with a minimum of 3 Save Opportunities

Reliever	Cheap	Regular	Tough	Reliever	Cheap	Regular	Tough
Aase, LA	1/1	0/1	2/2	Leach T, Min	0/0	1/1	1/5
Agosto, Hou	1/1	3/4	0/3	Lefferts, SD	3/3	13/18	7/9
Aguilera, Min	9/9	15/17	8/13	Long B, ChN	2/2	2/4	1/1
Akerfelds, Phi	0/0	1/1	2/2	Luecken, Tor	0/0	1/3	0/0
Aldrich, Bal	0/1	1/1	0/1	Machado, Mil	0/0	2/3	1/1
Andersen L, Bos	0/1	6/7	1/3	Mahler R, Cin	0/0	4/4	0/0
Arnsberg, Tex	0/0	3/3	2/3	McDowell R, Phi	7/7	9/13	6/8
Assenmacher, ChN	1/1	7/11	2/8	Mercker, Atl	2/2	4/6	1/2
Bedrosian, SF	6/6	7/9	4/7	Mohorcic, Mon	0/0	2/4	0/0
Belinda, Pit	1/2	6/6	1/5	Montgomery, KC	8/8	14/19	2/7
Boever, Phi	4/4	7/10	3/5	Murphy R, Bos	2/2	2/4	3/4
Brantley J, SF	0/0	12/15	7/9	Myers R, Cin	5/5	18/20	8/12
Burke, Mon	4/5	15/18	1/2	Nelson G, Oak	1/1	3/3	1/4
Burns, Oak	0/0	3/4	0/0	Niedenfuer, StL	1/1	1/2	0/0
Cadaret, NYA	0/0	1/1	2/3	Nunez E, Det	1/1	4/5	1/1
Candelaria, Tor	0/0	4/5	1/3	Olin, Cle	0/1	1/1	0/1
Charlton, Cin	0/0	2/3	0/0	Olson Gregg, Bal	20/20	14/17	3/5
Comstock, Sea	0/0	2/3	0/4	Orosco, Cle	0/0	2/3	0/0
Crews, LA	0/2	3/4	2/3	Palacios, Pit	0/0	2/2	1/1
Crim, Mil	2/2	6/8	3/6	Pall, ChA	0/0	1/1	1/2
Darwin, Hou	0/0	2/4	0/0	Parrett, Atl	0/0	2/5	0/3
Davis Mrk, KC	4/5	2/5	0/0	Patterson B, Pit	1/1	3/4	1/3
Dayley, StL	0/0	2/2	0/5	Pena A, NYN	1/1	3/3	1/1
Dibble, Cin	2/2	8/10	1/5	Pico, ChN	1/1	1/1	0/1
DiPino, StL	1/1	2/2	0/2	Plesac, Mil	8/8	11/17	5/9
Eckersley, Oak	21/21	21/23	6/6	Power, Pit	4/4	2/2	1/1
Eichhorn, Cal	2/2	5/6	6/8	Radinsky, ChA	2/2	2/2	0/1
Franco Jn, NYN	8/9	19/23	6/7	Reardon, Bos	9/9	9/13	3/6
Fraser, Cal	0/0	2/2	0/3	Reed Jr, Bos	0/0	2/2	0/1
Frey, Mon	0/0	8/8	1/1	Righetti, NYA	23/24	11/13	2/2
Gibson P, Det	0/0	3/3	0/3	Rogers, Tex	2/2	5/7	8/14
Gleaton, Det	0/0	10/11	3/5	Ruskin, Mon	0/0	2/7	0/1
Gott, LA	1/1	2/4	0/0	Russell Jf, Tex	3/3	5/5	2/4
Grant, Atl	0/0	3/5	0/1	Sampen, Mon	0/0	2/3	0/0
Gray, Bos	4/4	4/6	1/2	Savage, Min	0/0	1/1	0/2
Guetterman, NYA	0/0	1/3	1/4	Schilling, Bal	0/1	3/5	0/3
Hall D, Mon	0/0	2/4	1/1	Schmidt D, Mon	4/5	7/10	2/2
Harris GW, SD	1/1	6/9	2/6	Schooler, Sea	14/14	15/18	1/2
Harvey, Cal	10/10	8/13	7/8	Smith Dv, Hou	9/10	12/15	2/3
Henke, Tor	8/8	19/23	5/7	Smith Le, StL	7/8	22/24	2/5
Henneman, Det	4/5	16/20	2/3	Stanton M, Atl	0/1	1/1	1/1
Hesketh, Bos	1/2	2/4	2/3	Swift, Sea	0/0	5/5	1/2
Honeycutt, Oak	3/3	4/6	0/1	Terry, StL	0/0	1/2	1/1
Howell Jay, LA	2/2	14/19	0/3	Thigpen, ChA	29/32	20/23	8/10
Jackson M, Sea	2/3	1/5	0/4	Thurmond, SF	0/0	4/5	0/2
Jeffcoat, Tex	0/0	5/7	0/3	Ward D, Tor	0/1	11/15	0/2
Jones Ba, ChA	0/0	1/6	0/2	Wells, Tor	0/0	2/2	1/1
Jones D, Cle	14/15	28/33	1/3	Williams Mitch, ChN	4/4	7/9	5/7
Kipper, Pit	0/0	1/1	2/3	Williamson, Bal	0/1	1/3	0/1
Lancaster, ChN	1/1	3/7	2/3	Witt M, NYA	0/0	1/3	0/0
Landrum B, Pit	3/3	6/8	4/5	**MLB Average**	300/326	624/819	189/360

ARE GROUNDBALL PITCHERS MORE EFFECTIVE? (p. 160)

The table below includes all grounders and flies (hits and outs).

Both Leagues — Listed Alphabetically (125+ Innings Pitched)

Player, Team	Grd	Fly	G/F	Player, Team	Grd	Fly	G/F	Player, Team	Grd	Fly	G/F
Abbott, Cal	375	192	1.95	Hanson, Sea	295	218	1.35	Perez M, ChA	225	226	1.00
Anderson A, Min	297	208	1.43	Harkey, ChN	268	188	1.43	Rasmussen D, SD	256	230	1.11
Appier, KC	280	182	1.54	Harnisch, Bal	220	230	0.96	Rijo, Cin	243	194	1.25
Armstrong, Cin	213	194	1.10	Harris GA, Bos	291	167	1.74	Robinson D, SF	205	211	0.97
Assenmacher, ChN	128	87	1.47	Harris GW, SD	150	103	1.46	Robinson JM, Det	195	176	1.11
Ballard, Bal	184	185	0.99	Hawkins, NYA	196	239	0.82	Robinson R, Mil	242	236	1.03
Belcher, LA	174	190	0.92	Heaton, Pit	225	160	1.41	Ruffin, Phi	228	163	1.40
Benes, SD	238	227	1.05	Hibbard, ChA	331	222	1.49	Ryan, Tex	186	219	0.85
Berenguer, Min	98	128	0.77	Higuera, Mil	174	214	0.81	Saberhagen, KC	192	137	1.40
Bielecki, ChN	240	174	1.38	Holman B, Sea	287	195	1.47	Sanderson, Oak	253	292	0.87
Black, Tor	311	242	1.29	Hough, Tex	302	262	1.15	Schiraldi, SD	118	114	1.04
Blyleven, Cal	207	163	1.27	Howell K, Phi	177	93	1.90	Scott M, Hou	281	262	1.07
Boddicker, Bos	332	246	1.35	Hurst, SD	306	200	1.53	Show, SD	174	99	1.76
Bolton, Bos	169	128	1.32	Jackson Dan, Cin	198	108	1.83	Smiley, Pit	193	190	1.02
Bosio, Mil	193	128	1.51	Jeffcoat, Tex	153	130	1.18	Smith B, StL	233	144	1.62
Boyd, Mon	218	249	0.88	Johnson D, Bal	220	278	0.79	Smith Roy, Min	174	234	0.74
Brown Kev, Tex	361	105	3.44	Johnson R, Sea	237	253	0.94	Smith Z, Pit	374	175	2.14
Browning, Cin	269	354	0.76	Key, Tor	203	203	1.00	Smoltz, Atl	280	269	1.04
Burkett, SF	329	214	1.54	Kiecker, Bos	248	115	2.16	Stewart D, Oak	318	338	0.94
Cadaret, NYA	178	110	1.62	King E, ChA	224	173	1.29	Stieb, Tor	299	223	1.34
Candiotti, Cle	310	213	1.46	Knudson, Mil	257	218	1.18	Stottlemyre, Tor	282	242	1.17
Cary, NYA	135	217	0.62	Krueger, Mil	196	150	1.31	Swift, Sea	285	83	3.43
Cerutti, Tor	229	175	1.31	Lamp, Bos	186	106	1.75	Swindell, Cle	271	287	0.94
Charlton, Cin	227	135	1.68	Lancaster, ChN	158	116	1.36	Tanana, Det	220	201	1.09
Clary, Atl	196	103	1.90	Langston, Cal	265	238	1.11	Tapani, Min	215	183	1.17
Clemens, Bos	308	198	1.56	LaPoint, NYA	231	210	1.10	Terrell, Det	263	153	1.72
Combs, Phi	260	191	1.36	Leary, NYA	344	184	1.87	Tewksbury, StL	255	155	1.65
Cone, NYN	221	215	1.03	Leibrandt, Atl	237	200	1.18	Tudor, StL	202	176	1.15
Cook D, LA	200	215	0.93	Lilliquist, SD	149	164	0.91	Valdez, Cle	149	134	1.11
Crews, LA	162	109	1.49	Maddux G, ChN	425	164	2.59	Valenzuela, LA	285	240	1.19
Darling, NYN	172	123	1.40	Magrane, StL	319	211	1.51	Viola, NYN	365	224	1.63
Darwin, Hou	158	215	0.73	Mahler R, Cin	205	147	1.39	Walk, Pit	193	154	1.25
Davis Storm, KC	182	136	1.34	Martinez De, Mon	358	202	1.77	Ward D, Tor	186	95	1.96
DeJesus J, Phi	177	120	1.48	Martinez R, LA	230	278	0.83	Welch, Oak	325	277	1.17
DeLeon J, StL	158	223	0.71	McCaskill, Cal	280	186	1.51	Wells, Tor	215	247	0.87
Deshaies, Hou	217	280	0.77	McDonald, Bal	153	134	1.14	West, Min	173	184	0.94
Drabek, Pit	364	212	1.72	McDowell J, ChA	226	225	1.00	Whitson, SD	310	239	1.30
Erickson S, Min	201	106	1.90	Milacki, Bal	178	176	1.01	Wilson S, ChN	149	184	0.81
Farr, KC	140	131	1.07	Mitchell J, Bal	204	113	1.81	Wilson Tr, SF	162	108	1.50
Fernandez S, NYN	135	232	0.58	Moore M, Oak	342	217	1.58	Witt B, Tex	251	220	1.14
Finley C, Cal	302	258	1.17	Morgan M, LA	419	158	2.65	Witt M, NYA	205	96	2.14
Gardner M, Mon	182	164	1.11	Morris Jk, Det	331	278	1.19	Young C, Oak	171	152	1.13
Garrelts, SF	272	244	1.11	Moyer, Tex	147	112	1.31	Young Mt, Sea	366	164	2.23
Glavine, Atl	340	215	1.58	Mulholland, Phi	274	209	1.31	**MLB Average**			**1.28**
Gooden, NYN	329	175	1.88	Navarro, Mil	237	174	1.36				
Gordon, KC	246	206	1.19	Ojeda, NYN	197	109	1.81				
Gross K, Mon	213	185	1.15	Parrett, Atl	134	114	1.18				
Gullickson, Hou	289	247	1.17	Petry, Det	233	144	1.62				
Guthrie, Min	208	141	1.48	Portugal, Hou	300	190	1.58				

WHO ARE THE BEST HITTING PITCHERS IN BASEBALL? (p. 162)

Listed by Highest Lifetime Batting Averages — 50+ Plate Appearances

Pitcher, Team	AVG	AB	H	HR	RBI	Pitcher, Team	AVG	AB	H	HR	RBI
Cook D, LA	.253	95	24	1	7	Downs, SF	.138	174	24	0	10
Schatzeder, NYN	.240	242	58	5	29	Kipper, Pit	.138	94	13	0	2
Robinson D, SF	.232	573	133	13	64	Knepper, SF	.137	840	115	6	59
Harkey, ChN	.224	67	15	0	4	Smoltz, Atl	.137	153	21	1	10
Terry, StL	.222	90	20	2	6	Noles, Phi	.136	177	24	0	11
Leary, NYA	.221	163	36	1	19	Honeycutt, Oak	.133	181	24	0	8
Lilliquist, SD	.217	106	23	2	7	Eckersley, Oak	.133	180	24	3	12
Dayley, StL	.210	81	17	0	2	Martinez R, LA	.129	124	16	0	9
Rasmussen D, SD	.205	215	44	0	14	Garrelts, SF	.127	228	29	1	10
Aguilera, Min	.203	138	28	3	11	Martinez De, Mon	.126	294	37	0	22
Valenzuela, LA	.202	807	163	8	72	Whitson, SD	.125	552	69	1	26
Fernandez S, NYN	.199	377	75	1	29	Darwin, Hou	.124	193	24	1	16
Hershiser, LA	.189	456	86	0	29	Ojeda, NYN	.124	242	30	0	3
Sutcliffe, ChN	.189	507	96	4	52	Fisher, Hou	.124	105	13	2	10
Gooden, NYN	.183	513	94	3	39	Scott M, Hou	.124	652	81	2	45
Maddux G, ChN	.182	314	57	0	14	LaCoss, SF	.123	472	58	2	19
Pico, ChN	.182	66	12	0	2	Terrell, Det	.120	192	23	3	10
Mahler R, Cin	.180	567	102	1	37	Hammaker, SD	.118	304	36	0	10
Cone, NYN	.178	258	46	0	11	Tibbs, Pit	.117	180	21	0	4
Candelaria, Tor	.174	596	104	1	48	Smiley, Pit	.114	184	21	0	12
Reuschel, SF	.168	1113	187	4	79	Pena A, NYN	.114	176	20	1	7
Reuss, Pit	.167	1023	171	1	58	DiPino, StL	.113	71	8	0	2
Lefferts, SD	.162	74	12	1	3	Belcher, LA	.112	179	20	1	11
Heaton, Pit	.162	173	28	0	11	Schiraldi, SD	.111	108	12	2	10
Hill K, StL	.160	81	13	0	4	Horton, StL	.109	110	12	0	0
Portugal, Hou	.160	100	16	1	7	Morgan M, LA	.103	107	11	0	3
Show, SD	.160	506	81	4	28	Smith P, Atl	.102	128	13	0	3
Gross K, Mon	.159	460	73	4	23	Dunne, SD	.101	109	11	0	6
Leibrandt, Atl	.158	139	22	0	8	Sanderson, Oak	.100	460	46	2	26
Drabek, Pit	.155	296	46	1	18	DeLeon J, StL	.097	341	33	0	8
Smith Z, Pit	.155	323	50	0	14	Bedrosian, SF	.094	149	14	0	2
Tudor, StL	.154	384	59	0	18	Armstrong, Cin	.092	76	7	0	3
Robinson R, Mil	.153	144	22	0	6	Power, Pit	.091	154	14	1	6
Combs, Phi	.153	72	11	0	2	Ruffin, Phi	.088	239	21	0	6
Walk, Pit	.149	370	55	0	39	Hurst, SD	.080	137	11	0	1
Mathews, StL	.149	148	22	0	5	Lancaster, ChN	.080	100	8	0	3
Viola, NYN	.148	108	16	0	5	Howell K, Phi	.079	114	9	0	3
Glavine, Atl	.146	205	30	0	14	Deshaies, Hou	.077	297	23	0	12
Darling, NYN	.146	485	71	2	18	Bielecki, ChN	.076	197	15	0	5
Rijo, Cin	.146	137	20	1	4	Hesketh, Bos	.070	86	6	0	2
Benes, SD	.143	84	12	1	4	Mulholland, Phi	.069	131	9	0	3
Smith B, StL	.142	422	60	3	29	Grant, Atl	.067	104	7	0	2
Browning, Cin	.141	469	66	0	21	Carman, Phi	.059	204	12	0	4
Jackson Dan, Cin	.141	163	23	0	10	McGaffigan, KC	.048	126	6	0	5
Gullickson, Hou	.141	576	81	3	27	Burkett, SF	.047	64	3	0	3
Magrane, StL	.140	235	33	3	10	**MLB 1990**	**.139**	**4131**	**572**	**15**	**223**
Thurmond, SF	.139	158	22	0	13						

WHICH PITCHERS SHOULD SUE THEIR FIELDERS? (p. 164)

In the table below, **UER** stands for un-earned charged to the pitcher, **Err** is the number of errors committed while he was picthing, and **UERA** is his Un-Earned Run Average.

Both Leagues—Listed Alphabetically (Minimum 125 Innings Pitched)

Player, Team	IP	R	UER	Err	UERA	Player, Team	IP	R	UER	Err	UERA
Abbott, Cal	211.2	116	10	21	0.43	Langston, Cal	223.0	120	11	13	0.44
Anderson A, Mi	188.2	106	11	11	0.52	LaPoint, NYA	157.2	84	12	21	0.68
Appier, KC	185.2	67	10	16	0.48	Leary, NYA	208.0	105	10	13	0.43
Armstrong, Cin	166.0	72	9	14	0.49	Leibrandt, Atl	162.1	72	15	18	0.83
Ballard, Bal	133.1	79	6	14	0.41	Maddux G, ChN	237.0	116	25	27	0.95
Belcher, LA	153.0	76	8	6	0.47	Magrane, StL	203.1	86	5	15	0.22
Benes, SD	192.1	87	10	15	0.47	Mahler R, Cin	134.2	67	3	6.	0.20
Bielecki, ChN	168.0	101	9	14	0.48	Martinez De, M	226.0	80	6	19	0.24
Black, Tor	206.2	86	4	14	0.17	Martinez R, LA	234.1	89	13	21	0.50
Blyleven, Cal	134.0	85	7	11	0.47	McCaskill, Cal	174.1	77	14	26	0.72
Boddicker, Bos	228.0	92	7	16	0.28	McDowell J, Ch	205.0	93	6	17	0.26
Bosio, Mil	132.2	67	8	11	0.54	Milacki, Bal	135.1	73	6	9	0.40
Boyd, Mon	190.2	64	2	7	0.09	Moore M, Oak	199.1	113	10	17	0.45
Brown Kev, Tex	180.0	84	12	17	0.60	Morgan M, LA	211.0	100	12	17	0.51
Browning, Cin	227.2	98	2	16	0.08	Morris Jk, Det	249.2	144	19	31	0.68
Burkett, SF	204.0	92	6	12	0.26	Mulholland, Ph	180.2	78	11	17	0.55
Candiotti, Cle	202.0	92	10	20	0.45	Navarro, Mil	149.1	83	9	16	0.54
Cary, NYA	156.2	77	4	10	0.23	Perez M, ChA	197.0	111	10	22	0.46
Cerutti, Tor	140.0	77	3	8	0.19	Petry, Det	149.2	78	4	10	0.24
Charlton, Cin	154.1	53	6	14	0.35	Portugal, Hou	196.2	90	11	19	0.50
Clemens, Bos	228.1	59	10	22	0.39	Rasmussen D, S	187.2	110	16	24	0.77
Combs, Phi	183.1	90	7	13	0.34	Rijo, Cin	197.0	65	6	13	0.27
Cone, NYN	211.2	84	8	13	0.34	Robinson D, SF	157.2	84	4	8	0.23
Cook D, LA	156.0	74	6	7	0.35	Robinson JM, D	145.0	101	5	15	0.31
Darling, NYN	126.0	73	10	13	0.71	Robinson R, Mi	179.2	78	13	16	0.65
Darwin, Hou	162.2	42	2	13	0.11	Ruffin, Phi	149.0	99	10	9	0.60
DeJesus J, Phi	130.0	63	9	13	0.62	Ryan, Tex	204.0	86	8	10	0.35
DeLeon J, StL	182.2	96	6	13	0.30	Saberhagen, KC	135.0	52	3	7	0.20
Deshaies, Hou	209.1	93	5	17	0.21	Sanderson, Oak	206.1	99	10	14	0.44
Drabek, Pit	231.1	78	7	16	0.27	Scott M, Hou	205.2	102	15	18	0.66
Farr, KC	127.0	32	4	7	0.28	Smiley, Pit	149.1	83	6	11	0.36
Fernandez S, N	179.1	79	10	21	0.50	Smith B, StL	141.1	81	14	18	0.89
Finley C, Cal	236.0	77	14	20	0.53	Smith Roy, Min	153.1	91	9	14	0.53
Gardner M, Mon	152.2	62	4	10	0.24	Smith Z, Pit	215.1	77	16	21	0.67
Garrelts, SF	182.0	91	7	18	0.35	Smoltz, Atl	231.1	109	10	12	0.39
Glavine, Atl	214.1	111	9	15	0.38	Stewart D, Oak	267.0	84	8	11	0.27
Gooden, NYN	232.2	106	7	24	0.27	Stieb, Tor	208.2	73	5	15	0.22
Gordon, KC	195.1	99	18	18	0.83	Stottlemyre, T	203.0	101	3	9	0.13
Gross K, Mon	163.1	86	3	13	0.17	Swift, Sea	128.0	46	12	15	0.84
Gullickson, Ho	193.1	100	18	20	0.84	Swindell, Cle	214.2	110	5	10	0.21
Guthrie, Min	144.2	65	4	10	0.25	Tanana, Det	176.1	104	0	5	0.00
Hanson, Sea	236.0	88	3	19	0.11	Tapani, Min	159.1	75	3	8	0.17
Harkey, ChN	173.2	71	8	15	0.41	Terrell, Det	158.0	98	6	19	0.34
Harnisch, Bal	188.2	96	5	9	0.24	Tewksbury, StL	145.1	67	11	14	0.68
Harris GA, Bos	184.1	90	8	17	0.39	Tudor, StL	146.1	48	9	12	0.55
Hawkins, NYA	157.2	101	7	12	0.40	Valenzuela, LA	204.0	112	8	27	0.35
Heaton, Pit	146.0	66	10	14	0.62	Viola, NYN	249.2	83	9	20	0.32
Hibbard, ChA	211.0	80	6	21	0.26	Walk, Pit	129.2	59	5	12	0.35
Higuera, Mil	170.0	80	9	16	0.48	Ward D, Tor	127.2	51	2	10	0.14
Holman B, Sea	189.2	92	7	11	0.33	Welch, Oak	238.0	90	12	9	0.45
Hough, Tex	218.2	108	9	18	0.37	Wells, Tor	189.0	72	6	8	0.29
Hurst, SD	223.2	85	7	14	0.28	West, Min	146.1	88	5	12	0.31
Johnson D, Bal	180.0	83	1	8	0.05	Whitson, SD	228.2	73	7	16	0.28
Johnson R, Sea	219.2	103	14	24	0.57	Wilson S, ChN	139.0	77	3	10	0.19
Key, Tor	154.2	79	6	8	0.35	Witt B, Tex	222.0	98	15	23	0.61
Kiecker, Bos	152.0	74	7	9	0.41	Young Mt, Sea	225.1	106	18	25	0.72
King E, ChA	151.0	59	4	8	0.24	**MLB Average**					**0.44**
Knudson, Mil	168.1	84	7	16	0.37						
Krueger, Mil	129.0	70	13	19	0.91						

WHAT'S A SAVE-PLUS-HOLD PERCENTAGE? (p. 166)

The table below shows a pitchers Holds (H), Saves (S) and Blown Saves (BS). His Hold+Save Percentage (%) is the sum of his Holds and Saves divided by the sum of his Holds and Saves and Blown Saves.

Both Leagues — Listed Alphabetically
(4 or more Holds+Saves+Blown Saves)

Pitcher	H	Sv	BS	%
Aase, LA	2	3	1	83
Acker, Tor	7	1	1	89
Agosto, Hou	16	4	4	83
Aguilera, Min	0	32	7	82
Akerfelds, Phi	7	3	0	100
Andersen L, Bos	8	7	4	79
Arnsberg, Tex	11	5	1	94
Assenmacher,ChN	10	10	10	67
Bailes, Cal	4	0	0	100
Bair, Pit	4	0	0	100
Ballard, Bal	7	0	0	100
Bautista, Bal	5	0	0	100
Bedrosian, SF	2	17	5	79
Belinda, Pit	9	8	5	77
Berenguer, Min	9	0	2	82
Boever, Phi	5	14	5	79
Brantley J, SF	8	19	5	84
Burke, Mon	6	20	5	84
Burns, Oak	9	3	1	92
Cadaret, NYA	8	3	1	92
Candelaria, Tor	7	5	3	80
Carman, Phi	8	1	1	90
Castillo T, Atl	3	1	1	80
Charlton, Cin	9	2	1	92
Colby, Cle	2	1	1	75
Comstock, Sea	9	2	5	69
Cook D, LA	4	1	1	83
Crawford, KC	7	1	1	89
Crews, LA	5	5	4	71
Crim, Mil	19	11	5	86
Darwin, Hou	0	2	2	50
Davis Mrk, KC	7	6	4	76
Dayley, StL	14	2	5	76
Dibble, Cin	17	11	6	82
DiPino, StL	4	3	2	78
Eckersley, Oak	0	48	2	96
Edens, Mil	2	2	0	100
Edwards, ChA	4	2	0	100
Eichhorn, Cal	4	13	3	85
Farr, KC	7	1	1	89
Fossas, Mil	8	0	2	80
Franco Jn, NYN	0	33	6	85
Fraser, Cal	5	2	3	70
Frey, Mon	5	9	0	100
Gibson P, Det	9	3	3	80
Gleaton, Det	7	13	3	87
Gott, LA	6	3	2	82
Grant, Atl	1	3	3	57
Gray, Bos	3	9	3	80
Guante, Cle	1	0	3	25
Guetterman,NYA	12	2	5	74
Hall D, Mon	4	3	2	78
Harris GW, SD	10	9	7	73
Harvey, Cal	1	25	6	81
Henke, Tor	2	32	6	85
Henneman, Det	4	22	6	81
Hesketh, Bos	3	5	4	67
Hickey, Bal	7	1	0	100
Holton, Bal	3	0	1	75
Honeycutt, Oak	27	7	3	92
Horton, StL	2	1	1	75
Howell Jay, LA	1	16	8	68
Innis, NYN	2	1	1	75
Jackson M, Sea	13	3	9	64
Jeffcoat, Tex	4	5	5	64
Jones Ba, ChA	30	1	7	82
Jones D, Cle	0	43	8	84
Kerfeld, Atl	3	2	0	100
Kipper, Pit	3	3	1	86
Klink, Oak	4	1	0	100
Lamp, Bos	7	0	2	78
Lancaster, ChN	5	6	5	69
Landrum B, Pit	1	13	3	82
Layana, Cin	3	2	0	100
Leach T, Min	4	2	4	60
Lefferts, SD	1	23	7	77
Long B, ChN	4	5	2	82
Luecken, Tor	1	1	2	50
Machado, Mil	0	3	1	75
Mahler R, Cin	1	4	0	100
McClure, Cal	3	0	1	75
McDowell R, Phi	1	22	6	79
Mercker, Atl	0	7	3	70
Meyer B, Hou	3	1	0	100
Mielke, Tex	3	0	1	75
Mills A, NYA	3	0	2	60
Mirabella, Mil	4	0	1	80
Mohorcic, Mon	2	2	2	67
Montgomery, KC	7	24	10	76
Murphy R, Bos	16	7	3	88
Myers R, Cin	0	31	6	84
Navarro, Mil	3	1	1	80
Niedenfuer, StL	10	2	1	92
Nunez E, Det	6	6	1	92
Nelson G, Oak	18	5	3	88
Ojeda, NYN	3	0	2	60
Olin, Cle	4	1	2	71
Oliveras, SF	2	2	0	100
Olson Gregg, Bal	0	37	5	88
Orosco, Cle	2	2	1	80
Pall, ChA	13	2	1	94
Parrett, Atl	11	2	6	68
Patterson B, Pit	8	5	3	81
Patterson K, ChA	4	2	0	100
Pena A, NYN	6	5	0	100
Perez Mk, StL	2	1	1	75
Plesac, Mil	2	24	10	72
Plunk, NYA	3	0	1	75
Power, Pit	3	7	0	100
Price, Bal	3	0	2	60
Radinsky, ChA	10	4	1	93
Reardon, Bos	1	21	7	76
Reed Jr, Bos	2	2	1	80
Righetti, NYA	0	36	3	92
RobinsonJD,NYA	11	0	2	85
Rodriguez R, SD	3	1	0	100
Rogers, Tex	6	15	8	72
Ruskin, Mon	15	2	6	74
Russell Jf, Tex	1	10	2	85
Sampen, Mon	1	2	1	75
Schatzeder,NYN	4	0	0	100
Schilling, Bal	5	3	6	57
Schmidt D, Mon	2	13	4	79
Schooler, Sea	0	30	4	88
Smith Dv, Hou	0	23	5	82
Smith Le, StL	1	31	6	84
Swift, Sea	7	6	1	93
Thigpen, ChA	0	57	8	88
Thurmond, SF	8	4	3	80
Ward D, Tor	11	11	7	76
Wayne, Min	5	1	1	86
Wells, Tor	3	3	0	100
Whitehurst, NYN	4	2	0	100
Williams M, ChN	1	16	4	81
Williamson, Bal	8	1	4	69
Wilson S, ChN	3	1	1	80
Witt M, NYA	2	1	2	60
MLB Average				81

WHICH RELIEVERS MAKE THE LEAST OF THEIR INHERITANCE (p. 168)

The table below shows the percentage (%) of Inherited Runners (IR) each relief pitcher allowed to Score (SC).

Both Leagues — Listed Alphabetically (9+ Inherited Runners)

Pitcher, Team	IR	SC	%	Pitcher, Team	IR	SC	%	Pitcher, Team	IR	SC	%
Aase, LA	21	6	28.6	Gott, LA	22	6	27.3	Olin, Cle	59	22	37.3
Acker, Tor	41	16	39.0	Grant, Atl	52	25	48.1	Oliveras, SF	24	6	25.0
Agosto, Hou	59	10	16.9	Gray, Bos	27	6	22.2	Olson Gregg, Bal	37	10	27.0
Aguilera, Min	38	8	21.1	Guante, Cle	17	7	41.2	Orosco, Cle	50	13	26.0
Akerfelds, Phi	57	15	26.3	Guetterman, NYA	69	18	26.1	Pall, ChA	62	20	32.3
Andersen L, Bos	54	20	37.0	Hall D, Mon	16	1	6.3	Parker C, Det	24	12	50.0
Aquino, KC	16	7	43.8	Harris Ge, Sea	28	8	28.6	Parrett, Atl	34	14	41.2
Arnsberg, Tex	45	18	40.0	Harris GW, SD	42	21	50.0	Patterson B, Pit	39	12	30.8
Assenmacher, ChN	55	16	29.1	Harvey, Cal	28	6	21.4	Patterson K, ChA	54	17	31.5
Bailes, Cal	29	10	34.5	Henke, Tor	32	6	18.8	Pena A, NYN	21	7	33.3
Ballard, Bal	21	4	19.0	Henneman, Det	36	7	19.4	Pico, ChN	21	10	47.6
Barfield Jn, Tex	33	13	39.4	Henry, Atl	21	11	52.4	Plesac, Mil	48	15	31.3
Bautista, Bal	26	8	30.8	Hernandez X, Hou	17	6	35.3	Plunk, NYA	45	17	37.8
Bedrosian, SF	31	7	22.6	Hesketh, Bos	38	17	44.7	Power, Pit	23	8	34.8
Belinda, Pit	41	9	22.0	Hickey, Bal	35	6	17.1	Price, Bal	50	9	18.0
Berenguer, Min	37	10	27.0	Holton, Bal	33	13	39.4	Radinsky, ChA	59	14	23.7
Birtsas, Cin	19	6	31.6	Honeycutt, Oak	43	11	25.6	Reardon, Bos	21	8	38.1
Blair, Tor	20	6	30.0	Horton, StL	24	6	25.0	Reed Jr, Bos	40	15	37.5
Boever, Phi	38	14	36.8	Howell Jay, LA	15	9	60.0	Righetti, NYA	15	4	26.7
Brantley J, SF	41	10	24.4	Jackson M, Sea	62	25	40.3	Robinson JD, NYA	62	16	25.8
Burke, Mon	48	13	27.1	Jeffcoat, Tex	25	10	40.0	Rodriguez Rich, SD	20	7	35.0
Burns, Oak	34	12	35.3	Jones Ba, ChA	56	19	33.9	Rogers, Tex	54	18	33.3
Cadaret, NYA	55	16	29.1	Jones D, Cle	48	13	27.1	Rojas, Mon	18	3	16.7
Candelaria, Tor	41	13	31.7	Kipper, Pit	31	10	32.3	Ruskin, Mon	40	11	27.5
Carman, Phi	62	17	27.4	Klink, Oak	31	4	12.9	Russell Jf, Tex	24	5	20.8
Castillo T, Atl	50	21	42.0	Knackert, Sea	20	8	40.0	Sampen, Mon	28	10	35.7
Charlton, Cin	25	5	20.0	Krueger, Mil	19	9	47.4	Schatzeder, NYN	33	8	24.2
Clancy, Hou	22	6	27.3	Lamp, Bos	60	26	43.3	Schilling, Bal	30	11	36.7
Comstock, Sea	80	17	21.3	Lancaster, ChN	44	18	40.9	Schiraldi, SD	19	19	100
Cook D, LA	35	17	48.6	Landrum B, Pit	31	10	32.3	Seanez, Cle	18	6	33.3
Crawford, KC	33	12	36.4	Layana, Cin	25	10	40.0	Searage, LA	17	8	47.1
Crews, LA	38	13	34.2	Leach T, Min	60	16	26.7	Smith Dv, Hou	21	5	23.8
Crim, Mil	46	15	32.6	Lefferts, SD	45	10	22.2	Smith Le, StL	34	6	17.6
Darwin, Hou	20	6	30.0	Long B, ChN	31	8	25.8	Swift, Sea	57	21	36.8
Davis Mrk, KC	40	16	40.0	Luecken, Tor	20	9	45.0	Terry, StL	36	13	36.1
Dayley, StL	42	18	42.9	Machado, Mil	32	16	50.0	Thigpen, ChA	34	6	17.6
Dibble, Cin	52	18	34.6	McCullers, Det	18	11	61.1	Thurmond, SF	43	13	30.2
DiPino, StL	37	21	56.8	McDowell R, Phi	45	16	35.6	Valdez E, Cle	20	5	25.0
Drummond, Min	17	8	47.1	McMurtry, Tex	21	6	28.6	Valdez, Cle	20	5	25.0
Eckersley, Oak	29	4	13.8	Mercker, Atl	15	5	33.3	Veres, Mil	21	5	23.8
Edens, Mil	26	8	30.8	Mielke, Tex	28	16	57.1	Walsh, LA	22	7	31.8
Edwards, ChA	35	11	31.4	Mills A, NYA	26	9	34.6	Colby, Cle	25	10	40.0
Eichhorn, Cal	69	20	29.0	Mirabella, Mil	41	16	39.0	Ward D, Tor	31	12	38.7
Farr, KC	45	9	20.0	Mohorcic, Mon	23	9	39.1	Wayne, Min	33	11	33.3
Fetters, Cal	27	12	44.4	Montgomery, KC	31	12	38.7	Whitehurst, NYN	22	8	36.4
Fossas, Mil	28	21	75.0	Moyer, Tex	23	6	26.1	Williams M, ChN	36	14	38.9
Franco Jn, NYN	29	10	34.5	Murphy R, Bos	62	19	30.6	Williamson, Bal	52	15	28.8
Fraser, Cal	37	14	37.8	Musselman J, NYN	16	1	6.3	Wills, Tor	28	6	21.4
Freeman M, Atl	20	2	10.0	Myers R, Cin	32	3	9.4	Wilson S, ChN	26	6	23.1
Frey, Mon	24	4	16.7	Nelson G, Oak	32	8	25.0	Young Cli, Cal	26	10	38.5
Gardner W, Bos	18	5	27.8	Niedenfuer, StL	30	8	26.7	**MLB Average**			**32.9**
Gibson P, Det	68	16	23.5	Nunez E, Det	46	11	23.9				
Gleaton, Det	57	17	29.8	O'Neal, SF	23	14	60.9				

WHO KEEPS RUNNERS OFF BASE? (p. 170)

Both Leagues — Listed Alphabetically (125+ Innings Pitched)

Pitcher, Team	BR/9	IP	BR	Pitcher, Team	BR/9	IP	BR
Abbott, Cal	13.73	211.2	323	Langston, Cal	13.08	223.0	324
Anderson A, Min	12.31	188.2	258	LaPoint, NYA	13.59	157.2	238
Appier, KC	11.59	185.2	239	Leary, NYA	12.42	208.0	287
Armstrong, Cin	11.71	166.0	216	Leibrandt, Atl	11.25	162.1	203
Ballard, Bal	13.30	133.1	197	Maddux G, ChN	12.04	237.0	317
Belcher, LA	10.94	153.0	186	Magrane, StL	12.00	203.1	271
Benes, SD	11.56	192.1	247	Mahler R, Cin	11.76	134.2	176
Bielecki, ChN	14.09	168.0	263	Martinez De, Mon	9.80	226.0	246
Black, Tor	10.76	206.2	247	Martinez R, LA	10.06	234.1	262
Blyleven, Cal	13.10	134.0	195	McCaskill, Cal	12.13	174.1	235
Boddicker, Bos	12.00	228.0	304	McDowell J, ChA	11.99	205.0	273
Bosio, Mil	11.67	132.2	172	Milacki, Bal	13.57	135.1	204
Boyd, Mon	10.34	190.2	219	Moore M, Oak	13.14	199.1	291
Brown Kev, Tex	11.90	180.0	238	Morgan M, LA	11.99	211.0	281
Browning, Cin	11.54	227.2	292	Morris Jk, Det	12.04	249.2	334
Burkett, SF	11.74	204.0	266	Mulholland, Phi	10.76	180.2	216
Candiotti, Cle	11.94	202.0	268	Navarro, Mil	13.32	149.1	221
Cary, NYA	12.12	156.2	211	Perez M, ChA	12.11	197.0	265
Cerutti, Tor	13.82	140.0	215	Petry, Det	13.59	149.2	226
Charlton, Cin	11.95	154.1	205	Portugal, Hou	11.81	196.2	258
Clemens, Bos	10.01	228.1	254	Rasmussen D, SD	13.52	187.2	282
Combs, Phi	13.21	183.1	269	Rijo, Cin	10.55	197.0	231
Cone, NYN	10.33	211.2	243	Robinson D, SF	12.27	157.2	215
Cook D, LA	12.29	156.0	213	Robinson JM, Det	14.59	145.0	235
Darling, NYN	13.14	126.0	184	Robinson R, Mil	12.57	179.2	251
Darwin, Hou	9.46	162.2	171	Ruffin, Phi	14.56	149.0	241
DeJesus J, Phi	11.91	130.0	172	Ryan, Tex	9.62	204.0	218
DeLeon J, StL	12.76	182.2	259	Saberhagen, KC	11.67	135.0	175
Deshaies, Hou	11.95	209.1	278	Sanderson, Oak	12.00	206.1	275
Drabek, Pit	9.69	231.1	249	Scott M, Hou	11.42	205.2	261
Farr, KC	10.77	127.0	152	Smiley, Pit	11.99	149.1	199
Fernandez S, NYN	10.14	179.1	202	Smith B, StL	12.35	141.1	194
Finley C, Cal	11.17	236.0	293	Smith Roy, Min	13.97	153.1	238
Gardner M, Mon	11.73	152.2	199	Smith Z, Pit	10.41	215.1	249
Garrelts, SF	13.01	182.0	263	Smoltz, Atl	11.55	231.1	297
Glavine, Atl	13.06	214.1	311	Stewart D, Oak	10.58	267.0	314
Gooden, NYN	11.84	232.2	306	Stieb, Tor	10.91	208.2	253
Gordon, KC	13.55	195.1	294	Stottlemyre, Tor	12.90	203.0	291
Gross K, Mon	13.22	163.1	240	Swift, Sea	11.46	128.0	163
Gullickson, Hou	13.22	193.1	284	Swindell, Cle	12.28	214.2	293
Guthrie, Min	12.07	144.2	194	Tanana, Det	13.53	176.1	265
Hanson, Sea	10.49	236.0	275	Tapani, Min	11.01	159.1	195
Harkey, ChN	11.35	173.2	219	Terrell, Det	14.41	158.0	253
Harnisch, Bal	13.17	188.2	276	Tewksbury, StL	10.47	145.1	169
Harris GA, Bos	13.13	184.1	269	Tudor, StL	9.35	146.1	152
Hawkins, NYA	13.70	157.2	240	Valenzuela, LA	13.24	204.0	300
Heaton, Pit	11.28	146.0	183	Viola, NYN	10.42	249.2	289
Hibbard, ChA	11.22	211.0	263	Walk, Pit	12.22	129.2	176
Higuera, Mil	11.65	170.0	220	Ward D, Tor	10.15	127.2	144
Holman B, Sea	12.34	189.2	260	Welch, Oak	11.19	238.0	296
Hough, Tex	13.17	218.2	320	Wells, Tor	10.10	189.0	212
Hurst, SD	10.14	223.2	252	West, Min	13.78	146.1	224
Johnson D, Bal	12.10	180.0	242	Whitson, SD	10.35	228.2	263
Johnson R, Sea	12.25	219.2	299	Wilson S, ChN	11.98	139.0	185
Key, Tor	11.17	154.2	192	Witt B, Tex	12.61	222.0	311
Kiecker, Bos	12.32	152.0	208	Young Mt, Sea	12.42	225.1	311
King E, ChA	10.79	151.0	181	**MLB Average**	**12.3**		
Knudson, Mil	12.30	168.1	230				
Krueger, Mil	13.53	129.0	194				

WHO SHOULD NIBBLE MORE? (p. 172)

Both Leagues — Listed Alphabetically (Minimum 125 Innings Pitched)

Pitcher	Strike 1	Ball 1	Diff	Pitcher	Strike 1	Ball 1	Diff
Abbott, Cal	.296	.295	1	Maddux G, ChN	.248	.293	-45
Anderson A, Min	.251	.350	-99	Magrane, StL	.215	.328	-114
Appier, KC	.224	.293	-68	Mahler R, Cin	.272	.244	28
Armstrong, Cin	.262	.212	50	Martinez De, Mon	.217	.245	-28
Ballard, Bal	.303	.272	31	Martinez R, LA	.200	.248	-48
Belcher, LA	.248	.228	20	McCaskill, Cal	.235	.258	-23
Benes, SD	.233	.255	-21	McDowell J, ChA	.223	.277	-54
Bielecki, ChN	.265	.314	-50	Milacki, Bal	.233	.322	-89
Black, Tor	.207	.276	-69	Moore M, Oak	.268	.265	3
Blyleven, Cal	.293	.320	-28	Morgan M, LA	.238	.306	-68
Boddicker, Bos	.248	.271	-23	Morris Jk, Det	.226	.272	-46
Bosio, Mil	.266	.245	21	Mulholland, Phi	.254	.248	6
Boyd, Mon	.220	.256	-35	Navarro, Mil	.284	.306	-22
Brown Kev, Tex	.245	.271	-26	Perez M, ChA	.249	.229	20
Browning, Cin	.272	.257	15	Petry, Det	.275	.247	28
Burkett, SF	.239	.285	-46	Portugal, Hou	.226	.286	-60
Candiotti, Cle	.245	.283	-38	Rasmussen D, SD	.301	.280	21
Cary, NYA	.238	.286	-48	Rijo, Cin	.205	.223	-18
Cerutti, Tor	.304	.285	19	Robinson D, SF	.285	.273	12
Charlton, Cin	.244	.210	33	Robinson JM, Det	.245	.268	-23
Clemens, Bos	.210	.256	-46	Robinson R, Mil	.293	.258	35
Combs, Phi	.249	.268	-18	Ruffin, Phi	.301	.293	7
Cone, NYN	.209	.254	-45	Ryan, Tex	.170	.213	-43
Cook D, LA	.279	.240	39	Saberhagen, KC	.268	.299	-31
Darling, NYN	.242	.317	-75	Sanderson, Oak	.244	.274	-30
Darwin, Hou	.205	.267	-62	Scott M, Hou	.237	.262	-26
DeJesus J, Phi	.228	.187	42	Smiley, Pit	.265	.296	-31
DeLeon J, StL	.243	.250	-7	Smith B, StL	.287	.284	3
Deshaies, Hou	.246	.243	2	Smith Roy, Min	.294	.340	-46
Drabek, Pit	.232	.214	18	Smith Z, Pit	.214	.293	-78
Farr, KC	.221	.217	3	Smoltz, Atl	.217	.267	-50
Fernandez S, NYN	.205	.191	15	Stewart D, Oak	.230	.232	-2
Finley C, Cal	.242	.245	-3	Stieb, Tor	.211	.258	-47
Gardner M, Mon	.214	.252	-38	Stottlemyre, Tor	.268	.283	-15
Garrelts, SF	.247	.301	-54	Swift, Sea	.293	.240	54
Glavine, Atl	.300	.255	46	Swindell, Cle	.282	.298	-15
Gooden, NYN	.238	.288	-50	Tanana, Det	.244	.329	-85
Gordon, KC	.281	.227	53	Tapani, Min	.246	.296	-51
Gross K, Mon	.267	.279	-12	Terrell, Det	.266	.326	-60
Gullickson, Hou	.277	.304	-28	Tewksbury, StL	.268	.267	1
Guthrie, Min	.258	.302	-44	Tudor, StL	.216	.237	-20
Hanson, Sea	.237	.225	12	Valenzuela, LA	.273	.280	-7
Harkey, ChN	.222	.252	-30	Viola, NYN	.229	.264	-36
Harnisch, Bal	.259	.265	-6	Walk, Pit	.237	.311	-74
Harris GA, Bos	.230	.309	-80	Ward D, Tor	.196	.269	-73
Hawkins, NYA	.239	.289	-50	Welch, Oak	.233	.255	-22
Heaton, Pit	.263	.263	0	Wells, Tor	.222	.252	-30
Hibbard, ChA	.251	.261	-11	West, Min	.255	.258	-4
Higuera, Mil	.241	.280	-40	Whitson, SD	.251	.253	-2
Holman B, Sea	.271	.244	27	Wilson S, ChN	.245	.283	-38
Hough, Tex	.248	.222	27	Witt B, Tex	.217	.269	-52
Hurst, SD	.221	.241	-20	Young Mt, Sea	.248	.223	25
Johnson D, Bal	.273	.289	-16	**MLB Average**	**.249**	**.270**	**-21**
Johnson R, Sea	.218	.213	5				
Key, Tor	.265	.304	-39				
Kiecker, Bos	.251	.259	-8				
King E, ChA	.239	.234	5				
Knudson, Mil	.287	.274	13				
Krueger, Mil	.280	.272	7				
Langston, Cal	.234	.295	-61				
LaPoint, NYA	.307	.272	34				
Leary, NYA	.269	.242	27				
Leibrandt, Atl	.249	.280	-30				

WHO WAS BETTER IN '90 — DWIGHT GOODEN OR JIM DESHAIES? (p. 174)

In the table below, **Sup** stands for Run Support Per Nine Innings. **RS** is the total Runs In Support for that pitcher while he was in the game.

Both Leagues — Listed Alphabetically (20+ Games Started)

Pitcher, Team	W/L	ERA	Sup	IP	RS	Pitcher, Team	W/L	ERA	Sup	IP	RS
Abbott, Cal	10-14	4.51	4.08	211.2	96	LaPoint, NYA	7-10	4.12	4.41	155.0	76
Anderson A, Min	7-18	4.53	3.43	188.2	72	Leary, NYA	9-19	4.11	3.07	208.0	71
Appier, KC	12-8	2.59	4.66	170.0	88	Leibrandt, Atl	9-11	3.16	4.71	162.1	85
Armstrong, Cin	12-9	3.47	4.74	163.1	86	Maddux G, ChN	15-15	3.46	3.91	237.0	103
Avery, Atl	3-10	5.47	3.53	97.0	38	Magrane, StL	10-17	3.59	3.01	203.1	68
Belcher, LA	9-9	4.00	4.18	153.0	71	Martinez De, Mon	10-11	2.95	4.02	226.0	101
Benes, SD	10-11	3.50	4.07	190.1	86	Martinez R, LA	20-6	2.92	5.42	234.1	141
Bielecki, ChN	7-11	5.30	4.35	151.0	73	McCaskill, Cal	12-11	3.25	4.54	174.1	88
Black, Tor	12-11	3.56	4.27	204.2	97	McDowell J, ChA	14-9	3.82	5.22	205.0	119
Blyleven, Cal	8-7	5.24	4.84	134.0	72	Milacki, Bal	5-8	4.38	4.04	129.1	58
Boddicker, Bos	17-8	3.36	5.41	228.0	137	Moore M, Oak	13-15	4.65	4.20	199.1	93
Bosio, Mil	4-9	4.00	4.27	132.2	63	Morgan M, LA	11-15	3.75	4.05	211.0	95
Boyd, Mon	10-6	2.93	4.20	190.2	89	Morris Jk, Det	15-18	4.51	5.23	249.2	145
Brown Kev, Tex	12-10	3.60	5.20	180.0	104	Mulholland, Phi	9-10	3.52	4.15	171.1	79
Browning, Cin	15-9	3.80	3.83	227.2	97	Navarro, Mil	8-7	4.99	5.77	126.1	81
Burkett, SF	14-7	3.85	5.69	201.0	127	Perez M, ChA	13-14	4.61	4.75	197.0	104
Candiotti, Cle	15-11	3.63	5.20	195.2	113	Petry, Det	8-9	4.75	4.21	134.2	63
Cary, NYA	6-12	4.24	3.19	155.0	55	Portugal, Hou	11-10	3.62	3.48	196.2	76
Cerutti, Tor	8-9	4.74	4.94	133.0	73	Rasmussen D, SD	11-15	4.51	5.66	187.2	118
Clemens, Bos	21-6	1.93	4.49	228.1	114	Rijo, Cin	14-8	2.70	4.25	197.0	93
Combs, Phi	10-10	4.05	4.90	182.0	99	Robinson D, SF	10-7	4.42	4.02	156.2	70
Cone, NYN	14-10	3.25	4.74	210.2	111	Robinson R, Mil	14-6	3.24	5.91	175.0	115
Davis Storm, KC	7-10	4.67	5.67	108.0	68	Robinson JM, Det	10-9	5.96	7.08	145.0	114
DeJesus J, Phi	7-8	3.74	4.15	130.0	60	Ruffin, Phi	6-13	5.24	3.94	132.1	58
DeLeon J, StL	7-19	4.43	2.96	182.2	60	Ryan, Tex	13-9	3.44	4.46	204.0	101
Deshaies, Hou	7-12	3.78	3.53	209.1	82	Scott M, Hou	9-13	3.81	3.11	205.2	71
Drabek, Pit	22-6	2.76	5.91	231.1	152	Saberhagen, KC	5-9	3.27	3.67	135.0	55
Fernandez S, NYN	9-14	3.46	4.22	179.1	84	Sanderson, Oak	17-11	3.88	4.62	206.1	106
Finley C, Cal	18-9	2.40	4.54	236.0	119	Smiley, Pit	9-10	4.67	4.19	148.1	69
Gardner M, Mon	7-8	3.39	3.69	151.1	62	Smith B, StL	9-8	4.28	4.79	141.0	75
Garrelts, SF	12-11	4.15	3.66	182.0	74	Smith Roy, Min	5-10	4.77	5.54	128.1	79
Glavine, Atl	10-12	4.28	4.28	214.1	102	Smith Z, Pit	12-9	2.49	3.16	213.1	75
Gooden, NYN	19-7	3.83	6.77	232.2	175	Smoltz, Atl	14-11	3.85	5.14	231.1	132
Gordon, KC	12-11	3.73	5.02	195.1	109	Stewart D, Oak	22-11	2.56	5.02	267.0	149
Gross K, Mon	8-12	5.03	4.17	146.2	68	Stieb, Tor	18-6	2.93	4.36	208.2	101
Gullickson, Hou	10-14	3.82	3.68	193.1	79	Stottlemyre, Tor	13-17	4.34	5.81	203.0	131
Guthrie, Min	6-9	4.00	3.93	135.0	59	Swindell, Cle	12-9	4.40	4.40	214.2	105
Hanson, Sea	18-9	3.24	4.54	236.0	119	Tanana, Det	9-8	5.22	5.05	165.2	93
Harkey, ChN	12-6	3.26	4.61	173.2	89	Tapani, Min	12-8	4.07	4.80	159.1	85
Harnisch, Bal	11-11	4.34	5.77	188.2	121	Terrell, Det	8-11	5.19	4.85	156.0	84
Harris GA, Bos	12-9	4.07	5.02	179.1	100	Tewksbury, StL	10-9	3.23	4.47	131.0	65
Hawkins, NYA	5-12	5.44	3.02	149.0	50	Tudor, StL	11-4	2.54	4.81	138.1	74
Heaton, Pit	12-8	3.44	4.96	136.0	75	Valenzuela, LA	13-13	4.59	5.65	204.0	128
Hibbard, ChA	14-9	3.16	3.75	211.0	88	Viola, NYN	20-12	2.67	4.94	249.2	137
Higuera, Mil	11-10	3.76	4.66	170.0	88	Walk, Pit	7-5	3.82	4.74	127.1	67
Holman B, Sea	11-11	4.03	4.27	189.2	90	Welch, Oak	27-6	2.95	5.90	238.0	156
Hough, Tex	12-12	4.07	4.65	218.2	113	Wells, Tor	10-5	3.11	4.67	167.2	87
Hurst, SD	11-9	3.14	3.62	223.2	90	West, Min	7-9	5.10	5.22	143.0	83
Jackson Dan, Cin	6-6	3.67	4.53	115.1	58	Whitson, SD	14-9	2.60	4.41	228.2	112
Johnson D, Bal	13-9	4.10	4.85	180.0	97	Witt B, Tex	17-10	3.44	4.64	217.1	112
Johnson R, Sea	14-11	3.65	4.59	219.2	112	Young C, Oak	9-6	4.53	4.45	109.1	54
Key, Tor	13-7	4.25	5.53	154.2	95	Young Mt, Sea	8-18	3.49	3.77	224.1	94
Kiecker, Bos	8-9	3.68	4.66	137.0	71	**MLB Average**		**3.98**	**4.52**		
King E, ChA	12-4	3.28	4.41	151.0	74						
Knudson, Mil	9-9	4.20	4.20	160.2	75						
Langston, Cal	10-17	4.40	3.91	223.0	97						

WHAT'S LASORDA DOING WITH RAMON MARTINEZ? (p. 177)

Pitcher	GS	IP	Pit.	Pit/GS	Pitcher	GS	IP	Pit.	Pit/GS
Abbott, Cal	33	211.2	3260	99	King E, ChA	25	151.0	2194	88
Anderson A, Min	31	188.2	2750	89	Knudson, Mil	27	160.2	2420	90
Appier, KC	24	170.0	2519	105	Krueger, Mil	17	88.0	1311	77
Armstrong, Cin	27	163.1	2518	93	Langston, Cal	33	223.0	3743	113
Avery, Atl	20	97.0	1712	86	LaPoint, NYA	27	155.0	2299	85
Ballard, Bal	17	97.1	1456	86	Leary, NYA	31	208.0	3142	101
Belcher, LA	24	153.0	2376	99	Leibrandt, Atl	24	162.1	2471	103
Benes, SD	31	190.1	3034	98	Lilliquist, SD	18	102.0	1532	85
Bielecki, ChN	29	151.0	2592	89	Maddux G, ChN	35	237.0	3433	98
Black, Tor	31	204.2	3128	101	Magrane, StL	31	203.1	2992	97
Blyleven, Cal	23	134.0	1917	83	Mahler R, Cin	16	89.2	1348	84
Boddicker, Bos	34	228.0	3552	104	Martinez De, Mon	32	226.0	3189	100
Bolton, Bos	16	106.2	1632	102	Martinez R, LA	33	234.1	3802	115
Bosio, Mil	20	132.2	1953	98	McCaskill, Cal	29	174.1	2741	95
Boskie, ChN	15	97.2	1521	101	McDonald, Bal	15	109.0	1617	108
Boyd, Mon	31	190.2	2616	84	McDowell J, ChA	33	205.0	3362	102
Brown Kev, Tex	26	180.0	2572	99	Milacki, Bal	24	129.1	2058	86
Browning, Cin	35	227.2	3076	88	Mitchell J, Bal	17	99.1	1498	88
Burkett, SF	32	201.0	3099	97	Moore M, Oak	33	199.1	3128	95
Candiotti, Cle	29	195.2	3171	109	Morgan M, LA	33	211.0	3010	91
Cary, NYA	27	155.0	2542	94	Morris Jk, Det	36	249.2	3753	104
Cerutti, Tor	23	133.0	2075	90	Mulholland, Phi	26	171.1	2354	91
Charlton, Cin	16	103.2	1476	92	Navarro, Mil	22	126.1	1987	90
Clemens, Bos	31	228.1	3530	114	Perez M, ChA	35	197.0	3229	92
Combs, Phi	31	182.0	2941	95	Petry, Det	23	134.2	2091	91
Cone, NYN	30	210.2	3411	114	Portugal, Hou	32	196.2	3046	95
Cook D, LA	16	96.0	1431	89	Rasmussen D, SD	32	187.2	2913	91
Darling, NYN	18	96.2	1532	85	Rijo, Cin	29	197.0	3045	105
Darwin, Hou	17	117.2	1711	101	Robinson D, SF	25	156.2	2142	86
Davis Storm, KC	20	108.0	1722	86	Robinson JM, Det	27	145.0	2517	93
DeJesus J, Phi	22	130.0	2108	96	Robinson R, Mil	27	175.0	2802	104
DeLeon J, StL	32	182.2	2972	93	Ruffin, Phi	25	132.1	2063	83
Deshaies, Hou	34	209.1	3285	97	Ryan, Tex	30	204.0	3306	110
Drabek, Pit	33	231.1	3360	102	Saberhagen, KC	20	135.0	2066	103
Erickson S, Min	17	107.1	1593	94	Sanderson, Oak	34	206.1	3180	94
Farrell, Cle	17	96.2	1537	90	Scott M, Hou	32	205.2	2959	92
Fernandez S, NYN	30	179.1	2884	96	Smiley, Pit	25	148.1	2036	81
Finley C, Cal	32	236.0	3622	113	Smith B, StL	25	141.0	1991	80
Gardner M, Mon	26	151.1	2441	94	Smith Roy, Min	23	128.1	2154	94
Garrelts, SF	31	182.0	2753	89	Smith Z, Pit	31	213.1	2970	96
Glavine, Atl	33	214.1	3422	104	Smoltz, Atl	34	231.1	3611	106
Gooden, NYN	34	232.2	3690	109	Stewart D, Oak	36	267.0	3977	110
Gordon, KC	32	195.1	3215	100	Stieb, Tor	33	208.2	3181	96
Gross K, Mon	26	146.2	2386	92	Stottlemyre, Tor	33	203.0	3143	95
Gubicza, KC	16	94.0	1518	95	Swindell, Cle	34	214.2	3186	94
Gullickson, Hou	32	193.1	2802	88	Tanana, Det	29	165.2	2751	95
Guthrie, Min	21	135.0	2041	97	Tapani, Min	28	159.1	2277	81
Hanson, Sea	33	236.0	3739	113	Terrell, Det	28	156.0	2442	87
Harkey, ChN	27	173.2	2669	99	Tewksbury, StL	20	131.0	1623	81
Harnisch, Bal	31	188.2	3237	104	Tudor, StL	22	138.1	1797	82
Harris GA, Bos	30	179.1	2878	96	Valenzuela, LA	33	204.0	3440	104
Hawkins, NYA	26	149.0	2438	94	Viola, NYN	35	249.2	3684	105
Heaton, Pit	24	136.0	1892	79	Walk, Pit	24	127.1	1972	82
Hibbard, ChA	33	211.0	3054	93	Welch, Oak	35	238.0	3461	99
Higuera, Mil	27	170.0	2562	95	Wells, Tor	25	167.2	2485	99
Holman B, Sea	28	189.2	2917	104	West, Min	27	143.0	2340	87
Hough, Tex	32	218.2	3561	111	Whitson, SD	32	228.2	2942	92
Howell K, Phi	18	106.2	1640	91	Wilson S, ChN	15	79.1	1379	92
Hurst, SD	33	223.2	3109	94	Wilson Tr, SF	17	96.2	1453	85
Jackson Dan, Cin	21	115.1	1779	85	Witt B, Tex	32	217.1	3706	116
Johnson D, Bal	29	180.0	2582	89	Witt M, NYA	16	96.2	1468	92
Johnson R, Sea	33	219.2	3734	113	Young C, Oak	21	109.1	1764	84
Key, Tor	27	154.2	2364	88	Young Mt, Sea	33	224.1	3594	109
Kiecker, Bos	25	137.0	1953	78	MLB Average	4210			94

WHO WINS THE PITCHERS' "STAR WARS"? (p. 180)

Shown below are pitchers' performances against the top hitters in baseball.

Player, Team	AB	H	HR	RBI	Avg	Player, Team	AB	H	HR	RBI	Avg
Abbott, Cal	118	46	4	22	.390	McCaskill, Cal	92	29	3	18	.315
Appier, KC	83	26	3	8	.313	McDowell J, ChA	101	34	3	13	.337
Armstrong, Cin	61	17	1	10	.279	Moore M, Oak	78	25	2	11	.321
Avery, Atl	63	19	1	11	.302	Morgan M, LA	101	36	3	10	.356
Ballard, Bal	72	27	2	5	.375	Morris Jk, Det	102	31	2	10	.304
Belcher, LA	75	19	0	9	.253	Mulholland, Phi	93	37	5	15	.398
Benes, SD	93	30	1	12	.323	Navarro, Mil	67	20	1	8	.299
Bielecki, ChN	60	20	1	9	.333	Perez M, ChA	94	24	1	8	.255
Black, Tor	76	21	3	7	.276	Petry, Det	64	20	4	8	.313
Blyleven, Cal	70	23	1	10	.329	Portugal, Hou	135	46	4	19	.341
Boddicker, Bos	88	29	4	10	.330	Rasmussen D, SD	93	30	3	10	.323
Boyd, Mon	108	33	4	9	.306	Rijo, Cin	101	31	3	10	.307
Brown Kev, Tex	73	17	2	9	.233	Robinson D, SF	89	34	3	11	.382
Browning, Cin	116	24	2	5	.207	Robinson JM, Det	70	24	3	12	.343
Burkett, SF	111	35	5	15	.315	Robinson R, Mil	91	30	1	9	.330
Candiotti, Cle	82	33	4	14	.402	Ruffin, Phi	87	31	2	16	.356
Cary, NYA	77	25	3	9	.325	Ryan, Tex	69	18	2	10	.261
Charlton, Cin	85	20	2	12	.235	Sanderson, Oak	94	28	7	16	.298
Clemens, Bos	85	29	2	5	.341	Scott M, Hou	121	37	4	16	.306
Combs, Phi	71	20	2	10	.282	Smiley, Pit	74	22	1	11	.297
Cone, NYN	104	35	6	16	.337	Smith B, StL	81	27	0	9	.333
Cook D, LA	63	12	0	6	.190	Smith Z, Pit	89	23	2	8	.258
Darwin, Hou	74	25	0	9	.338	Smoltz, Atl	110	32	3	8	.291
DeLeon J, StL	99	37	5	15	.374	Stewart D, Oak	127	40	1	9	.315
Deshaies, Hou	115	35	2	15	.304	Stieb, Tor	81	24	1	12	.296
Drabek, Pit	110	36	1	11	.327	Stottlemyre, Tor	95	36	2	13	.379
Fernandez S, NYN	94	23	4	16	.245	Swindell, Cle	92	30	4	11	.326
Finley C, Cal	112	24	1	5	.214	Tanana, Det	80	21	2	9	.262
Gardner M, Mon	86	24	2	11	.279	Terrell, Det	103	32	7	18	.311
Garrelts, SF	98	34	2	14	.347	Tewksbury, StL	64	19	2	11	.297
Glavine, Atl	104	32	2	11	.308	Tudor, StL	70	18	0	8	.257
Gooden, NYN	124	43	0	17	.347	Valdez, Cle	61	18	3	8	.295
Gordon, KC	82	27	0	6	.329	Valenzuela, LA	110	33	2	10	.300
Gross K, Mon	85	34	4	19	.400	Viola, NYN	117	40	3	11	.342
Gullickson, Hou	109	41	3	17	.376	Walk, Pit	67	23	4	8	.343
Guthrie, Min	67	28	0	4	.418	Welch, Oak	97	28	2	7	.289
Hanson, Sea	82	30	2	13	.366	Wells, Tor	83	20	0	6	.241
Harkey, ChN	75	21	1	7	.280	Whitson, SD	98	33	1	12	.337
Harnisch, Bal	88	29	2	11	.330	Wilson S, ChN	68	17	1	11	.250
Harris GA, Bos	66	26	2	7	.394	Witt B, Tex	75	18	2	8	.240
Hawkins, NYA	68	30	4	11	.441	Young C, Oak	62	20	3	17	.323
Hibbard, ChA	77	17	0	9	.221	Young Mt, Sea	75	14	2	7	.187
Higuera, Mil	76	19	2	13	.250						
Hough, Tex	72	15	1	4	.208	**AL Avg**	**8388**	**2543**	**230**	**1123**	**.303**
Hurst, SD	82	25	4	9	.305	**NL Avg**	**8208**	**2557**	**244**	**1132**	**.312**
Jackson Dan, Cin	62	17	2	10	.274						
Johnson D, Bal	91	31	6	11	.341						
Johnson R, Sea	91	18	1	9	.198						
Key, Tor	80	16	2	10	.200						
Kiecker, Bos	68	27	0	9	.397						
King E, ChA	64	13	0	4	.203						
Knudson, Mil	65	25	3	15	.385						
LaPoint, NYA	66	17	3	7	.258						
Langston, Cal	90	29	3	12	.322						
Leary, NYA	108	24	1	8	.222						
Leibrandt, Atl	60	16	2	6	.267						
Maddux G, ChN	91	34	3	17	.374						
Magrane, StL	87	25	2	9	.287						
Mahler R, Cin	75	20	2	8	.267						
Martinez De, Mon	135	29	3	11	.215						
Martinez R, LA	101	23	2	10	.228						

WHOSE HEATER IS THE HOTTEST? (p. 182)

Both Leagues — Alphabetical (25 Starts/50 Relief Games)

Pitcher,Team	K	IP	K/9
Abbott, Cal	105	211.2	4.5
Acker, Tor	54	91.2	5.3
Agosto, Hou	50	92.1	4.9
Aguilera, Min	61	65.1	8.4
Akerfelds, Phi	42	93.0	4.1
Andersen L, Bos	93	95.2	8.7
Anderson A, Min	82	188.2	3.9
Armstrong, Cin	110	166.0	6.0
Arnsberg, Tex	44	62.2	6.3
Assenmacher, ChN	95	103.0	8.3
Bedrosian, SF	43	79.1	4.9
Belinda, Pit	55	58.1	8.5
Benes, SD	140	192.1	6.6
Berenguer, Min	77	100.1	6.9
Bielecki, ChN	103	168.0	5.5
Black, Tor	106	206.2	4.6
Boddicker, Bos	143	228.0	5.6
Boever, Phi	75	88.1	7.6
Boyd, Mon	113	190.2	5.3
Brantley J, SF	61	86.2	6.3
Brown Kev, Tex	88	180.0	4.4
Browning, Cin	99	227.2	3.9
Burke, Mon	47	75.0	5.6
Burkett, SF	118	204.0	5.2
Candiotti, Cle	128	202.0	5.7
Carman, Phi	58	86.2	6.0
Cary, NYA	134	156.2	7.7
Clemens, Bos	209	228.1	8.2
Combs, Phi	108	183.1	5.3
Comstock, Sea	50	56.0	8.0
Cone, NYN	233	211.2	9.9
Crews, LA	76	107.1	6.4
Crim, Mil	39	85.2	4.1
Davis Mrk, KC	73	68.2	9.6
Dayley, StL	51	73.1	6.3
DeLeon J, StL	164	182.2	8.1
Deshaies, Hou	119	209.1	5.1
Dibble, Cin	136	98.0	12.5
DiPino, StL	49	81.0	5.4
Drabek, Pit	131	231.1	5.1
Eckersley, Oak	73	73.1	9.0
Eichhorn, Cal	69	84.2	7.3
Farr, KC	94	127.0	6.7
Fernandez S, NYN	181	179.1	9.1
Finley C, Cal	177	236.0	6.8
Franco Jn, NYN	56	67.2	7.4
Frey, Mon	29	55.2	4.7
Gardner M, Mon	135	152.2	8.0
Garrelts, SF	80	182.0	4.0
Gibson P, Det	56	97.1	5.2
Glavine, Atl	129	214.1	5.4
Gleaton, Det	56	82.2	6.1
Gooden, NYN	223	232.2	8.6
Gordon, KC	175	195.1	8.1
Gott, LA	44	62.0	6.4
Grant, Atl	69	91.1	6.8
Gross K, Mon	111	163.1	6.1
Guetterman, NYA	48	93.0	4.6
Gullickson, Hou	73	193.1	3.4
Hanson, Sea	211	236.0	8.0
Harkey, ChN	94	173.2	4.9
Harnisch, Bal	122	188.2	5.8
Harris GA, Bos	117	184.1	5.7
Harris GW, SD	97	117.1	7.4
Harvey, Cal	82	64.1	11.5
Hawkins, NYA	74	157.2	4.2
Henke, Tor	75	74.2	9.0
Henneman, Det	50	94.1	4.8
Hibbard, ChA	92	211.0	3.9
Higuera, Mil	129	170.0	6.8
Holman B, Sea	121	189.2	5.7
Honeycutt, Oak	38	63.1	5.4
Hough, Tex	114	218.2	4.7
Hurst, SD	162	223.2	6.5
Jackson M, Sea	69	77.1	8.0
Johnson D, Bal	68	180.0	3.4
Johnson R, Sea	194	219.2	7.9
Jones Ba, ChA	45	74.0	5.5
Jones D, Cle	55	84.1	5.9
Key, Tor	88	154.2	5.1
Kiecker, Bos	93	152.0	5.5
King E, ChA	70	151.0	4.2
Knudson, Mil	56	168.1	3.0
Landrum B, Pit	39	71.2	4.9
Langston, Cal	195	223.0	7.9
LaPoint, NYA	67	157.2	3.8
Layana, Cin	53	80.0	6.0
Leach T, Min	46	81.2	5.1
Lefferts, SD	60	78.2	6.9
Maddux G, ChN	144	237.0	5.5
Magrane, StL	100	203.1	4.4
Martinez De, Mon	156	226.0	6.2
Martinez R, LA	223	234.1	8.6
McCaskill, Cal	78	174.1	4.0
McDowell J, ChA	165	205.0	7.2
McDowell R, Phi	39	86.1	4.1
Montgomery, KC	94	94.1	9.0
Moore M, Oak	73	199.1	3.3
Morgan M, LA	106	211.0	4.5
Morris Jk, Det	162	249.2	5.8
Mulholland, Phi	75	180.2	3.7
Murphy R, Bos	54	57.0	8.5
Myers R, Cin	98	86.2	10.2
Nelson G, Oak	38	74.2	4.6
Niedenfuer, StL	32	65.0	4.4
Olson Gregg, Bal	74	74.1	9.0
Orosco, Cle	55	64.2	7.7
Pall, ChA	39	76.0	4.6
Parrett, Atl	86	108.2	7.1
Patterson B, Pit	70	94.2	6.7
Pena A, NYN	76	76.0	9.0
Perez M, ChA	161	197.0	7.4
Plesac, Mil	65	69.0	8.5
Portugal, Hou	136	196.2	6.2
Price, Bal	54	65.1	7.4
Radinsky, ChA	46	52.1	7.9
Rasmussen D, SD	86	187.2	4.1
Righetti, NYA	43	53.0	7.3
Rijo, Cin	152	197.0	6.9
Robinson D, SF	78	157.2	4.5
Robinson JD, NYA	43	88.2	4.4
Robinson JM, Det	76	145.0	4.7
Robinson R, Mil	71	179.2	3.6
Rogers, Tex	74	97.2	6.8
Ruffin, Phi	79	149.0	4.8
Ruskin, Mon	57	75.1	6.8
Ryan, Tex	232	204.0	10.2
Sampen, Mon	69	90.1	6.9
Sanderson, Oak	128	206.1	5.6
Scott M, Hou	121	205.2	5.3
Smiley, Pit	86	149.1	5.2
Smith B, StL	78	141.1	5.0
Smith Le, StL	87	83.0	9.4
Smith Z, Pit	130	215.1	5.4
Smoltz, Atl	170	231.1	6.6
Stewart D, Oak	166	267.0	5.6
Stieb, Tor	125	208.2	5.4
Stottlemyre, Tor	115	203.0	5.1
Swindell, Cle	135	214.2	5.7
Tanana, Det	114	176.1	5.8
Tapani, Min	101	159.1	5.7
Terrell, Det	64	158.0	3.6
Thigpen, ChA	70	88.2	7.1
Valenzuela, LA	115	204.0	5.1
Viola, NYN	182	249.2	6.6
Ward D, Tor	112	127.2	7.9
Welch, Oak	127	238.0	4.8
Wells, Tor	115	189.0	5.5
West, Min	92	146.1	5.7
Whitson, SD	127	228.2	5.0
Williams Mitch, ChN	55	66.1	7.5
Witt B, Tex	221	222.0	9.0
Young Mt, Sea	176	225.1	7.0
MLB Avg			**5.7**

WHAT IS THE "RED BARRETT TROPHY"? (p. 184)

Most Pitches In a Game By Starting Pitchers in 1990

Pitcher	Opp	Date	Score	W/L	IP	H	R	ER	BB	SO	#Pit
Clemens, Bos	Det	8/04	3- 1	W	8.2	9	1	1	2	8	165
Harkey, ChN	StL	6/24	3- 2	L	9.0	6	2	1	5	6	155
McDowell J, ChA	Bos	9/14	4- 0	W	7.0	4	0	0	4	10	154
Martinez R, LA	ChN	4/28	5- 4	W	9.0	7	4	3	1	10	152
Smoltz, Atl	ChN	8/26	4- 3	W	9.0	6	3	1	2	8	152
Valenzuela, LA	@Cin	9/14	10- 4	W	9.0	9	4	4	4	4	151
Black, Tor	@Det	6/12	7- 3	W	9.0	8	3	3	3	4	151
Johnson R, Sea	@ChA	9/28	13- 4	W	9.0	10	4	3	2	11	151
Johnson R, Sea	Oak	9/11	2- 10	L	7.2	9	6	3	4	11	150
Finley C, Cal	KC	9/28	1- 2	L	8.0	6	2	0	5	9	150
Farrell, Cle	@Bos	6/08	3- 4	L	8.0	6	4	4	4	6	149
Martinez R, LA	SD	6/16	5- 2	W	9.0	4	2	1	4	8	149
Magrane, StL	@ChN	6/22	7- 0	W	9.0	3	0	0	3	11	149
Martinez R, LA	Cin	9/09	6- 4	W	9.0	8	4	4	3	8	148
Drabek, Pit	Phi	7/29	2- 1	W	9.0	2	1	1	7	8	147
Witt B, Tex	Oak	6/07	3- 1	W	8.0	6	1	1	3	11	147
Ryan, Tex	@Mil	7/31	11- 3	W	7.2	6	3	1	2	8	147
Witt B, Tex	NYA	7/24	4- 1	W	9.0	7	1	1	3	10	146
Finley C, Cal	@Oak	7/26	4- 2	L	9.0	8	2	1	4	9	146
Finley C, Cal	@Bal	9/08	4- 5	L	8.0	9	4	4	4	10	146
Harkey, ChN	StL	8/08	4- 3	L	9.0	8	0	0	7	3	146

Fewest Pitches In a Complete Game By Starting Pitchers in 1990

Pitcher	Opp	Date	Score	W/L	IP	H	R	ER	BB	SO	#Pit
Lancaster, ChN	Atl	5/09	4- 0	W	5.0	4	0	0	0	2	58
Candiotti, Cle	@Det	9/06	6- 0	W	5.0	7	0	0	0	1	62
Smith P, Atl	@ChN	5/09	0- 4	L	4.0	6	4	4	0	2	69
Tewksbury, StL	@Cin	8/29	9- 1	W	9.0	6	1	1	0	0	76
Drabek, Pit	@Atl	8/29	10- 0	W	6.0	2	0	0	0	5	79
Brown Kev, Tex	Min	6/20	8- 0	W	9.0	4	0	0	0	4	79
Whitson, SD	@ChN	5/06	8- 3	W	9.0	8	3	3	0	1	80
Ruffin, Phi	@Pit	6/26	0- 1	L	8.0	6	1	1	0	2	80
Tewksbury, StL	Hou	8/17	5- 0	W	9.0	1	0	0	0	3	80
Drabek, Pit	@StL	9/30	2- 0	W	9.0	3	0	0	0	2	80
Drabek, Pit	ChN	6/06	6- 1	W	7.0	5	1	1	0	2	81
Whitson, SD	SF	4/20	9- 2	W	9.0	9	2	2	0	3	85
Scott M, Hou	NYN	7/18	1- 0	W	9.0	4	0	0	0	4	85
Swindell, Cle	@Min	5/10	2- 3	L	8.0	7	3	3	2	3	86
McDonald, Bal	ChA	7/21	2- 0	W	9.0	4	0	0	1	5	86
Morris Jk, Det	@Oak	6/26	2- 3	L	8.0	4	3	2	2	8	87
Smiley, Pit	@SF	4/26	2- 1	W	9.0	3	1	1	0	6	88
Smiley, Pit	@NYN	9/12	1- 2	L	8.0	5	2	2	1	2	89
Petry, Det	@KC	5/30	3- 4	L	8.0	7	4	4	2	0	89
LaPoint, NYA	@Min	7/20	1- 2	L	8.1	8	2	2	1	1	89
Brown Kev, Tex	@Min	6/26	4- 5	L	8.0	6	5	3	1	4	90
McDowell J, ChA	@Mil	8/05	6- 1	W	9.0	5	1	1	1	0	90
Robinson D, SF	Mon	8/20	4- 2	W	9.0	4	2	1	1	7	90
Smith Z, Pit	NYN	9/05	1- 0	W	9.0	1	0	0	1	7	91
Gordon, KC	Mil	8/12	7- 1	W	9.0	5	1	1	1	4	92
Brown Kev, Tex	@Cal	6/10	2- 1	W	9.0	5	1	1	1	2	93
Tewksbury, StL	@Pit	8/12	6- 0	W	9.0	6	0	0	0	4	93
Hurst, SD	@LA	4/09	2- 4	L	8.0	4	4	4	2	1	94
Smoltz, Atl	LA	6/27	4- 0	W	9.0	3	0	0	0	6	94
Abbott, Cal	Tor	7/13	2- 0	W	9.0	4	0	0	0	3	94
McCaskill, Cal	Tex	8/28	2- 0	W	9.0	4	0	0	1	4	94
Milacki, Bal	@Min	6/30	6- 0	W	9.0	3	0	0	2	4	95
Knudson, Mil	KC	8/19	7- 2	W	9.0	3	2	2	1	5	95
Leibrandt, Atl	Cin	6/19	3- 0	W	9.0	6	0	0	0	1	95
Morgan M, LA	@StL	5/26	8- 0	W	9.0	5	0	0	1	3	96
Ruffin, Phi	ChN	6/15	7- 0	W	9.0	3	0	0	3	2	96
Hurst, SD	@Cin	9/28	2- 1	W	9.0	4	1	1	1	4	96
Aquino, KC	Bos	7/20	1- 3	L	9.0	5	3	3	2	2	96
Perez M, ChA	@NYA	7/12	8- 0	W	6.0	0	0	0	4	9	96

WHO'S TOUGHEST TO HIT? (p. 186)

Both Leagues — Listed Alphabetically (125+Innings Pitched)

Pitcher, Team	AB	H	Opponent Batting AVG	Pitcher, Team	AB	H	Opponent Batting AVG
Abbott, Cal	833	246	.295	LaPoint, NYA	617	180	.292
Anderson A, Min	741	214	.289	Leary, NYA	785	202	.257
Appier, KC	710	179	.252	Leibrandt, Atl	628	164	.261
Armstrong, Cin	626	151	.241	Maddux G, ChN	913	242	.265
Ballard, Bal	526	152	.289	Magrane, StL	774	204	.264
Belcher, LA	566	136	.240	Mahler R, Cin	514	134	.261
Benes, SD	730	177	.242	Martinez De, Mon	839	191	.228
Bielecki, ChN	654	188	.287	Martinez R, LA	867	191	.220
Black, Tor	778	181	.233	McCaskill, Cal	660	161	.244
Blyleven, Cal	538	163	.303	McDowell J, ChA	776	189	.244
Boddicker, Bos	873	225	.258	Milacki, Bal	523	143	.273
Bosio, Mil	508	131	.258	Moore M, Oak	764	204	.267
Boyd, Mon	703	164	.233	Morgan M, LA	811	216	.266
Brown Kev, Tex	685	175	.255	Morris Jk, Det	953	231	.242
Browning, Cin	882	235	.266	Mulholland, Phi	683	172	.252
Burkett, SF	781	201	.257	Navarro, Mil	600	176	.293
Candiotti, Cle	788	207	.263	Perez M, ChA	735	177	.241
Cary, NYA	597	155	.260	Petry, Det	563	148	.263
Cerutti, Tor	546	162	.297	Portugal, Hou	747	187	.250
Charlton, Cin	567	131	.231	Rasmussen D, SD	742	217	.292
Clemens, Bos	847	193	.228	Rijo, Cin	712	151	.212
Combs, Phi	696	179	.257	Robinson D, SF	618	173	.280
Cone, NYN	784	177	.226	Robinson JM, Det	552	141	.255
Cook D, LA	591	155	.262	Robinson R, Mil	696	194	.279
Darling, NYN	495	135	.273	Ruffin, Phi	599	178	.297
Darwin, Hou	605	136	.225	Ryan, Tex	729	137	.188
DeJesus J, Phi	461	97	.210	Saberhagen, KC	524	146	.279
DeLeon J, StL	683	168	.246	Sanderson, Oak	803	205	.255
Deshaies, Hou	760	186	.245	Scott M, Hou	789	194	.246
Drabek, Pit	846	190	.225	Smiley, Pit	585	161	.275
Farr, KC	451	99	.220	Smith B, StL	559	160	.286
Fernandez S, NYN	650	130	.200	Smith Roy, Min	611	191	.313
Finley C, Cal	864	210	.243	Smith Z, Pit	801	196	.245
Gardner M, Mon	561	129	.230	Smoltz, Atl	858	206	.240
Garrelts, SF	698	190	.272	Stewart D, Oak	980	226	.231
Glavine, Atl	827	232	.281	Stieb, Tor	778	179	.230
Gooden, NYN	889	229	.258	Stottlemyre, Tor	781	214	.274
Gordon, KC	746	192	.257	Swift, Sea	496	135	.272
Gross K, Mon	628	171	.272	Swindell, Cle	850	245	.288
Gullickson, Hou	769	221	.287	Tanana, Det	678	190	.280
Guthrie, Min	557	154	.276	Tapani, Min	621	164	.264
Hanson, Sea	883	205	.232	Terrell, Det	629	184	.293
Harkey, ChN	653	153	.234	Tewksbury, StL	565	151	.267
Harnisch, Bal	723	189	.261	Tudor, StL	534	120	.225
Harris GA, Bos	703	186	.265	Valenzuela, LA	808	223	.276
Hawkins, NYA	599	156	.260	Viola, NYN	938	227	.242
Heaton, Pit	543	143	.263	Walk, Pit	503	136	.270
Hibbard, ChA	792	202	.255	Ward D, Tor	457	101	.221
Higuera, Mil	653	167	.256	Welch, Oak	886	214	.242
Holman B, Sea	724	188	.260	Wells, Tor	701	165	.235
Hough, Tex	807	190	.235	West, Min	554	142	.256
Hurst, SD	823	188	.228	Whitson, SD	855	215	.251
Johnson D, Bal	700	196	.280	Wilson S, ChN	540	140	.259
Johnson R, Sea	806	174	.216	Witt B, Tex	829	197	.238
Key, Tor	602	169	.281	Young Mt, Sea	836	198	.237
Kiecker, Bos	572	145	.253				
King E, ChA	570	135	.237	AL Avg			.259
Knudson, Mil	664	187	.282	NL Avg			.256
Krueger, Mil	496	137	.276				
Langston, Cal	829	215	.259				

WHO'S EASIEST TO STEAL ON? (p. 188)

Both Leagues — Alphabetical (140 Innings Pitched)

Pitcher, Team	SB	CS	SB%	SB/9	PkO	Pitcher, Team	SB	CS	SB%	SB/9	PkO
Abbott, Cal	15	4	78.9	0.64	0	Langston, Cal	22	14	61.1	0.89	5
Anderson A, Min	10	11	47.6	0.48	0	LaPoint, NYA	10	9	52.6	0.57	0
Appier, KC	13	1	92.9	0.63	0	Leary, NYA	18	8	69.2	0.78	5
Armstrong, Cin	14	6	70.0	0.76	0	Leibrandt, Atl	21	3	87.5	1.16	1
Ballard, Bal	8	6	57.1	0.54	0	Maddux G, ChN	13	4	76.5	0.49	3
Belcher, LA	11	7	61.1	0.65	2	Magrane, StL	21	16	56.8	0.93	0
Benes, SD	23	5	82.1	1.08	0	Mahler R, Cin	9	4	69.2	0.60	1
Bielecki, ChN	17	9	65.4	0.91	2	Martinez De, Mon	19	9	67.9	0.76	0
Black, Tor	12	8	60.0	0.52	0	Martinez R, LA	22	13	62.9	0.84	2
Blyleven, Cal	4	9	30.8	0.27	1	McCaskill, Cal	6	10	37.5	0.31	4
Boddicker, Bos	13	10	56.5	0.51	1	McDowell J, ChA	23	11	67.6	1.01	2
Bosio, Mil	7	4	63.6	0.47	1	Milacki, Bal	19	3	86.4	1.26	0
Boyd, Mon	25	6	80.6	1.18	0	Moore M, Oak	17	6	73.9	0.77	0
Brown Kev, Tex	7	4	63.6	0.35	1	Morgan M, LA	16	13	55.2	0.68	0
Browning, Cin	12	10	54.5	0.47	1	Morris Jk, Det	45	6	88.2	1.62	0
Burkett, SF	18	7	72.0	0.79	1	Mulholland, Phi	3	3	50.0	0.15	2
Candiotti, Cle	18	7	72.0	0.80	0	Navarro, Mil	11	4	73.3	0.66	0
Cary, NYA	14	10	58.3	0.80	0	Perez M, ChA	12	11	52.2	0.55	1
Cerutti, Tor	6	3	66.7	0.39	2	Petry, Det	13	6	68.4	0.78	0
Charlton, Cin	17	4	81.0	0.99	1	Portugal, Hou	23	9	71.9	1.05	1
Clemens, Bos	14	14	50.0	0.55	1	Rasmussen D, SD	21	16	56.8	1.01	0
Combs, Phi	11	10	52.4	0.54	1	Rijo, Cin	19	4	82.6	0.87	6
Cone, NYN	23	9	71.9	0.98	3	Robinson D, SF	19	8	70.4	1.08	2
Cook D, LA	16	4	80.0	0.92	2	Robinson JM, Det	10	9	52.6	0.62	1
Darling, NYN	24	4	85.7	1.71	5	Robinson R, Mil	15	11	57.7	0.75	1
Darwin, Hou	17	6	73.9	0.94	1	Ruffin, Phi	3	4	42.9	0.18	0
DeJesus J, Phi	10	6	62.5	0.69	1	Ryan, Tex	25	9	73.5	1.10	0
DeLeon J, StL	20	12	62.5	0.99	0	Saberhagen, KC	2	5	28.6	0.13	2
Deshaies, Hou	21	9	70.0	0.90	2	Sanderson, Oak	13	5	72.2	0.57	0
Drabek, Pit	18	9	66.7	0.70	3	Scott M, Hou	53	7	88.3	2.32	0
Farr, KC	8	3	72.7	0.57	1	Smiley, Pit	13	6	68.4	0.78	0
Fernandez S, NYN	20	6	76.9	1.00	0	Smith B, StL	21	4	84.0	1.34	0
Finley C, Cal	15	18	45.5	0.57	0	Smith Roy, Min	15	13	53.6	0.88	0
Gardner M, Mon	16	6	72.7	0.94	0	Smith Z, Pit	27	4	87.1	1.13	0
Garrelts, SF	18	5	78.3	0.89	1	Smoltz, Atl	31	10	75.6	1.21	2
Glavine, Atl	22	9	71.0	0.92	0	Stewart D, Oak	13	6	68.4	0.44	0
Gooden, NYN	60	16	78.9	2.32	1	Stieb, Tor	6	8	42.9	0.26	1
Gordon, KC	8	10	44.4	0.37	1	Stottlemyre, Tor	23	13	63.9	1.02	1
Gross K, Mon	31	5	86.1	1.71	0	Swift, Sea	0	2	0.0	0.00	0
Gullickson, Hou	23	9	71.9	1.07	0	Swindell, Cle	3	12	20.0	0.13	0
Guthrie, Min	17	12	58.6	1.06	2	Tanana, Det	9	15	37.5	0.46	0
Hanson, Sea	18	8	69.2	0.69	1	Tapani, Min	9	9	50.0	0.51	0
Harkey, ChN	8	6	57.1	0.41	0	Terrell, Det	10	6	62.5	0.57	0
Harnisch, Bal	18	10	64.3	0.86	1	Tewksbury, StL	8	5	61.5	0.50	0
Harris GA, Bos	15	7	68.2	0.73	3	Tudor, StL	8	9	47.1	0.49	1
Hawkins, NYA	11	8	57.9	0.63	1	Valenzuela, LA	19	7	73.1	0.84	1
Heaton, Pit	15	13	53.6	0.92	0	Viola, NYN	25	15	62.5	0.90	1
Hibbard, ChA	11	8	57.9	0.47	0	Walk, Pit	13	9	59.1	0.90	1
Higuera, Mil	15	4	78.9	0.79	0	Ward D, Tor	12	6	66.7	0.85	0
Holman B, Sea	8	8	50.0	0.38	1	Welch, Oak	10	7	58.8	0.38	0
Hough, Tex	33	6	84.6	1.36	3	Wells, Tor	11	11	50.0	0.52	1
Hurst, SD	19	7	73.1	0.76	1	West, Min	5	5	50.0	0.31	0
Johnson D, Bal	1	4	20.0	0.05	0	Whitson, SD	12	7	63.2	0.47	0
Johnson R, Sea	28	8	77.8	1.15	1	Wilson S, ChN	6	8	42.9	0.39	0
Key, Tor	6	4	60.0	0.35	0	Witt B, Tex	36	7	83.7	1.46	1
Kiecker, Bos	15	6	71.4	0.89	1	Young Mt, Sea	20	14	58.8	0.80	0
King E, ChA	8	5	61.5	0.48	0						
Knudson, Mil	8	9	47.1	0.43	0	**MLB**	**3290**	**1510**	**68.5**	**0.79**	**167**
Krueger, Mil	9	6	60.0	0.63	0						

WHO ARE THE MOST EFFICIENT RELIEF PITCHERS? (p. 192)

Both Leagues — Listed Alphabetically (30+ First Batters Faced)

Pitcher, Team	AVG	AB	H	HR	BB	K	Pitcher, Team	AVG	AB	H	HR	BB	K
Acker, Tor	.382	55	21	2	4	5	Layana, Cin	.356	45	16	2	8	11
Agosto, Hou	.208	72	15	0	9	10	Leach T, Min	.125	48	6	0	3	5
Aguilera, Min	.260	50	13	0	4	11	Lefferts, SD	.196	51	10	0	5	13
Akerfelds, Phi	.133	60	8	0	7	8	Long B, ChN	.300	40	12	1	6	6
Andersen L, Bos	.210	62	13	0	1	19	Luecken, Tor	.250	32	8	1	5	6
Arnsberg, Tex	.265	49	13	0	3	8	Machado, Mil	.303	33	10	3	4	6
Assenmacher,ChN	.194	62	12	4	4	17	McDowell R, Phi	.262	61	16	0	5	7
Bedrosian, SF	.230	61	14	2	7	6	Mercker, Atl	.233	30	7	1	6	9
Belinda, Pit	.146	48	7	1	6	16	Mills A, NYA	.323	31	10	2	4	2
Berenguer, Min	.186	43	8	1	6	13	Mirabella, Mil	.324	37	12	2	5	6
Boever, Phi	.220	59	13	0	8	9	Montgomery, KC	.185	65	12	1	3	17
Brantley J, SF	.234	47	11	0	6	8	Murphy R, Bos	.371	62	23	3	4	15
Burke, Mon	.296	54	16	0	2	8	Myers R, Cin	.197	61	12	2	3	23
Burns, Oak	.400	35	14	2	5	8	Nelson G, Oak	.205	44	9	1	4	8
Cadaret, NYA	.256	39	10	0	7	7	Niedenfuer, StL	.304	46	14	0	6	6
Candelaria, Tor	.231	39	9	1	3	8	Nunez E, Det	.200	35	7	1	6	7
Carman, Phi	.149	47	7	1	8	9	Olin, Cle	.239	46	11	0	3	7
Castillo T, Atl	.233	43	10	1	4	10	Olson Gregg, Bal	.241	58	14	1	5	11
Charlton, Cin	.250	36	9	0	3	8	Orosco, Cle	.200	45	9	1	7	12
Comstock, Sea	.216	51	11	1	7	12	Pall, ChA	.224	49	11	1	4	6
Crawford, KC	.286	42	12	1	3	5	Parrett, Atl	.235	51	12	0	8	13
Crews, LA	.203	59	12	1	3	13	Patterson B, Pit	.214	42	9	0	5	13
Crim, Mil	.302	63	19	1	4	11	Patterson K, ChA	.290	31	9	1	9	7
Davis Mrk, KC	.186	43	8	1	6	21	Pena A, NYN	.250	48	12	1	3	10
Dayley, StL	.224	49	11	0	8	9	Plesac, Mil	.228	57	13	1	7	15
Dibble, Cin	.190	63	12	2	3	26	Plunk, NYA	.289	38	11	2	6	12
DiPino, StL	.352	54	19	2	5	11	Power, Pit	.256	39	10	1	1	12
Eckersley, Oak	.206	63	13	0	0	19	Price, Bal	.239	46	11	0	2	9
Edwards, ChA	.231	26	6	1	8	6	Radinsky, ChA	.255	51	13	0	10	13
Eichhorn, Cal	.293	58	17	0	1	13	Reardon, Bos	.209	43	9	1	4	10
Farr, KC	.159	44	7	1	5	10	Righetti, NYA	.191	47	9	3	6	8
Franco Jn, NYN	.216	51	11	0	4	9	Robinson JD,NYA	.262	42	11	0	5	9
Fraser, Cal	.154	39	6	1	5	4	Rogers, Tex	.291	55	16	1	8	12
Frey, Mon	.250	44	11	1	6	7	Ruskin, Mon	.211	57	12	1	9	12
Gibson P, Det	.283	53	15	0	4	8	Sampen, Mon	.346	52	18	2	3	11
Gleaton, Det	.204	49	10	1	6	5	Schatzeder, NYN	.333	42	14	1	5	7
Gott, LA	.255	47	12	0	2	8	Schilling, Bal	.233	30	7	1	3	6
Grant, Atl	.283	53	15	2	4	8	Schooler, Sea	.130	46	6	0	2	9
Gray, Bos	.231	39	9	0	2	9	Smith Dv, Hou	.277	47	13	2	2	7
Guetterman, NYA	.232	56	13	1	5	10	Smith Le, StL	.300	60	18	1	4	17
Hall D, Mon	.289	38	11	0	4	5	Swift, Sea	.220	41	9	0	2	3
Harris GW, SD	.286	63	18	2	6	11	Terry, StL	.349	43	15	1	3	4
Harvey, Cal	.209	43	9	0	11	16	Thigpen, ChA	.127	63	8	2	9	12
Henke, Tor	.228	57	13	2	2	15	Thurmond, SF	.257	35	9	1	2	8
Henneman, Det	.242	62	15	1	5	7	Ward D, Tor	.129	70	9	1	3	22
Hesketh, Bos	.250	40	10	1	2	8	Wayne, Min	.125	32	4	1	3	7
Hickey, Bal	.242	33	8	1	4	7	Whitehurst, NYN	.243	37	9	1	1	6
Honeycutt, Oak	.169	59	10	0	1	11	Williams M, ChN	.234	47	11	0	9	10
Howell Jay, LA	.359	39	14	3	4	6	Williamson, Bal	.175	40	7	0	6	8
Jackson M, Sea	.308	52	16	2	7	16	Wills, Tor	.278	36	10	0	4	11
Jones Ba, ChA	.276	58	16	0	4	11							
Jones D, Cle	.207	58	12	2	7	7	MLB	.250					
Kipper, Pit	.162	37	6	1	1	6							
Klink, Oak	.250	36	9	0	3	3							
Lamp, Bos	.350	40	14	0	2	3							
Lancaster, ChN	.304	46	14	3	2	6							
Landrum B, Pit	.423	52	22	2	1	5							

WHO (STILL) THROWS TO FIRST? (p. 194)

Both Leagues — Listed Alphabetically (Minimum 125 IP)

Pitcher	Pickoff Throws			Stolen Bases		Pitcher	Pickoff Throws			Stolen Bases	
	Total	Per 9	PO	SB	Per 9		Total	Per 9	PO	SB	Per 9
Abbott, Cal	105	4.5	0	15	0.6	Langston, Cal	183	7.4	5	22	0.9
Anderson A, Min	125	6.0	0	10	0.5	LaPoint, NYA	107	6.1	0	10	0.6
Appier, KC	94	4.6	0	13	0.6	Leary, NYA	173	7.5	5	18	0.8
Armstrong, Cin	196	10.6	0	14	0.8	Leibrandt, Atl	111	6.2	1	21	1.2
Ballard, Bal	111	7.5	0	8	0.5	Maddux G, ChN	91	3.5	3	13	0.5
Belcher, LA	91	5.4	2	11	0.6	Magrane, StL	107	4.7	0	21	0.9
Benes, SD	94	4.4	0	23	1.1	Mahler R, Cin	85	5.7	1	9	0.6
Bielecki, ChN	148	7.9	2	17	0.9	Martinez De, Mon	127	5.1	0	19	0.8
Black, Tor	166	7.2	0	12	0.5	Martinez R, LA	147	5.6	2	22	0.8
Blyleven, Cal	31	2.1	1	4	0.3	McCaskill, Cal	145	7.5	4	6	0.3
Boddicker, Bos	89	3.5	1	13	0.5	McDowell J, ChA	209	9.2	2	23	1.0
Bosio, Mil	82	5.6	1	7	0.5	Milacki, Bal	111	7.4	0	19	1.3
Boyd, Mon	106	5.0	0	25	1.2	Moore M, Oak	85	3.8	0	17	0.8
Brown Kev, Tex	209	10.4	1	7	0.3	Morgan M, LA	152	6.5	0	16	0.7
Browning, Cin	135	5.3	1	12	0.5	Morris Jk, Det	82	3.0	0	45	1.6
Burkett, SF	280	12.4	1	18	0.8	Mulholland, Phi	67	3.3	2	3	0.1
Candiotti, Cle	144	6.4	0	18	0.8	Navarro, Mil	58	3.5	0	11	0.7
Cary, NYA	116	6.7	0	14	0.8	Perez M, ChA	128	5.8	1	12	0.5
Cerutti, Tor	147	9.4	2	6	0.4	Petry, Det	98	5.9	0	13	0.8
Charlton, Cin	90	5.2	1	17	1.0	Portugal, Hou	170	7.8	1	23	1.1
Clemens, Bos	269	10.6	1	14	0.6	Rasmussen D, SD	175	8.4	0	21	1.0
Combs, Phi	43	2.1	1	11	0.5	Rijo, Cin	191	8.7	6	19	0.9
Cone, NYN	208	8.8	3	23	1.0	Robinson D, SF	209	11.9	2	19	1.1
Cook D, LA	85	4.9	2	16	0.9	Robinson JM, Det	83	5.2	1	10	0.6
Darling, NYN	162	11.6	5	24	1.7	Robinson R, Mil	90	4.5	1	15	0.8
Darwin, Hou	158	8.7	1	17	0.9	Ruffin, Phi	0	0.0	0	3	0.2
DeJesus J, Phi	16	1.1	1	10	0.7	Ryan, Tex	36	1.6	0	25	1.1
DeLeon J, StL	13	0.6	0	20	1.0	Saberhagen, KC	48	3.2	2	2	0.1
Deshaies, Hou	341	14.7	2	21	0.9	Sanderson, Oak	41	1.8	0	13	0.6
Drabek, Pit	90	3.5	3	18	0.7	Scott M, Hou	151	6.6	0	53	2.3
Farr, KC	97	6.9	1	8	0.6	Smiley, Pit	110	6.6	0	13	0.8
Fernandez S, NYN	52	2.6	0	20	1.0	Smith B, StL	77	4.9	0	21	1.3
Finley C, Cal	48	1.8	0	15	0.6	Smith Roy, Min	101	5.9	0	15	0.9
Gardner M, Mon	85	5.0	0	16	0.9	Smith Z, Pit	172	7.2	0	27	1.1
Garrelts, SF	160	7.9	1	18	0.9	Smoltz, Atl	115	4.5	2	31	1.2
Glavine, Atl	272	11.4	0	22	0.9	Stewart D, Oak	68	2.3	0	13	0.4
Gooden, NYN	205	7.9	1	60	2.3	Stieb, Tor	137	5.9	1	6	0.3
Gordon, KC	58	2.7	1	8	0.4	Stottlemyre, Tor	162	7.2	1	23	1.0
Gross K, Mon	85	4.7	0	31	1.7	Swift, Sea	99	7.0	0	0	0.0
Gullickson, Hou	116	5.4	0	23	1.1	Swindell, Cle	88	3.7	0	3	0.1
Guthrie, Min	143	8.9	2	17	1.1	Tanana, Det	203	10.4	0	9	0.5
Hanson, Sea	116	4.4	1	18	0.7	Tapani, Min	67	3.8	0	9	0.5
Harkey, ChN	101	5.2	0	8	0.4	Terrell, Det	31	1.8	0	10	0.6
Harnisch, Bal	154	7.3	1	18	0.9	Tewksbury, StL	71	4.4	0	8	0.5
Harris GA, Bos	201	9.8	3	15	0.7	Tudor, StL	131	8.1	1	8	0.5
Hawkins, NYA	157	9.0	1	11	0.6	Valenzuela, LA	137	6.0	1	19	0.8
Heaton, Pit	117	7.2	0	15	0.9	Viola, NYN	114	4.1	1	25	0.9
Hibbard, ChA	151	6.4	0	11	0.5	Walk, Pit	106	7.4	1	13	0.9
Higuera, Mil	58	3.1	0	15	0.8	Ward D, Tor	64	4.5	0	12	0.8
Holman B, Sea	126	6.0	1	8	0.4	Welch, Oak	96	3.6	0	10	0.4
Hough, Tex	368	15.1	3	33	1.4	Wells, Tor	123	5.9	1	11	0.5
Hurst, SD	177	7.1	1	19	0.8	West, Min	34	2.1	0	5	0.3
Johnson D, Bal	104	5.2	0	1	0.1	Whitson, SD	105	4.1	0	12	0.5
Johnson R, Sea	114	4.7	1	28	1.1	Wilson S, ChN	120	7.8	0	6	0.4
Key, Tor	89	5.2	0	6	0.3	Witt B, Tex	140	5.7	1	36	1.5
Kiecker, Bos	64	3.8	1	15	0.9	Young Mt, Sea	45	1.8	0	20	0.8
King E, ChA	109	6.5	0	8	0.5						
Knudson, Mil	63	3.4	0	8	0.4	MLB	23905	5.7	167	3290	0.8
Krueger, Mil	89	6.2	0	9	0.6						

WHICH PITCHERS CAN REST IN PEACE? (p. 198)

Shown below are pitchers who left 16 or more runners on base.

Pitcher	Left	Sc	Sc%	Pitcher	Left	Sc	Sc%	Pitcher	Left	Sc	Sc%
Abbott, Cal	36	12	33.3	Frey, Mon	21	5	23.8	Nelson G, Oak	23	1	4.3
Acker, Tor	17	6	35.3	Gardner W, Bos	24	10	41.7	Niedenfuer, StL	35	7	20.0
Agosto, Hou	53	11	20.8	Garrelts, SF	22	12	54.5	Nunez E, Det	27	5	18.5
Akerfelds, Phi	37	9	24.3	Gibson P, Det	45	5	11.1	Nunez J, ChN	16	8	50.0
Andersen L, Bos	16	3	18.8	Glavine, Atl	27	9	33.3	Olin, Cle	34	9	26.5
Anderson A, Min	19	4	21.1	Gordon, KC	20	11	55.0	Orosco, Cle	24	9	37.5
Appier, KC	22	4	18.2	Gross K, Mon	20	10	50.0	Pall, ChA	39	12	30.8
Armstrong, Cin	17	6	35.3	Guetterman, NYA	25	12	48.0	Parker C, Det	16	2	12.5
Arnsberg, Tex	35	7	20.0	Gullickson, Hou	27	5	18.5	Parrett, Atl	29	11	37.9
Assenmacher, ChN	33	6	18.2	Guthrie, Min	24	10	41.7	Patterson B, Pit	25	6	24.0
				Hall D, Mon	30	11	36.7	Patterson K, ChA	28	6	21.4
Avery, Atl	19	11	57.9	Hammaker, SD	23	11	47.8	Perez M, ChA	37	14	37.8
Bailes, Cal	22	7	31.8	Hanson, Sea	27	8	29.6	Peterson, ChA	18	8	44.4
Ballard, Bal	41	14	34.1	Harkey, ChN	18	6	33.3	Petry, Det	26	11	42.3
Barfield Jn, Tex	21	10	47.6	Harnisch, Bal	32	12	37.5	Plunk, NYA	26	5	19.2
Bedrosian, SF	19	8	42.1	Harris GA, Bos	34	15	44.1	Poole, LA	16	2	12.5
Belinda, Pit	29	7	24.1	Harris GW, SD	28	4	14.3	Portugal, Hou	18	7	38.9
Benes, SD	21	13	61.9	Hawkins, NYA	37	11	29.7	Price, Bal	34	9	26.5
Berenguer, Min	25	10	40.0	Hesketh, Bos	18	7	38.9	Radinsky, ChA	51	16	31.4
Bielecki, ChN	26	7	26.9	Hibbard, ChA	27	12	44.4	Rasmussen D, SD	22	12	54.5
Black, Tor	24	13	54.2	Hickey, Bal	24	7	29.2	Rijo, Cin	16	5	31.3
Blyleven, Cal	18	7	38.9	Holman B, Sea	27	10	37.0	Robinson D, SF	15	7	46.7
Boddicker, Bos	23	12	52.2	Honeycutt, Oak	23	7	30.4	Robinson JD, NYA	34	10	29.4
Bolton, Bos	19	4	21.1	Horton, StL	19	7	36.8	Robinson JM, Det	29	11	37.9
Boskie, ChN	17	7	41.2	Hough, Tex	22	10	45.5	Rogers, Tex	19	7	36.8
Brown Kev, Tex	16	9	56.3	Hurst, SD	19	9	47.4	Ruffin, Phi	34	8	23.5
Browning, Cin	19	5	26.3	Jackson M, Sea	23	12	52.2	Ruskin, Mon	40	9	22.5
Burkett, SF	24	11	45.8	Jeffcoat, Tex	28	10	35.7	Sanderson, Oak	20	4	20.0
Burns, Oak	26	4	15.4	Johnson D, Bal	27	11	40.7	Schatzeder, NYN	17	3	17.6
Cadaret, NYA	37	13	35.1	Johnson R, Sea	34	16	47.1	Searage, LA	16	1	6.3
Candelaria, Tor	27	6	22.2	Jones Ba, ChA	23	2	8.7	Shaw, Cle	18	6	33.3
Candiotti, Cle	17	5	29.4	Kerfeld, Atl	20	5	25.0	Show, SD	18	8	44.4
Carman, Phi	27	6	22.2	Kiecker, Bos	27	14	51.9	Smiley, Pit	21	9	42.9
Cary, NYA	19	3	15.8	King E, ChA	20	4	20.0	Smith Roy, Min	23	7	30.4
Castillo T, Atl	22	7	31.8	Kipper, Pit	20	4	20.0	Smoltz, Atl	18	3	16.7
Cerutti, Tor	30	2	6.7	Knudson, Mil	27	12	44.4	Stieb, Tor	19	5	26.3
Charlton, Cin	30	6	20.0	Krueger, Mil	20	6	30.0	Swift, Sea	37	7	18.9
Clary, Atl	29	17	58.6	Lamp, Bos	23	8	34.8	Swindell, Cle	30	9	30.0
Clemens, Bos	19	9	47.4	Lancaster, ChN	24	10	41.7	Tanana, Det	26	11	42.3
Combs, Phi	24	7	29.2	Langston, Cal	22	12	54.5	Tapani, Min	22	11	50.0
Comstock, Sea	49	7	14.3	LaPoint, NYA	33	10	30.3	Terrell, Det	28	13	46.4
Cone, NYN	18	8	44.4	Layana, Cin	19	4	21.1	Terry, StL	25	7	28.0
Cook D, LA	40	13	32.5	Leach T, Min	19	7	36.8	Tewksbury, StL	16	6	37.5
Crawford, KC	17	5	29.4	Leary, NYA	25	10	40.0	Valdez, Cle	16	7	43.8
Crews, LA	16	9	56.3	Lilliquist, SD	23	14	60.9	Walk, Pit	17	5	29.4
Crim, Mil	36	11	30.6	Maddux G, ChN	23	8	34.8	Walker MC, Cle	19	8	42.1
Davis Mrk, KC	33	8	24.2	Magrane, StL	17	8	47.1	Ward D, Tor	22	7	31.8
Davis Storm, KC	16	5	31.3	McCaskill, Cal	21	6	28.6	Wayne, Min	21	1	4.8
Dayley, StL	17	8	47.1	McDowell J, ChA	26	8	30.8	Welch, Oak	18	3	16.7
DeJesus J, Phi	16	11	68.8	McGaffigan, KC	17	3	17.6	Wells, Tor	17	7	41.2
DeLeon J, StL	23	7	30.4	Mielke, Tex	22	6	27.3	West, Min	23	3	13.0
Deshaies, Hou	20	9	45.0	Milacki, Bal	29	8	27.6	Williams Mitch, ChN	17	3	17.6
Dibble, Cin	17	1	5.9	Mills A, NYA	19	3	15.8				
DiPino, StL	18	5	27.8	Mirabella, Mil	31	7	22.6	Williamson, Bal	18	1	5.6
Drabek, Pit	18	6	33.3	Mitchell J, Bal	25	5	20.0	Wills, Tor	22	6	27.3
Edens, Mil	20	12	60.0	Moore M, Oak	24	11	45.8	Wilson S, ChN	27	10	37.0
Edwards, ChA	33	8	24.2	Morgan M, LA	20	10	50.0	Wilson Tr, SF	19	7	36.8
Erickson S, Min	16	5	31.3	Morris Jk, Det	18	8	44.4	Witt B, Tex	20	7	35.0
Farrell, Cle	18	1	5.6	Moyer, Tex	26	13	50.0	Witt M, NYA	16	4	25.0
Fernandez S, NYN	17	6	35.3	Murphy R, Bos	56	14	25.0	Young C, Oak	30	10	33.3
Finley C, Cal	19	6	31.6	Musselman J, NYN	18	5	27.8	Young Mt, Sea	31	13	41.9
Fraser, Cal	21	5	23.8	Navarro, Mil	28	10	35.7	MLB			32.9

WHICH SOUTHPAWS EAT LEFTIES? (p. 200)

Lefthanders with 1 or more games in relief

Left-Handed Relievers	Vs. LHB		Vs. RHB		Left-Handed Relievers	Vs. LHB		Vs. RHB	
Pitcher, Team	BFP	Avg	BFP	Avg	Pitcher, Team	BFP	Avg	BFP	Avg
Agosto, Hou	127	.227	277	.276	McWilliams, KC	19	.385	24	.263
Assenmacher, ChN	135	.223	291	.247	Mercker, Atl	58	.250	153	.231
Bailes, Cal	58	.286	115	.330	Minutelli, Cin	2	----	4	.000
Ballard, Bal	148	.294	430	.287	Mirabella, Mil	82	.235	185	.299
Barfield Jn, Tex	52	.340	126	.236	Moses, Min	2	.000	11	.556
Birtsas, Cin	87	.275	152	.356	Moyer, Tex	90	.222	357	.308
Bohanon, Tex	29	.200	129	.318	Mulholland, Phi	110	.277	636	.247
Bolton, Bos	106	.242	395	.253	Munoz, Det	11	.333	13	.273
Boone D, Bal	5	.200	38	.324	Murphy R, Bos	101	.241	184	.404
Brown K, Mil	25	.136	71	.206	Musselman J, NYN	52	.229	92	.358
Cadaret, NYA	138	.252	387	.274	Myers R, Cin	86	.181	267	.197
Candelaria, Tor	84	.253	261	.284	Novoa, SF	16	.071	72	.333
Carman, Phi	117	.175	251	.239	Ojeda, NYN	123	.168	377	.307
Casian, Min	11	.333	79	.303	Orosco, Cle	82	.224	207	.244
Castillo T, Atl	105	.284	232	.310	Osuna, Hou	22	.188	26	.333
Cerutti, Tor	121	.277	488	.302	Otto, Oak	2	.000	11	.333
Charlton, Cin	136	.224	514	.233	Patterson B, Pit	111	.204	275	.267
Clark Br, Sea	23	.316	25	.158	Patterson K, ChA	79	.194	204	.260
Clarke S, StL	5	.200	7	.143	Perry P, LA	12	.250	24	.333
Clements P, SD	30	.296	33	.414	Plesac, Mil	71	.161	228	.286
Comstock, Sea	84	.250	144	.180	Poole, LA	11	.182	35	.185
Cook D, LA	153	.296	510	.252	Powell, Mil	46	.256	168	.368
Corbett, Cal	7	.500	19	.313	Price, Bal	100	.267	173	.245
Davis Mrk, KC	69	.200	265	.274	Radinsky, ChA	71	.177	166	.271
Dayley, StL	115	.283	192	.201	Reuss, Pit	10	.125	24	.318
DiPino, StL	148	.293	212	.294	Righetti, NYA	44	.244	191	.232
Edwards, ChA	108	.183	288	.253	Rodriguez Rich, SD	72	.231	129	.319
Elvira, Mil	4	.000	21	.333	Rodriguez Ro, Cin	20	.368	27	.348
Fossas, Mil	43	.300	103	.344	Rogers, Tex	104	.219	324	.259
Franco Jn, NYN	67	.228	220	.259	Rosenberg, ChA	12	.400	32	.207
Frey, Mon	74	.274	162	.194	Ruffin, Phi	139	.292	539	.299
Gibson P, Det	136	.263	286	.272	Ruskin, Mon	129	.281	207	.246
Gleaton, Det	99	.242	226	.200	Sanchez Z, KC	14	.250	33	.433
Guetterman, NYA	111	.253	265	.229	Schatzeder, NYN	99	.261	184	.261
Gunderson, SF	19	.294	75	.292	Searage, LA	52	.255	84	.247
Guthrie, Min	102	.343	501	.262	Searcy, Det	55	.326	286	.258
Hall D, Mon	77	.270	177	.230	Sherill, StL	11	.444	14	.500
Hammaker, SD	76	.194	287	.276	Smith Z, Pit	126	.164	734	.258
Heaton, Pit	104	.311	495	.254	Stanton M, Atl	10	.250	32	.500
Hesketh, Bos	83	.260	186	.296	Swan, Sea	43	.231	170	.265
Hickey, Bal	52	.261	61	.269	Tanana, Det	125	.230	638	.290
Honeycutt, Oak	94	.163	162	.230	Thurmond, SF	71	.233	167	.267
Horton, StL	80	.279	113	.340	Tudor, StL	131	.214	444	.228
Jeffcoat, Tex	97	.233	369	.296	Valdez E, Cle	38	.188	66	.259
Kaiser, Cle	22	.353	38	.286	Vosberg, SF	32	.192	72	.250
Kilgus, Tor	20	.294	54	.311	Walsh, LA	31	.222	39	.257
Kipper, Pit	94	.225	166	.178	Wayne, Min	53	.174	113	.291
Klink, Oak	59	.255	106	.221	Wells, Tor	120	.264	639	.230
Knepper, SF	26	.200	176	.329	West, Min	102	.244	544	.259
Kraemer, ChN	40	.273	79	.328	Wickander, Cle	19	.400	34	.258
Krueger, Mil	98	.237	468	.285	Williams Mitch, ChN	87	.227	223	.243
Lee, Mil	27	.304	58	.236	Wilson S, ChN	146	.219	451	.273
Lefferts, SD	97	.207	230	.237	Wilson Tr, SF	71	.219	386	.218
Leiter, Tor	5	.000	17	.067	Young Cli, Cal	37	.394	100	.300
Lilliquist, SD	104	.326	433	.275	Young C, Oak	103	.260	424	.268
Lovelace, Sea	6	.500	11	.250	MLB		.251		.265
Macdonald, Tor	3	.000	5	.000					
McClure, Cal	14	.333	16	.214					
McElroy, Phi	25	.286	51	.409					

WHO'S BEST AT HOLDING THE FORT? (p. 206)

A hold (H) is a Save Opportunity passed on to the next pitcher. If a pitcher comes into the game in a Save Situation and leaves the game having gotten at least 1 out and without having blown the lead, this is a "passed-on" Save Opportunity and the pitcher is credited with a Hold.

Both Leagues — Listed Alphabetically (pitchers with 1+ Holds)

Pitcher, Team	H	Pitcher, Team	H	Pitcher, Team	H	Pitcher, Team	H
Aase, LA	2	Fraser, Cal	5	Long B, ChN	4	Radinsky, ChA	10
Acker, Tor	7	Freeman M, Atl	1	Luecken, Tor	1	Reardon, Bos	1
Agosto, Hou	16	Frey, Mon	5	Lugo, Det	1	Reed Jr, Bos	2
Akerfelds, Phi	7	Frohwirth, Phi	1	Maddux M, LA	1	Reed Rk, Pit	1
Andersen L, Bo	8	Gibson P, Det	9	Mahler R, Cin	1	Robinson JD, N	11
Aquino, KC	1	Gleaton, Det	7	Maldonado C, K	1	Rodriguez Rich, SD	3
Arnsberg, Tex	11	Gott, LA	6	McClure, Cal	3	Rogers, Tex	6
Assenmacher, C	10	Gozzo, Cle	1	McDowell R, Ph	1	Rojas, Mon	1
Bailes, Cal	4	Grant, Atl	1	McGaffigan, KC	1	Ruskin, Mon	15
Bair, Pit	4	Gray, Bos	3	McWilliams, KC	2	Russell Jf, Te	1
Ballard, Bal	7	Guante, Cle	1	Meyer B, Hou	3	Sampen, Mon	1
Bautista, Bal	5	Guetterman, NY	12	Mielke, Tex	3	Sanchez Z, KC	1
Bedrosian, SF	2	Hall D, Mon	4	Mills A, NYA	3	Schatzeder, NY	4
Belinda, Pit	9	Hammaker, SD	2	Minton, Cal	1	Schilling, Bal	5
Berenguer, Min	9	Harris Ge, Sea	1	Mirabella, Mil	4	Schiraldi, SD	1
Birtsas, Cin	2	Harris GW, SD	10	Mohorcic, Mon	2	Schmidt D, Mon	2
Blair, Tor	1	Hartley, LA	1	Montgomery, KC	7	Seanez, Cle	3
Boever, Phi	5	Harvey, Cal	1	Moyer, Tex	1	Searcy, Det	1
Boone D, Bal	1	Heaton, Pit	1	Munoz, Det	2	Sebra, Mil	1
Brantley J, SF	8	Henke, Tor	2	Murphy R, Bos	16	Smith B, StL	1
Burke, Mon	6	Henneman, Det	4	Musselman J, N	1	Smith Le, StL	1
Burns, Oak	9	Henry, Atl	1	Navarro, Mil	3	Stottlemyre M, Tor	1
Cadaret, NYA	8	Hernandez X, H	1	Nelson G, Oak	18	Swan, Sea	1
Candelaria, To	7	Hesketh, Bos	3	Niedenfuer, St	10	Swift, Sea	7
Carman, Phi	8	Hickey, Bal	7	Nipper, Cle	1	Tewksbury, StL	2
Castillo T, At	3	Hill K, StL	1	Norris, Oak	1	Thurmond, SF	8
Charlton, Cin	9	Hillegas, ChA	1	Nunez E, Det	6	Tudor, StL	2
Clancy, Hou	1	Holton, Bal	3	O'Neal, SF	1	Valdez, Cle	1
Clary, Atl	1	Honeycutt, Oak	27	Ojeda, NYN	3	Veres, Mil	1
Colby, Cle	2	Horton, StL	2	Olin, Cle	4	Walsh, LA	1
Comstock, Sea	9	Howell Jay, LA	1	Olivares, StL	1	Ward D, Tor	11
Cook D, LA	4	Innis, NYN	2	Oliveras, SF	2	Wayne, Min	5
Costello, Mon	1	Jackson M, Sea	13	Ontiveros, Phi	1	Wells, Tor	3
Crawford, KC	7	Jeffcoat, Tex	4	Orosco, Cle	2	Weston, Bal	1
Crews, LA	5	Jones Ba, ChA	30	Osuna, Hou	1	Whitehurst, NY	4
Crim, Mil	19	Kerfeld, Atl	3	Pall, ChA	13	Wickander, Cle	1
Darling, NYN	2	Kiecker, Bos	1	Parker C, Det	1	Williams M, ChN	1
Davis Mrk, KC	7	Kilgus, Tor	1	Parrett, Atl	11	Williamson, Bal	8
Dayley, StL	14	Kipper, Pit	3	Patterson B, P	8	Wills, Tor	3
Dewey, SF	1	Klink, Oak	4	Patterson K, C	4	Wilson S, ChN	3
Dibble, Cin	17	Knackert, Sea	1	Pavlas, ChN	1	Wilson Tr, SF	2
DiPino, StL	4	Kraemer, ChN	1	Pena A, NYN	6	Witt M, NYA	2
Drummond, Min	1	LaCoss, SF	1	Perez Mk, StL	2		
Edens, Mil	2	Lamp, Bos	7	Perry P, LA	1	MLB	818
Edwards, ChA	4	Lancaster, ChN	5	Petry, Det	3		
Eichhorn, Cal	4	Landrum B, Pit	1	Plesac, Mil	2		
Farr, KC	7	Layana, Cin	3	Plunk, NYA	3		
Fetters, Cal	1	Leach T, Min	4	Poole, LA	2		
Filer, Mil	1	Lee, Mil	1	Power, Pit	3		
Fossas, Mil	8	Lefferts, SD	1	Price, Bal	3		

WHO'S BEST ON SHORT REST? (p. 208)

Both Leagues — Listed Alphabetically
(Pitchers with 3+ Starts on 3 Days Rest)

Name	3 Days Rest				4 Days Rest			
	ERA	IP	W	L	ERA	IP	W	L
Anderson A, Min	3.24	25.0	3	0	6.22	81.0	1	11
Appier, KC	3.06	17.2	1	1	2.04	88.1	7	4
Bielecki, ChN	8.40	15.0	0	1	5.23	96.1	5	8
Boskie, ChN	2.83	28.2	2	1	6.48	25.0	0	2
Browning, Cin	5.60	37.0	4	2	3.17	150.1	9	5
Burkett, SF	4.56	49.1	3	2	3.34	116.0	8	3
Charlton, Cin	1.80	20.0	1	1	3.07	61.2	3	4
Clancy, Hou	3.86	14.0	0	2	3.38	21.1	2	2
Cone, NYN	2.57	21.0	1	2	3.16	108.1	8	5
Farr, KC	2.02	22.1	3	1	1.69	5.1	1	0
Garrelts, SF	3.47	49.1	3	2	4.48	80.1	5	5
Glavine, Atl	7.41	17.0	0	2	4.71	120.1	6	6
Gross K, Mon	4.86	16.2	1	2	4.87	94.1	6	8
Harkey, ChN	4.67	27.0	3	2	2.67	104.2	6	2
Jackson Dan, Cin	4.30	14.2	2	1	2.68	57.0	1	2
Knudson, Mil	3.20	39.1	2	2	3.71	77.2	5	5
Maddux G, ChN	1.30	48.1	5	1	4.01	128.0	7	11
Mahler R, Cin	5.06	26.2	2	1	4.11	46.0	2	4
McDonald, Bal	3.20	19.2	2	1	2.69	60.1	3	4
Mitchell J, Bal	3.38	21.1	2	1	4.53	57.2	4	3
Moore M, Oak	6.92	27.1	1	1	4.54	113.0	9	9
Morris Jk, Det	4.94	27.1	2	0	4.23	178.2	11	14
Mulholland, Phi	6.07	29.2	2	2	3.23	100.1	4	7
Navarro, Mil	2.49	21.2	1	1	6.08	66.2	4	4
Ojeda, NYN	5.57	21.0	0	4	3.18	22.2	3	0
Perez M, ChA	9.00	14.0	0	3	4.12	129.0	9	7
Petry, Det	6.00	15.0	0	2	4.67	88.2	6	6
Pico, ChN	3.00	18.0	2	1	5.40	18.1	1	1
Reuschel, SF	3.95	27.1	1	2	4.69	48.0	1	4
Robinson D, SF	3.93	18.1	2	1	5.24	89.1	6	4
Sanderson, Oak	3.95	27.1	2	1	3.99	144.1	12	8
Scott M, Hou	6.32	15.2	0	2	3.89	115.2	5	7
Smith Z, Pit	2.25	36.0	3	0	2.55	116.2	7	7
Smoltz, Atl	4.37	22.2	1	2	3.84	159.1	11	5
Stewart D, Oak	0.72	25.0	3	0	3.01	209.1	16	10
Viola, NYN	2.89	28.0	2	2	2.91	163.2	12	8
Welch, Oak	8.59	14.2	1	2	2.87	181.2	20	4
Wilson S, ChN	8.31	13.0	0	3	6.16	30.2	1	2
Wilson Tr, SF	2.78	45.1	3	2	6.32	31.1	3	3
Witt B, Tex	3.98	20.1	2	1	3.58	98.0	7	4
Young C, Oak	4.02	15.2	1	1	7.53	20.1	1	2
Young Mt, Sea	1.74	20.2	0	2	3.29	147.2	6	9
MLB	4.08	1775.1	116	109	3.93	15259.2	904	904

WHO ARE THE QUALITY STARTERS? (p. 210)

Minimum 20 Starts

Player,Team	Games Started	Quality Starts	Pct.
Abbott, Cal	33	17	51.5
Anderson A, Min	31	16	51.6
Appier, KC	24	17	70.8
Armstrong, Cin	27	17	63.0
Avery, Atl	20	6	30.0
Belcher, LA	24	12	50.0
Benes, SD	31	21	67.7
Bielecki, ChN	29	14	48.3
Black, Tor	31	19	61.3
Blyleven, Cal	23	10	43.5
Boddicker, Bos	34	23	67.6
Bosio, Mil	20	7	35.0
Boyd, Mon	31	22	71.0
Brown Kev, Tex	26	17	65.4
Browning, Cin	35	20	57.1
Burkett, SF	32	18	56.3
Candiotti, Cle	29	17	58.6
Cary, NYA	27	15	55.6
Cerutti, Tor	23	7	30.4
Clemens, Bos	31	27	87.1
Combs, Phi	31	16	51.6
Cone, NYN	30	19	63.3
Davis Storm, KC	20	7	35.0
DeJesus J, Phi	22	12	54.5
DeLeon J, StL	32	18	56.3
Deshaies, Hou	34	18	52.9
Drabek, Pit	33	24	72.7
Fernandez S, NYN	30	18	60.0
Finley C, Cal	32	24	75.0
Gardner M, Mon	26	15	57.7
Garrelts, SF	31	16	51.6
Glavine, Atl	33	19	57.6
Gooden, NYN	34	20	58.8
Gordon, KC	32	18	56.3
Gross K, Mon	26	12	46.2
Gullickson, Hou	32	16	50.0
Guthrie, Min	21	9	42.9
Hanson, Sea	33	23	69.7
Harkey, ChN	27	18	66.7
Harnisch, Bal	31	16	51.6
Harris GA, Bos	30	12	40.0
Hawkins, NYA	26	9	34.6
Heaton, Pit	24	13	54.2
Hibbard, ChA	33	19	57.6
Higuera, Mil	27	14	51.9
Holman B, Sea	28	16	57.1
Hough, Tex	32	15	46.9
Hurst, SD	33	20	60.6
Jackson Dan, Cin	21	12	57.1
Johnson D, Bal	29	14	48.3
Johnson R, Sea	33	22	66.7
Key, Tor	27	14	51.9
Kiecker, Bos	25	12	48.0
King E, ChA	25	14	56.0
Knudson, Mil	27	14	51.9
Langston, Cal	33	17	51.5
LaPoint, NYA	27	12	44.4
Leary, NYA	31	17	54.8
Leibrandt, Atl	24	15	62.5
Maddux G, ChN	35	22	62.9
Magrane, StL	31	20	64.5
Martinez De, Mon	32	23	71.9
Martinez R, LA	33	23	69.7
McCaskill, Cal	29	17	58.6
McDowell J, ChA	33	19	57.6
Milacki, Bal	24	13	54.2
Moore M, Oak	33	17	51.5
Morgan M, LA	33	21	63.6
Morris Jk, Det	36	18	50.0
Mulholland, Phi	26	16	61.5
Navarro, Mil	22	9	40.9
Perez M, ChA	35	19	54.3
Petry, Det	23	8	34.8
Portugal, Hou	32	23	71.9
Rasmussen D, SD	32	13	40.6
Rijo, Cin	29	20	69.0
Robinson D, SF	25	16	64.0
Robinson JM, Det	27	10	37.0
Robinson R, Mil	27	16	59.3
Ruffin, Phi	25	9	36.0
Ryan, Tex	30	17	56.7
Saberhagen, KC	20	14	70.0
Sanderson, Oak	34	16	47.1
Scott M, Hou	32	18	56.3
Smiley, Pit	25	12	48.0
Smith B, StL	25	12	48.0
Smith Roy, Min	23	9	39.1
Smith Z, Pit	31	24	77.4
Smoltz, Atl	34	19	55.9
Stewart D, Oak	36	27	75.0
Stieb, Tor	33	24	72.7
Stottlemyre, Tor	33	15	45.5
Swindell, Cle	34	17	50.0
Tanana, Det	29	14	48.3
Tapani, Min	28	14	50.0
Terrell, Det	28	12	42.9
Tewksbury, StL	20	11	55.0
Tudor, StL	22	17	77.3
Valenzuela, LA	33	16	48.5
Viola, NYN	35	25	71.4
Walk, Pit	24	9	37.5
Welch, Oak	35	24	68.6
Wells, Tor	25	18	72.0
West, Min	27	11	40.7
Whitson, SD	32	27	84.4
Witt B, Tex	32	20	62.5
Young C, Oak	21	6	28.6
Young Mt, Sea	33	19	57.6
MLB	4210	2202	52.3

WHICH STARTING STAFFS STAR, AND WHICH RELIEF STAFFS REEK? (p. 212)

Team Pitching Statistics — Listed Alphabetically by Team

American League Starters

Team	ERA	W	L	IP	H	R	ER	HR	BB	K	BA
Baltimore	4.35	52	62	949.1	987	489	459	116	358	447	.270
Boston	3.32	69	48	995.2	947	412	367	56	347	677	.251
California	3.92	62	63	1048.0	1072	519	456	78	381	665	.268
Chicago	3.83	65	47	973.2	927	450	414	72	339	607	.251
Cleveland	4.50	56	62	963.1	1057	523	482	118	316	530	.279
Detroit	5.00	55	68	925.1	941	555	514	115	438	550	.266
Kansas City	3.93	51	65	944.2	983	477	413	75	361	622	.268
Milwaukee	4.20	55	57	958.1	1061	508	447	81	278	482	.280
Minnesota	4.38	46	68	938.1	1014	505	457	90	300	546	.279
New York	4.47	42	71	946.1	950	518	470	96	385	578	.264
Oakland	3.51	89	49	1038.2	972	448	405	99	369	552	.249
Seattle	3.67	57	62	1048.1	939	478	427	88	417	775	.239
Texas	3.96	60	60	1037.2	960	511	456	87	440	751	.246
Toronto	3.93	66	52	968.1	985	448	423	93	285	520	.265

National League Starters

Team	ERA	W	L	IP	H	R	ER	HR	BB	K	BA
Atlanta	4.39	48	69	982.1	1016	542	479	85	356	599	.268
Chicago	4.48	51	65	933.1	990	518	465	79	342	517	.273
Cincinnati	3.61	64	49	983.2	934	429	395	88	346	579	.251
Houston	3.71	48	62	990.0	979	466	408	99	332	554	.259
Los Angeles	3.92	65	57	1002.2	967	492	437	99	310	678	.253
Montreal	3.47	49	51	1000.00	905	412	386	88	320	695	.242
New York	3.55	73	56	1050.2	975	459	414	90	322	934	.245
Philadelphia	4.14	51	60	942.2	912	477	434	82	409	524	.256
Pittsburgh	3.60	67	49	971.1	939	434	388	96	241	519	.255
St. Louis	3.87	53	69	966.1	951	467	415	63	292	543	.259
San Diego	3.72	53	62	1000.0	995	459	413	102	308	601	.260
San Francisco	4.21	62	53	962.0	988	481	450	91	354	501	.267

American League Relievers

Team	ERA	W	L	IP	H	R	ER	HR	BB	K	BA
Baltimore	3.52	24	23	486.0	458	209	190	45	179	329	.251
Boston	4.62	19	26	446.1	492	252	229	36	172	320	.281
California	3.55	18	19	406.0	410	187	160	28	163	279	.265
Chicago	3.18	29	21	475.2	386	183	168	34	209	307	.227
Cleveland	3.78	21	23	464.0	434	214	195	45	202	330	.251
Detroit	3.26	24	15	505.0	460	199	183	39	223	306	.246
Kansas City	3.93	24	21	476.0	466	232	208	41	199	384	.256
Milwaukee	3.94	19	31	486.2	497	252	213	40	191	289	.264
Minnesota	3.67	28	20	497.1	495	224	203	44	189	326	.262
New York	3.77	25	24	498.1	480	231	209	48	233	331	.256
Oakland	2.35	14	10	417.1	315	122	109	24	125	279	.210
Seattle	3.87	20	23	395.0	380	202	170	32	189	289	.255
Texas	3.52	23	19	407.0	383	185	159	26	183	246	.253
Toronto	3.65	20	24	485.2	449	213	197	50	160	372	.248

National League Relievers

Team	ERA	W	L	IP	H	R	ER	HR	BB	K	BA
Atlanta	5.01	17	28	447.1	511	279	249	43	223	339	.290
Chicago	4.06	26	20	509.1	520	256	230	42	230	360	.267
Cincinnati	2.93	27	22	472.2	404	168	154	36	197	450	.233
Houston	3.42	27	25	460.0	417	190	175	31	164	300	.245
Los Angeles	3.32	21	19	439.1	397	193	162	38	168	343	.240
Montreal	3.14	36	26	473.1	444	186	165	39	190	296	.250
New York	3.10	18	15	389.1	364	154	134	29	122	283	.248
Philadelphia	4.00	26	25	506.1	469	252	225	42	242	316	.249
Pittsburgh	2.99	28	18	475.2	428	185	158	39	172	329	.243
St. Louis	3.91	17	23	477.0	481	231	207	35	183	290	.264
San Diego	3.61	22	25	461.2	442	214	185	45	199	327	.254
San Francisco	3.81	23	24	484.1	489	229	205	40	199	287	.265

WHO'S BEST IN THE INFIELD ZONE? (p. 218)

1990 Infielders — Listed by Zone Rating
(600 or more defensive innings)

FIRST BASE

Player, Team	Innings	PO	A	E	Range Factor	In Zone	Outs	Zone Rating
Magadan, NYN	900.1	830	71	2	--	194	180	.928
Bream, Pit	975.2	971	104	8	--	230	213	.926
Mattingly, NYA	778.1	800	78	3	--	215	199	.926
McGwire, Oak	1334.2	1329	95	5	--	311	286	.920
Hrbek, Min	1021.0	1057	81	3	--	198	180	.909
O'Brien P, Sea	800.0	850	76	5	--	177	159	.898
Brett, KC	877.0	865	66	7	--	233	207	.888
Brock, Mil	899.2	885	63	5	--	225	199	.884
Galarraga, Mon	1318.1	1300	94	10	--	320	283	.884
Grace, ChN	1315.1	1324	180	12	--	397	351	.884
Milligan, Bal	846.2	846	87	9	--	245	216	.882
Benzinger, Cin	746.0	707	52	6	--	177	155	.876
Jordan, Phi	690.2	743	37	4	--	177	155	.876
McGriff F, Tor	1299.0	1246	126	6	--	320	280	.875
Palmeiro, Tex	1255.2	1215	91	7	--	284	248	.873
Quintana, Bos	1201.1	1188	137	17	--	376	328	.872
Clark Jk, SD	888.2	855	69	6	--	231	199	.861
Murray E, LA	1286.0	1180	113	10	--	316	269	.851
Davis G, Hou	774.1	796	55	4	--	214	182	.850
Morris H, Cin	632.2	589	53	3	--	120	102	.850
Fielder, Det	1225.1	1190	111	14	--	292	248	.849
Joyner, Cal	725.0	727	62	4	--	170	144	.847
Clark W, SF	1338.1	1456	119	12	--	355	300	.845
Martinez Crl, ChA	626.0	632	38	8	--	141	119	.844
Guerrero, StL	1083.1	1083	73	13	--	269	209	.777
								.869

SECOND BASE

Player, Team	Innings	PO	A	E	Range Factor	In Zone	Outs	Zone Rating
Franco Ju, Tex	1308.2	310	444	19	5.32	647	622	.961
Ripken B, Bal	1047.0	250	366	8	5.36	595	571	.960
Whitaker, Det	1037.1	286	372	6	5.76	552	526	.953
Lee M, Tor	956.2	259	286	4	5.16	491	465	.947
Reed Jd, Bos	984.2	215	374	6	5.44	604	572	.947
Sandberg, ChN	1315.0	278	469	8	5.17	716	677	.946
Browne J, Cle	1180.0	286	382	10	5.17	646	610	.944
Oquendo, StL	1202.2	285	393	3	5.10	607	572	.942
Randolph, Oak	920.0	198	313	11	5.11	499	470	.942
Alomar R, SD	1226.1	311	392	17	5.28	609	573	.941
Reynolds H, Sea	1406.1	330	499	19	5.43	772	725	.939
Gallego, Oak	661.1	153	258	4	5.65	409	384	.939
Sax S, NYA	1355.2	292	457	10	5.04	772	716	.927
Fletcher S, ChA	1321.1	305	436	9	5.11	694	639	.921
Lind, Pit	1275.1	330	449	7	5.55	681	626	.919
Ray, Cal	854.1	241	295	7	5.72	462	424	.918
White F, KC	627.2	142	218	8	5.28	346	317	.916
Gantner, Mil	675.2	164	220	7	5.21	354	324	.915
Treadway, Atl	989.1	241	360	15	5.60	576	527	.915
Deshields, Mon	1115.0	236	371	12	5.00	613	560	.914
Duncan, Cin	924.2	245	287	15	5.32	485	435	.897
Thompson Ro, SF	1167.0	287	441	8	5.68	725	650	.897
Doran, Cin	932.0	198	302	6	4.89	520	466	.896
Samuel, LA	881.2	194	258	13	4.75	471	422	.896
Herr, NYN	1170.0	275	349	7	4.85	586	525	.896
Jefferies, NYN	996.1	219	278	12	4.60	480	425	.885
Liriano, Min	830.0	176	260	11	4.85	446	391	.877
					5.13			.925

THIRD BASE

Player, Team	Innings	PO	A	E	Range Factor	In Zone	Outs	Zone Rating
Gaetti, Min	1291.0	102	318	18	3.05	473	440	.930
Hayes C, Phi	1236.2	121	324	20	3.38	443	409	.923
Williams MD, SF	1372.2	140	306	19	3.05	415	381	.918
Ventura, ChA	1210.0	116	268	25	3.04	405	365	.901
Pendleton, StL	1010.0	91	248	19	3.19	361	319	.884
Caminiti, Hou	1249.1	118	243	21	2.75	359	315	.877
Pagliarulo, SD	950.0	79	200	13	2.77	307	267	.870
King J, Pit	840.2	58	215	18	3.12	313	272	.869
Gruber, Tor	1267.2	123	280	19	3.00	421	365	.867
Martinez E, Sea	1196.1	89	259	27	2.82	375	325	.867
Wallach, Mon	1425.2	128	309	21	2.89	433	375	.866
Jacoby, Cle	772.2	44	158	4	2.40	237	204	.861
Worthington, Bal	1074.1	90	218	18	2.73	356	305	.857
Buechele, Tex	685.2	70	157	8	3.08	223	191	.857
Salazar L, ChN	727.0	55	136	10	2.49	204	174	.853
Lansford, Oak	1032.0	100	194	9	2.64	327	278	.850
Phillips, Det	793.1	69	200	20	3.28	286	243	.850
Seitzer, KC	1257.2	100	262	18	2.72	401	340	.848
Sharperson, LA	690.0	70	153	12	3.07	240	202	.842
Sabo, Cin	1269.0	70	273	12	2.52	411	344	.837
Boggs W, Bos	1340.2	108	241	20	2.48	385	319	.829
Sheffield, Mil	1069.0	98	254	25	3.17	398	323	.812
Harris L, LA	639.1	77	133	9	3.08	217	176	.811
Johnson H, NYN	771.2	52	159	20	2.69	233	188	.807
Howell Jk, Cal	817.0	70	193	17	3.08	299	237	.793
Presley, Atl	1095.0	101	231	25	2.93	409	309	.756
					2.74			.853

SHORTSTOP

Player, Team	Innings	PO	A	E	Range Factor	In Zone	Outs	Zone Rating
Schofield, Cal	865.1	170	318	17	5.25	523	503	.962
Ripken C, Bal	1404.1	242	435	3	4.36	734	705	.960
Guillen, ChA	1361.1	252	474	17	4.91	801	768	.959
Trammell, Det	1213.1	232	409	14	4.86	665	635	.955
Smith O, StL	1203.1	212	378	12	4.50	660	623	.944
Fernandez T, Tor	1384.0	297	480	9	5.11	805	759	.943
Larkin B, Cin	1344.0	254	469	17	4.96	780	733	.940
Spiers, Mil	929.2	159	326	12	4.81	557	523	.939
Weiss, Oak	1154.0	194	373	12	4.52	663	622	.938
Vizquel, Sea	680.0	103	239	7	4.62	394	368	.934
Espinoza, NYA	1209.1	268	447	17	5.45	694	643	.927
Fermin, Cle	1180.0	213	421	16	4.96	707	653	.924
Thon, Phi	1262.0	222	439	25	4.89	748	689	.921
Templeton, SD	1165.2	214	367	26	4.69	610	561	.920
Gagne, Min	1074.0	184	377	14	4.82	637	585	.918
Huson, Tex	795.1	157	254	17	4.84	453	414	.914
Thomas A, Atl	606.0	103	193	10	4.54	335	306	.913
Owen S, Mon	1194.1	216	340	6	4.23	622	567	.912
Dunston, ChN	1247.2	255	392	20	4.81	680	618	.909
Bell Jay, Pit	1377.0	260	459	22	4.84	803	728	.907
Rivera L, Bos	928.2	186	310	18	4.98	505	448	.887
Elster, NYN	795.1	159	251	17	4.83	413	364	.881
Griffin Alf, LA	1153.2	221	382	26	4.91	663	583	.879
Stillwell, KC	1138.2	181	350	24	4.39	628	550	.876
Ramirez R, Hou	1058.0	190	321	25	4.56	638	553	.867
Uribe, SF	1036.1	182	373	20	4.99	668	579	.867
Blauser, Atl	778.2	141	257	16	4.79	416	355	.853
					4.67			.916

WHO ARE THE BEST-THROWING CATCHERS? (p. 222)

Both Leagues — Alphabetical (250 Innings Caught)

Catcher, Team	SB	CS	CS%	PkO	SB/9	Without Pitcher CS Pit CS	%
Alomar S, Cle	77	41	34.7	0	0.66	10	28.7
Biggio, Hou	117	38	24.5	1	1.16	6	21.5
Boone, KC	32	10	23.8	0	0.86	0	23.8
Borders, Tor	54	40	42.6	2	0.61	6	38.6
Bradley S, Sea	43	17	28.3	0	0.86	5	21.8
Carter G, SF	66	21	24.1	0	1.11	4	20.5
Cerone, NYA	13	16	55.2	1	0.46	7	40.9
Daulton, Phi	78	42	35.0	3	0.63	1	34.5
Dempsey, LA	34	17	33.3	0	0.97	2	30.6
Fisk, ChA	71	42	37.2	1	0.66	7	33.0
Fitzgerald, Mon	103	26	20.2	0	1.19	3	18.3
Gedman, Hou	48	17	26.2	0	1.30	0	26.2
Geren, NYA	55	42	43.3	1	0.66	6	39.6
Girardi, ChN	80	47	37.0	0	0.67	12	30.4
Goff, Mon	34	7	17.1	0	1.07	2	12.8
Harper B, Min	86	50	36.8	0	0.79	18	27.1
Hassey, Oak	20	12	37.5	0	0.37	1	35.5
Heath, Det	84	34	28.8	0	0.85	7	24.3
Karkovice, ChA	18	18	50.0	2	0.34	0	50.0
Kennedy, SF	63	24	27.6	1	0.78	6	22.2
Lavalliere, Pit	68	36	34.6	0	0.81	13	25.3
Macfarlane, KC	68	14	17.1	0	0.67	1	16.0
Melvin, Bal	44	19	30.2	0	0.62	3	26.7
Mercado, Mon	40	6	13.0	0	1.33	2	9.1
Myers G, Tor	40	26	39.4	0	0.57	9	29.8
Nokes, NYA	41	30	42.3	1	0.85	15	26.8
O'Brien C, NYN	40	30	42.9	1	0.61	4	39.4
Oliver, Cin	64	43	40.2	2	0.61	9	34.7
Olson Greg, Atl	75	23	23.5	0	0.94	6	18.5
Ortiz, Min	21	15	41.7	3	0.44	3	36.4
Pagnozzi, StL	40	33	45.2	0	0.69	5	41.2
Parent, SD	52	18	25.7	2	0.99	6	18.8
Parrish Ln, Cal	62	55	47.0	2	0.51	5	44.6
Pena T, Bos	99	46	31.7	1	0.75	5	29.3
Petralli, Tex	58	35	37.6	2	0.63	7	32.6
Quirk, Oak	10	11	52.4	0	0.36	1	50.0
Reed Jf, Cin	67	15	18.3	0	1.23	3	15.2
Salas, Det	36	15	29.4	1	0.84	4	23.4
Santiago, SD	60	31	34.1	4	0.68	6	29.4
Santovenia, Mon	51	11	17.7	0	1.21	1	16.4
Sasser, NYN	91	38	29.5	0	1.40	6	26.0
Scioscia, LA	99	38	27.7	2	0.83	6	24.4
Skinner J, Cle	20	13	39.4	1	0.48	2	35.5
Slaught, Pit	58	26	31.0	1	0.93	4	27.5
Stanley M, Tex	41	12	22.6	0	1.02	5	14.6
Steinbach, Oak	43	20	31.7	0	0.57	4	27.1
Surhoff BJ, Mil	89	31	25.8	1	0.76	5	22.6
Tettleton, Bal	55	21	27.6	0	0.66	5	22.5
Valle, Sea	65	28	30.1	0	0.69	7	24.4
Whitt, Atl	70	31	30.7	1	1.42	6	26.3
Zeile, StL	93	43	31.6	0	0.95	8	27.3
	3290	1510	68.5	42	0.79	292	73.0

WHICH OUTFIELDERS HAVE THE CANNONS? (p. 224)

Both Leagues — Listed by Hold Percentage
(25 or more Baserunner Opportunities)

Player, Team	Opp	XB	Pct	Player, Team	Opp	XB	Pct	Player, Team	Opp	XB	Pct
Right Field				**Center Field**				**Left Field**			
Jose, StL	41	12	29.3	Reynolds RJ, Pit	27	10	37.0	Briley, Sea	44	8	18.2
Canseco, Oak	59	18	30.5	Mack, Min	40	16	40.0	Eisenreich, KC	45	9	20.0
Felix, Tor	59	22	37.3	Felix, Tor	29	13	44.8	Roberts Bip, SD	65	13	20.0
Sosa, ChA	127	49	38.6	Javier, LA	79	36	45.6	Orsulak, Bal	29	6	20.7
Bichette, Cal	31	12	38.7	Davis E, Cin	69	32	46.4	Cotto, Sea	28	6	21.4
Moses, Min	28	11	39.3	Samuel, LA	28	13	46.4	Bichette, Cal	31	7	22.6
Hayes V, Phi	85	34	40.0	Miller K, NYN	32	15	46.9	Bonds, Pit	114	28	24.6
Briley, Sea	50	20	40.0	Anderson B, Bal	25	12	48.0	Hatcher B, Cin	44	11	25.0
Barfield Je, NYA	136	55	40.4	Griffey Jr, Sea	193	94	48.7	Jackson B, KC	48	13	27.1
Walker L, Mon	83	34	41.0	Henderson D, Oak	98	48	49.0	Hamilton, Mil	33	9	27.3
Mack, Min	29	12	41.4	Carter J, SD	126	63	50.0	Stubbs, Hou	36	10	27.8
Brunansky, Bos	139	61	43.9	Martinez Da, Mon	100	50	50.0	Vaughn G, Mil	111	32	28.8
Gwynn T, SD	107	47	43.9	Jackson B, KC	67	34	50.7	Coleman, StL	102	31	30.4
Deer, Mil	100	44	44.0	Puckett, Min	141	73	51.8	Carter J, SD	41	13	31.7
Braggs, Cin	43	19	44.2	Pettis, Tex	108	56	51.9	Gant, Atl	50	16	32.0
Hill G, Tor	37	17	45.9	Wilson M, Tor	134	70	52.2	Kruk, Phi	49	16	32.7
Lemon, Det	76	35	46.1	Jose, StL	42	22	52.4	Bell Geo, Tor	116	38	32.8
Bonilla B, Pit	95	44	46.3	Van Slyke, Pit	118	62	52.5	Smith Lo, Atl	141	47	33.3
Felder, Mil	28	13	46.4	Burks, Bos	182	96	52.7	Hayes V, Phi	42	14	33.3
Snyder C, Cle	103	48	46.6	Mcrae B, KC	64	34	53.1	Raines, Mon	98	33	33.7
Orsulak, Bal	64	30	46.9	Shelby, Det	30	16	53.3	Anderson B, Bal	35	12	34.3
Kingery, SF	44	21	47.7	White D, Cal	142	76	53.5	Daniels, LA	104	36	34.6
O'Neill, Cin	122	59	48.4	Dykstra, Phi	168	90	53.6	McReynolds, NYN	115	40	34.8
Thompson M, StL	93	45	48.4	Wilson W, KC	37	20	54.1	Davis E, Cin	37	13	35.1
Tartabull, KC	51	25	49.0	Webster M, Cle	85	46	54.1	Gladden, Min	135	48	35.6
Buhner, Sea	29	15	51.7	Walton, ChN	129	70	54.3	Maldonado, Cle	117	42	35.9
Strawberry, NYN	101	53	52.5	Grissom, Mon	29	16	55.2	Braggs, Cin	39	14	35.9
Murphy Dl, Phi	151	80	53.0	Young G, Hou	38	21	55.3	Daugherty, Tex	39	14	35.9
Wilson G, Hou	62	33	53.2	McGee, Oak	161	89	55.3	Henderson R, Oak	75	27	36.0
Dawson, ChN	143	77	53.8	Gibson K, LA	65	36	55.4	Hall M, NYA	36	13	36.1
Anthony, Hou	52	28	53.8	Nixon O, Mon	43	24	55.8	Smith Dw, ChN	58	21	36.2
Finley S, Bal	74	41	55.4	Hatcher B, Cin	62	35	56.5	Bradley P, ChA	69	25	36.2
Cotto, Sea	32	18	56.3	Kelly, NYA	145	82	56.6	Mitchell K, SF	154	56	36.4
Justice, Atl	45	26	57.8	Boston, NYN	106	60	56.6	Felder, Mil	38	14	36.8
Sierra, Tex	126	73	57.9	Cole, Cle	56	32	57.1	Calderon, ChA	116	43	37.1
Brooks, LA	110	64	58.2	Butler, SF	189	109	57.7	Leonard J, Sea	59	22	37.3
Larkin G, Min	53	31	58.5	Venable, Cal	26	15	57.7	Clark D, ChN	32	12	37.5
Eisenreich, KC	59	35	59.3	Winningham, Cin	38	22	57.9	Incaviglia, Tex	125	47	37.6
Bass K, SF	55	33	60.0	Devereaux, Bal	81	47	58.0	Jones Tr, Sea	37	14	37.8
Litton, SF	32	20	62.5	Yount, Mil	195	114	58.5	Lynn, SD	34	13	38.2
Maldonado, Cle	36	24	66.7	Abner, SD	29	17	58.6	Polonia, Cal	68	26	38.2
Winfield, Cal	96	66	68.8	Dascenzo, ChN	46	27	58.7	Ward G, Det	60	23	38.3
Tabler, NYN	36	25	69.4	Lankford, StL	34	20	58.8	Dascenzo, ChN	31	12	38.7
			49.2	Romine, Bos	27	16	59.3	Greenwell, Bos	150	59	39.3
				Finley S, Bal	55	33	60.0	Sheets, Det	48	19	39.6
				Johnson L, ChA	126	78	61.9	Azocar, NYA	37	15	40.5
				Gant, Atl	147	91	61.9	Griffey, Sea	32	13	40.6
				Biggio, Hou	37	23	62.2	Wilson W, KC	41	17	41.5
				Yelding, Hou	98	61	62.2	Davis C, Cal	36	17	47.2
				Jackson Dar, SD	26	17	65.4				**32.6**
				Wynne, ChN	44	29	65.9				
				McDowell O, Atl	91	60	65.9				
				Moseby, Det	99	67	67.7				
							55.1				

WHICH CATCHERS HELP A PITCHER'S ERA? (p. 226)

1990 Catchers with 250 Innings Caught

Catcher	Innings	Own ERA	Others ERA	Diff
Alomar S, Cle	1052.1	4.34	4.06	+ 0.28
Biggio, Hou	904.2	3.62	3.61	+ 0.01
Boone, KC	335.0	3.57	4.05	- 0.48
Borders, Tor	799.2	3.97	3.67	+ 0.30
Bradley S, Sea	448.1	3.69	3.74	- 0.05
Carter G, SF	534.2	3.64	4.33	- 0.69
Cerone, NYA	256.2	4.24	4.23	+ 0.01
Daulton, Phi	1115.0	4.20	3.75	+ 0.45
Dempsey, LA	314.2	4.23	3.60	+ 0.63
Fisk, ChA	970.0	3.70	3.44	+ 0.26
Fitzgerald, Mon	778.2	3.38	3.36	+ 0.02
Gedman, Hou	332.0	3.61	3.69	- 0.08
Geren, NYA	750.2	3.92	4.56	- 0.64
Girardi, ChN	1070.1	4.19	4.76	- 0.57
Goff, Mon	286.1	3.77	3.27	+ 0.50
Harper B, Min	985.2	4.46	3.42	+ 1.04
Hassey, Oak	489.2	2.89	3.32	- 0.43
Heath, Det	890.1	4.44	4.30	+ 0.14
Karkovice, ChA	478.1	3.44	3.70	- 0.26
Kennedy, SF	727.1	4.21	3.94	+ 0.27
Lavalliere, Pit	751.0	3.49	3.30	+ 0.19
Macfarlane, KC	910.2	3.81	4.15	- 0.34
Melvin, Bal	633.2	3.89	4.21	- 0.32
Mercado, Mon	271.2	3.08	3.39	- 0.31
Myers G, Tor	635.0	3.71	3.93	- 0.22
Nokes, NYA	434.1	4.79	4.36	+ 0.43
O'Brien C, NYN	592.2	3.71	4.14	- 0.43
Oliver, Cin	943.0	3.53	3.14	+ 0.39
Olson Greg, Atl	718.1	4.40	4.77	- 0.37
Ortiz, Min	432.0	3.50	4.41	- 0.91
Pagnozzi, StL	520.0	4.03	3.79	+ 0.24
Parent, SD	473.2	3.53	3.75	- 0.22
Parrish Ln, Cal	1098.0	3.47	4.88	- 1.41
Pena T, Bos	1186.0	3.65	4.04	- 0.39
Petralli, Tex	827.2	3.77	3.91	- 0.14
Quirk, Oak	252.0	3.75	3.06	+ 0.69
Reed Jf, Cin	490.1	3.21	3.48	- 0.27
Salas, Det	384.0	4.57	4.32	+ 0.25
Santiago, SD	799.2	3.65	3.73	- 0.08
Santovenia, Mon	378.2	3.11	3.45	- 0.34
Sasser, NYN	583.1	3.66	3.27	+ 0.39
Scioscia, LA	1069.0	3.63	4.05	- 0.42
Skinner J, Cle	375.0	4.06	4.34	- 0.28
Slaught, Pit	562.2	3.57	3.29	+ 0.28
Stanley M, Tex	360.2	4.09	3.74	+ 0.35
Steinbach, Oak	681.1	3.29	3.08	+ 0.21
Surhoff BJ, Mil	1048.1	4.17	3.95	+ 0.22
Tettleton, Bal	753.2	4.29	3.83	+ 0.46
Valle, Sea	843.0	3.85	3.54	+ 0.31
Whitt, Atl	444.1	5.04	4.38	+ 0.66
Zeile, StL	884.1	3.79	4.03	- 0.24

WHEN IS AN ERROR NOT AN ERROR? (p. 228)

Players with 6 or more errors

Player, Team	Err	Runs	Player, Team	Err	Runs	Player, Team	Err	Runs
Alomar Jr, Cle	14	4	Gregg, Atl	6	4	Reed J, Bos	16	11
Alomar R, SD	19	7	Griffey Jr, Sea	7	2	Reynolds H, Sea	19	14
Anderson K, Cal	9	14	Griffin, LA	26	24	Ripken B, Bal	8	5
Backman, Pit	12	13	Gruber, Tor	19	7	Rivera, Bos	18	14
Baerga, Cle	17	8	Guerrero, StL	13	7	Roberts B, SD	13	11
Barfield, NYA	9	4	Guillen, ChA	17	11	Sabo, Cin	12	6
Bell J, Pit	22	17	Harper, Min	11	2	Salazar, ChN	12	11
Benzinger, Cin	6	5	Harris, LA	11	11	Samuel, LA	16	11
Bichette, Cal	7	3	Hayes C, Phi	20	18	Sandberg, ChN	8	4
Biggio, Hou	13	8	Hayes V, Phi	6	2	Santiago, SD	12	1
Blauser, Atl	16	19	Heath, Det	13	5	Santovenia, Mon	6	1
Blowers, NYA	10	15	Herr, NYN	7	8	Sasser, NYN	14	7
Boggs, Bos	20	13	Hill, Cal	11	9	Sax S, NYA	10	6
Bonds, Pit	6	1	Howell J, Cal	18	11	Schofield, Cal	17	7
Bonilla, Pit	15	5	Huson, Tex	19	10	Schu, Cal	11	7
Braggs, Cin	7	7	Incaviglia, Tex	8	5	Scioscia, LA	10	2
Bream, Pit	8	7	Jackson, KC	12	10	Seitzer, KC	19	16
Brett, KC	7	3	Jacoby, Cle	6	1	Sharperson, LA	15	7
Brookens, Cle	6	2	Jefferies, NYN	16	6	Sheffield, Mil	25	19
Brooks, LA	10	6	Johnson H, NYN	28	16	Sierra, Tex	10	10
Browne, Cle	10	10	Johnson L, ChA	10	5	Slaught, NYA	8	7
Brunansky, Bos	7	6	Jones T, StL	7	0	Smith L, Atl	12	4
Buechele, Tex	8	3	Justice, Atl	14	6	Smith O, StL	12	8
Butler, SF	6	2	King, Pit	18	15	Snyder, Cle	7	5
Calderon, ChA	7	3	Kunkel, Tex	11	4	Sosa, ChA	13	7
Caminiti, Hou	21	9	Lansford, Oak	9	6	Spiers, Mil	12	10
Carter, SD	11	7	Larkin B, Cin	17	8	Stillwell, KC	24	30
Clark Ja, SD	6	2	Lemon, Det	6	4	Stubbs, Hou	6	2
Clark W, SF	12	4	Leyritz, NYA	13	12	Surhoff, Mil	12	6
Cole, Cle	6	1	Lind, Pit	7	5	Sveum, Mil	6	2
Coles, Sea	9	11	Liriano, Tor	11	8	Templeton, SD	26	19
Coolbaugh, Tex	10	6	Maas, NYA	9	9	Thomas, Atl	10	4
Cora, SD	11	11	Macfarlane, KC	6	5	Thompson, StL	7	4
Daulton, Phi	8	2	Manrique, Min	7	8	Thompson R, SF	8	6
Deer, Mil	10	4	Martinez, ChA	8	3	Thon, Phi	25	15
Deshields, Mon	12	12	Martinez, Sea	27	19	Trammell, Det	14	11
Diaz E, Sea	17	16	McGee, Oak	17	15	Treadway, Atl	15	14
Doran, Cin	8	8	McGriff, Tor	6	2	Uribe, SF	20	13
Duncan, Cin	18	9	Milligan, Bal	9	8	Van Slyke, Pit	8	2
Dunston, ChN	20	18	Mitchell, SF	9	6	Vaughn, Mil	7	5
Dykstra, Phi	6	3	Molitor, Mil	10	14	Velarde, NYA	12	2
Elster, NYN	17	6	Murray, LA	10	4	Ventura, ChA	25	16
Espinoza, NYA	17	9	Naehring, Bos	9	9	Vizquel, Sea	7	7
Felix, Tor	9	6	Newman, Min	13	4	Wallach, Mon	21	13
Fermin, Cle	16	11	Oliver, Cin	6	2	Walton, ChN	6	1
Fernandez, Tor	9	6	Olson, Atl	7	3	Weiss, Oak	12	5
Fielder, Det	14	9	Owen, Mon	6	4	Whitaker, Det	6	2
Finley S, Bal	7	2	Pagliarulo, SD	13	9	White, Cal	9	7
Fitzgerald, Mon	6	3	Palmeiro, Tex	7	9	White, KC	8	9
Fletcher, ChA	9	2	Parrish, Cal	6	3	Wilkerson, ChN	14	15
Franco Ju, Tex	19	18	Pendleton, StL	19	18	Williams M, SF	19	12
Fryman, Det	14	7	Perry, KC	6	2	Wilson G, Hou	6	2
Gaetti, Min	18	14	Petralli, Tex	6	2	Worthington, Bal	18	10
Gagne, Min	14	20	Phillips, Oak	23	12	Yelding, Hou	17	8
Galarraga, Mon	10	4	Presley, Atl	26	30	Young Mt, Sea	9	7
Gallego, Oak	13	12	Quinones, Cin	6	2	Zeile, StL	15	7
Gant, Atl	8	5	Quintana, Bos	17	19			
Gantner, Mil	9	7	Raines, Mon	6	0			
Girardi, ChN	11	3	Ramirez, Hou	25	20			
Gladden, Min	6	6	Ramos, ChN	10	5			
Goff, Mon	9	3	Randolph, Oak	11	11			
Grace, ChN	12	6	Ray, Cal	7	2			
Greenwell, Bos	7	1	Redus, Pit	8	9			

WHO BOOTS 'EM, AND WHO TOSSES 'EM AWAY? (p. 230)

Throwing Errors (T) and Fielding Errors (F) — 1990 (5+ Errors in '90)

Fielder	T	F	Fielder	T	F	Fielder	T	F	Fielder	T	F
Alomar R, SD	5	14	Fielder, Det	4	10	Leyritz, NYA	6	7	Santiago, SD	10	2
Alomar S, Cle	11	3	Finley C, Cal	5	0	Lind, Pit	3	4	Santovenia, Mon	6	0
Anderson K, Cal	3	6	Finley S, Bal	0	7	Liriano, Min	4	7	Sasser, NYN	12	2
Backman, Pit	4	8	Fitzgerald, Mon	4	2	Lyons S, ChA	1	4	Sax S, NYA	3	7
Baerga, Cle	4	13	Fletcher S, ChA	6	3	Maas, NYA	3	6	Schaefer, Sea	2	3
Barfield Je, NYA	1	8	Foley T, Mon	2	3	Macfarlane, KC	3	3	Schofield, Cal	6	11
Bell Geo, Tor	1	4	Franco Ju, Tex	6	13	Manrique, Min	3	4	Schu, Cal	2	9
Bell Jay, Pit	7	15	Fryman T, Det	4	10	Martinez Crl, ChA	1	7	Scioscia, LA	8	2
Benzinger, Cin	0	6	Gaetti, Min	6	12	Martinez E, Sea	6	21	Seitzer, KC	6	13
Bichette, Cal	0	7	Gagne, Min	5	9	McDowell R, Phi	3	2	Sharperson, LA	4	11
Biggio, Hou	9	4	Galarraga, Mon	3	7	McGee, Oak	5	12	Sheffield, Mil	9	16
Blankenship L, Oak	2	3	Gallego, Oak	0	13	McGriff F, Tor	2	4	Sierra, Tex	0	10
			Gant, Atl	2	6	McGwire, Oak	2	3	Slaught, Pit	6	2
Blauser, Atl	8	8	Gantner, Mil	2	7	Milligan, Bal	2	7	Smith Lo, Atl	0	12
Blowers, NYA	1	9	Girardi, ChN	8	3	Mitchell K, SF	1	8	Smith O, StL	7	5
Boggs W, Bos	7	13	Gladden, Min	1	5	Molitor, Mil	2	8	Snyder C, Cle	2	5
Bonds, Pit	1	5	Goff, Mon	6	3	Moseby, Det	1	4	Sojo, Tor	2	3
Bonilla B, Pit	6	9	Grace, ChN	5	7	Murphy Dl, Phi	3	2	Sosa, ChA	2	11
Braggs, Cin	0	7	Green G, Tex	0	7	Murray E, LA	4	6	Spiers, Mil	3	9
Bream, Pit	4	4	Greenwell, Bos	3	4	Naehring, Bos	2	7	Steinbach, Oak	5	0
Brett, KC	1	6	Gregg, Atl	4	2	Newman A, Min	8	5	Stillwell, KC	6	18
Brock, Mil	1	4	Griffey Jr, Sea	1	6	O'Brien C, NYN	4	1	Stubbs, Hou	1	5
Brookens, Cle	1	5	Griffin Alf, LA	7	19	O'Brien P, Sea	0	5	Surhoff BJ, Mil	10	2
Brooks, LA	3	7	Gruber, Tor	10	9	Oliver, Cin	4	2	Sveum, Mil	1	5
Browne J, Cle	3	7	Guerrero, StL	3	10	Olson Greg, Atl	5	2	Templeton, SD	8	18
Brumley, Sea	0	5	Guillen, ChA	5	12	Owen S, Mon	3	3	Tettleton, Bal	4	1
Brunansky, Bos	1	6	Gwynn T, SD	0	5	Pagliarulo, SD	2	11	Thomas A, Atl	2	8
Buechele, Tex	3	5	Harper B, Min	8	3	Palmeiro, Tex	1	6	Thomas F, ChA	1	4
Butler, SF	3	3	Harris L, LA	5	6	Parrish Ln, Cal	4	2	Thompson M, StL	0	7
Calderon, ChA	1	6	Hayes C, Phi	9	11	Pecota, KC	0	5	Thompson Ro, SF	1	7
Caminiti, Hou	9	12	Hayes V, Phi	1	5	Pena T, Bos	3	2	Thon, Phi	8	17
Carter J, SD	2	9	Heath, Det	11	2	Pendleton, StL	9	10	Trammell, Det	5	9
Clark Jk, SD	3	3	Henderson R, Oak	1	4	Perry G, KC	0	6	Treadway, Atl	5	10
Clark W, SF	2	10				Petralli, Tex	3	3	Uribe, SF	5	15
Cole, Cle	1	5	Herr, NYN	0	7	Phillips, Det	8	15	Van Slyke, Pit	1	7
Coleman, StL	1	4	Hill D, Cal	2	9	Presley, Atl	7	19	Vaughn G, Mil	1	6
Coles, Det	5	4	Howell Jk, Cal	1	17	Quinones L, Cin	1	5	Velarde, NYA	5	7
Coolbaugh, Tex	4	6	Hudler, StL	3	2	Quintana, Bos	2	15	Ventura, ChA	14	11
Cora, SD	2	9	Huson, Tex	8	10	Quirk, Oak	2	3	Vizquel, Sea	3	4
Daulton, Phi	5	3	Incaviglia, Tex	1	7	Raines, Mon	2	4	Wallach, Mon	10	11
Dawson, ChN	2	3	Jackson B, KC	0	12	Ramirez R, Hou	7	18	Walton, ChN	0	6
Deer, Mil	2	8	Jacoby, Cle	2	4	Ramos D, ChN	3	7	Webster M, Cle	0	5
Deshields, Mon	2	10	Jefferies, NYN	5	11	Randolph, Oak	4	7	Weiss, Oak	6	6
Devereaux, Bal	1	4	Johnson H, NYN	16	12	Ray, Cal	2	5	Whitaker, Det	1	5
Diaz E, Mil	6	11	Johnson L, ChA	1	9	Redus, Pit	2	6	White D, Cal	3	6
Doran, Cin	2	6	Johnson R, Sea	5	0	Reed Jd, Bos	6	10	White F, KC	2	6
Duncan, Cin	6	12	Jones Tim, StL	4	3	Reed Jf, Cin	3	2	Wilkerson, ChN	3	11
Dunston, ChN	9	11	Jose, StL	0	5	Reynolds H, Sea	8	11	Williams MD, SF	6	13
Dykstra, Phi	0	6	Justice, Atl	4	10	Ripken B, Bal	3	5	Wilson G, Hou	1	5
Elster, NYN	9	8	Kelly, NYA	2	3	Rivera L, Bos	8	10	Witt B, Tex	4	1
Esasky, Atl	1	4	King J, Pit	8	10	Roberts Bip, SD	6	7	Worthington, Bal	10	8
Espinoza, NYA	4	13	Kunkel, Tex	4	7	Sabo, Cin	4	8	Yelding, Hou	7	10
Felder, Mil	1	4	Lansford, Oak	6	3	Salazar L, ChN	2	10	Young Mt, Sea	8	1
Felix, Tor	3	6	Larkin B, Cin	10	7	Samuel, LA	6	10	Zeile, StL	7	8
Fermin, Cle	2	14	Lavalliere, Pit	4	1	Sandberg, ChN	3	5			
Fernandez T, Tor	6	3	Lemon, Det	1	5						

WHO LED THE LEAGUE IN FUMBLES? (p. 232)

Both Leagues — Listed by Most Games per Error (G/E) — 1990
(750 or more defensive innings)

Name	Inn	E	G/E
Catchers			
Valle, Sea	843.0	2	46.8
Fisk, ChA	970.0	4	26.9
Pena T, Bos	1186.0	5	26.4
Borders, Tor	799.2	4	22.2
Tettleton, Bal	753.2	4	20.9
Geren, NYA	750.2	4	20.9
Parrish Ln, Cal	1098.0	6	20.3
Oliver, Cin	943.0	6	17.5
Macfarlane, KC	910.2	6	16.9
Lavalliere, Pit	751.0	5	16.7
Daulton, Phi	1115.0	8	15.5
Petralli, Tex	827.2	6	15.3
Fitzgerald, Mon	778.2	6	14.4
Zeile, StL	884.1	7	14.0
Scioscia, LA	1069.0	10	11.9
Surhoff BJ, Mil	1048.1	10	11.6
Biggio, Hou	904.2	9	11.2
Girardi, ChN	1070.1	11	10.8
Harper B, Min	985.2	11	10.0
Alomar S, Cle	1052.1	14	8.4
Heath, Det	890.1	13	7.6
Santiago, SD	799.2	12	7.4
First Basemen			
Magadan, NYN	900.1	2	50.0
Hrbek, Min	1021.0	3	37.8
McGwire, Oak	1334.2	5	29.7
Mattingly, NYA	778.1	3	28.8
McGriff F, Tor	1299.0	6	24.1
Davis G, Hou	774.1	4	21.5
Brock, Mil	899.2	5	20.0
Palmeiro, Tex	1255.2	7	19.9
O'Brien P, Sea	800.0	5	17.8
Clark Jk, SD	888.2	6	16.5
Galarraga, Mon	1318.1	10	14.6
Murray E, LA	1286.0	10	14.3
Brett, KC	877.0	7	13.9
Bream, Pit	975.2	8	13.6
Clark W, SF	1338.1	12	12.4
Grace, ChN	1315.1	12	12.2
Milligan, Bal	846.2	9	10.5
Fielder, Det	1225.1	14	9.7
Guerrero, StL	1083.1	13	9.3
Quintana, Bos	1201.1	17	7.9
Second Basemen			
Oquendo, StL	1202.2	3	44.5
Lee M, Tor	956.2	4	26.6
Lind, Pit	1275.1	7	20.2
Whitaker, Det	1037.1	6	19.2
Herr, NYN	1170.0	7	18.6
Sandberg, ChN	1315.0	8	18.3
Reed Jd, Bos	984.2	6	18.2
Doran, Cin	932.0	6	17.3
Fletcher S, ChA	1321.1	9	16.3
Thompson Ro, SF	1167.0	8	16.2
Sax S, NYA	1355.2	10	15.1
Ripken B, Bal	1047.0	8	14.5
Ray, Cal	854.1	7	13.6
Browne J, Cle	1180.0	10	13.1

Name	Inn	E	G/E
Deshields, Mon	1115.0	12	10.3
Randolph, Oak	920.0	11	9.3
Jefferies, NYN	996.1	12	9.2
Liriano, Min	830.0	11	8.4
Reynolds H, Sea	1406.1	19	8.2
Alomar R, SD	1226.1	17	8.0
Franco Ju, Tex	1308.2	19	7.7
Samuel, LA	881.2	13	7.5
Treadway, Atl	989.1	15	7.3
Duncan, Cin	924.2	15	6.8
Third Basemen			
Jacoby, Cle	772.2	4	21.5
Lansford, Oak	1032.0	9	12.7
Sabo, Cin	1269.0	12	11.7
Pagliarulo, SD	950.0	13	8.1
Williams MD, SF	1372.2	19	8.0
Gaetti, Min	1291.0	18	8.0
Seitzer, KC	1257.2	18	7.8
Wallach, Mon	1425.2	21	7.5
Boggs W, Bos	1340.2	20	7.4
Gruber, Tor	1267.2	19	7.4
Hayes C, Phi	1236.2	20	6.9
Worthington, Bal	1074.1	18	6.6
Caminiti, Hou	1249.1	21	6.6
Pendleton, StL	1010.0	19	5.9
Ventura, ChA	1210.0	25	5.4
Howell Jk, Cal	817.0	17	5.3
King J, Pit	840.2	18	5.2
Martinez E, Sea	1196.1	27	4.9
Presley, Atl	1095.0	25	4.9
Sheffield, Mil	1069.0	25	4.8
Phillips, Det	793.1	20	4.4
Johnson H, NYN	771.2	20	4.3
Shortstops			
Ripken C, Bal	1404.1	3	52.0
Owen S, Mon	1194.1	6	22.1
Fernandez T, Tor	1384.0	9	17.1
Smith O, StL	1203.1	12	11.1
Weiss, Oak	1154.0	12	10.7
Trammell, Det	1213.1	14	9.6
Guillen, ChA	1361.1	17	8.9
Larkin B, Cin	1344.0	17	8.8
Spiers, Mil	929.2	12	8.6
Gagne, Min	1074.0	14	8.5
Fermin, Cle	1180.0	16	8.2
Espinoza, NYA	1209.1	17	7.9
Bell Jay, Pit	1377.0	22	7.0
Dunston, ChN	1247.2	20	6.9
Uribe, SF	1036.1	20	5.8
Rivera L, Bos	928.2	18	5.7
Schofield, Cal	865.1	17	5.7
Thon, Phi	1262.0	25	5.6
Blauser, Atl	778.2	16	5.4
Stillwell, KC	1138.2	24	5.3
Elster, NYN	795.2	17	5.2
Huson, Tex	795.1	17	5.2
Templeton, SD	1165.2	26	5.0
Griffin Alf, LA	1153.2	26	4.9
Ramirez R, Hou	1058.0	25	4.7

Name	Inn	E	G/E
Left Fielders			
Maldonado, Cle	837.1	1	93.0
McReynolds, NYN	1238.0	3	45.9
Daniels, LA	985.0	3	36.5
Bonds, Pit	1275.0	6	23.6
Coleman, StL	1008.0	5	22.4
Henderson R, Oak	993.1	5	22.1
Greenwell, Bos	1381.0	7	21.9
Bell Geo, Tor	922.0	5	20.5
Gladden, Min	1100.0	6	20.4
Raines, Mon	1059.2	6	19.6
Calderon, ChA	1113.0	7	17.7
Incaviglia, Tex	1080.1	7	17.1
Mitchell K, SF	1180.0	9	14.6
Vaughn G, Mil	834.1	7	13.2
Smith Lo, Atl	992.2	12	9.2
Center Fielders			
Burks, Bos	1267.1	2	70.4
Pettis, Tex	1032.0	2	57.3
Wilson M, Tor	1171.0	3	43.4
Webster M, Cle	773.0	2	42.9
Puckett, Min	1042.1	3	38.6
Yount, Mil	1362.2	4	37.9
Kelly, NYA	1294.1	4	36.0
Carter J, SD	950.0	3	35.2
Boston, NYN	796.1	3	29.5
Martinez Da, Mon	788.2	3	29.2
Henderson D, Oak	943.1	4	26.2
Butler, SF	1391.1	6	25.8
Dykstra, Phi	1287.2	6	23.8
Griffey Jr, Sea	1332.2	7	21.2
Gant, Atl	950.0	5	21.1
Moseby, Det	862.2	5	19.2
Devereaux, Bal	845.1	5	18.8
Van Slyke, Pit	1134.2	8	15.8
Walton, ChN	850.0	6	15.7
Johnson L, ChA	1169.2	10	13.0
White D, Cal	1013.2	9	12.5
McGee, Oak	1268.0	17	8.3
Right Fielders			
O'Neill, Cin	1165.1	2	64.7
Winfield, Cal	921.2	2	51.2
Strawberry, NYN	1263.0	3	46.8
Murphy Dl, Phi	1289.1	5	28.7
Gwynn T, SD	1265.2	5	28.1
Walker L, Mon	1003.1	4	27.9
Dawson, ChN	1164.1	5	25.9
Brunansky, Bos	1180.0	7	18.7
Snyder C, Cle	984.1	6	18.2
Thompson M, StL	772.2	5	17.2
Barfield Je, NYA	1193.1	8	16.6
Sierra, Tex	1308.2	10	14.5
Lemon, Det	765.0	6	14.2
Brooks, LA	1252.0	10	13.9
Deer, Mil	912.2	8	12.7
Bonilla B, Pit	1300.0	12	12.0
Sosa, ChA	1253.0	13	10.7
Felix, Tor	860.1	9	10.6

WHO ARE THE PRIME PIVOT MEN? (p. 234)

All Major League Second Basemen, 1990 — Listed Alphabetically

Player, Team	DP Opp	DP	Pct.	Player, Team	DP Opp	DP	Pct.
Alomar R, SD	73	41	.562	Manrique, Min	35	28	.800
Anderson K, Cal	4	2	.500	McKnight, Bal	2	1	.500
Backman, Pit	6	3	.500	McLemore, Cle	6	4	.667
Baerga, Cle	5	5	1.000	Miller K, NYN	3	1	.333
Barrett M, Bos	19	12	.632	Molitor, Mil	41	19	.463
Bates, Cin	6	3	.500	Morandini, Phi	8	5	.625
Belliard, Pit	6	3	.500	Newman A, Min	40	27	.675
Blankenship L, Oak	5	4	.800	Noboa, Mon	8	6	.750
Blauser, Atl	6	3	.500	Oberkfell, Hou	4	2	.500
Booker R, Phi	2	1	.500	Oester, Cin	15	4	.267
Bordick, Oak	1	0	0.000	Oquendo, StL	72	38	.528
Brookens, Cle	14	8	.571	Paredes, Mon	3	2	.667
Browne J, Cle	80	36	.450	Pecota, KC	21	12	.571
Brumley, Sea	3	3	1.000	Pena G, StL	5	4	.800
Candaele, Hou	18	11	.611	Petralli, Tex	2	2	1.000
Cerone, NYA	1	0	0.000	Phillips, Det	38	27	.711
Cora, SD	12	9	.750	Quinones L, Cin	10	5	.500
Deshields, Mon	56	31	.554	Randolph, Oak	60	41	.683
Diaz E, Mil	12	7	.583	Ray, Cal	77	41	.532
Disarcina, Cal	2	1	.500	Ready, Phi	12	6	.500
Doran, Cin	48	23	.479	Reed Jd, Bos	59	38	.644
Duncan, Cin	62	32	.516	Reynolds H, Sea	100	56	.560
Faries, SD	3	1	.333	Riles, SF	8	2	.250
Fletcher S, ChA	98	69	.704	Ripken B, Bal	78	52	.667
Foley T, Mon	6	2	.333	Roberts Bip, SD	5	4	.800
Franco Ju, Tex	88	50	.568	Rohde, Hou	7	5	.714
Gallego, Oak	41	27	.659	Samuel, LA	59	21	.356
Gantner, Mil	54	33	.611	Sandberg, ChN	64	39	.609
Giles, Sea	3	2	.667	Sax S, NYA	84	52	.619
Gonzales R, Bal	17	11	.647	Schaefer, Sea	1	1	1.000
Grebeck, ChA	3	1	.333	Seitzer, KC	7	3	.429
Green G, Tex	2	1	.500	Sharperson, LA	2	1	.500
Hale, Min	2	2	1.000	Shumpert, KC	16	10	.625
Harris L, LA	13	6	.462	Smith G, ChN	2	2	1.000
Herr, NYN	79	57	.722	Sojo, Tor	3	2	.667
Hill D, Cal	42	27	.643	Sveum, Mil	9	6	.667
Hudler, StL	4	3	.750	Teufel, NYN	7	4	.571
Hulett, Bal	10	6	.600	Thompson Ro, SF	73	46	.630
Huson, Tex	2	2	1.000	Tolleson, NYA	3	3	1.000
Infante, Atl	4	1	.250	Treadway, Atl	71	37	.521
Jefferies, NYN	53	20	.377	Vizcaino, LA	1	1	1.000
Jeltz, KC	7	5	.714	Whitaker, Det	96	57	.594
Jones Tim, StL	1	0	0.000	White F, KC	45	33	.733
Kunkel, Tex	1	1	1.000	Wilkerson, ChN	4	2	.500
Kutcher, Bos	2	1	.500	Wilson C, StL	1	1	1.000
Lawless, Tor	1	0	0.000	Yelding, Hou	2	1	.500
Lee M, Tor	62	28	.452		2481	1446	.583
Lemke, Atl	19	10	.526				
Lind, Pit	83	46	.554				
Liriano, Min	56	33	.589				
Litton, SF	6	6	1.000				
Lyons S, ChA	9	3	.333				

WHICH SHORTSTOPS ARE BEST AT GOING INTO THE HOLE? (p. 236)

All 1990 Shortstops — Listed Alphabetically

Shortstop	Balls In Hole	Outs Made	Percent	Shortstop	Balls In Hole	Outs Made	Percent
Alomar R, SD	3	1	0.333	Miller K, NYN	1	0	0.000
Anderson D, SF	36	21	0.583	Naehring, Bos	20	10	0.500
Anderson K, Cal	27	14	0.519	Newman A, Min	47	25	0.532
Baerga, Cle	45	25	0.556	Nixon O, Mon	2	2	1.000
Baez, NYN	7	5	0.714	Noboa, Mon	5	3	0.600
Bell Jay, Pit	167	88	0.527	Offerman, LA	28	13	0.464
Bell Ju, Bal	2	0	0.000	Oquendo, StL	5	3	0.600
Belliard, Pit	7	6	0.857	Owen S, Mon	131	62	0.473
Benjamin, SF	16	8	0.500	Parker R, SF	2	0	0.000
Blauser, Atl	117	33	0.282	Pecota, KC	12	8	0.667
Booker R, Phi	22	11	0.500	Perezchica, SF	2	1	0.500
Bordick, Oak	5	3	0.600	Phillips, Det	13	10	0.769
Brookens, Cle	4	2	0.500	Polidor, Mil	2	2	1.000
Brumley, Sea	45	25	0.556	Puckett, Min	2	1	0.500
Candaele, Hou	12	5	0.417	Quinones L, Cin	12	4	0.333
Cedeno A, Hou	1	1	1.000	Ramirez R, Hou	104	53	0.510
Cochrane, Sea	1	0	0.000	Ramos D, ChN	13	8	0.615
Cora, SD	14	2	0.143	Reed Jd, Bos	46	27	0.587
Diaz E, Mil	71	33	0.465	Riles, SF	20	10	0.500
Diaz Mar, NYN	10	7	0.700	Ripken C, Bal	140	84	0.600
Disarcina, Cal	18	10	0.556	Rivera L, Bos	109	58	0.532
Duncan, Cin	6	3	0.500	Roberts Bip, SD	12	7	0.583
Dunston, ChN	103	57	0.553	Rohde, Hou	2	1	0.500
Elster, NYN	97	57	0.588	Rosario, Atl	4	2	0.500
Espinoza, NYA	130	77	0.592	Santana, Cle	8	2	0.250
Faries, SD	4	0	0.000	Santana A, SF	4	1	0.250
Fermin, Cle	182	98	0.538	Schaefer, Sea	29	13	0.448
Fernandez T, Tor	162	94	0.580	Schofield, Cal	120	75	0.625
Foley T, Mon	42	23	0.548	Sharperson, LA	23	14	0.609
Fryman T, Det	20	14	0.700	Smith G, ChN	1	1	1.000
Gaetti, Min	1	1	1.000	Smith O, StL	140	66	0.471
Gagne, Min	149	96	0.644	Snyder C, Cle	6	2	0.333
Gallego, Oak	30	20	0.667	Sojo, Tor	1	0	0.000
Garcia C, Pit	4	2	0.500	Spiers, Mil	131	70	0.534
Giles, Sea	39	24	0.615	Stillwell, KC	137	87	0.635
Gonzales R, Bal	11	5	0.455	Sveum, Mil	7	4	0.571
Grebeck, ChA	21	16	0.762	Templeton, SD	131	53	0.405
Green G, Tex	66	39	0.591	Thomas A, Atl	60	27	0.450
Griffin Alf, LA	155	88	0.568	Thon, Phi	137	58	0.423
Guillen, ChA	155	101	0.652	Tolleson, NYA	40	25	0.625
Harris L, LA	0	0	0.000	Trammell, Det	148	87	0.588
Heath, Det	0	0	0.000	Uribe, SF	147	90	0.612
Hill D, Cal	32	17	0.531	Velarde, NYA	16	9	0.563
Howell Jk, Cal	3	1	0.333	Vizcaino, LA	16	12	0.750
Hudler, StL	1	1	1.000	Vizquel, Sea	77	43	0.558
Huson, Tex	110	65	0.591	Walewander, NYA	1	0	0.000
Infante, Atl	2	0	0.000	Weiss, Oak	130	77	0.592
Jeltz, KC	20	12	0.600	Wilkerson, ChN	1	0	0.000
Johnson H, NYN	78	46	0.590	Yelding, Hou	41	25	0.610
Jones Tim, StL	32	12	0.375				
Kunkel, Tex	62	33	0.532		**4847**	**2647**	**.546**
Larkin B, Cin	147	70	0.476				
Lee M, Tor	14	12	0.857				
Leius, Min	16	10	0.625				
Lemke, Atl	3	0	0.000				
Liriano, Min	2	1	0.500				
Litton, SF	15	8	0.533				
Lyons S, ChA	1	1	1.000				
McKnight, Bal	1	1	1.000				
McLemore, Cle	15	7	0.467				

WHO'S BEST IN THE OUTFIELD ZONE (p. 239)

Range Factors and Zone Ratings, 1990 — Outfielders
(600 or more defensive innings)

LEFT FIELD

Player, Team	Innings	PO	A	E	Range Factor	In Zone	Balls Handled	Zone Rating
Henderson R, Oak	993.1	291	5	5	2.73	314	281	.895
Roberts Bip, SD	610.2	161	8	3	2.53	185	157	.849
Bradley P, ChA	728.1	185	4	3	2.37	226	191	.845
Raines, Mon	1059.2	239	3	6	2.11	261	219	.839
Gladden, Min	1100.0	284	12	6	2.47	338	279	.825
Coleman, StL	1008.0	240	10	5	2.28	265	218	.823
Maldonado, Cle	837.1	202	8	1	2.27	240	197	.821
Incaviglia, Tex	1080.1	252	11	7	2.25	295	242	.820
Daniels, LA	985.0	207	13	3	2.04	258	211	.818
Bonds, Pit	1275.0	333	14	6	2.49	400	326	.815
Vaughn G, Mil	834.1	196	8	7	2.28	237	192	.810
Bell Geo, Tor	922.0	224	4	5	2.27	270	218	.807
Mitchell K, SF	1180.0	293	9	9	2.37	358	284	.793
Leonard J, Sea	600.0	107	0	1	1.62	139	109	.784
Smith Lo, Atl	992.2	252	6	12	2.45	323	250	.774
Calderon, ChA	1113.0	267	7	7	2.27	348	268	.770
Greenwell, Bos	1381.0	287	12	7	1.99	382	289	.757
McReynolds, NYN	1238.0	237	14	3	1.85	322	237	.736
					2.19			.804

CENTER FIELD

Player, Team	Innings	PO	A	E	Range Factor	In Zone	Balls Handled	Zone Rating
Webster M, Cle	773.0	287	1	2	3.38	367	326	.888
Devereaux, Bal	845.1	279	4	5	3.07	358	311	.869
Wilson M, Tor	1171.0	352	5	3	2.77	455	394	.866
Johnson L, ChA	1169.2	351	5	10	2.82	473	409	.865
Henderson D, Oak	943.1	310	4	4	3.03	407	347	.853
White D, Cal	1013.2	302	11	9	2.86	389	331	.851
Pettis, Tex	1032.0	287	9	2	2.60	367	312	.850
Dykstra, Phi	1287.2	439	8	6	3.17	550	464	.844
Yelding, Hou	662.0	215	5	7	3.09	285	240	.842
Puckett, Min	1042.1	319	6	3	2.83	413	347	.840
Griffey Jr, Sea	1332.2	331	9	7	2.34	474	397	.838
Boston, NYN	796.1	199	3	3	2.32	261	218	.835
Kelly, NYA	1294.1	400	4	4	2.84	535	446	.834
McGee, Oak	1268.0	400	13	17	3.05	529	440	.832
Butler, SF	1391.1	418	4	6	2.77	547	454	.830
Van Slyke, Pit	1134.2	325	7	8	2.70	431	357	.828
Carter J, SD	950.0	294	9	3	2.90	388	321	.827
Martinez Da, Mon	788.2	247	5	3	2.91	312	257	.824
Moseby, Det	862.2	265	6	5	2.88	334	275	.823
Yount, Mil	1362.2	422	3	4	2.83	601	492	.819
Walton, ChN	850.0	249	3	6	2.73	322	263	.817
Gant, Atl	950.0	279	6	5	2.75	407	323	.794
Burks, Bos	1267.1	322	7	2	2.35	468	364	.778
					2.74			.832

RIGHT FIELD

Player, Team	Innings	PO	A	E	Range Factor	In Zone	Balls Handled	Zone Rating
Hayes V, Phi	677.1	175	6	2	2.43	189	166	.878
Thompson M, StL	772.2	187	2	5	2.26	186	163	.876
Gwynn T, SD	1265.2	327	11	5	2.44	376	321	.854
Orsulak, Bal	643.1	209	2	2	2.98	252	214	.849
Strawberry, NYN	1263.0	268	11	3	2.01	304	258	.849
Wilson G, Hou	681.1	190	11	5	2.72	220	186	.845
Sosa, ChA	1253.0	313	14	13	2.44	369	311	.843
Sierra, Tex	1308.2	282	7	10	2.06	339	284	.838
Brooks, LA	1252.0	255	9	10	1.97	310	256	.826
Lemon, Det	765.0	204	7	6	2.55	247	203	.822
O'Neill, Cin	1165.1	272	12	2	2.21	317	259	.817
Brunansky, Bos	1180.0	305	6	7	2.43	369	301	.816
Bonilla B, Pit	1300.0	290	8	12	2.15	340	277	.815
Murphy Dl, Phi	1289.1	318	7	5	2.30	381	310	.814
Walker L, Mon	1003.1	247	11	4	2.35	297	240	.808
Barfield Je, NYA	1193.1	299	17	8	2.44	370	297	.803
Canseco, Oak	742.0	183	6	1	2.30	230	184	.800
Snyder C, Cle	984.1	222	11	6	2.19	271	216	.797
Felix, Tor	860.1	183	9	9	2.10	238	188	.790
Deer, Mil	912.2	242	14	8	2.60	315	248	.787
Winfield, Cal	921.2	164	7	2	1.69	211	162	.768
Dawson, ChN	1164.1	249	11	5	2.05	306	231	.755
					2.22			**.815**

About STATS, Inc.

It all starts with the **system.** The STATS scoring method, which includes pitch-by-pitch and the direction, distance, and velocity of each ball hit into play, yields an immense amount of information. Sure, we have all the statistics you're used to seeing, but where other statistics sources quit, STATS is just getting started.

Then, there is the **network.** Our information is timely because our game reporters send their information by computer as soon as the game is over. Statistics are checked and rechecked, updated and available daily.

Analysis comes next. STATS constantly searches for new ways to use this wealth of information to open windows into the workings of Baseball. Accurate numbers, intelligent computer programming, and a large dose of imagination all help coax the most valuable information from its elusive cover.

Finally, **distribution!**

STATS has served Major League teams for 11 years now, including the White Sox, Yankees, and Athletics. The boxscores that STATS provides exclusively to *USA Today* have revolutionized what Baseball fans expect from a boxscore. *Sports Illustrated, The Sporting News,* and *The National* regularly feature STATS, Inc. ESPN's nightly baseball coverage is supported by a full-time STATS statistician. We provide statistics for Earl Weaver Baseball, the nationally syndicated newspaper games Dugout Derby[TM] and Pigskin Playoff[TM], and other baseball games and fantasy leagues all over the country.

For the baseball fan, STATS continues a great tradition with *The Scouting Report: 1991,* available in book stores in the Spring of 1991. You'll find scouting reports on over 700 players in this book.

STATS publishes monthly and year-end reports on each Major League team. We offer a host of year-end statistical breakdowns on paper or disk that cover hitting, pitching, catching, baserunning, throwing, and more. STATS produces custom reports on request.

Computer users with modems can access the STATS computer with STATS On-Line. If you own a computer with a modem, there is no other source with the scope of baseball information that STATS can offer.

STATS and Bill James enjoy an on-going affiliation that has produced several baseball products including the *STATS 1991 Major League Handbook* and Bill James Fantasy Baseball, a game designed by Bill which allows you to own and manage your own team and compete with other team owners around the country.

Keep an eye out for other exciting future projects, such as STATS Fantasy Football and Basketball.

It is STATS, Inc.'s purpose to make the best possible Baseball information available to all Baseball interests: fans, players, teams, or media. Write to:

STATS, Inc.
7366 North Lincoln Ave.
Lincolnwood, IL 60646-1708

. . . or call us at 1-708-676-3322. We can send you a STATS brochure, a free Bill James Fantasy Baseball information kit, and/or information on STATS On-Line.

To maintain its information, STATS hires reporters around the country to cover games. If you are interested in applying for a reporter's position, please write or call STATS.

Index